AGENTIC INTELLIGENCE

Custom AI Solutions for Identity, Innovation, and Adaptive Learning

James Hutson
Professor of Art History, AI, and Visual Culture
Lindenwood University, USA

CRC Press
Taylor & Francis Group
Boca Raton London New York

CRC Press is an imprint of the
Taylor & Francis Group, an **informa** business
A SCIENCE PUBLISHERS BOOK

Cover credit: The image used on the cover is created by the author, Dr. James Hutson.

First edition published 2026
by CRC Press
2385 NW Executive Center Drive, Suite 320, Boca Raton FL 33431

and by CRC Press
4 Park Square, Milton Park, Abingdon, Oxon, OX14 4RN

CRC Press is an imprint of Taylor & Francis Group, LLC

Library of Congress Cataloging-in-Publication Data (applied for)

ISBN: 978-1-041-12309-5 (hbk)
ISBN: 978-1-041-17116-4 (pbk)
ISBN: 978-1-003-68801-3 (ebk)

DOI: 10.1201/9781003688013

Typeset in Times New Roman
by Prime Publishing Services

Dedication

This manuscript is dedicated with deepest gratitude to my wife, Piper, and to my children, Bishop and Aurora. Your love, patience, and unwavering support have been my constant source of strength throughout this journey. Piper, your encouragement and partnership have sustained me through the long hours of research and writing. Bishop and Aurora, your joy and curiosity remind me daily of the importance of this work and inspire me to strive for excellence.

This book stands as a testament to your sacrifices, your understanding, and the boundless love that makes every endeavor meaningful. With all my heart, I dedicate this work to you.

Epigraph

"Some people call this artificial intelligence, but the reality is this technology will enhance us. So instead of artificial intelligence, I think we'll augment our intelligence."

—Ginni Rometty, Former CEO of IBM

Preface

The present moment can be summed up by a scene that is quickly becoming commonplace: a small team hands an "agent" an open-ended brief—"design a pilot for reducing patient wait times across three clinics"—and watches as it drafts hypotheses, calls external tools, proposes experiments, and schedules stakeholder interviews. Early exemplars, such as Anthropic's Claude Code and OpenAI's Agent Mode, are still nascent, bounded by safety rails, limited context horizons, brittle planning, and uneven reliability, yet they foreshadow a shift in how problems will be approached. These systems do more than fetch facts or summarize documents; they orchestrate steps, negotiate trade-offs, and adapt workflows in response to feedback. Their limitations are real and worth naming: decomposition can be myopic, verification can lag behind generation, and tool-use can fall apart at the seams of poorly specified APIs. Still, multi-agent patterns—planners, critics, solvers, and verifiers—demonstrate tantalizing promise for long-horizon tasks that outgrow single-pass prompting. In these early vignettes, one sees the line between "assistant" and "colleague" blur, especially when agents coordinate with humans in the loop. The point is not that today's agents already solve ambiguous problems; rather, it is that the workflow itself is being reimagined around them. That reimagining, more than any single capability, signals where we are headed.

One of the most significant contributions of agent-based systems to education and work lies in their role as mirrors of identity. Training an AI agent to "think like oneself" requires learners to articulate their assumptions, ethical commitments, and personal heuristics in explicit, testable form. In doing so, identity is externalized as something both malleable and observable—a living construct that can be critiqued, revised, and refined through dialogue with an intelligent counterpart. This recursive process transforms the agent from a neutral utility into a site of ethical authorship and self-examination, aligning with theories of self-authorship and moral development. What students often discover is that the act of building an agent surfaces tensions between intuitive beliefs and codified rules, creating moments of dissonance that become catalysts for deeper reflection. In this way, the agent is not simply a tool for accelerating tasks but a developmental partner in cultivating self-awareness.

Parallel to this developmental function is the role of agents as prototypes for the workplace of tomorrow. Employers are already experimenting with "knowledge clones"—digital assistants trained to replicate employee workflows, decision heuristics, and domain expertise. From Salesforce's Einstein GPT to enterprise copilots in Microsoft 365, organizations are converging on a vision where every professional carries a personalized agent tuned to their tasks. Embedding this practice within higher education ensures graduates are not only literate in AI but already adept at shaping and governing their own digital extensions. The act of building and iterating a custom agent during one's studies simulates the very processes industries are adopting: decomposing tasks, auditing outputs, and codifying decision logics for reuse. Thus, the developmental arc of agent training doubles as professional rehearsal, giving learners both a portfolio artifact and a durable skillset in orchestrating human–machine collaboration.

Perhaps the most far-reaching contribution of agentic practice is its capacity to anchor lifelong learning. Contemporary neuroscience confirms that emerging adults are still consolidating executive function and metacognitive capacity well into their mid-twenties. Iteratively refining a personal agent provides an ongoing scaffold for this growth, compelling learners to plan, monitor, and evaluate both their own reasoning and the system's outputs. This is heutagogy in action: learning how to learn, not once, but continually, across shifting contexts. By encoding one's strategies, preferences, and blind spots into an agent, the learner effectively builds a metacognitive twin—an artifact that can persist beyond graduation and adapt as new challenges arise. Unlike static résumés or transcripts, such agents evolve with their creators, offering a pathway for self-directed reinvention in a volatile labor market. In this sense, the lifelong learning clone is less a novelty than a rite of passage: a structured means of cultivating the resilience, reflection, and adaptability demanded by the AI-mediated century.

At the same time, it is important to be candid about the state of play: agents remain in their infancy. They struggle with robust memory, with calibrated confidence, with generalizable planning under uncertainty, and with auditability that satisfies regulated environments. They require careful scaffolding—role definitions, tool schemas, guardrails, and explicit evaluation loops—to deliver dependable value. They excel when tasks are decomposable and when high-quality artifacts or feedback are available at each step; they falter when the space of possible futures explodes or when objectives are poorly specified. Reliability improves when organizations invest in orchestration layers, test harnesses, and human-verified checkpoints rather than relying on single-shot outputs. Even so, the direction is clear: multi-step reasoning, tool-mediated action, and socialized collaboration among specialized agents are becoming normal features of intelligent systems, not exotic research demos. As these capabilities mature, the handoff from human intention to machine-led exploration will become both safer and more routine. The central question is not whether agents will matter, but how institutions will adapt so that their strengths are amplified and their weaknesses are contained.

If adoption has felt "slow," the explanation lies less in technology than in people, processes, and incentives. Enterprises run on compliance regimes, budget cycles, procurement rules, and entrenched habits that do not pivot on a press release. Classrooms run on syllabi, assessment norms, accreditation, and cultural expectations that take semesters—sometimes years—to revise. Many AI engineers, often with good intentions, design systems around how they believe people ought to think and work—linear, rational, perfectly documented—rather than around how real teams actually behave under deadlines and constraints. The next wave of productivity will not come from bending human workflows to fit an idealized pipeline; it will come from teaching humans how to pair effectively with systems that decompose messily, search widely, and iterate quickly. That means foregrounding orchestration and verification as everyday skills, not afterthoughts. It means building feedback channels that convert tacit know-how into explicit signals agents can use. It also means resisting the urge to "perfect" a process diagram before experimenting with small, reversible trials. Culture change, not model choice, is the bottleneck.

The hybridization of learning offers a powerful lens for this change. Daniel Kahneman's dual-process theory—fast, intuitive System 1 and slow, deliberative System 2—maps cleanly onto emerging human-AI workflows. Generative systems are breathtaking at fast ideation: surfacing options, analogies, outlines, sketches, and candidate code within seconds. Deliberative systems—human or machine—shine when evaluating, testing, refuting, and refining those candidates against constraints and evidence. Effective teams now choreograph exchanges between fast and slow modes: rapid divergence to explore the space of possibilities, then purposeful convergence to critique, measure, and decide. In education, that looks like studio-style cycles of draft, critique, and revision where AI is neither shortcut nor oracle but a catalyst for iteration. In industry, it looks like sprint rituals that incorporate AI-generated alternatives and automated checks before human sign-off. The real skill is learning when to accelerate and when to resist acceleration, when to accept "good enough" and when to summon a slower, deeper pass. Teaching this cadence is as central to the future of work as any single technical tool.

Because generative media systems have made knowledge cheap and abundant, academic value propositions are already shifting. When retrieval and summarization are utilities, differentiation moves upstream to problem framing, data stewardship, experimental design, and evaluation, and downstream to implementation, integration, and change management. Institutions that define learning as fact recall will find themselves in a race they cannot win against machines with perfect recall and tireless synthesis. At the same time, labor markets are signaling preferences for demonstrable skills, portfolios, and proof-of-work rather than seat time alone. Competency-based credentialing, micro-credentials tied to authentic artifacts, and AI-verifiable evidence are beginning to complement—and in some roles supplant—the traditional degree as the primary hiring proxy. None of this negates the liberal arts case for broad, reflective education; it reframes it as a foundation for judgment, ethics, and integrative thinking atop a new layer of technical fluency. The winners will be institutions that bind these elements into coherent pathways rather than treating them as electives bolted to an unchanged core.

These pedagogical shifts are not happening in isolation; they are being shaped by powerful internal and external forces. Economically, organizations face pressure to raise productivity while navigating talent shortages and cost constraints. Politically, debates over academic integrity, content moderation, and AI governance are reshaping norms and policies. Legally, emerging standards for transparency, safety, bias mitigation, and data provenance are changing how intelligent systems are evaluated and deployed. Culturally, public attitudes oscillate between exuberance and anxiety, producing waves of enthusiasm followed by precaution—each wave leaving behind new practices and guardrails. Within institutions, leaders must reconcile strategic ambition with operational reality: budgets, training, cybersecurity, accessibility, and procurement. Across all of these, the pattern is consistent: the technology's curve rises quickly, while the human systems that must absorb it change through negotiation, not decree. This book treats those negotiations as central, not peripheral, to the future of learning and work.

To make progress, we must lift our gaze from the microcosm to the macrocosm. Too many conversations fixate on whether students "cheat" with chatbots or whether employees use automated drafting tools to skip the "hard part." The obsession is misplaced and, as argued later in this volume, often ludicrous. The operative questions are systemic: What capabilities should graduates and employees possess when intelligent tools are ubiquitous? How should institutions measure learning and performance when process is augmented and outputs are co-authored? What governance and evaluation frameworks allow teams to embrace speed without sacrificing rigor or equity? How can organizations redesign roles and workflows so that human judgment is preserved for the moments that matter most? By asking these questions, we trade a whack-a-mole posture for institutional design. We stop policing edge cases and start engineering robust systems.

A systems view also clarifies the architectural turn underway. Monolithic models are giving way to modular and multi-agent compositions: specialized components that plan, retrieve, simulate, write, test, critique, and verify. In this world, work looks less like "prompt in, answer out" and more like orchestration: routing tasks, managing state, enforcing checks, and capturing evidence. Identity changes, too. Instead of static résumés, learners and professionals present dynamic, evidence-linked profiles—portfolios, badges, and agent-maintained records that articulate skills in context. Education becomes an ecosystem of co-learning with automated tutors, synthetic media engines, and domain-specific evaluators that scaffold both fast and slow thinking. The boundary between classroom and workplace thins as apprenticeships, live datasets, and real clients enter the curriculum through secure sandboxes. This is less a revolution than an integration: aligning tools, content, and assessment so that learning produces directly usable capability.

The path forward requires cultures that are both ambitious and careful. Organizations need common language for capability maturity, model risk, and value capture; they also need rituals that make experimentation safe and reversible. Workforce development must emphasize orchestration, evaluation, data literacy, and change navigation—not just "prompting." Governance should be enabling, not paralyzing: model cards, audit trails, human-in-the-loop criteria, and tiered release gates that match risk to oversight. Leaders should start small—bounded pilots with clear metrics—then scale what works while pruning what does not. Educators should redesign assessments to reward process visibility, critique, and revision, encouraging students to show their work with and without tools. Industry partners should co-create authentic challenges and datasets, trading access and mentoring for a better-prepared talent pipeline. None of this is automatic; all of it is doable.

This volume is organized to help readers make those moves with clarity and confidence. It begins by mapping the evolution from monolithic systems to modular, agentic compositions and by framing the fast/slow dynamics that govern productive human-AI collaboration. It then turns to identity and credentialing, arguing for evidence-linked profiles that travel with the learner and update as skills deepen. Subsequent chapters examine organizational culture and adoption, including training programs that develop orchestration and evaluation as core competencies. Sector case studies illustrate both promise and pitfalls, highlighting where intelligent systems have already delivered value and where caution remains warranted. The penultimate chapters focus on designing, training, and maintaining agents for personal and professional use, with practical patterns for reliability and governance. The conclusion offers a strategic outlook and concrete recommendations for educators, leaders, technologists, and policymakers. Together, these chapters sketch a pragmatic, hopeful path through a period of rapid change.

What follows is not a manifesto for technology, but a guide for institutions that want to align human potential with intelligent tools. The central bet is simple: by blending fast generation with slow evaluation, by teaching orchestration and judgment, and by measuring what matters, we can raise both productivity and dignity at work and in school. By rethinking credentials as living representations of ability, we can make pathways more porous and opportunity more fairly distributed. By treating culture change as a first-class problem, we can avoid the cynicism that follows failed rollouts and instead build confidence through visible wins. And by zooming out from micro-controversies to systemic design, we can replace fragile patchwork with resilient, transparent, and adaptive institutions. The agents will get better; the question is whether we will get wiser in how we use them. This book is an invitation to do just that.

James Hutson

Contents

Acknowledgements

I express profound appreciation to the many individuals and institutions whose contributions and unwavering support were pivotal to the genesis and development of this volume. At the vanguard of acknowledgment stands Dr. John Porter, whose innovative leadership in aligning the adoption of emergent technologies with educational initiatives left an indelible mark on this work's evolution. I also extend special gratitude to Dr. Kathi Vosevich, Dean of the College of Arts and Humanities, for steadfast encouragement and for championing the research that culminates here; her guidance and confidence in my academic endeavors significantly shaped the contours of this book. I am indebted to the research collaborators and colleagues whose insights informed key sections, including Professors Ben Fulcher, Jeremiah Ratican, Joe Weber, and Ben Scholle, as well as Dr. Trent Olsen. I further thank Drs. Daniel Plate and Emily Barnes, whose thoughtful feedback helped refine arguments and sharpen direction throughout. I am grateful to the administrative leaders across participating institutions—Presidents, Provosts, and Deans—whose commitment to scholarly excellence furnished the conditions under which this project could thrive. To leaders in industry and education who generously shared experiences during a period of rapid technological change, your candor and time were invaluable in grounding these pages in practice as well as theory. Finally, I offer sincere thanks to colleagues and fellow researchers whose constructive critiques and encouragement enriched the work and helped clarify its aims. Any remaining errors or oversights are mine alone.

List of Figures

List of Tables

Chapter 1

Introduction—Agentic AI and the Evolution of Learning

1.1 OVERVIEW OF AI INTEGRATION ACROSS EDUCATION AND INDUSTRY

The story of emerging technologies is rarely a straight line. Each wave of innovation begins with promises that outpace practice, followed by a reckoning when institutions must translate potential into results. Today, artificial intelligence (AI) systems stand at this inflection point. Executives, educators, and policymakers speak urgently of transformation, yet the tools are still more often piloted than embedded. What emerges is less a tale of technical limits than of organizational readiness: data pipelines, governance, training, and workflow design determine outcomes far more than algorithmic horsepower. For both companies and universities, the central challenge is not whether to use these systems but how to build the scaffolds that make adoption sustainable. This chapter opens by surveying the terrain of stalled integration, mapping the distance between boardroom ambition and frontline reality. That distance frames the questions of transformation, governance, and practice that guide the volume.

Across industries in 2025, AI adoption is broad in pilots yet shallow in enterprise impact. McKinsey (2025) reports that "most respondents have yet to see organization-wide, bottom-line impact from gen AI use," underscoring the gap between experimentation and value. Organizations are slowly building the structures that enable durable returns, suggesting movement from novelty toward operating practice. Gartner (2025) captures this phase as the "Trough of Disillusionment," a reset in which inflated expectations meet implementation

DOI: 10.1201/9781003688013-1

realities. This period should be read less as a technology failure than as a governance and workflow bottleneck. The question is not what models are capable of, but how institutions are designed to use them effectively. Framed this way, adoption becomes a problem of management transformation rather than simple tooling. The evidence reviewed in this section reveals the persistent divide between executive urgency and operational readiness.

C-suite sentiment reflects strong momentum: leaders believe adoption must advance. The 2025 Thomson Reuters C-Suite Survey lists "exploring the potential for & implementing AI" among the top near-term priorities. Yet nearly one-third of executives admit their organizations are progressing "too slowly." An enablement gap widens the problem: 82% report that AI is embedded in workflows, but only 34% have equipped employees with the tools to use it. Slack's Workforce Index (2024) adds clarity, noting that two-thirds of workers have yet to try any generative tools despite executive directives. Deloitte (2025) emphasizes the skills gap, with 45% of technology leaders citing generative fluency as the most urgently needed competency. Taken together, the evidence signals a common story: boardroom will is outpacing workforce readiness. The decisive barrier is not intention but enablement.

Obstacles to adoption are pragmatic yet decisive: data quality, budgets, security, and ROI clarity. Reuters finds that "quality and structure of data" and "available budget" are the most frequent obstacles cited by leaders. Gartner reports that fewer than 30% of digital intelligence leaders say their CEOs are satisfied with returns, highlighting the demand for disciplined value capture. McKinsey underscores that many firms are still laying the foundations of governance and MLOps required for scale. Yet the momentum is shifting: Slack's June 2025 update shows that 60% of workers now use generative systems, with daily use up 233% in six months (Salesforce Newsroom, 2025). Still, enthusiasm without workflow design rarely matures into dependable value. The next chapters focus on mapping tasks, integrating human-in-the-loop checks, and ensuring traceable evaluation. These practices translate ambition into repeatable, governed outcomes.

Patterns vary by sector but follow a recognizable arc. Manufacturing and logistics teams are embedding intelligence into supply-chain decisions while remaining cautious about returns (Reuters, 2025). Cybersecurity adoption continues, but MIT Sloan (2025) finds that "only 2% of organizations worldwide are fully prepared to scale AI securely." Finance leaders, historically conservative, are beginning to shift budgets toward autonomous capabilities, though ethics and privacy remain paramount (IT Pro, 2025). Gartner's "Trough" framing captures the moment: expectations are resetting, not retreating. For executives, the imperative is to invest in data, controls, and orchestration before scaling pilots. For educators and public-sector leaders, the parallel is policy and assessment scaffolds before mandates. Across domains, throughput aligns more closely with organizational design than with algorithmic sophistication.

Higher education demonstrates the paradox in a different register. EDUCAUSE (2025) observes that the community "continues to grapple with questions related to using artificial intelligence (AI) in learning and work." UNESCO warns that rapid developments "have so far outpaced policy debates and regulatory frameworks." Students, however, are moving faster: Cengage (2025) finds that 65% of students believe they know more about AI than their instructors and want explicit skills included in courses. Faculty, by contrast, identify integrity, bias, and training as their leading concerns, echoing enterprise anxieties about risk and readiness. The friction created by policy gaps, uneven legitimacy, and skill divides slows curricular integration despite evident benefits. Slack (2024) shows that training fosters trust, a lesson transferable to faculty development and assessment redesign. The principle is simple: treat intelligent tools like lab equipment, providing scaffolds for access, provenance checks, and competency-based evaluation.

This anecdotal evidence long circulated by consulting firms such as McKinsey, Deloitte, and Gartner is now substantiated by a growing body of academic research. Recent studies confirm that the barriers slowing adoption—misalignment, skill shortages, poor data quality, and weak governance—are not merely executive complaints but measurable, systemic obstacles. For instance, El Arab et al. (2025) conducted an umbrella review on nursing education, identifying resistance to change, absence of standardized curricula, and privacy concerns as common impediments. These findings mirror corporate frustrations where employees lack sufficient preparation and leadership struggles with integration strategies. The implication is straightforward: institutions cannot purchase intelligent systems and expect transformation without redesigning structures, competencies, and ethical frameworks. The decisive variable is alignment across technology, governance, and training, without which investments stall at the pilot stage. Both higher education and industry converge on the same conclusion: culture and governance, not technical maturity, dictate outcomes. Technology succeeds only when embedded into supportive organizational ecosystems.

Within education, systematic reviews highlight that teachers recognize the potential of digital systems for personalization and engagement but remain constrained by inadequate training and infrastructure. García et al. (2025) found in their review of primary education that enthusiasm for integration is consistently tempered by lack of institutional support, resources, and professional development. Their conclusion—that integration is a "necessity" rather than an optional enhancement—echoes industry assessments that adoption is inevitable but delayed by misalignment. Dulundu (2024) identifies the dual trajectory: extraordinary potential for inclusion and efficiency, balanced by risks of bias and inequity if not carefully managed. The consistent lesson across these studies is that smart systems do not fail because of technical incapacity but because institutions lack scaffolds to support their use. Skills training, policy development, and assessment frameworks are required to translate capacity into value. The challenge, therefore, lies not in computing capability but in institutional orchestration. Effective adoption means designing the environment in which tools can succeed.

In health sciences, this paradox is especially acute. Turner et al. (2025) describes it as the "alignment paradox," where intelligent systems enable personalized learning yet may conflict with standardized curricular goals unless supported by ethics, interpretability, and oversight. This observation parallels Gartner's warning of a "Trough of Disillusionment," in which initial optimism is tempered by implementation barriers. Babur (2025) further notes that while adaptive systems and clinical simulations promise major benefits, their adoption has been slow due to limited systematic evidence, insufficient safeguards, and gaps in faculty expertise. These findings emphasize that governance and capacity-building are as urgent as technological deployment. The alignment paradox is not an abstract concept but the daily reality faced by deans, regulators, and CIOs attempting to modernize without undermining standards. What emerges is a picture of systemic tension between potential and preparedness. The health sciences highlight why successful adoption must be anchored in oversight frameworks and collaborative governance. Without these, integration risks stagnation.

Industry-focused research reinforces the same dynamics. Vudugula et al. (2023) demonstrate in their systematic review that predictive models only generate reliable benefits when paired with governance mechanisms such as explainability and ethical alignment. They stress that the "black box dilemma" erodes trust unless organizations adopt transparent practices like SHAP or LIME interpretability. Similarly, Mohammadi (2025) shows that industry-university partnerships accelerate innovation only when supported by joint committees, shared platforms, and transparent data arrangements. These findings validate Deloitte's recurring conclusion: governance and cross-functional collaboration are prerequisites for scaling adoption. Predictive power, in isolation, is never enough. Organizational trust and decision architectures determine whether tools enhance or undermine value. In this light, governance is not peripheral but central to sustainable integration. It becomes the stage upon which adoption either flourishes or fails.

Finally, multiple studies underscore the centrality of public perception and workforce readiness. Omri et al. (2025) demonstrate that governance quality directly shapes whether algorithmic systems worsen or mitigate unemployment among vulnerable populations, illustrating the social stakes of alignment. García, García et al. (2025) further confirm that teachers' willingness to adopt depends on adequate training and systemic support, spotlighting workforce development as a critical enabler. Together, these studies align with industry surveys that show leadership urgency outpaces employee readiness. Integration thus emerges as a negotiated trajectory shaped by trust, training, and governance rather than a binary of adoption or rejection. The lesson across academic research from 2023 to 2025 is unambiguous: technological novelty is not the source of value. Instead, it is the alignment of systems with people, processes, and ethical imperatives that delivers transformation. Industry and academia alike reveal that without this foundation, adoption will continue to stall. The future of integration hinges less on innovation speed than on institutional readiness.

In essence, the slowdown in adoption arises not only from governance and structural bottlenecks but also from the way humans think and make decisions (Figure 1.1). Cognitive psychology shows that decision-making often oscillates between rapid, intuitive moves and slower, more reflective judgments. Kahneman's dual-process theory captures this duality, distinguishing between fast, automatic reasoning and deliberate, analytical thought. This framework helps explain why organizations struggle to integrate new technologies: leaders may act quickly on enthusiasm while employees hesitate, requiring reflection, training, and evidence before committing. The tension between speed and deliberation mirrors the broader adoption gap—executives push for acceleration while practitioners proceed cautiously. Agentic systems can be positioned not as replacements but as complements, balancing intuitive leaps with rigorous analysis. When embedded in workflows with oversight, these tools can extend both modes of reasoning, supporting quick responses without losing reflective depth. Framed this way, adoption challenges become as much about cognitive alignment as about technical or structural readiness.

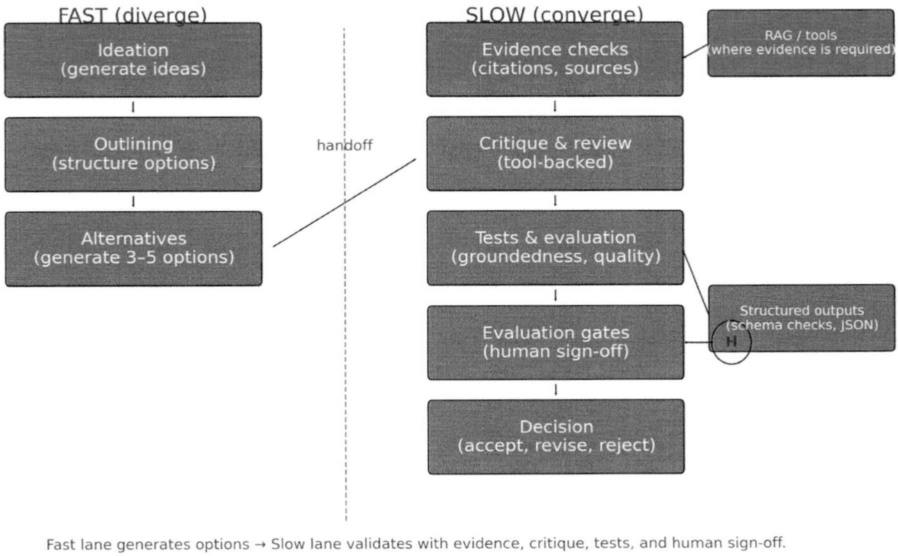

Figure 1.1 Why Adoption Lags Capability.

1.2 THEORETICAL FRAMEWORK: FAST (RAPID) AND SLOW (REFLECTIVE) LEARNING PARADIGMS

The theoretical foundation of this book begins with Daniel Kahneman's influential dual-process theory of cognition, articulated in *Thinking, Fast and Slow*. Kahneman distinguishes between two systems of thought: System 1, which is rapid, automatic, and intuitive, and System 2, which is slower, deliberate, and reflective (Figure 1.2) (Tversky, 2025; Fischhoff, 2024). System 1 provides efficiency, enabling quick judgments, but is vulnerable to heuristics and cognitive biases that may reduce accuracy. By contrast, System 2 provides analytical rigor, allowing for deeper evaluation, though it requires significantly more cognitive resources and time (Dhaliwal, 2017). This duality is particularly useful as a metaphor for understanding generative technologies. Generative systems can be seen as fast, intuitive processors, producing immediate outputs, while human oversight and structured evaluation represent the reflective dimension. Workflows in organizations frequently demand this balance—rapid ideation must be followed by careful, deliberate review. In this way, dual-process theory provides a bridge between human cognition and organizational adoption, linking psychology with governance and practice.

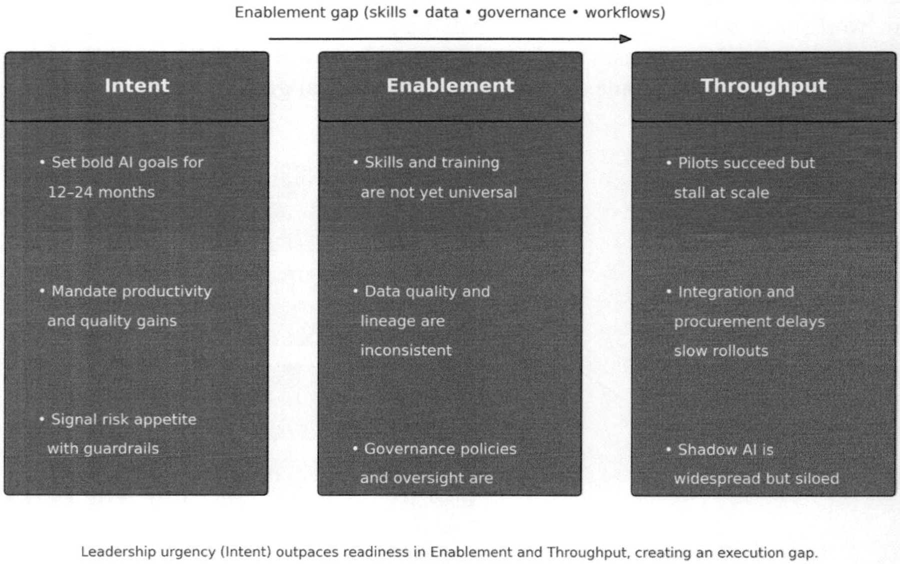

Figure 1.2 Fast/Slow Choreography for Human-AI Workflows.

Recent scholarship builds directly upon Kahneman's insight by modeling "fast" and "slow" processes within computational architectures. Zhong et al. (2025) present Dyve, a dynamic process verifier inspired by the dual-process model, which applies System 1-style rapid confirmation for routine steps while reserving System 2-style deep analysis for more complex reasoning tasks. Their results demonstrate significant improvements in reasoning accuracy when hybrid modes are used, compared with reliance on either fast or slow processing alone. Fabiano et al. (2021) introduce SOFAI, a system that arbitrates between rapid and reflective solvers in multi-agent planning, effectively mirroring human metacognition. These studies underscore how computational models can operationalize cognitive duality, pairing speed with rigor in ways that humans already practice. The design principle is simple but profound: fast components generate possibilities, slow components test their validity, and meta-agents mediate transitions between the two. For emerging agentic systems, this principle is essential for ensuring reliability, transparency, and trust. The theoretical implication is that intelligent systems of the future will not only augment human cognition but also reproduce parallel forms of dual-process reasoning in their own architectures.

In education, researchers emphasize that effective teaching requires guiding learners between intuitive and reflective modes of thought. Schwab et al. (2022) observe that many student errors occur when intuitive heuristics are misapplied to problems requiring deliberate reasoning, such as mathematical proofs or scientific analysis. To address this, they propose instructional strategies that scaffold transitions, encouraging students to pause, reflect, and engage System 2 when accuracy matters most. Brosnan and Ashwin (2023) extend this perspective to autism research, finding that autistic individuals often display a preference for deliberative processing. This tendency can be an advantage in contexts requiring resistance to bias and detailed reasoning, but it may create challenges in fast-paced social situations that rely on intuition. These insights are particularly relevant for the design of intelligent tutors, which must learn when to prompt students toward reflective engagement and when to encourage intuitive exploration. The broader implication is that intelligent systems can act as moderators, dynamically shifting learners between modes to optimize understanding. By operationalizing dual-process theory at scale, these tools can personalize education in ways that align with cognitive science.

Other applied fields further illustrate the value of balancing fast and slow paradigms to mitigate risks. In finance, Ferri et al. (2021) demonstrate that experimental financial bubbles are reduced when participants are nudged toward System 2 reflection, highlighting the stabilizing role of deliberate reasoning. In medicine, Dhaliwal (2017) documents how premature closure—the tendency to jump quickly to intuitive diagnoses—can be avoided by intentionally engaging reflective processes. Intelligent systems can directly support such practices, detecting signs of premature closure and nudging clinicians to review alternative hypotheses before finalizing decisions. Conversely, in emergency contexts such as trauma care, systems can support rapid responses while flagging elements that require slower, more detailed analysis. This mirrors organizational adoption more broadly, where leaders prize speed but must also safeguard accuracy, accountability, and ethical responsibility. By embedding dual-process insights into governance structures, institutions can design agents that balance urgency with oversight. In this way, dual-process theory functions not only as a cognitive framework but also as an institutional blueprint for high-stakes decision-making.

Beyond Kahneman's original model, contemporary theorists have extended dual-process theory into multi-layered or hybrid frameworks. Gulati et al. (2021) propose a "System 0," a supervisory layer that governs transitions between fast and slow cognition, echoing Kahneman's own acknowledgment that metacognition regulates these shifts. This idea parallels modern multi-agent architectures in digital systems, where supervisory agents decide when to deploy rapid generation versus deeper evaluation. Venkatraman et al. (2020) caution against simplistic applications of the System 1/2 model in marketing, arguing that intuition and deliberation interact in more complex ways than the binary suggests. In design science, Kannengiesser and Gero (2019) map System 1 to pattern-based creativity and System 2 to structured analysis, using this framework to explain the process of design thinking. These disciplinary perspectives demonstrate that dual-process theory is neither static nor one-dimensional but continually reinterpreted and tested. Each domain adapts the framework to its needs, producing richer variations of fast/slow interaction. For intelligent architectures, the implication is clear: the future lies in hybrid systems capable of balancing creativity with caution, speed with accuracy.

The fast/slow framework (Table 1.1) also carries important implications for organizational culture and workforce development. Strannegård et al. (2013)

propose a cognitive architecture that combines symbolic reasoning, akin to slow reflective thought, with subsymbolic reasoning, analogous to rapid intuitive responses. This structure is directly applicable to human-technology collaboration, where employees must learn when to trust fast outputs and when to slow down for deeper review. Training programs can explicitly teach this cadence, aligning with growing calls for "AI literacy" across industries. Dual-process theory thus functions as a pedagogical blueprint, equipping workers with the ability to alternate between modes of thinking. Employees who learn to recognize when they are in "fast" mode and when to shift into "slow" are better positioned to coordinate effectively with automated systems. Institutions can build workflows that scaffold these alternations, ensuring efficiency without losing rigor or accountability. In this way, Kahneman's framework informs both the design of computational systems and the cultivation of human competencies needed to work alongside them.

Table 1.1 Fast vs. Slow: Tasks, Tools, and Evidence

Task	*Fast Move*	*Slow Move*	*Required Evidence/ Artifacts*	*Human Gate*
Draft policy brief	Generate outline with 3-5 policy options; draft executive-summary variants; retrieve 5-7 recent sources via RAG; produce initial talking points.	Evidence checks on every claim; quote-check and add citations; stakeholder/ bias analysis; tool-backed fact-check; finalize structured references and rationale.	Evidence brief with citations and RAG trace; source quality notes; decision/ change log; final bibliography.	Policy subject-matter + legal review sign-off.
Code utility (function or script)	Generate function and docstring; sketch API; scaffold unit tests and usage examples.	Run unit and property-based tests; static analysis/lint; security scan; benchmark expected inputs; containerized or reproducible environment.	Test suite and results with coverage; linter/ security reports; benchmark numbers; requirements/ environment file and run notes.	Maintainer code review (PR) with merge approval.
Rubric feedback (assignment)	Draft criterion-by-criterion formative feedback; highlight strengths and next steps; offer 2-3 tone variants if needed.	Align language to rubric descriptors; compare against gold/exemplar set; bias/fairness pass; redact speculative claims; finalize release copy.	Annotated rubric with criterion scores; exemplar comparison sheet; feedback trace log referencing evidence in the student work.	Instructor approval before release to learner.

In healthcare, Turner et al. (2025) describe what they call the "alignment paradox": intelligent systems can personalize education and training but risk undermining structured curricular goals without ethical oversight. This paradox is best understood through a dual-process lens, where fast personalization provides speed and flexibility, while slow oversight preserves consistency, fairness, and accountability. Babur (2025) warns that without reflective governance, integration can exacerbate inequities, particularly in developing nations where resources and safeguards are limited. These findings reinforce the necessity of slow, deliberative systems in domains where human lives are directly affected. At the same time, rapid diagnostic support demonstrates the clear value of fast systems in situations where minutes or seconds determine outcomes. The theoretical lesson is not that one mode should dominate, but that both must be deliberately integrated into design and deployment. Only through this balance does alignment emerge, ensuring safety without sacrificing efficiency. This reality underscores the broader argument of the book: agentic models must be anchored in dual-process cognition if they are to deliver on both promise and protection.

At the societal level, dual-process frameworks also help explain public perception of emerging technologies. Omri et al. (2025) demonstrate that governance quality shapes whether adoption is experienced as threatening or enabling, paralleling System 1 fear responses with System 2 reflective evaluation. Public trust hinges on managing this interplay—balancing intuitive anxieties with transparent, structured explanations. UNESCO (n.d.) has noted that policy debates often lag behind technological developments, leaving many governments stuck in reactive, "fast" modes of governance. Addressing this gap requires embedding structured, "slow" deliberation in regulatory spaces while retaining the agility to respond quickly to shifting innovations. For institutions, this balance translates into cultivating procedures that allow for both urgency and reflection. In practice, it means developing policies that can react swiftly to risks while simultaneously creating long-term frameworks for accountability. As agentic systems advance, such duality will be required not only in cognition but also in societal, political, and regulatory contexts.

Agentic systems, in particular, bring the fast/slow dynamic to the forefront of design and governance. These systems excel at decomposing problems quickly, generating options with remarkable speed, but without reflective layers they risk producing brittle or harmful solutions. Research on Dyve and SOFAI demonstrates that hybrid architectures, which combine fast and slow processes, consistently outperform single-mode approaches (Zhong et al., 2025; Fabiano et al., 2021). For human collaboration, the implication is straightforward: effectiveness comes not from privileging speed or reflection alone but from orchestrating their interaction. In governance, this translates into checkpoints, evaluation criteria, and rollback plans that mirror reflective, System 2 oversight. In pedagogy, it means encouraging students to use automated systems for rapid ideation while ensuring that their assessments reward slow, critical evaluation. The fast/slow paradigm thus operates simultaneously as a cognitive metaphor and a design principle. By embedding this cadence into both architectures and institutions, it becomes possible to combine agility with accountability at scale.

In sum, Kahneman's dual-process theory offers a powerful theoretical foundation for understanding the role of intelligent systems in learning, work, and governance. It functions not only as a psychological model but also as a design philosophy for building hybrid human-machine systems. Empirical studies demonstrate that applying fast/slow frameworks improves reasoning accuracy, reduces risks of bias, and supports more equitable governance outcomes. The future of agentic intelligence depends on embedding this cadence—deploying speed where it creates value and reflection where it guarantees safety. Organizations that learn to treat fast and slow as complementary rather than opposing unlock both creativity and reliability. The theoretical argument is therefore pragmatic: dual-process cognition provides a blueprint for modular architectures that can scale responsibly. This framework also supplies the connective tissue for the book, guiding analysis of current adoption barriers as well as strategies for building future-ready institutions. By grounding the discussion in cognitive theory, the volume situates technical adoption within broader human and organizational dynamics.

1.3 AGENTIC IDENTITY FORMATION IN AI-ENHANCED LEARNING ENVIRONMENTS

A natural extension of the fast/slow framework is to consider how identity itself is shaped when humans work in tandem with intelligent collaborators. The rise of generative systems with persistent memory has blurred the line between tool and collaborator, creating environments where dialogue is continuous and adaptive. Advances in conversational engines now allow continuity across interactions, enabling systems to recall, refine, and mirror user traits over time. Ethan Mollick (2024) describes this phenomenon as "co-intelligence," in which systems do not merely generate text but act as adaptive partners in thought. This dynamic positions them as both shapers and reflectors of identity, capturing fragments of personality, style, and cognitive preference. Studies in education confirm that the integration of machine collaborators influences the identities of both students and teachers, altering traditional distributions of authority, expertise, and creativity (Mureșan, 2023). At the same time, the agents themselves increasingly embody identities, whether as digital clones, extensions, or semi-autonomous workers. Identity, in this context, becomes reciprocal: humans shape digital counterparts, and digital counterparts reshape human self-concept.

This reciprocal model aligns with the framework of "agentic identity" articulated in recent scholarship on human-centered AI. For instance, requiring students to iteratively build and refine custom agents compels a deeper articulation of their own values, epistemologies, and priorities, thereby turning the act of agent training into a developmental crucible. In this process, students externalize fragments of their reasoning and ethical orientation, encounter the tension between intention and system response, and refine their identity through iterative correction. The agent becomes both a record of evolving selfhood and a mirror that reflects inconsistencies back to its human author. Rather than treating identity as a fixed attribute, this framework situates identity as a living record—portable, inspectable, and co-evolving with intelligent systems.

Professional identity formation provides an important analogue. In medicine, nursing, and pharmacy, identity has historically been cultivated through structured learning environments that emphasize mentorship, lived practice, and institutional culture (Rehman et al., 2024; Copeland et al., 2023). In AI-infused contexts, these formative structures are joined by intelligent collaborators who can simulate professional tasks, model ethical dilemmas, and provide scaffolding for decision-making. Kellogg et al. (2024) describe how companies already deploy "GPT pods" to mirror employee workflows, suggesting that readiness to collaborate with non-human colleagues is itself becoming part of professional identity. The implication is that professional formation is no longer confined to human mentorship and community of practice; it now includes apprenticeship with, and adaptation to, digital counterparts. Identity formation becomes hybrid, blending human judgment with machine-mediated extension.

The tripartite framework further demonstrates that this identity work is inseparable from workforce readiness and lifelong learning. By developing agents that reflect their cognitive strategies and disciplinary expertise, students rehearse the very practices that employers now demand: the ability to externalize knowledge into modular, reusable, and transparent systems. In parallel, the process of tuning and refining one's agent fosters metacognition, as learners must plan their inputs, monitor outputs, and evaluate misalignments. This cycle of planning, monitoring, and evaluating aligns directly with Flavell's (1979) foundational account of metacognition and is amplified in AI-rich environments where feedback loops are immediate and iterative. The result is that identity formation, professional rehearsal, and lifelong metacognitive practice converge in a single practice: the sustained development of one's agentic counterpart.

For lifelong learning, the significance is profound. Rather than a static résumé or transcript, the agent itself becomes a living artifact of identity—an evolving record of competencies, values, and adaptive strategies. García et al. (2025) have shown that teachers increasingly define themselves as mediators in AI-enhanced classrooms, and this same mediation applies to learners constructing lifelong "learning clones." These artifacts persist beyond graduation, enabling individuals to continue rehearsing, revising, and reinventing their professional and personal selves across changing labor markets. In this respect, identity formation is no longer a stage confined to adolescence or early adulthood but an ongoing process scaffolded by intelligent collaborators. Identity is, in short, a lifelong negotiation—between human agency, institutional frameworks, and machine partners—anchored by the deliberate cultivation of agentic extensions.

Scholars argue that this new dynamic introduces both opportunities and tensions. Cheng (2022) advances the notion of "Artificial Agential Intelligence," contending that only when digital systems are reframed as agents rather than tools can they participate meaningfully in identity construction. Such reframing expands the scope of professional formation to include practical reasoning and imaginative understanding distributed across human and non-human actors. Maroteau et al. (2023) show that generative writing tools have already altered academic publishing identities, forcing institutions to reconsider originality, authorship, and intellectual labor. The ethical implications are significant: if identities are co-authored, who bears responsibility for outcomes? Mureşan (2023) documents how educators in Latin America perceive identity itself—both for teachers and students—as being reshaped by these integrations, with results ranging from empowerment to disorientation. These findings suggest that identity formation in enhanced environments is no longer a unidirectional process but a reciprocal and contested one. The dynamic is evolutionary, adaptive, and deeply tied to ethical design.

Education provides some of the clearest evidence of identity reshaping in practice. Burstein et al. (2021) note that testing platforms now embed responsible-use standards, shifting student identity from passive test-taker to co-navigator of human–machine evaluation. Similarly, García et al. (2025) observe that teachers increasingly identify themselves as mediators rather than gatekeepers when classrooms are infused with automated tutoring systems. This shift requires educators to align their professional identities with systems capable of personalization and even instructional substitution. As a result, the teacher's role is no longer defined by exclusive authority but by the ability to guide and frame machine collaboration. For students, adaptive systems expand opportunities for identity to evolve alongside changing skills and professions, offering a flexibility that traditional education rarely achieved. Identity thus becomes iterative and modular, shaped dynamically by interaction. Both teachers and learners are repositioned within an ecology of shared agency.

Parallel challenges emerge in the workforce, where professional identity is increasingly hybrid. Ali et al. (2024) project journalism programs redesigned to prepare students for dual identities, where the role of "reporter" combines human investigation with curating content co-produced with digital agents. Rehman et al. (2024) note that pandemic disruptions delayed—but did not erase—professional identity formation in medical education, highlighting its resilience under pressure. Workers across industries are now expected to adopt fluid identities, shifting between specialist, orchestrator, creator, and verifier depending on the operations of digital collaborators. Romero (2024) underscores that lifelong learning is essential in this environment, with professionals continually reconstructing their identities to stay aligned with evolving technologies and labor markets. This means identity is no longer static or role-bound; it becomes a living negotiation between human agency, market forces, and machine collaborators. The workforce thus provides a mirror to education, revealing identity as both adaptive and contingent.

At the organizational level, identity reshaping is mediated through governance frameworks and institutional culture. Nickerson et al. (2025) emphasize that agents are unpredictable, producing outcomes not always anticipated by designers, which forces organizations to rethink responsibility and authorship. Professional identity therefore extends into organizational identity, as firms themselves begin to be seen as co-actors with their digital infrastructures. Ta'an et al. (2025) confirm that interprofessional collaboration now explicitly includes machine colleagues, effectively making identity formation a multi-species endeavor. Institutions that ignore this dual identity—human and digital—risk eroding trust and legitimacy among employees and students. The presence of digital collaborators reconfigures organizational norms around accountability, responsibility, and creativity. Identity thus becomes not only individual but institutional, reflected in how organizations structure their practices. In this sense, organizational identity is inseparable from the technologies with which it operates.

Ethical considerations must remain central to identity formation in enhanced environments. Landau et al. (2024) stress the importance of contestability in decision-making systems, ensuring that individuals retain the ability to challenge machine-determined outcomes. This safeguard is more than procedural; it protects the existential integrity of individuals as agents of their own trajectories. Without it, identity risks becoming subordinated to algorithmic authority. Cheng (2022) advances the vision of agential intelligence grounded in virtue epistemology, where systems embody accountability and reflective knowledge. In this framing, professional identity formation cannot be separated from the ethical frameworks guiding system design. Autonomy, dignity, and human agency must be embedded into collaborations if identities are to remain robust. Ethics, therefore, is not supplemental to identity but its very foundation.

Emerging research also highlights the emotional dimensions of identity formation. Larose-Pierre et al. (2023) argue that emotional intelligence—self-awareness, empathy, and stress management—is essential for professional identity in pharmacy education. If digital collaborators now co-shape professional identities, emotional intelligence becomes the buffer that preserves authenticity and resilience in hybrid contexts. Maroteau et al. (2023) raise concerns about originality and authorship, reinforcing the need to reframe identity to account for shared intellectual labor. Mureșan (2023) emphasizes that trust and human centrality are critical for stabilizing identity when systems permeate classrooms. These findings suggest that identity formation is as much relational and emotional as it is cognitive and technical. The human element—awareness, empathy, and agency—remains indispensable, even as systems mirror personality traits and preferences. Without attention to these dimensions, identity risks becoming hollowed out by the very tools designed to enhance it.

Looking ahead, identity must be understood as iterative, modular, and dynamic. Cheng (2022) describes the transition from task-based to agent-based frameworks, in which collaborators act as enduring partners rather than disposable tools. This vision resonates with Omri et al. (2025), who show that governance determines whether automation shapes identity inclusively or exacerbates exclusion, particularly for vulnerable populations. Romero (2024) highlights that lifelong learning has become a baseline condition, with identity formation tied to continuous upskilling and reskilling. Professional and personal identities will increasingly be defined by the capacity to orchestrate relationships with digital counterparts. In this future, identity is both an asset and an obligation, constantly renegotiated across contexts. Such adaptability is necessary for resilience in fast-changing markets and institutions. Identity will no longer be inherited or static but co-authored and dynamic.

Thus, agentic identity formation in enhanced learning environments is inherently bidirectional. Humans construct and reconstruct their identities through interactions with intelligent collaborators, while these collaborators themselves increasingly embody semi-autonomous extensions of identity. Identity is therefore not simply learned, inherited, or achieved but co-produced across human and digital actors. The implications extend to education, workforce development, and organizational culture, making identity a central axis of adaptation in the twenty-first century. Future-ready identities will be hybrid, relational, and adaptable, characterized by resilience and flexibility. The challenge for institutions and individuals is to ensure that this co-production preserves human agency, dignity, and equity. Without such safeguards, identity risks becoming fragmented or hollow. With them, identity becomes resilient, dynamic, and future-proof, capable of thriving in hybrid human–machine environments.

1.4 BRIDGING MODULARITY AND IDENTITY: A STRATEGIC FRAMEWORK

A useful way to extend the earlier discussion of cognition and identity is to ask how people and institutions can remain resilient when technologies, markets, and roles shift faster than they can fully anticipate. Modularity provides the technical and organizational scaffolding, while identity offers the human and cultural counterpart. In practice, modularity allows systems to scale and adapt by swapping specialized components without overhauling entire infrastructures—much like replacing one app in a smartphone ecosystem without redesigning the phone itself. Identity, in parallel, allows individuals to reskill, reposition, and re-present themselves as careers evolve—like a nurse who retrains into health informatics or a teacher who becomes an instructional designer using digital tutors. Without modular systems, identities have nowhere to grow; without adaptive identities, modular systems remain underused. The two work best in tandem, ensuring that organizations and individuals can change without collapsing under volatility. Together they form a strategic posture: technical architectures that bend without breaking, and human identities that evolve without losing coherence.

Modularity is not only a software principle but an institutional philosophy. In software, modular design prevents monolithic programs from collapsing under complexity by breaking them into smaller, interchangeable parts. In organizations, modular thinking enables new processes or roles to be added without erasing prior structures. For instance, universities can embed short-format micro-credentials inside traditional degree programs, allowing students to accumulate specialized skills like data visualization or digital storytelling alongside broad disciplinary training. In industry, companies increasingly deploy families of specialized agents—compliance checkers, knowledge retrievers, or customer simulators—rather than relying on one oversized model to handle every task. This mirrors how human teams distribute expertise across individuals rather than concentrating it in one role. By recombining modules as needs change, organizations can shift direction without destabilizing their foundations. Modularity thus fosters a culture where adaptation is routine rather than disruptive.

Identity functions as the human mirror of modularity. Just as systems are built from separable functions, individuals increasingly present themselves through modular identities composed of skills, projects, and evolving roles. A marketing professional may alternate between roles as analyst, storyteller, and orchestrator of automated collaborators, depending on the demands of a campaign. A student might view herself not only as a learner of history but also as a co-creator of simulations with generative tools. These layered identities are not contradictions but composites, shifting in salience as circumstances demand. Credentialing systems reflect this trend by capturing evidence of specific competencies, such as project management or programming, rather than presenting a singular degree label. Professional development becomes less about climbing a single ladder and more about curating a portfolio of capabilities. Identity, when viewed modularly, is not fragmented but orchestrated—like instruments in an ensemble playing in harmony.

The tripartite framework of agentic development (identity reflection, professional rehearsal, and lifelong metacognition) offers a practical means of enacting modular identity formation in both educational and professional contexts. When students train agents that embody fragments of their reasoning, they are in effect constructing modular identity units—discrete yet connected representations of values, disciplinary skills, and problem-solving strategies. These units can be recombined as careers shift, much like technical modules in a software architecture. In the workforce, professionals continually refine their agentic clones, layering new competencies onto older ones, thereby creating modular cognitive portfolios that remain adaptive and portable. Identity becomes less a singular narrative than an evolving constellation of agentic modules, each responsive to different contexts but anchored in a coherent self-concept.

Bridging modularity and identity helps reconcile the tension between stability and flexibility. Organizations seek consistent performance but must adapt to shifting markets; workers seek coherent self-concepts but must reskill to stay relevant. A modular identity framework offers stability through enduring competencies—communication, ethical reasoning, analytical literacy—while permitting flexibility through new skill modules such as coding or prompt engineering. Similarly, modular system architectures preserve core baselines—data governance, compliance checks, security layers—while allowing experimental tools to be layered in and swapped out. This parallel ensures that both systems and people evolve without losing their foundations. For example, a hospital may retain its stable ethical protocols but adopt modular diagnostic agents, while its staff reskill to interpret and manage these outputs. Both sides adapt without chaos. Stability is anchored, but renewal is possible.

Credentialing illustrates how modularity and identity converge in practical terms. Evidence-linked portfolios increasingly act as modular "snapshots" of professional identity, documenting skills as they are gained, refined, or retired. A software engineer might present not only a degree but a record of cloud certifications, design projects, and leadership modules. Employers benefit by seeing a more dynamic picture of adaptability, while institutions gain data that reveal which competencies are in highest demand. This feedback loop ties modular learning architectures directly to labor-market relevance. As credentials grow more granular, identities grow more fluid, with degrees serving as scaffolds and modular badges supplying real-time updates. A career then becomes less of a single path and more of an evolving mosaic. Learning shifts from an endpoint to a continuous, identity-driven process.

Governance provides the connective tissue that keeps modularity and identity credible. Without shared standards, modular systems risk fragmentation and modular identities risk incoherence. For systems, governance means transparent APIs, ethical oversight boards, and routine audits to ensure interoperability. For individuals, it involves verifiable credentials, contestable evaluations, and privacy protections that preserve ownership of identity. Governance is what transforms modularity from scattered parts into strategy and identity from improvisation into coherent narrative. For example, digital badges only hold value when anchored in trusted frameworks such as 1EdTech standards. Similarly, organizations gain legitimacy when their modular systems are subject to independent review. Trust elevates modularity and identity from abstractions into functioning realities.

Pedagogical practices provide another arena where modularity and identity converge. Instead of rigid, siloed courses, curricula can be structured as modular pathways that students combine to shape individualized trajectories. Assessments can move from final verdicts to evidence nodes, contributing to living portfolios. Teachers, too, adopt modular roles: facilitator in one context, critic in another, and orchestrator of collaborative machine tools in a third. These roles flex as student needs evolve, creating classrooms that act as laboratories for iterative identity formation. A student might graduate not just as a "psychology major" but as someone with a modular toolkit spanning behavioral analysis, data visualization, and human-computer interaction. Such design prepares graduates for workplaces already organized around modularity. Education and work mirror each other, reinforcing adaptability across domains.

Workplace cultures also evolve when modularity and identity are aligned. Teams can be composed dynamically, pulling in specialists as needed instead of relying on rigid hierarchies. A worker may adopt identity modules such as analyst, project lead, or collaborator with digital agents depending on the project phase. Organizations increasingly frame careers as modular progressions rather than fragile ladders, reducing fears of obsolescence. For example, a journalist might rotate between reporting, curating AI-generated content, and serving as a verifier of automated outputs. Modularity provides the organizational infrastructure, and identity supplies the flexibility to inhabit new roles. Careers become resilient mosaics rather than brittle trajectories. This synergy allows both individuals and institutions to respond nimbly to disruption.

Strategically, the convergence of modularity and identity prepares organizations and individuals for volatility. Economic shocks, political instability, or technological disruptions demand systems capable of quick reconfiguration and people capable of redefining themselves without collapse. Modularity supplies the structure for resilience, while identity provides the narrative coherence that makes change meaningful. When the two are aligned, disruptions become redesigns rather than breakdowns. A disrupted profession, such as traditional publishing, can recombine skills into new forms like digital content orchestration. A disruptive technology, such as generative video, becomes a module integrated into existing creative infrastructures rather than a threat to them. Leaders who approach modularity and identity as interdependent move from defensive adaptation to proactive design. Growth becomes the natural outcome of volatility, not its casualty.

Therefore, this first chapter has demonstrated that adoption of intelligent systems is rarely held back by technical limitations alone. Instead, the real barriers are cultural, organizational, and cognitive, often rooted in governance gaps and uneven readiness. Dual-process theory provides a lens to understand why fast, intuitive action must always be paired with slow, reflective oversight for sustainable outcomes. Identity adds another dimension by showing that learners and professionals are no longer shaped exclusively by human institutions but also by their interactions with machine collaborators. These collaborations shift the way expertise, authorship, and creativity are distributed, making identity itself adaptive and co-constructed. The link between modularity and identity reveals a dual framework: modular systems allow structural flexibility, while adaptive identities allow individuals and organizations to reconfigure without collapse. Together, they provide a strategic foundation for resilience in times of rapid change. This insight anchors the book and sets the stage for the chapters that follow.

Chapter 2 explores the shift from monolithic to modular architectures, charting the historical development of system design. Early centralized models were powerful but brittle, prone to failure when stressed by complexity or scale. Modular and multi-agent designs, by contrast, distribute work across specialized components, allowing systems to adapt incrementally. The advantages of modularity include task-specific specialization, purpose-built efficiency, and scalability that avoids the collapse of monolithic structures. Deterministic safeguards in high-stakes environments demonstrate that modularity is not just about efficiency but also about trust and reliability. Standards and operating models further stabilize modular adoption, preventing fragmentation while enabling growth. Examples from education, healthcare, and industry highlight why modular systems are increasingly indispensable. By emphasizing modularity, this chapter provides the architectural scaffolding that supports every argument that follows.

Chapter 3 turns to the fast learning paradigm, focusing on rapid generation and iterative refinement. Generative systems are shown to accelerate brainstorming, creative production, and agile problem-solving. Weak models can still be valuable for idea generation, while advanced systems allow sophisticated outputs with speed. Human-in-the-loop oversight ensures that rapid ideation is not confused with final results but instead forms the raw material for refinement. Iterative workflows demonstrate how individuals and teams use these tools for quick upskilling, reducing the time from novice to competent practitioner. Case studies from both education and industry illustrate how fast learning is applied in practice. These examples reveal the value of speed when structured within guided processes. The fast paradigm is therefore positioned as essential, but always incomplete without its slower counterpart.

Chapter 4 complements this discussion by examining the slow learning paradigm, which focuses on deliberate analysis and critical thinking. Intelligent systems can scaffold reflective engagement by providing critique, counterarguments, and structured reasoning. Processes such as staged analysis, metacognitive scaffolding, and simulated "dreaming" emulate the slow, deliberative qualities of human cognition. Evaluative criteria are introduced to measure how effectively systems support deep learning, both in classrooms and research contexts. Case studies illustrate how immersive exemplars encourage learners to slow down, reflect, and evaluate more carefully. The contrast with fast workflows shows why both paradigms are necessary in tandem. Institutions that overemphasize one at the expense of the other risk imbalance, either in speed without accuracy or reflection without agility. This chapter therefore deepens the dual-process framework introduced in the opening.

Chapter 5 extends the theme of identity by examining credentialing systems that evolve alongside learners and workers. Traditional degrees are contrasted with dynamic, evidence-linked credentials that represent identity as a portfolio rather than a fixed label. Personal agents play an active role by helping individuals articulate skills, curate portfolios, and navigate career choices. This creates opportunities for more precise alignment between personal identity and labor market needs. Yet ethical, privacy, and governance challenges emerge as credentials become more agentic and data-driven. Professionals must now manage not only their competencies but also the digital infrastructures that record and present them. Lifelong learning becomes a process of continuous credentialing, reshaping identity with every new module acquired. This chapter frames identity as dynamic, modular, and inseparable from evolving systems of recognition.

Chapter 6 shifts attention to organizational culture, showing how institutions either accelerate or stall adoption depending on readiness. Leadership urgency often collides with resistance at the cultural level, where workers hesitate or lack skills to engage. Structured training programs provide pathways for competency development, ensuring literacy in prompting, evaluation, and modular fluency. Overcoming resistance depends on creating inclusive environments where experimentation is normalized and trust is built. Case studies highlight organizations that have succeeded by aligning executive vision with workforce development. These examples show that adoption is not simply a technical challenge but a cultural one. Without culture-building, even modular systems and adaptive credentials fail to gain traction. This chapter demonstrates that institutions must cultivate readiness across every role to unlock value.

Chapter 7 provides concrete illustrations by examining custom solutions across domains such as healthcare, education, the public sector, and creative industries. Each sector faces unique challenges that call for specialized tools, from assistive agents to predictive systems and autonomous solutions. Evidence of measurable return on investment is presented, demonstrating workflow optimization and improved user experiences. Sector-specific solutions also highlight tensions between efficiency and ethics, showing how governance mediates adoption. Case studies provide vivid accounts of both successes and failures, offering transferable lessons. The diversity of applications illustrates how modularity and identity interact in different contexts. Institutions that adopt tailored strategies find greater value than those that rely on generic implementations. This chapter grounds abstract frameworks in the practical realities of adoption across industries.

Chapter 8 turns back to individuals and teams, focusing on the training and deployment of personal and professional agents. Methodologies for developing, refining, and maintaining agents are outlined, emphasizing adaptability and long-term sustainability. Applications include experiential learning, productivity augmentation, and enhanced workforce preparedness. Workers must develop power skills—such as collaboration, orchestration, and evaluation—alongside technical competencies. Case studies demonstrate how personal agents extend human capacity while requiring oversight to prevent errors or drift. Evaluative criteria provide benchmarks for best practices in long-term strategy. This chapter shows how individuals can integrate agents into their professional and personal lives responsibly. It bridges organizational adoption with the lived practices of daily work.

The final chapter, Chapter 9, synthesizes these threads into a new paradigm for learning and work. Fast and slow cognition, modular architectures, and evolving identities are drawn together into a unified framework. Strategic visions for education and industry highlight how institutions can design for resilience rather than react defensively to disruption. Actionable recommendations are presented for educators, policymakers, technologists, and organizational leaders. Ethical imperatives such as contestability, inclusion, and dignity are emphasized as non-negotiable conditions for sustainable futures. Case studies and forecasts illustrate possible trajectories if these principles are followed. The book concludes with a pragmatic optimism: volatility can be turned into redesign when modularity and identity evolve in alignment. Identity-driven systems emerge as the foundation for thriving in an uncertain future. This final synthesis closes the loop, connecting the opening questions of adoption to a coherent strategic vision.

REFERENCES

Ali, W., Khan, A.Z., Ahmad, F. and Mahmood, F. 2024. Exploring artificial intelligence readiness framework for public sector organizations: An expert opinion methodology. Journal of Business and Management Research. 3(3): 85–129.

Babur, M.N. 2025. AI in education: A luxury or a necessity for developing nations? Journal of Biological and Allied Health Sciences. 5(1): 1–2.

Brosnan, M. and Ashwin, C. 2023. Thinking, fast and slow on the autism spectrum. Autism. 27(5): 1245–1255.

Burstein, J., LaFlair, G.T., Kunnan, A.J. and von Davier, A.A. 2021. A theoretical assessment ecosystem for a digital-first assessment—The Duolingo English Test. DRR-21-04.

Cengage Group. 2025. AI's impact on education in 2025. https://www.cengagegroup.com/news/perspectives/2025/ais-impact-on-education-in-2025/

Cheng, T. 2022. Artificial agential intelligence. Journal of Artificial Intelligence and Consciousness. 9(03): 285–295.

Copeland, D., Gonyeau, M.J., Van Amburgh, J. and Bronich, T. 2023. Professional identity formation: Using an institutional EPA based IPPE assessment. American Journal of Pharmaceutical Education. 87(8).

Deloitte. 2025. New Deloitte tech exec survey spotlights a moment of reinvention for the tech C-suite as need for GenAI skills, cross-functional collaboration becomes critical [Press release]. https://www.deloitte.com/us/en/about/press-room/new-deloitte-tech-exec-survey-spotlights-a-moment-of-reinvention.html

Dhaliwal, G. 2017. Premature closure? Not so fast. BMJ Quality & Safety. 26(2): 87–89.

Dulundu, A. 2024. AI in education: benefits and concerns. Next Generation Journal for the Young Researchers. 8: 81.

EDUCAUSE. 2025. 2025 EDUCAUSE AI Landscape Study: Introduction and key findings. https://www.educause.edu/content/2025/2025-educause-ai-landscape-study/introduction-and-key-findings

El Arab, R.A., Al Moosa, O.A., Abuadas, F.H. and Somerville, J. 2025. The role of AI in nursing education and practice: Umbrella review. Journal of Medical Internet Research. 27: e69881.

Fabiano, F., Ganapini, M.B., Horesh, L., Loreggia, A., Murugesan, K., Pallagani, V., et al. 2021. Epistemic planning in a fast and slow setting. *In*: TFSOCTAI@ AAAI Fall Symposium.

Ferri, G., Ploner, M. and Rizzolli, M. 2021. Trading fast and slow: The role of deliberation in experimental financial markets. Journal of Behavioral and Experimental Finance. 32: 100593.

Fischhoff, B. 2024. Daniel Kahneman (1934–2024). Science. 384(6695): 515–515.

Flavell, J.H. 1979. Metacognition and cognitive monitoring: A new area of cognitive–developmental inquiry. American Psychologist. 34(10): 906.

García, O.A., García, M.D.C.R. and Alonso-Secades, V. 2025. Perceptions, strategies, and challenges of teachers in the integration of artificial intelligence in primary education: A systematic review. Journal of Information Technology Education: Research. 24: 006.

Gartner. 2025. Generative AI hits the Trough of Disillusionment as adoption surges into production. https://www.gartner.com/en/articles/generative-ai-hits-the-trough-of-disillu sionment-and-adoption-surges-into-production

Gulati, A., Soni, S. and Rao, S. 2021. Interleaving fast and slow decision making. *In*: 2021 IEEE International Conference on Robotics and Automation (ICRA), pp. 1535–1541. IEEE.

IT Pro. 2025. CFOs were skeptical about AI investment, but they've changed their tune since the arrival of agents. https://www.itpro.com/business/business-strategy/cfos-were-skeptical-about-ai-investment-but-theyve-changed-their-tune-since-the-arrival-of-agents

Kannengiesser, U. and Gero, J.S. 2019. Design thinking, fast and slow: A framework for Kahneman's dual-system theory in design. Design Science. 5: e10.

Kellogg, K., Bach, N., Ciccarelli, L.J. and Mollick, E. 2024. No shortcuts for generative AI upskilling. MIT Sloan School of Management and Boston Consulting Group. Retrieved: https://mitsloan.mit.edu/press/no-shortcuts-generative-ai-upskilling

Landau, S., Dempsey, J.X., Kamar, E., Bellovin, S.M. and Pool, R. 2024. Challenging the machine: Contestability in government AI systems. arXiv preprint arXiv:2406.10430.

Larose-Pierre, M., Cleven, A.J., Renaud, A., Hughes, J.A., McQuade, B., Griffin, B.L. and Johnson, C. 2023. Reevaluating core elements of emotional intelligence in professional identity formation for inclusion in pharmacy education. American Journal of Pharmaceutical Education. 87(6): 100082.

Maroteau, G., An, J.S., Murgier, J., Hulet, C., Ollivier, M. and Ferreira, A. 2023. Evaluation of the impact of large language learning models on articles submitted to Orthopaedics & Traumatology: Surgery & Research (OTSR): A significant increase in the use of artificial intelligence in 2023. Orthopaedics & Traumatology: Surgery & Research. 109(8): 103720.

McKinsey & Company. 2025. The state of AI: How organizations are rewiring to capture value. https://www.mckinsey.com/capabilities/quantumblack/our-insights/the-state-of-ai-how-organizations-are-rewiring-to-capture-value

MIT Sloan Management Review Middle East. 2025. Only 2% of global organizations ready to scale AI securely, new report reveals. https://www.mitsloanme.com/article/only-2-of-global-organizations-ready-to-scale-ai-securely-new-report-reveals/

Mohammadi, A. 2025. New AI Technology Integration for Industry-University Cooperation. Journal of Comprehensive Business Administration Research. https://doi.org/10.47852/bonviewJCBAR52024118

Mollick, E. 2024. Co-Intelligence: Living and Working with AI. Penguin.

Mureșan, M. 2023. Impact of artificial intelligence on education. *In*: Proceedings of the 32nd International RAIS Conference on Social Sciences and Humanities, pp. 81–85. Scientia Moralitas Research Institute.

Nickerson, J., Saltz, J., Lindberg, A. and Seidel, S. 2025. Introduction to the Minitrack on AI, Organizing, and Management. *In*: Proceedings of the 57th Hawaii International Conference on System Sciences. https://hdl.handle.net/10125/107082

Omri, A., Omri, H. and Afi, H. 2025. Exploring the impact of AI on unemployment for people with disabilities: do educational attainment and governance matter? Frontiers in Public Health. 13: 1559101.

Rehman, M., Khalid, F., Sheth, U., Al-Duaij, L., Chow, J., Azim, A., et al. 2024. Quarantining from professional identity: How did COVID-19 impact professional identity formation in undergraduate medical education? Perspectives on Medical Education. 13(1): 130.

Reuters. 2025. AI is driving change in supply chains, but investment remains cautious. https://www.reuters.com/world/us/ai-driving-change-supply-chains-cautious-investment-2025-07-xx/

Romero, M. 2024. Lifelong learning challenges in the era of artificial intelligence: A computational thinking perspective. arXiv preprint arXiv:2405.19837.

Salesforce Newsroom. 2025. New Slack research: Daily AI usage among workers surges 233%. https://www.salesforce.com/news/stories/daily-ai-workforce-use-growth/

Schwab, K., Meerts-Brandsma, L., Qwynne Lackey, N., Povilaitis, V., Zajchowski, C., Moseley, B., et al. 2022. Learning, fast and slow. SCHOLE: A Journal of Leisure Studies and Recreation Education. 37(3): 186–193.

Slack Workforce Lab. 2024. Despite AI enthusiasm, Workforce Index reveals workers aren't yet unlocking its benefits. https://slack.com/blog/news/the-workforce-index-june-2024

Strannegård, C., von Haugwitz, R., Wessberg, J. and Balkenius, C. 2013. A cognitive architecture based on dual process theory. *In*: International Conference on Artificial General Intelligence, pp. 140–149. Berlin, Heidelberg: Springer Berlin Heidelberg.

Ta'an, W.A., Damrah, S., Al-Hammouri, M.M. and Williams, B. 2025. Professional identity and its relationships with AI readiness and interprofessional collaboration. PLoS One. 20(5): e0322794.

Thomson Reuters Institute. 2025. 2025 C-Suite survey: Digital transformation & AI [PDF]. https://www.thomsonreuters.com/en-us/posts/wp-content/uploads/sites/20/2025/05/C-Suite-Report-2025.pdf

Turner, L., Knopp, M.I., Mendonca, E.A. and Desai, S. 2025. Bridging artificial intelligence and medical education: Navigating the alignment paradox. ATS Scholar. 6(2): 135–148.

Tversky, B. 2025. Daniel Kahneman (1934–2024).

UNESCO. (n.d.). Artificial intelligence in education. https://www.unesco.org/en/digital-education/artificial-intelligence

Venkatraman, V., Timpone, R., Garcia-Garcia, M., Godard, O., Baldo, D., Schoeller, M., et al. 2020. Disrupting system 1 thinking: Better science for smarter marketing. ESOMAR Festival. 140.

Vudugula, S., Chebrolu, S.K., Bhuiyan, M. and Rozony, F.Z. 2023. Integrating artificial intelligence in strategic business decision-making: A systematic review of predictive models. International Journal of Scientific Interdisciplinary Research. 4(1): 01–26.

Zhong, J., Li, Z., Xu, Z., Wen, X. and Xu, Q. 2025. Dyve: Thinking fast and slow for dynamic process verification. arXiv preprint arXiv:2502.11157.

Chapter 2

Foundations of Modular AI—Shifting from Monolithic Systems

2.1 HISTORICAL DEVELOPMENT FROM MONOLITHIC MODELS TO MODULAR AND MULTI-AGENT SOLUTIONS

Architecture—not just raw capability—now determines the outcomes of intelligent systems. Many organizations still attempt to deploy a single, all-purpose model, only to encounter brittleness, opaque errors, and governance headaches. The alternative is modular composition: a system in which specialized components plan, retrieve, synthesize, test, critique, and verify, all coordinated by an orchestration layer (Figure 2.1). This separation of concerns improves reliability, reduces cost, and makes compliance and audit trails feasible rather than aspirational. It also mirrors human workflows: quick ideation balanced by slower evaluation, with clear handoffs and checkpoints. In practical terms, this means pairing deterministic services such as search, rule-based filters, or calculators with probabilistic generators that handle creativity and reasoning. Everyday examples include customer service bots that retrieve policies from a database while generating natural language responses, or tutoring systems that combine rule-based grading rubrics with adaptive, generative feedback. Prompts, tools, memory, and evaluators become versioned components that can be tested and swapped without rebuilding the entire system. This marks a decisive shift away from the monolithic model toward multi-agent compositions that evolve safely over time (Table 2.1).

DOI: 10.1201/9781003688013-2

Table 2.1 Evolution of Modular AI Principles

Stage/ Paradigm	*Core Contribution*	*Example/Analogy*	*Modern Analogue in Generative AI*
Expert Systems (1970s–80s)	Monolithic knowledge bases bundling rules, facts, and control logic	Early medical diagnostic programs	Oversized LLMs treated as "one-box" solvers
Blackboard Systems	Independent knowledge sources coordinated via shared workspace	Hearsay-II for speech recognition	Orchestration layers routing outputs of multiple agents
Distributed Problem Solving	Protocols for autonomous agents to self-organize tasks	Contract Net Protocol (Smith, 1980)	Ride-sharing platforms; agent bidding in workflows
Software Engineering/ Microservices	Encapsulation, modular services, swappable functions	Replacing a washing machine motor without buying a new appliance	Modular pipelines, prompt+tool separation, versioned components
Transformer Scaling Era	General-purpose models with vast parameters	"Universal solver" temptation	GPT-4/Claude large models—impressive but brittle alone
Retrieval-Augmented Generation (RAG)	Pairing deterministic retrieval with probabilistic synthesis	Legal assistant fetching case law before drafting	Indexed corpora + LLMs for factual grounding
Structured Tool Use	Function calls, schema validation, connectors for predictable integrations	Pilot's pre-flight checklist	OpenAI Function Calling, LangChain Tools
Planning–Action Hybrids	Interleaving reasoning, acting, and self-critique	Student solving a math problem with scratch work + textbook check	ReAct, Tree-of-Thoughts, Reflexion
Operational Frameworks	Packaged orchestration for reproducibility, audit, and human oversight	Assembly line with quality control at each station	AutoGen, LangGraph, Hugging Face Agents
Embodied/ Exploratory Systems	Curriculum-building, skill libraries, self-verification	Voyager in Minecraft exploration	Modular skill reuse and lifelong learning clones

Early generations of knowledge systems were built as tightly coupled, single-box programs that bundled facts, rules, and control logic into one structure. Flagship expert systems performed impressively in narrow domains but became brittle and expensive to maintain as requirements changed. A shift began with the blackboard paradigm, which split problem-solving into independent "knowledge sources" coordinated over a shared workspace. This mattered because contributors could be swapped or upgraded without rewriting the entire program (McManus, 1991). Projects like Hearsay-II showed how opportunistic, modular control outperformed rigid pipelines for messy tasks such as speech understanding.

The blackboard lineage seeded a core idea: multiple specialists cooperating could outperform one giant program attempting everything (Lesser and Erman, 1977). Modern readers might compare this to a hospital team: a speech therapist, neurologist, and psychologist working together outperform one generalist doctor. The blackboard approach foreshadowed today's orchestration layers that mediate tools and skills, marking the first break from single-engine designs.

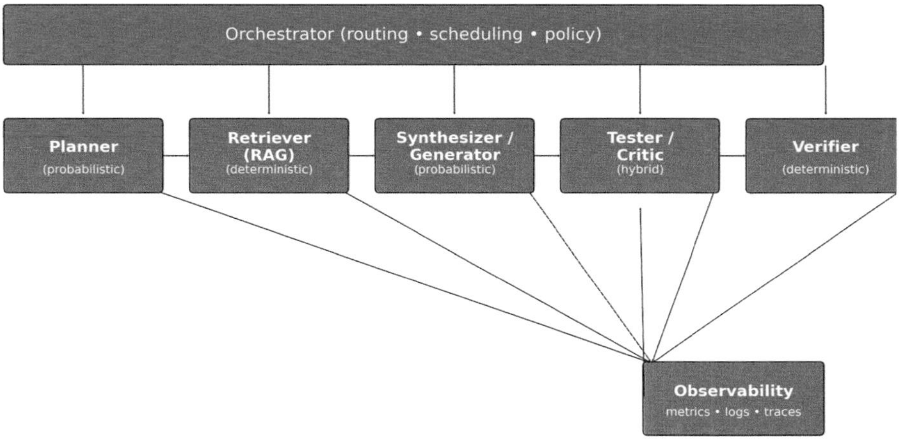

Figure 2.1 From Monolith to Orchestra: Modular Architecture.

A second stream emerged through distributed problem solving, where autonomous processes coordinate through protocols instead of shared memory. The Contract Net Protocol formalized task announcements, bids, and awards, showing how loosely coupled processes could self-organize around work (Smith, 1980). Theories of rational agents soon followed, framing decision-making with explicit beliefs, desires, and intentions (Rao and Georgeff, 1995). Standards such as KQML and the FIPA Agent Communication Language defined common semantics for communication across agents (Finn et al., 1997; FIPA, 2002). These innovations made multi-party systems designable and testable rather than ad hoc experiments. Just as importantly, they normalized the view that competence could be distributed across peers instead of centralized in a single solver (Wooldridge and Jennings, 1995). A relatable example is how ride-sharing platforms dispatch drivers: each driver-agent coordinates through shared protocols instead of one central dispatcher handling every decision. Coordination primitives matured alongside inference formalisms, creating a foundation for modern multi-agent systems.

Principles from software engineering provided another durable stream of influence. Parnas argued that modules should conceal design decisions likely to change, effectively inventing modern encapsulation as a hedge against uncertainty (Parnas, 1972). This ethos later drove service-oriented architectures and microservices, which broke applications into separable services at internet scale (Fowler and Lewis, 2015). For learning systems, the lesson was clear: isolate functions behind interfaces, version them, and compose them at runtime (Porter et al., 2016). When generative engines began calling external tools, they inherited these proven practices. Continuous delivery now extended beyond software code to prompts, retrievers, and evaluators (Newman, 2021). This allowed engineers to update parts of a pipeline without freezing the entire stack. An analogy here is modern home appliances: a faulty washing machine motor can be swapped out without replacing the whole appliance. Modularity shifted from philosophy to practical engineering discipline.

Neural breakthroughs, especially the transformer architecture, briefly re-centralized power into large, general-purpose models (Vaswani et al., 2017; Zhu et al., 2021). Scaling laws encouraged ever-bigger models, tempting organizations to treat them as universal solutions. Yet even highly capable systems struggled with arithmetic accuracy, factual consistency, and external tool use—precisely the areas where smaller deterministic components excelled. The pendulum swung back toward splitting "think, look up, and act" into separate, testable steps. Modern deployments typically pair a strong general model with specialized fetchers, planners, and verifiers (Lewis et al., 2020). This echoes the team metaphor: a capable generalist surrounded by domain specialists is more effective than the generalist working alone. The general-purpose model became a component, not the system.

Retrieval-augmented generation (RAG) crystallized modular composition into a repeatable design pattern. RAG externalizes knowledge into indexes and constrains synthesis to retrieved passages, reducing fabricated content and improving updateability. Because retrieval is deterministic and auditable, it satisfies governance far better than embedding every fact inside a model's parameters (Cheng et al., 2025). The generator focuses on reasoning and phrasing, while retrieval guarantees provenance and currency. Toolkits extended RAG into pipelines with chunkers, rankers, and evaluators, making the division of labor concrete. A familiar example is a legal assistant that retrieves case law documents before drafting arguments, ensuring accuracy and citations. From there, routing to calculators, code interpreters, or databases became natural extensions. RAG normalized modularity at the center of generative workflows (Lewis et al., 2020).

Once models learned when to call tools, composition matured into an operating norm. Structured function calls and schema-validated outputs made integrations predictable and testable in production (OpenAI, 2023; 2024). Connectors and discovery protocols broadened the attachable ecosystem (Anthropic, 2024; 2025). These advances let builders wire calculators, search engines, or APIs into a conversational plan while evaluators checked each step. Conversations shifted from free-flowing text to programmable state machines with observable checkpoints (Choi et al., 2023). An analogy is a pilot's pre-flight checklist: every step is explicit, observable, and correctable. This shift underpins most production-grade assistants and agentic services today. A runtime can now swap tools or validators without retraining the underlying model, lowering costs and improving safety.

Research soon fused planning and action within inference itself. ReAct demonstrated that interleaving reasoning with environment actions outperformed purely reflective or purely reactive methods (Yao et al., 2023). Tree-of-Thoughts generalized problem-solving into exploratory search with backtracking, allowing models to reconsider paths before committing. Reflexion introduced self-critique and memory, enabling systems to learn from prior attempts without retraining (Qu et al., 2024). Toolformer showed that models could learn when to call APIs by training on their own outputs (Schick et al., 2023). Together, these patterns defined the inner life of a capable assistant: propose, act, observe, and revise (Shinn et al., 2023). For non-specialists, this is akin to how a student solves a math problem: sketch an answer, check against resources, adjust, and try again. Planning became integral to inference rather than a separate design step (Yao et al., 2023).

Enterprise and open-source frameworks then packaged these ideas into usable scaffolds. AutoGen orchestrated multi-agent conversations and human-in-the-loop feedback for safer long-running tasks (Wu et al., 2024). LangGraph represented assistants as state machines with cycles and checkpoints, aligning with compliance and audit needs (LangChain, 2024; 2025). Hugging Face's Agents offered composable tools and transparent prompts, emphasizing reproducibility (Hugging Face, 2024). These runtimes turned abstract research into production practice: keep components small and swappable, coordinate them through protocols, and monitor them closely. Just as manufacturing lines rely on interchangeable parts rather than custom-built machines, these frameworks reduced complexity while increasing reliability. Builders could now scale systems through structure, not just by adding parameters. Observability hooks at each step gave operations teams new levers for governance (Allam, 2024).

Embodied and open-ended exemplars pushed composition further. Voyager decomposed gameplay into an evolving curriculum, growing skill libraries, and iterative self-verification, outperforming prior systems in exploration (Wang et al., 2023). Instead of reinventing each action, Voyager retrieved, modified, and reused code skills as modules, echoing the modular learning patterns of human problem-solvers. Later projects extended multi-agent teams into collaborative planning for real-world tasks, often embedding evaluators to control repetition and side effects (Wu et al., 2021). These cases demonstrate why modular control shells matter for safety and governance. Capabilities can be audited at the module boundary rather than only at the final output, making accountability feasible. An accessible analogy is an assembly line where each station can be checked independently rather than only inspecting the final product. Systems that learn to organize their own skills advance fastest, proving that composition itself is capability (Wang et al., 2023).

By 2024–2025, the field had converged on a hybrid model: a strong general-purpose engine surrounded by modular services, tools, and collaborating agents. Legacy standards such as FIPA's messaging protocols provided inspiration for interoperability, while modern cloud and open-source ecosystems stabilized interfaces for planning, memory, and evaluation (FIPA, 2002; OpenAI, 2024; LangChain, 2025). The continuity from blackboards to tool-calling is striking: semi-independent contributors coordinate, arbitrate control, and surface state for review (McManus, 1991; Finn et al., 1997). Organizationally, this mirrors human teams where retrievers, planners, and verifiers collaborate more effectively than one polymath attempting everything (Wooldridge and Jennings, 1995).

Continuous integration now applies to prompts and tools as much as to code, allowing constant iteration without retraining entire models (OpenAI, 2024). For non-specialists, this is similar to updating an app's plug-ins rather than rewriting the whole program. The monolith has given way to the orchestra, where many players combine under structured direction.

The historical trajectory from monolithic expert systems to modular, multi-agent compositions reveals a recurring lesson: composition outperforms concentration. Early one-box programs, while impressive in narrow domains, collapsed under complexity and change. Successive innovations—from blackboard systems and distributed protocols to microservices and retrieval-augmented generation—shifted intelligence into separable, auditable components that can be recombined as needs evolve. This modular ethos now defines the state of practice: a general-purpose model functions as one contributor within an orchestrated ensemble of planners, retrievers, evaluators, and verifiers.

The benefits are twofold. First, modularity improves technical reliability, lowering costs, reducing brittleness, and enabling compliance through visible checkpoints. Second, it mirrors human workflows, in which rapid idea generation is balanced by deliberate evaluation and role specialization. Just as organizations thrive when expertise is distributed across diverse teams, intelligent systems mature when roles are clearly defined and independently testable.

By 2025, the field has converged on hybrid architectures that treat large models as powerful but partial components. Continuous integration now applies not only to code but to prompts, tools, and evaluators, reflecting a cultural shift toward orchestration as the true capability. For institutions, this evolution underscores a crucial point: trustworthy automation depends less on model size than on the design of the surrounding architecture. The question is no longer "Which model is best?" but "How should specialized roles, interfaces, and governance mechanisms be composed into a resilient whole?"

2.2 ADVANTAGES OF MODULAR AI: PURPOSE-BUILT EFFICIENCY, SCALABILITY, TASK-SPECIFICITY

The move from single, all-purpose models to modular designs is not just an engineering preference—it is a response to real-world demands. Organizations today need systems that are reliable, affordable, and explainable, not just powerful in the abstract. Modularity achieves this by breaking work into clear roles: planning, retrieving information, synthesizing responses, testing, critiquing, and verifying (Figure 2.2). In the same way a newsroom assigns different tasks to reporters, editors, and fact-checkers, modular AI routes work to the right specialist at the right time. Each part of the system can be tuned for its job, making the whole process more predictable. Mixture-of-Experts designs provide one clear example: instead of waking up every "expert" at once, the system activates only the few it needs, saving resources and speeding up responses (Mu and Lin, 2025). Experiments in translation and language modeling show that this approach improves performance while lowering hardware costs (Huang et al., 2024). The end result is a system that runs faster and more cheaply while remaining easier to monitor and adjust.

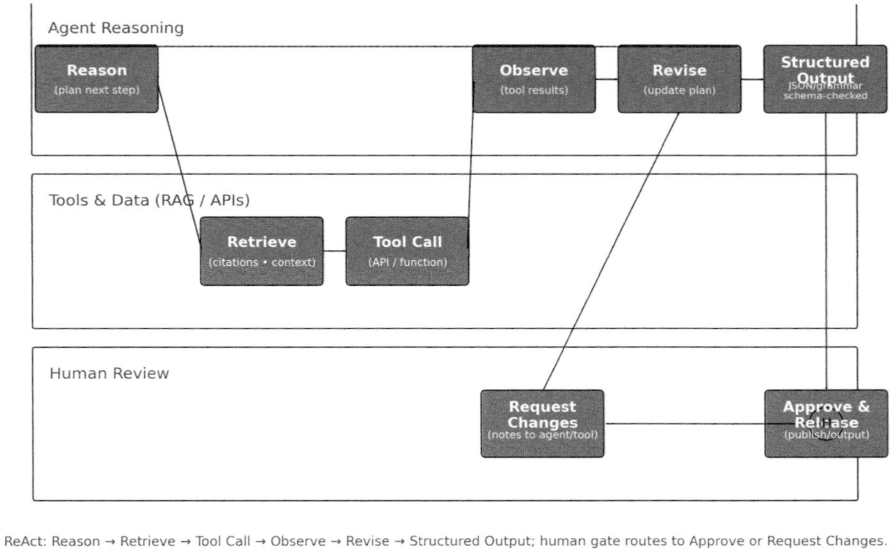

Figure 2.2 Plan-Think-Act with RAG and Tools.

Scalability, one of the hardest challenges in production, also benefits from modular thinking. In cloud systems, decomposed services can be deployed and maintained independently, so a single failure does not take everything down (Agrawal, 2025; Tadi, 2022). This is like designing a modern airplane with multiple redundant engines: if one fails, the rest keep the plane in the air. By scaling each service based on actual demand—extra GPUs for retrieval, simple CPUs for routing—teams spend resources where they matter most. Governance improves too, because every module has an owner responsible for monitoring, error handling, and updates. This means outages are localized, fixes are faster, and accountability is clearer. Platform teams increasingly adopt templates that include resilience checks from the start, much like builders follow standard codes to ensure bridges and buildings are safe (Souza, 2024). The system scales not through brute force, but through careful design that contains problems before they spread.

Specialization also helps systems succeed at the level of individual tasks. Research shows that multi-agent teams with distinct roles—planner, retriever, solver, critic—complete tasks more reliably than one all-in-one model (Wang et al., 2024). The analogy here is a medical team: the surgeon, anesthesiologist, and nurse each contribute in different ways, and together their coordination produces better outcomes than a generalist doctor working alone. With explicit roles, developers can improve one piece, such as the retriever, without risking the rest of the pipeline. Over time, these roles become reusable assets, a catalog of specialists that can be plugged into new projects. For organizations, this makes systems easier to audit, since responsibilities are assigned to modules rather than hidden in a single "black box." Transparency of responsibility fosters trust among regulators, clients, and users. In practice, this division of labor brings both reliability and accountability. Specialization, in short, makes systems stronger by embracing diversity rather than collapsing everything into one model.

One of the biggest benefits of modularity lies in grounding—making sure outputs are accurate and traceable. RAG is a prime example: it splits fact-finding from text generation. The retriever pulls in current, verifiable information, while the generator focuses on weaving that information into clear language (Lewis et al., 2020; Cheng et al., 2025). For users, this means answers that cite sources, like a student paper with footnotes, instead of unsupported guesses. Diagnostic tools such as RAGChecker can even score retrieval and generation separately, turning "something went wrong" into a specific engineering question (Ru et al., 2024). This makes improvement faster and cheaper, since updating the retrieval index is easier than retraining a giant model. Non-specialists can think of this like separating the roles of librarian and writer: accuracy depends on both, but each can be evaluated independently. This clarity transforms reliability from aspiration into routine practice. Grounding, therefore, becomes a hallmark of trustworthy modular design.

Verification also becomes more practical in modular designs. Instead of treating critique as optional, systems can assign it to a dedicated module. Studies show that when generators call tools like calculators, code checkers, or search engines to revise their answers, accuracy improves across a wide range of tasks (Gou et al., 2023). In human terms, this is like a writer fact-checking their own article with reference books before submitting it to an editor. In production, the same principle resembles reliability checks in engineering: trial runs, stress tests, or safety valves. By treating evaluation as a separate service, organizations can decide when it is worth slowing down for extra scrutiny. This makes it possible to balance efficiency with safety, building systems that users can trust without paralyzing the workflow (Souza, 2024). Verification as a service is one of the clearest proofs that modularity improves governance. A system that critiques itself is more likely to be trusted by others.

Efficiency gains extend into computing itself. Expert-based architectures that route tasks dynamically show dramatic improvements in speed and memory use (Huang et al., 2024). Because experts are modular, they can be distributed across different hardware, with heavier tasks running on premium accelerators and lighter ones handled by cheaper machines. This is not unlike a delivery company sending semi-trucks for cross-country shipments and bicycles for local deliveries: each vehicle is chosen for the job at hand. Costs become more predictable, and underused components can be retired to keep the system lean. Purpose-built efficiency here means every specialist earns its place in the system or is replaced. For businesses, that translates into lower operating costs without compromising performance. At the same time, efficiency unlocks wider access, as cheaper deployment lowers the barrier for smaller firms and public institutions. Purpose-built architecture ensures AI can scale to society, not just to tech giants.

Adaptability is another dividend of modular pipelines, especially in specialized fields. Studies comparing retrieval-augmented pipelines to fine-tuned models show that the modular approach performs better across key metrics like BLEU and ROUGE, often by double-digit margins (Briman and Yildiz, 2024). In applied settings such as construction safety, retrieval modules ensured outputs included critical details—like specific measurements or hazard conditions—that fine-tuned models often missed (Krütli and Hanne, 2025). The reason is simple: retrieval brings in domain-specific context on demand without needing to re-train the whole system. For regulated industries, retrieval logs also provide an audit trail for compliance. For non-specialists, this is like updating a library catalog instead of rewriting every book to add new information. Adaptation becomes a matter of updating inputs rather than re-engineering the entire engine. This makes modular designs both agile and compliant. Flexibility, in this sense, is built into the architecture itself.

Security and governance also find firmer footing in modular systems. When every module has explicit roles and observable outputs, security teams can isolate vulnerabilities and patch them without halting the entire pipeline. Logs at the module level give auditors granular insight into what went wrong and when, reducing the risks of opaque "black box" failures (Souza, 2024). Developers can implement tiered safeguards, with sensitive tasks routed through high-trust evaluators and routine tasks handled by lightweight agents. In practical terms, this mirrors airport security: routine bags go through scanners, while suspicious ones are pulled aside for deeper inspection. The layered approach balances throughput with protection. Crucially, modular governance satisfies regulatory expectations for transparency, which is increasingly a prerequisite for adoption in healthcare, finance, and education. A modular system can show its work at every step, making accountability possible where monoliths only offer end results. This builds the foundation for both trust and compliance.

Modularity also supports innovation by enabling experimentation at the edges. Because components can be swapped in and out, researchers can test new retrieval models, evaluation techniques, or orchestration strategies without risking production stability. This is akin to musicians rehearsing with different instruments while the orchestra continues to play the core symphony uninterrupted. Sandboxed testing environments make it possible to innovate continuously while maintaining dependable operations. Innovation cycles accelerate because new ideas can be tried at the module level rather than requiring full-stack redesigns. In academic research, modular design makes reproducibility more achievable, since datasets, prompts, and evaluators can be versioned and shared independently (Porter et al., 2016). For businesses, this means lower R&D costs and faster routes from prototype to production. Modularity does not slow change; it accelerates it by lowering the risk of failure. In effect, modularity turns innovation from disruption into evolution.

Another advantage is cultural alignment within organizations. Modular systems make it easier to distribute responsibility across specialized teams, each accountable for their own service. This parallels how agile methods distribute roles across product owners, scrum masters, and developers. Employees gain clarity about where they fit in the system, reducing both overlap and confusion. Training programs can be tailored to specific modules, allowing employees to upskill in focused areas rather than attempting to master everything. Culturally, this fosters collaboration rather than competition, since success depends on modules coordinating effectively. Leaders also gain clearer levers for management, since performance metrics can be tied to module-level outcomes rather than diffuse system behavior. This transparency supports not just governance but morale, aligning technical structure with human culture. In many ways, modularity is as much an organizational philosophy as a software architecture.

Modularity, therefore, provides a repeatable pathway from pilot projects to enterprise-scale platforms. Because components can be tested and improved independently, organizations can introduce continuous integration, A/B testing, and progressive rollouts in ways that are impossible with monolithic black boxes (Souza, 2024). Budgets become easier to plan, since investment is directed toward specific modules rather than an undifferentiated stack. Hiring plans also align with modules—retrieval engineers, evaluation leads, orchestration developers—reducing pressure on generalists. Over time, asset reuse accelerates development of new solutions, much like Lego blocks being reassembled into new designs. For leaders, this means innovation becomes structured rather than chaotic. Teams can scale their systems without betting everything on a single model or risking catastrophic failure. Modularity, in short, is not just a technical fix but a strategic framework for sustainable growth.

The advantages of modular AI span efficiency, scalability, specialization, grounding, verification, adaptability, security, innovation, culture, and governance. Systems designed as coordinated ensembles of modules outperform monolithic approaches by reducing costs, localizing errors, and making accountability tractable. For developers, modularity offers technical clarity; for leaders, it provides strategic flexibility; and for users, it delivers reliability and trust. The recurring theme is that modularity mirrors the way human teams already operate: distributed expertise coordinated through orchestration. By building systems as ensembles rather than monoliths, organizations gain both resilience and agility. Governance becomes enforceable, innovation becomes safer, and identity formation aligns with flexible skill-building. The lesson is consistent across technical and organizational domains: modularity is not just good engineering but good strategy. It is the architecture of adaptability, ensuring that systems evolve gracefully while remaining transparent and trustworthy.

2.3 DETERMINISTIC OUTPUTS IN HIGH-REGULATION ENVIRONMENTS

Before exploring efficiency and scale, the last section argued that decomposition wins because it routes the right work to the right capability. High-regulation domains prize predictability, traceability, and repeatability over cleverness or novelty. In these settings, deterministic components—rule engines, grammar-constrained decoding, typed schemas, and auditable retrieval—anchor systems that must behave the same way today and tomorrow given the same inputs. Healthcare, finance, and public administration have converged on that principle through a growing literature on uncertainty management, abstention, and formal verification. The governing idea is simple: allow probabilistic learners to explore, but force the final act of decision or formatting through deterministic gates. Constraining surface forms (e.g., JSON that always validates) and admissible actions (e.g., clinically approved orders) converts free-form generation into bounded, testable behavior (Wang et al., 2025). In practice, this approach reduces incident risk and simplifies audits because outputs are schema-checked, logged, and reproducible. The section synthesizes evidence showing how structured outputs, selective prediction, conformal coverage, provenance, and formal methods convert stochastic inference into compliant workflows (Table 2.2). The through-line is governance by design, not governance by after-the-fact review (Bodnari and Travis, 2025; Lambert et al., 2024).

Table 2.2 Deterministic vs. Probabilistic Components and Controls

Component	***Typical Risk Control (Schema, Rules, Abstention)***	***Audit Artifact***
Calculator (deterministic)	Implementation bug; arithmetic precision error	Test log; requirements traceability
Rules engine (deterministic)	Incomplete or outdated rule coverage	Ruleset version history; compliance review notes
Generator (probabilistic LLM)	Hallucination; bias; inconsistent output	Model card; evaluation benchmark results; annotated gold set
Classifier (probabilistic ML model)	Misclassification; data drift; fairness gaps	Confusion matrix; drift monitoring dashboard; audit log

Structured output methods are one of the most direct ways to achieve determinism in intelligent systems. When an output must follow a fixed grammar or schema, whole categories of errors vanish by design. Research in natural language generation demonstrates that grammar-constrained decoding enforces adherence to context-free rules, dramatically improving validity and reducing brittle post-processing steps (Tuccio et al., 2025). Recent decoding techniques go further by masking invalid tokens during generation, ensuring that only syntactically correct sequences are produced, which lowers downstream failure rates (Park et al., 2025). Complementary approaches reshape free-form generations into structured records, prioritizing schema compliance over stylistic variation (Wang et al., 2025). In regulated settings, the simple guarantee of always-valid JSON can be transformative, making audit trails and replay possible at scale. The principle is straightforward: schemas function as contracts and decoding becomes enforcement, not an optional safeguard. Once that discipline is established, reliability at the surface ripples through the entire system.

A second pillar of determinism is selective prediction, sometimes described as the "right to abstain." Instead of forcing a model to offer an answer when uncertainty is high, the system can emit "no decision" under defined thresholds. Clinical studies show that this approach improves accuracy by sending borderline extractions from patient notes to human review rather than risking error (Swaminathan et al., 2024). Broader research confirms that abstention strategies stabilize outcomes in finance and healthcare, where inconsistency across models can otherwise produce harmful handoffs (Black et al., 2021). The compliance value is clear: abstention is not a bug but a specified outcome, supported by rationale, much like a cautious doctor ordering further tests instead of guessing. Operational teams can monitor abstain rates, tune thresholds, and trace overrides, turning uncertainty into a governed choice. Determinism, in this sense, includes the decision not to decide. That deliberate restraint translates into clearer service-level agreements and fewer escalations in high-stakes environments.

Conformal prediction adds a third layer by wrapping predictions with mathematically grounded coverage guarantees. Instead of a single number, the output includes a calibrated interval or a set of possible outcomes that satisfy a user-chosen error rate (Olsson et al., 2022; Sreenivasan et al., 2025). Clinical applications show that conformal wrappers improve reliability by flagging out-of-distribution cases and reducing overconfident errors. New integrations combine calibration with conformal methods to strengthen process monitoring, producing timelier and more trustworthy alerts in healthcare analytics (Majlatow et al., 2025). In practice, this means institutions can act when the prediction set is small and confident, but defer when it is large and ambiguous. Because the error budget is explicit, compliance teams can document risk thresholds and defend them as transparent trade-offs. This transforms statistical uncertainty into a policy tool rather than a hidden liability. Conformal prediction thus bridges probabilistic inference with deterministic governance.

Hybrid systems in clinical decision support illustrate how deterministic logic constrains risk even when machine learning is involved. Reviews emphasize that rule-based CDS tools, while sometimes limited, remain valuable for their predictability and ease of validation (Thayer et al., 2024). Many deployments combine supervised models with post-hoc rules for safety-critical tasks such as allergy detection, ensuring that edge cases are handled conservatively (Berge et al., 2023). The operational rhythm is clear: learned models propose, rules constrain, and humans finalize. Scholars consistently recommend deterministic “if-then-else” logic for critical decisions, while upstream classification or ranking is left to adaptive modules (Bayor et al., 2025). This layering makes failures observable and remediation responsibilities clear. Predictability, not raw flexibility, becomes the defining safeguard. The result is a system that regulators can validate, clinicians can trust, and organizations can maintain over time.

Formal verification pushes determinism beyond outputs into the realm of behavior. Recent research explores verifying plans against temporal logic or safety constraints before execution, effectively turning generative models into components of provably safe pipelines (Lee et al., 2025). Surveys of neural network verification show growing success in bounding robustness and safety over specified input regions, aligning with certification needs in aviation, finance, and medicine (Sbai, 2025). Scholars also propose cryptographic auditing and privacy-preserving proofs, shifting compliance from “trust us” to “prove it” (Thurzo, 2025). The common thread is a move from demonstration to guarantee: the system cannot violate property X under defined assumptions. While proofs are typically local, they cover the most critical properties such as ordering constraints or access permissions. These guarantees narrow the scope of potential failure, reducing both legal and ethical exposure. Verification therefore complements grammar and abstention with enforceable claims of safety.

Provenance and audit trails transform deterministic rules into organizational memory. Biomedical reviews highlight lineage graphs, standardized metadata, and structured logs as essential to reproducibility and post-hoc analysis (Gierend et al., 2024). Governance studies in low-resource settings show that even basic identity and consent tracking allow reliable lineage, reinforcing that traceability is not only for wealthy systems (Li et al., 2024). In practice, provenance makes each decision explainable: which data were retrieved, what rules fired, and which human or system approved the result. Because deterministic modules emit predictable events, the logs are cleaner and easier to interpret. This moves audits from detective work to procedural confirmation. Institutions can align provenance schemas directly with regulatory frameworks and quality standards, ensuring that compliance is continuous rather than episodic. Determinism at the module level thus becomes a foundation for organizational trust.

Updating and change control reveal why deterministic boundaries matter as systems evolve. Methodological reviews stress recalibration and modular revision as ways to maintain validity without full retraining (Meijerink et al., 2025). Bioethics arguments propose that continuously learning systems should be treated as research unless strict governance and control plans are in place (Sparrow, 2024). Large-scale recall studies underscore how many failures stemmed from unclear update protocols rather than from model flaws themselves (Chen et al., 2025). Deterministic interfaces contain this risk by localizing change: a retriever can be swapped, a rule set revised, or a threshold adjusted without destabilizing the entire stack. Institutions then gain the ability to document, test, and roll back safely. In operational terms, this is like upgrading a single component of an aircraft engine rather than replacing the entire plane. The effect is confidence that systems will remain predictable even under constant evolution.

Knowledge-graph–augmented retrieval extends this pattern by grounding outputs in structured facts and relations. Studies report that when retrieval is constrained by graph schemas, customer service response times improve by nearly 29% and coverage becomes more reliable (Xu et al., 2024). Graph constraints also make behavior testable: required entities and connections can be verified before a system generates an answer. In clinical contexts, structured retrieval aligns directly with coding standards and quality documentation, easing integration with compliance requirements. The principle is consistent with structured outputs: schemas at input reduce ambiguity just as schemas at output reduce brittleness. When paired together, pipelines become structured end-to-end, making errors rarer and easier to diagnose. This approach shifts reliability from ad hoc tuning to systemic property. Graph grounding demonstrates that determinism scales with structure, not just with size.

Governance frameworks translate these techniques into operational routines. Reviews highlight risk registers, decision rights, and change-control gates as central features for machine-learning services in enterprise healthcare (Bodnari and Travis, 2025; Stetson et al., 2025). Regulatory syntheses stress validation, explainability appropriate to the context, and robust post-market monitoring—all easier when outputs are structured and rules explicit (Ebad et al., 2025). Clinical surveys confirm that calibrated uncertainty and transparent pathways increase confidence among practitioners (Mienye and Sun, 2024). Across domains, best practices converge on rule-first designs in safety-critical steps and schema-first designs in communication pipelines (Bayor et al., 2025; Labkoff et al., 2024). These patterns show that determinism is not a feature bolted on at the end but the architecture of trustworthy adoption. Institutions that internalize this lesson transform governance from reactive policing into proactive design. Reliability becomes a property of the system's very structure.

Emergency and point-of-care contexts underscore why these measures matter most when time is short. Research on sensor-embedded learning stresses the need for calibrated uncertainty and standardized interfaces to protect patients at the bedside (Han et al., 2025). Emergency medicine literature emphasizes predictable behavior, escalation rules, and conservative defaults when lives are at stake (Amiot et al., 2025). Together, these findings point toward bounded autonomy: allow systems to propose but force outputs through deterministic contracts before action. This balance protects speed without compromising safety, ensuring that urgency does not lead to silent failures. Outcomes include fewer invalid outputs, quicker incident response, and higher trust from frontline clinicians. The larger message is that determinism is not just a technical safeguard but an operational habit. In high-regulation domains, it is the difference between tools that experiment and tools that institutions can depend on.

The trajectory of research and practice shows that determinism is not an optional refinement but the backbone of responsible AI in regulated settings. By enforcing schemas, abstention rules, and verifiable constraints, institutions convert unpredictable statistical variation into governed workflows. The consistent theme across healthcare, finance, and public administration is that predictability must be engineered at the architectural level rather than patched on after deployment. Deterministic modules enable clean audit trails, localized updates, and reproducible performance that regulators can evaluate with confidence. They also clarify accountability: engineers own modules, compliance officers review logs, and practitioners operate with transparent boundaries. This design philosophy turns uncertainty into manageable choice rather than hidden liability. What results is a system in which reliability is not a by-product of luck but an intentional, measurable property. For high-stakes contexts, that transformation is what separates prototypes from production systems.

At the same time, determinism enables organizations to evolve without sacrificing trust. By treating structured outputs, conformal coverage, and provenance as systemic guarantees, institutions gain the ability to document, test, and revise while maintaining compliance. This approach redefines governance from reactive enforcement into proactive design, where risk is mitigated at the point of generation. Importantly, it creates room for innovation, since probabilistic models can still explore as long as deterministic gates constrain final decisions. That balance supports both efficiency and safety, aligning the incentives of developers, regulators, and end-users. The synthesis of techniques—schema enforcement, abstention, formal verification, and structured retrieval—establishes a coherent toolbox for trustworthy automation. Ultimately, the lesson is straightforward: in domains where errors carry systemic costs, determinism is the only viable foundation. Institutions that adopt this principle secure both operational resilience and social legitimacy. In short, determinism converts high-regulation environments from barriers to adoption into laboratories of best practice for safe AI design.

2.4 STANDARDS AND OPERATING MODELS GUIDING MODULAR ADOPTION IN ACADEMIA AND INDUSTRY

Not surprisingly, modular adoption accelerates when institutions can point to shared rulebooks rather than bespoke playbooks. The most widely cited cross-sector framework is the U.S. National Institute of Standards and Technology's Risk Management Framework, which organizes trustworthy-system work into four functions—Govern, Map, Measure, Manage—and provides outcomes that teams can operationalize (Table 2.3) (NIST, 2023). NIST complements the core text with a living Playbook that turns those outcomes into concrete actions, references, and artifacts teams can tailor to their context (NIST, 2022/2023). Because modular stacks split planning, retrieval, synthesis, testing, and verification, a risk framework that is function-oriented rather than model-oriented is a natural fit. For generative engines specifically, NIST has also published a companion

Table 2.3 Standards Crosswalk for Modular Adoption

Standard	*Team Artifact*	*Purpose*	*Where Stored*
NIST AI RMF Govern	Model card	Document system scope, capabilities, limitations, intended use, and risks	Project repository; model registry
NIST AI RMF Map	Datasheet	Summarize dataset provenance, composition, intended uses, and data governance	Data catalog; dataset documentation hub
NIST AI RMF Measure	Gold set (evaluation benchmark)	Provide consistent basis for measuring performance and fairness	Evaluation suite; test repository
NIST AI RMF Manage	Drift huddle agenda	Define triggers, processes, and decision rights when monitoring drift and incidents	Governance wiki; monitoring dashboard
ISO/IEC 42001	Model card; governance policy	Align with AI management system requirements; ensure accountable documentation	Quality management system repository
ISO/IEC 5338	Datasheet; system lifecycle record	Ensure human oversight and lifecycle documentation across development stages	Lifecycle management records; compliance system
ISO/IEC 23894	Risk register; impact assessment form	Track risks, mitigations, and residual impacts; provide basis for audits	Risk management system; audit log

"Generative AI Profile," translating the high-level risk outcomes into scenario-specific practices for content synthesis, grounding, and evaluation (NIST, 2024a). Together, these resources create a governance spine to which organizations can attach service interfaces, audit trails, and evaluation harnesses. The key shift is from tool-first decisions to outcome-first designs. That move aligns engineering with policy and makes scaling safer and repeatable.

International standards bodies have converged on guidance that directly supports modular design. ISO/IEC 42001, known as the Artificial Intelligence Management System (AIMS), establishes requirements for building and improving an organization's intelligence-management program, much like ISO 27001 did for information security (ISO/IEC, 2023a). Its focus is process: risk registers, defined roles, internal controls, and continual improvement. This process-centered structure means modular systems can be wrapped in compliant management routines without mandating a specific technology. In parallel, NIST has published a "crosswalk" mapping its Risk Management Framework (RMF) to ISO 5338 and 5339, aligning life-cycle processes across standards (NIST, 2024b). Harmonization matters because universities, vendors, and enterprises often operate across multiple jurisdictions and supply chains. Shared mappings allow artifacts such as risk logs or evaluation reports to count for more than one framework. The net effect is less duplication, smoother audits, and modular components that can be standardized at their interfaces.

Risk and life-cycle standards provide the scaffolding for how intelligent systems should be built and maintained. ISO/IEC 5338:2023 codifies an end-to-end system life cycle for machine-learning–enabled software, extending traditional systems-engineering practice with learning-specific gates (ISO/IEC, 2023b). Its vocabulary—requirements, verification and validation, operations, and improvement—aligns naturally with modular orchestration, where each service exposes its own typed interface and acceptance criteria. A companion standard, ISO/IEC 23894:2023, adapts general risk-management principles to intelligent systems, assigning responsibility for risk identification, evaluation, and treatment to specific components or owners (ISO/IEC, 2023c). Data quality is similarly standardized through ISO/IEC 5259 (parts 1–4), which define metrics, contracts, and process vocabularies for analytic and machine-learning pipelines (ISO/IEC, 2024a; 2024b). Applied to modular systems, these documents clarify what "done" means: the retriever must meet freshness and coverage targets, while the verifier must meet precision and abstention thresholds. This turns good engineering habits into auditable practices. Regulators, vendors, and educators can then align expectations without reinventing procedures.

Law and policy set the outer boundary conditions that make modularity essential rather than optional. The European Union's Artificial Intelligence Act, in force since August 2024, phases in obligations over several years, starting with bans and transparency duties and extending to strict requirements for high-risk systems (European Commission, 2024). Official timelines confirm publication in July 2024, entry into force August 1, and staged application dates stretching into 2025 and 2026, including coverage of general-purpose models (AI Act, 2024). Despite lobbying for delays, EU officials reaffirmed deadlines, signaling that ready-to-audit designs are now the expectation. Modular architectures simplify compliance by isolating sensitive data in non-parametric stores, logging provenance at retrieval, and ensuring that verification steps leave their own traceable evidence. Instead of one opaque test of a giant model, regulators can examine specific components. For universities or public agencies, this structure is especially useful because obligations arrive gradually, giving them time to adopt standards-backed operating models. Architecture, in this sense, becomes a compliance strategy.

Education has its own maturing standards that fit naturally with modular credentials and digital identity. The W3C's Verifiable Credentials Data Model 2.0, finalized in May 2025, provides a tamper-evident, privacy-preserving way to issue and verify records such as degrees, skills, and licenses (W3C, 2025). Building on this, 1EdTech's Open Badges 3.0 and Comprehensive Learner Record (CLR) 2.0 translate those concepts into interoperable records for schools and workforce systems (1EdTech, 2024; 2025a). Learning Tools Interoperability (LTI) 1.3/Advantage secures integrations between tools and learning platforms, crucial in classrooms that rely on modular services for retrieval, simulation, or assessment (1EdTech, 2019; 2025b). The Credential Engine's CTDL vocabulary adds a discovery layer by making credentials machine-readable for search and analytics (Credential Engine, 2024). Combined, these standards create an identity stack: verifiable records for learners, secure interoperability for tools, and searchable metadata for the ecosystem. Modular academic programs can then mix badges, CLRs, and transcripts into evidence-linked learner profiles. Employers receive portable and verifiable skill signals, while registrars retain control because issuance and revocation are encoded.

Operating models translate standards into daily routines. The NIST RMF Playbook offers catalogs of actions that map directly to system development: "Govern" covers policies and roles, "Map" covers system diagrams and data lineage, "Measure" covers evaluation and telemetry, and "Manage" covers incident response and improvement (NIST, 2022; 2023). These functions can be applied flexibly to retrieval-augmented generation, tool-calling, or multi-agent teams without changing the framework itself. For organizations, this means that checklists, RACI charts, and sprint acceptance criteria can all reference standardized categories. Adoption can be staged: begin with governance and data lineage, then layer in evaluation and rollback policies. This is especially important in universities, where faculty and administrators must align syllabi, accreditation, and assessment with new services gradually. Enterprises mirror the pattern through product councils or advisory boards that treat prompts, tools, and evaluators as versioned assets. The Playbook thus serves as a bridge between compliance documents and operational practice.

Public evaluators are reinforcing this modular turn by releasing test infrastructure. The U.K.'s AI Safety Institute (AISI) launched Inspect, an open platform for model and agent evaluations across coding, reasoning, autonomy, and multimodal tasks (AISI, 2024a; 2024b). AISI supplements the tool with methodology reports and progress updates covering cybersecurity, chemical and biological safeguards, and autonomous behaviors (AISI, 2024c). Because Inspect is scenario-based and capability-specific, it pairs naturally with modular architectures where each component is testable. Institutions can probe the retriever, verifier, or orchestration logic separately instead of only measuring final outputs. This granularity speeds remediation because weak links are isolated quickly. It also supports regulatory requirements for continuous monitoring and post-market assurance. In effect, public infrastructure is making testable modules the default expectation.

Data quality and bias guidance are central to responsible operation, and here too modular systems have an advantage. NIST Special Publication 1270 frames bias as a socio-technical challenge and catalogs mitigation strategies that can be assigned to different services in a modular stack (NIST, 2022). The ISO/IEC 5259 series similarly provides common vocabularies and metrics for data quality across analytics and machine learning (ISO/IEC, 2024a; 2024b). Applied in practice, retrieval and ranking services can inherit ISO metrics as service-level objectives, while predictive modules adopt abstention or calibration targets from risk frameworks. This allocation clarifies responsibility: when quality drifts, teams know who owns the fix. Vendor contracts can then specify expectations in standardized, testable terms, making procurement more objective. Universities benefit as well, since the same metrics align student-success analytics with the language of industry. A shared vocabulary shortens the path from standard to syllabus.

MLOps literature now codifies adoption sequences that institutions can follow rather than invent. Reviews in Information and Software Technology outline maturity models and common pitfalls in productionizing machine-learning systems, from version control to continuous evaluation and rollback (John et al., 2025; Zarour et al., 2025). New frameworks extend these ideas to large language models and retrieval-augmented pipelines, clarifying roles, tooling, and cost drivers. Across studies, one message is consistent: modularity requires CI/CD not just for code, but for prompts, tools, and evaluators. Policy hooks—risk sign-offs, red-team gates, and rollback criteria—are essential to connect engineering practice with governance frameworks like NIST RMF and ISO 5338. Organizations can benchmark against maturity models, schedule upgrades, and prioritize gaps quarter by quarter. Educational programs can run parallel processes, sequencing curriculum revisions with lab infrastructure upgrades. The adoption path thus becomes a planned journey rather than a reactive scramble.

Identity and credentialing close the loop between modular operating models and human development. W3C Verifiable Credentials 2.0 and 1EdTech's Open Badges 3.0/CLR 2.0 provide portable, cryptographically secure records of achievement that can move across borders and platforms (W3C, 2025; 1EdTech, 2024; 2025a). The CTDL vocabulary standardizes how credentials and competencies are described, making them searchable across ecosystems (Credential Engine, 2024). LTI 1.3/Advantage secures integration of external tools in learning platforms, ensuring that modular services for assessment or simulation can plug in without breaking continuity (1EdTech, 2019; 2025b). Together, these standards enable learner identities that are modular, evidence-linked, and portable. Employers gain verified skill signals that reduce uncertainty in hiring. Students gain pathways to stack credentials and demonstrate growth over time. Institutions retain governance because issuance, verification, and revocation are encoded in the standards themselves. Identity thus becomes the human face of interoperability in modular ecosystems.

The survey of standards and operating models demonstrates that modular adoption is not simply a technical preference but an institutional necessity. Frameworks such as the NIST AI RMF and ISO/IEC 42001 provide rulebooks that translate abstract values like trust and transparency into operational artifacts such as model cards, datasheets, and risk registers. The convergence of these standards allows organizations to manage prompts, tools, and evaluators as versioned components subject to governance rather than ad hoc experimentation. In practice, harmonization reduces duplication, accelerates audits, and allows a single artifact to satisfy multiple regulatory obligations across borders. For educators, interoperability standards like Open Badges, CLRs, and verifiable credentials provide the scaffolding for modular academic identity. The recurring principle is alignment: system components map onto governance categories, and learner evidence maps onto credentialing taxonomies. By adopting shared rulebooks, institutions build confidence internally and externally that modularity can be trusted. Standards thus transform innovation into a manageable, repeatable process rather than a fragile experiment.

At the same time, operating models and evaluative infrastructures embed these standards into daily practice. Playbooks, maturity models, and MLOps pipelines ensure that governance becomes routine rather than episodic. Public testbeds such as AISI's Inspect reinforce the expectation that each module should be independently auditable, making orchestration a matter of design rather than faith. This shift carries cultural implications: teams are organized around service ownership, procurement specifies modular criteria, and curricula prepare students for verifiable, stackable credentials. The wider message is that compliance is not a drag on progress but the architecture that allows modular systems to scale safely. With predictable governance and interoperable credentials, both industry and academia can innovate without losing legitimacy. The modular turn is therefore reinforced at every level: technical interfaces, institutional processes, policy frameworks, and learner identities. Together, these layers anchor modular AI in standards that are portable across contexts and durable over time. In short, operating models and standards give modular adoption its spine, ensuring resilience in both technological and human ecosystems.

Therefore, the main argument of this chapter is that architecture, not sheer size, determines whether intelligent systems are reliable, affordable, and governable. Larger models may be impressive, but they often become brittle, opaque, and expensive to manage. History shows that progress came when systems moved from single "do-everything" engines to modular designs such as blackboards, agent protocols, and retrieval-based pipelines. In each case, dividing work into clear roles—planning, retrieving, synthesizing, testing, verifying—outperformed one model guessing at everything. This is much like how hospitals rely on specialists instead of one person treating every patient. The payoff is systems that are easier to test, easier to update, and easier to explain. When pieces can be swapped or improved independently, organizations gain agility without losing trust. The lesson is simple: distributed roles build resilient systems.

The significance of this shift is most visible in high-stakes areas like healthcare, finance, and education. In these settings, it is not enough for an answer to sound plausible—it must be correct, documented, and explainable. Deterministic components such as schema-bound outputs, abstention policies, and calibrated error guarantees ensure that systems provide predictable results. For example, requiring a medical record system to always produce valid JSON is like requiring lab forms to always have the patient's name and date of birth—it reduces simple but dangerous errors. Selective abstention further prevents harmful mistakes by routing uncertain cases to human experts, just as a cautious pilot diverts a flight when weather is unsafe. Conformal prediction wraps outputs with statistical guarantees, similar to weather forecasts that show confidence intervals. Audit trails capture each decision, so investigators can reconstruct how an answer was reached. Together, these safeguards turn experimental systems into dependable tools.

Standards and operating models now make modular practices repeatable across industries and institutions. NIST's Risk Management Framework provides a playbook for governance, mapping, measuring, and managing risks with clear routines. ISO/IEC standards extend these principles to life cycles, risk handling, and data quality, ensuring consistency across modules. The EU's AI Act has added urgency, setting phased deadlines that reward modular, auditable designs. In practice, modularity makes compliance easier by isolating sensitive data, logging retrievals, and producing verifiable records. For universities, the W3C's Verifiable Credentials and 1EdTech's Open Badges 3.0/CLR 2.0 make it possible to issue stackable, tamper-evident learning records. This means a student can carry modular evidence of their skills, much like a worker can show certifications in first aid, cybersecurity, or project management. Employers gain clearer hiring signals, while registrars retain control through secure issuance and revocation. Standards thus connect architecture with trust, benefiting both education and industry.

The actionable takeaway is to build systems and programs as portfolios of well-defined parts, each with clear ownership, metrics, and change controls. For industry, this means procurement teams should ask whether each component has interfaces, whether risk is documented, and whether updates can be rolled back safely. For instance, a bank adopting a fraud-detection system should verify that the retriever of transaction data and the model scoring risk are separate, testable services. For academia, the same principle applies to learning technologies: course tools should integrate through standards like LTI so that one malfunctioning module does not crash the whole learning platform. Educators should also ensure that student records are portable and evidence-linked, so achievements can be verified outside the campus system. Both sectors should plan staged adoption, layering governance first and expanding capabilities as teams grow more comfortable. The advantage of modularity is that institutions can adapt without disruption. It shifts adoption from one-off projects into continuous, reliable practice.

The cultural implication is just as important as the technical one. Modularity forces organizations to value clarity over size, cooperation over concentration, and evidence over assumption. It encourages leaders to think like orchestra conductors, ensuring every section plays its part in harmony rather than relying on one soloist to cover everything. In education, this means blending badges, transcripts, and credentials into richer learner profiles. In industry, it means blending retrievers, planners, and verifiers into orchestrated services. Both reflect the same philosophy: complex systems work best when broken into parts that can be improved, tested, and trusted. By adopting this approach, institutions gain resilience in a volatile environment. Architecture becomes the foundation for scaling ambition responsibly. The stage is now set to examine how "fast learning" practices make these modular designs even more powerful.

REFERENCES

1EdTech. 2019/2025b. Learning Tools Interoperability (LTI)® Core Spec v1.3 / LTI Advantage implementation. https://www.imsglobal.org/spec/lti/v1p3; https://www.imsglobal.org/spec/lti/v1p3/impl

1EdTech. 2024. Open Badges 3.0. https://www.1edtech.org/standards/open-badges; news release: https://www.1edtech.org/1edtech-article/new-open-badges-30-standard-provides-enhanced-security-and-mobility/411060

1EdTech. 2025a. Comprehensive Learner Record (CLR) Standard 2.0. https://www.imsglobal.org/spec/clr/v2p0; overview: https://www.1edtech.org/standards/clr

AI Act. 2024. Implementation timeline. https://artificialintelligenceact.eu/implementation-timeline/; Historic timeline. https://artificialintelligenceact.eu/developments/

AISI—UK AI Safety Institute. 2024a. Inspect evaluations platform. https://inspect.aisi.org.uk/

AISI—UK AI Safety Institute. 2024b. AI Safety Institute releases new evaluations platform. https://www.gov.uk/government/news/ai-safety-institute-releases-new-ai-safety-evaluations-platform

AISI—UK AI Safety Institute. 2024c. Approach to evaluations & progress reports. https://www.gov.uk/government/publications/ai-safety-institute-approach-to-evaluations/ai-safety-institute-approach-to-evaluations; https://www.aisi.gov.uk/work/fourth-progress-report/; https://www.aisi.gov.uk/work/advanced-ai-evaluations-may-update

Allam, H. 2024. Shift-left observability: Embedding insights from code to production. International Journal of AI, BigData, Computational and Management Studies. 5(2): 58–69.

Amiot, F., Nshimyimana, J.P. and Soloviev, A. 2025. Artificial intelligence and emergency medicine: Balancing innovation and ethics. JMIR Medical Informatics. 13(1): e70903.

Anthropic. 2024. Model context protocol. https://www.anthropic.com/news/model-context-protocol

Anthropic. 2025. Tool use with Claude. https://docs.anthropic.com/en/docs/agents-and-tools/tool-use/overview

Agrawal, P. 2025. Microservices architecture: A modern approach to cloud-native development. Journal of Computer Science and Technology Studies. 7(6): 709–716.

Bayor, A.A., Li, J., Yang, I.A. and Varnfield, M. 2025. Designing Clinical Decision Support Systems (CDSS)—A user-centered lens of the design characteristics, challenges, and implications: Systematic review. Journal of Medical Internet Research. 27: e63733.

Berge, G.T., Granmo, O.C., Tveit, T.O., Ruthjersen, A.L. and Sharma, J. 2023. Combining unsupervised, supervised and rule-based learning: The case of detecting patient allergies in electronic health records. BMC Medical Informatics and Decision Making. 23(1): 188.

Black, E., Leino, K. and Fredrikson, M. 2021. Selective ensembles for consistent predictions. arXiv preprint arXiv:2111.08230.

Bodnari, A. and Travis, J. 2025. Scaling enterprise AI in healthcare: The role of governance in risk mitigation frameworks. NPJ Digital Medicine. 8(1): 272.

Briman, M.K.H. and Yildiz, B. 2024. Beyond ROUGE: A comprehensive evaluation metric for abstractive summarization leveraging similarity, entailment, and acceptability. International Journal on Artificial Intelligence Tools. 33(05): 2450017.

Chen, W.P., Teng, W.G., Kuo, C.B., Yen, Y.J., Lian, J.Y., Sing, M., et al. 2025. Regulatory insights from 27 years of Artificial Intelligence/Machine Learning–enabled medical device recalls in the United States: Implications for future governance. JMIR Medical Informatics. 13(1): e67552.

Cheng, M., Luo, Y., Ouyang, J., Liu, Q., Liu, H., Li, L., et al. 2025. A survey on knowledge-oriented retrieval-augmented generation. arXiv preprint arXiv:2503.10677.

Choi, D., Shavit, Y. and Duvenaud, D.K. 2023. Tools for verifying neural models' training data. Advances in Neural Information Processing Systems. 36: 1154–1188.

Credential Engine. 2024. CTDL Handbook/Fact sheet. https://credreg.net/ctdl/handbook; https://credentialengine.org/resources/credential-transparency-description-language-fact-sheet/

Ebad, S.A., Alhashmi, A., Amara, M., Miled, A.B. and Saqib, M. 2025. Artificial intelligence-based software as a medical device (AI-SaMD): A systematic review. Healthcare. 13:(7): 817.

European Commission. 2024. AI Act enters into force. https://commission.europa.eu/news-and-media/news/ai-act-enters-force-2024-08-01_en

Finn, T., Labrou, Y. and Mayfield, J. 1997. KQML as an agent communication language. Software Agents. 291–316.

FIPA, A.C.L. 2002. FIPA ACL message structure specification. Foundation for Intelligent Physical Agents. http://www.fipa.org/specs/fipa00061/SC00061G.html(30.6. 2004).

Fowler, M. and Lewis, J. 2015. Microservices: Nur ein weiteres Konzept in der Softwarearchitektur oder mehr. Objektspektrum. 1: 14–20.

Gierend, K., Krüger, F., Genehr, S., Hartmann, F., Siegel, F., Waltemath, D., et al. 2024. Provenance information for biomedical data and workflows: Scoping review. Journal of Medical Internet Research. 26: e51297.

Gou, Z., Shao, Z., Gong, Y., Shen, Y., Yang, Y., Duan, N., et al. 2023. Critic: Large language models can self-correct with tool-interactive critiquing. arXiv preprint arXiv:2305.11738.

Han, G.R., Goncharov, A., Eryilmaz, M., Ye, S., Palanisamy, B., Ghosh, R., et al. 2025. Machine learning in point-of-care testing: Innovations, challenges, and opportunities. Nature Communications. 16(1): 3165.

Huang, H., Ardalani, N., Sun, A., Ke, L., Bhosale, S., Lee, H.H., et al. 2024. Toward efficient inference for mixture of experts. Advances in Neural Information Processing Systems. 37: 84033–84059.

Hugging Face. 2024. License to Call: Introducing Transformers Agents 2.0. https://huggingface.co/blog/agents

ISO/IEC. 2023a. ISO/IEC 42001: Artificial Intelligence Management System (AIMS). https://www.iso.org/standard/42001

ISO/IEC. 2023b. ISO/IEC 5338: AI system life cycle processes. https://www.iso.org/standard/81118.html; sample PDF: https://cdn.standards.iteh.ai/samples/81118/8e53a667079f4d959e93119fdbe84434/ISO-IEC-5338-2023.pdf

ISO/IEC. 2023c. ISO/IEC 23894: Guidance on AI risk management. https://www.iso.org/standard/77304.html; sample PDF: https://cdn.standards.iteh.ai/samples/77304/cb803ee4e9624430a5db177459158b24/ISO-IEC-23894-2023.pdf

ISO/IEC. 2024a. ISO/IEC 5259-1: Data quality for analytics and ML—Overview. https://www.iso.org/standard/81088.html; sample PDF: https://cdn.standards.iteh.ai/samples/81088/f4aab019dc5843dbb7fecf362e6bf83e/ISO-IEC-5259-1-2024.pdf

ISO/IEC. 2024b. ISO/IEC 5259-4: Process framework for data quality in ML. https://www.iso.org/standard/81093.html

John, M.M., Olsson, H.H. and Bosch, J. 2025. An empirical guide to MLOps adoption: Framework, maturity model and taxonomy. Information and Software Technology. 183: 107725.

Krütli, D. and Hanne, T. 2025. Augmenting LLMs to securely retrieve information for construction and facility management. Information. 16(2): 76.

Labkoff, S., Oladimeji, B., Kannry, J., Solomonides, A., Leftwich, R., Koski, E., et al. 2024. Toward a responsible future: recommendations for AI-enabled clinical decision support. Journal of the American Medical Informatics Association. 31(11): 2730–2739.

Lambert, B., Forbes, F., Doyle, S., Dehaene, H. and Dojat, M. 2024. Trustworthy clinical AI solutions: A unified review of uncertainty quantification in Deep Learning models for medical image analysis. Artificial Intelligence in Medicine. 150: 102830.

LangChain. 2024. LangGraph. https://blog.langchain.com/langgraph/

LangChain. 2025. LangGraph documentation. https://langchain-ai.github.io/langgraph/

Lee, C.P., Porfirio, D., Wang, X.J., Zhao, K.C. and Mutlu, B. 2025. Veriplan: Integrating formal verification and LLMs into end-user planning. *In*: Proceedings of the 2025 CHI Conference on Human Factors in Computing Systems, pp. 1–19.

Lesser, V.R. and Erman, L.D. 1977. A retrospective view of the Hearsay-II architecture. *In*: International Joint Conference on Artificial Intelligence, Vol. 5, pp. 790–800.

Lewis, P., Perez, E., Piktus, A., Petroni, F., Karpukhin, V., Goyal, N., et al. 2020. Retrieval-augmented generation for knowledge-intensive NLP tasks. Advances in Neural Information Processing Systems. 33: 9459–9474.

Li, T., Wandella, A., Gomer, R. and Al-Mafazy, M.H. 2024. Operationalizing health data governance for AI innovation in low-resource government health systems: A practical implementation perspective from Zanzibar. Data & Policy. 6: e63.

Majlatow, M., Shakil, F.A., Emrich, A. and Mehdiyev, N. 2025. Uncertainty-aware predictive process monitoring in healthcare: Explainable insights into probability calibration for conformal prediction. Applied Sciences. 15(14): 7925.

McManus, J.W. 1991. Design and analysis tools for concurrent blackboard systems. *In*: IEEE/AIAA 10th Digital Avionics Systems Conference, pp. 432–439. IEEE.

Meijerink, L.M., Dunias, Z.S., Leeuwenberg, A.M., de Hond, A.A., Jenkins, D.A., Martin, G., et al. 2025. Updating methods for artificial intelligence–based clinical prediction models: A scoping review. Journal of Clinical Epidemiology. 178: 111636.

Mienye, I.D. and Sun, Y. 2024. A survey of explainable artificial intelligence in healthcare. Informatics in Medicine Unlocked. 45: 101473.

Mu, S. and Lin, S. 2025. A comprehensive survey of mixture-of-experts: Algorithms, theory, and applications. arXiv preprint arXiv:2503.07137.

Newman, S. 2021. Building microservices: designing fine-grained systems. O'Reilly Media, Inc.

NIST. 2022. Special Publication 1270: Towards a standard for identifying and managing bias in AI. https://nvlpubs.nist.gov/nistpubs/SpecialPublications/NIST.SP.1270.pdf

NIST. 2022/2023. AI RMF Playbook. https://www.nist.gov/itl/ai-risk-management-framework/nist-ai-rmf-playbook; AIRC Playbook mirror: https://airc.nist.gov/airmf-resources/playbook/

NIST. 2023. AI Risk Management Framework (AI RMF 1.0). https://nvlpubs.nist.gov/nistpubs/ai/nist.ai.100-1.pdf; overview: https://www.nist.gov/itl/ai-risk-management-framework

NIST. 2024a. AI RMF Generative AI Profile (NIST.AI.600-1. https://nvlpubs.nist.gov/nistpubs/ai/NIST.AI.600-1.pdf

NIST. 2024b. Crosswalk between NIST AI RMF 1.0 and ISO/IEC 5338/5339. https://airc.nist.gov/docs/Crosswalk_NIST_AI_RMF_and_ISO_5338_5339.pdf

Olsson, H., Kartasalo, K., Mulliqi, N., Capuccini, M., Ruusuvuori, P., Samaratunga, H., et al. 2022. Estimating diagnostic uncertainty with conformal prediction in pathology. Nature Communications. 13: 6137.

OpenAI. 2023. Function calling and other API updates. https://openai.com/index/function-calling-and-other-api-updates/

OpenAI. 2024. Introducing Structured Outputs in the API. https://openai.com/index/introducing-structured-outputs-in-the-api/

Park, K., Zhou, T. and D'Antoni, L. 2025. Flexible and efficient grammar-constrained decoding. arXiv preprint arXiv:2502.05111.

Parnas, D.L. 1972. On the criteria to be used in decomposing systems into modules. Communications of the ACM. 15(12): 1053–1058.

Porter, B., Grieves, M., Rodrigues Filho, R. and Leslie, D. 2016. {REX}: A development platform and online learning approach for runtime emergent software systems. *In*: 12th USENIX Symposium on Operating Systems Design and Implementation (OSDI 16): pp. 333–348.

Qu, Y., Zhang, T., Garg, N. and Kumar, A. 2024. Recursive introspection: Teaching foundation model agents how to self-improve. *In*: Automated Reinforcement Learning: Exploring Meta-Learning, AutoML, and LLMs.

Rao, A.S. and Georgeff, M.P. 1995. BDI agents: From theory to practice. ICMAS. 95: 312–319.

Ru, D., Qiu, L., Hu, X., Zhang, T., Shi, P., Chang, S., et al. 2024. Ragchecker: A fine-grained framework for diagnosing retrieval-augmented generation. Advances in Neural Information Processing Systems. 37: 21999–22027.

Sbai, Z. 2025. Model checking deep neural networks: Opportunities and challenges. Frontiers in Computer Science. 7: 1557977.

Schick, T., Dwivedi-Yu, J., Dessì, R., Raileanu, R., Lomeli, M., Hambro, E., et al. 2023. Toolformer: Language models can teach themselves to use tools. Advances in Neural Information Processing Systems. 36: 68539–68551.

Shinn, N., Cassano, F., Gopinath, A., Narasimhan, K. and Yao, S. 2023. Reflexion: Language agents with verbal reinforcement learning. Advances in Neural Information Processing Systems. 36: 8634–8652.

Smith, R.G. 1980. The contract net protocol: High-level communication and control in a distributed problem solver. IEEE Transactions on Computers. 29(12): 1104–1113.

Sparrow, R. 2024. Should adaptive machine-learning systems in medicine be regulated as research? The American Journal of Bioethics. 24(7): 3–15.

Souza, A. 2024. Observability and monitoring. *In*: Tech Leadership Playbook: Building and Sustaining High-Impact Technology Teams, pp. 171–191. Berkeley, CA: Apress.

Sreenivasan, A.P., Vaivade, A., Noui, Y., Khoonsari, P.E., Burman, J., Spjuth, O., et al. 2025. Conformal prediction enables disease course prediction and allows individualized diagnostic uncertainty in multiple sclerosis. NPJ Digital Medicine. 8(1): 224.

Stetson, P.D., Choy, J., Summerville, N., Baldwin-Medsker, A., Mak, J., Chatterjee, A., et al. 2025. Responsible Artificial Intelligence governance in oncology. npj Digital Medicine. 8(1): 407.

Swaminathan, A., Lopez, I., Wang, W., Srivastava, U., Tran, E., Bhargava-Shah, A., et al. 2024. Selective prediction for extracting unstructured clinical data. Journal of the American Medical Informatics Association. 31(1): 188–197.

Tadi, S.R.C.C.T. 2022. Architecting resilient cloud-native APIs: Autonomous fault recovery in event-driven microservices ecosystems. Journal of Scientific and Engineering Research. 9(3): 293–305.

Thayer, J.G., Franklin, A., Miller, J.M., Grundmeier, R.W., Rogith, D. and Wright, A. 2024. A scoping review of rule-based clinical decision support malfunctions. Journal of the American Medical Informatics Association. 31(10): 2405–2413.

Thurzo, A. 2025. Provable AI ethics and explainability in medical and educational AI agents: Trustworthy ethical firewall. Electronics. 14(7): 1294.

Tuccio, G., Bulla, L., Madonia, M., Gangemi, A. and Mongiovi, M. 2025. Grammar-constrained NLG. Findings of the Association for Computational Linguistics. 177: 2152–2170.

Vaswani, A., Shazeer, N., Parmar, N., Uszkoreit, J., Jones, L., Gomez, A.N., et al. 2017. Attention is all you need. Advances in Neural Information Processing Systems. 30.

W3C. 2025. Verifiable Credentials Data Model v2.0 (Recommendation). https://www.w3.org/TR/vc-data-model-2.0/; overview/news: https://www.w3.org/news/2025/the-verifiable-credentials-2-0-family-of-specifications-is-now-a-w3c-recommendation/

Wang, G., Xie, Y., Jiang, Y., Mandlekar, A., Xiao, C., Zhu, Y., et al. 2023. Voyager: An open-ended embodied agent with large language models. arXiv preprint arXiv:2305.16291.

Wang, F., Zhang, Z., Zhang, X., Wu, Z., Mo, T., Lu, Q., et al. 2024. A comprehensive survey of small language models in the era of large language models: Techniques, enhancements, applications, collaboration with LLMs, and trustworthiness. arXiv preprint arXiv:2411.03350.

Wang, D.Y.B., Shen, Z., Mishra, S.S., Xu, Z., Teng, Y. and Ding, H. 2025. SLOT: Structuring the output of large language models. arXiv preprint arXiv:2505.04016.

Wooldridge, M. and Jennings, N.R. 1995. Intelligent agents: Theory and practice. The Knowledge Engineering Review. 10(2): 115–152.

Wu, Q., Bansal, G., Zhang, J., Wu, Y., Li, B., Zhu, E., et al. 2024. Autogen: Enabling next-gen LLM applications via multi-agent conversations. *In*: First Conference on Language Modeling.

Xu, Z., Cruz, M.J., Guevara, M., Wang, T., Deshpande, M., Wang, X., et al. 2024. Retrieval-augmented generation with knowledge graphs for customer-service QA. *In*: Proceedings of SIGIR 2024. 2363–2367.

Yao, S., Zhao, J., Yu, D., Du, N., Shafran, I., Narasimhan, K., et al. 2023. React: Synergizing reasoning and acting in language models. *In*: International Conference on Learning Representations (ICLR).

Zhu, C., Ping, W., Xiao, C., Shoeybi, M., Goldstein, T., Anandkumar, A., et al. 2021. Long-short transformer: Efficient transformers for language and vision. Advances in Neural Information Processing Systems. 34: 17723–17736.

Chapter 3

Fast Learning and AI —Rapid Generation and Iterative Refinement

3.1 RAPID CONTENT GENERATION FOR CREATIVE AND ANALYTICAL TASKS

Fast learning begins with what cognitive scientists call "divergence"—the deliberate broadening of possibilities before narrowing toward a solution. In practice, intelligent systems now serve as accelerators for this stage, producing multiple outlines, alternative framings, or rough code sketches in minutes. The purpose is not polish but volume under constraint, generating structured variety that humans can then refine. This mirrors brainstorming sessions in classrooms or design studios, where the rule is "quantity first, quality later." Research shows that scaffolded prompts, tool use for factual accuracy, multi-sample decoding, and rubric-based critique consistently expand the idea space without sacrificing relevance (Noy and Zhang, 2023; Doshi et al., 2024). Controlled studies confirm that AI-assisted drafting reduces cycle time and raises average quality, especially for novice writers. In professional settings, such as marketing, teams gain more viable campaign concepts faster when evaluators score alternatives against explicit rubrics (Cillo et al., 2024; Hartmann and Heitmann, 2025). A simple but effective practice is a 15-minute sprint producing five options, followed by a quick screen to keep only those that meet must-have criteria (Figure 3.1).

The most reliable way to guide early drafts is through scaffolding—short, carefully prepared demonstrations that show the model the structure, tone, and boundaries of the desired output (Table 3.1). Few-shot prompts, which provide two to six examples of the task at hand, reduce irrelevant text and help the system

DOI: 10.1201/9781003688013-3

stay on topic by teaching it the format in advance (Brown et al., 2020). For tasks that require reasoning, chain-of-thought prompts make intermediate steps explicit—like showing your work in a math problem—which has been shown to improve accuracy in mathematical and logical domains (Wei et al., 2022). More advanced are hybrid approaches such as ReAct, which combines "reasoning" with "acting" by letting the model think through a step and then call a tool, such as a search engine or calculator, before moving forward. This method reduces the risk of fluent but false answers because the system grounds its reasoning with external evidence (Yao et al., 2023). Similarly, Program-Aided Prompting (PAL) shifts numerical or procedural tasks from the language model to a Python interpreter, ensuring calculations are correct rather than linguistically plausible guesses (Gao et al., 2023). Toolformer goes a step further by allowing the model to learn when and how to call external APIs—such as a database lookup or a web query—using only a handful of demonstrations, which makes it much easier for non-experts to use effectively (Schick et al., 2023). The overarching implication is that the "first mile" of drafting matters most: the inputs, required sections, and allowable tools should be templated before generation begins. Much like a recipe card keeps a cook from skipping steps, well-designed scaffolds keep drafts coherent, domain-appropriate, and ready for refinement.

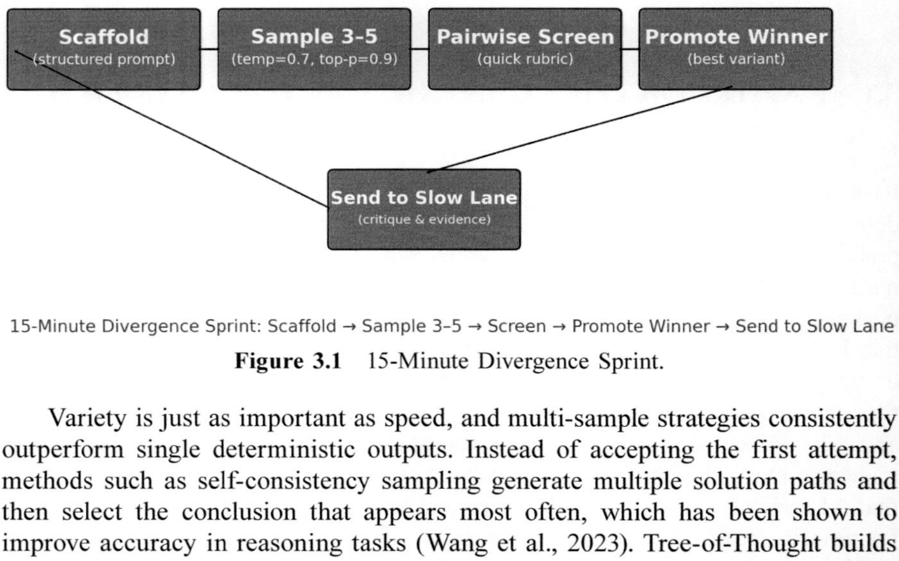

Figure 3.1 15-Minute Divergence Sprint.

Variety is just as important as speed, and multi-sample strategies consistently outperform single deterministic outputs. Instead of accepting the first attempt, methods such as self-consistency sampling generate multiple solution paths and then select the conclusion that appears most often, which has been shown to improve accuracy in reasoning tasks (Wang et al., 2023). Tree-of-Thought builds on this principle by allowing the model to explore several branching reasoning paths at once, much like mapping different possible moves in a chess game before choosing the best one. This branching structure makes the model better at solving puzzles and planning problems because it considers alternatives before settling on a final answer (Yao et al., 2023). In creative work, generating several drafts at once gives evaluators the chance to compare options side by side, a process known to improve human judgment. Researchers caution, however, that overusing "best-of-n" filtering—where only the single "best" output is chosen from a large set—can backfire by reinforcing the evaluator's own biases and discarding useful diversity (Le Bronnec et al., 2024). Broader evaluations recommend mixing sampling settings to reveal both the system's strengths and its hidden weaknesses. A practical balance is to produce three to five drafts, use a rubric or pairwise comparisons to select the strongest, and archive the rest for later adaptation. This creates a disciplined approach to creativity that mirrors human brainstorming while adding the scale and speed of machines.

Table 3.1 Techniques for Rapid Content Generation

Technique/ Approach	***Core Purpose***	***How It Works***	***Example Application***
Few-shot & Chain-of-Thought Prompts	Provide structure and reduce irrelevant output	Show 2–6 examples or step-by-step reasoning to guide the model	Drafting an academic essay outline with explicit sections
ReAct/PAL/ Toolformer	Ground reasoning in external tools	Interleave reasoning with tool calls (search, calculator, APIs)	Policy brief with real citations and correct statistics
Multi-sample Generation (Self-Consistency, Tree-of-Thoughts)	Expand idea space through variety	Generate multiple solution paths, select most frequent or best	Brainstorming five campaign slogans, then narrowing
Decoding Controls (Temperature, Top-p, Min-p)	Balance creativity vs. precision	Adjust randomness or restrict token selection probabilities	Exploratory class discussion questions vs. formal compliance memo
Retrieval-Augmented Generation (RAG, REALM)	Improve factual accuracy & currency	Pair generator with deterministic retriever	Literature review citing most recent journal articles
Self-Critique (Self-Refine, Reflexion)	Improve quality iteratively	Model critiques its own draft and revises	Refining a grant proposal draft through multiple passes
Automated Testing & Logs (SWE-bench, Unit Tests)	Validate technical correctness	Run generated code through test suites, record errors	Debugging a Python script before integration
Performance Metrics (Time-to-First-Draft, Edit Distance)	Track efficiency & quality	Measure draft speed and revision effort	Monitoring student essays or workplace reports
Human-in-the-Loop Evaluation	Ensure accountability and nuance	Rubric-based review or pairwise comparisons	Teacher evaluating AI-generated quiz questions

The way outputs are decoded also matters because decoding controls determine how adventurous or conservative a model will be in generating text. Temperature adjusts how much randomness is introduced when choosing the next word: a higher temperature makes the system more exploratory and creative, while a lower temperature makes it more predictable and precise. Nucleus sampling (top-p) works differently by narrowing the choice of possible next words to only those that together make up a set probability (for example, the top 90%), which ensures variety while avoiding rare and incoherent words. Newer methods such as min-p sampling refine this balance by discarding options that fall below a certain probability threshold, filtering out highly unlikely tokens without collapsing overall diversity (Fu et al., 2025). Evidence shows that the right settings depend on the task: open-ended brainstorming is stronger with exploratory decoding, while formal summaries and compliance briefs require conservative settings. For instance, a teacher generating five discussion questions for class might use a moderate temperature (around 0.7) with broad top-p to spark variety, while a university administrator writing a policy memo would reduce temperature (around 0.3) to ensure consistency. Regardless of the settings, outputs should always be constrained by audience, tone, and length to prevent drift. In effect, decoding functions like a set of dials that balance creativity with control, and documenting these choices allows teams to reproduce quality and compare results over time.

Analytical work benefits most when generation is combined with external tools rather than relying on the model alone. RAG connects the system to up-to-date databases or document indexes, pulling in verified information that reduces hallucinations and raises factual accuracy (Lewis et al., 2020). REALM (Retrieval-Augmented Language Model) takes a slightly different approach: it "pretrains" the model with a built-in retriever that learns to fetch relevant passages during training, and then fine-tunes the system for downstream tasks like answering questions or synthesizing evidence (Guu et al., 2020). This design makes REALM especially effective for producing research summaries, literature reviews, or policy briefs, because the retriever has already been optimized to find contextually relevant material. ReAct extends the principle further by interleaving reasoning with actions—such as searching the web, citing documents, or running a calculator—ensuring that answers are grounded in evidence rather than text prediction alone (Yao et al., 2023). PAL reinforces the same logic by outsourcing arithmetic to an interpreter, guaranteeing accurate calculations instead of leaving them to the probabilistic model (Gao et al., 2023). Toolformer goes a step further by teaching models to autonomously learn when to call APIs—structured connections to external software or databases—so they can, for instance, check a calendar, query a dataset, or retrieve real-time information (Schick et al., 2023). Together, these methods mean that analytical drafts should include citations, records of tool calls, and calculation logs, creating a transparent trail that others can verify. Just as a lab report must document its methods and data, a well-structured policy brief or technical memo should show its evidence so that the output moves from being merely plausible to being genuinely defensible.

Self-critique methods add another important layer of quality control by allowing models to review and improve their own drafts. Self-Refine is one such framework: instead of producing an answer in a single pass, the model first generates a draft, then creates feedback on that draft, and finally produces a revised version based on its own critique. This loop can be repeated several times, often leading to outputs that are more accurate and better aligned with task requirements (Madaan et al., 2023). Reflexion builds on a similar idea but adds memory—models "remember" past mistakes, critiques, and corrections across multiple attempts. By learning from their own prior errors, models can improve not just one draft but their approach over time. In educational settings, rubric-aligned prompts apply the same principle by asking models to evaluate work against clear criteria, simulating the grading process. While these automated evaluations can approximate human judgment, their reliability depends on the complexity of the rubric and the importance of nuance in the task (Zhang et al., 2024; Lee et al., 2024). Large-scale studies confirm that models are more consistent when making pairwise comparisons—judging which of two drafts is better—than when assigning absolute scores (Watts et al., 2024). The best practice in consequential contexts is to combine these methods with human oversight, using logs of criteria and decisions to ensure transparency. In effect, self-critique frameworks echo the process of peer review but compress it into much shorter cycles.

Technical fields like software engineering and data analysis illustrate the limits of outputs that are not rigorously verified. SWE-bench—short for Software Engineering Benchmark—is a large-scale test suite that evaluates how well models handle realistic programming problems. Unlike toy examples, it requires systems to fix bugs or add features across multiple files in real-world codebases, a task that exposes where models break down in handling complex dependencies (Jimenez et al., 2023). Results show that even advanced systems often stumble here, underscoring the need for unit tests and execution traces to catch errors before deployment. Research on automated code review similarly suggests that while AI can spot bugs and improve quality, too much automation can generate false positives, which lengthens review cycles instead of shortening them (Lu et al., 2024). A safer workflow is to let the model propose a patch, automatically run the relevant tests, and then revise based on error logs. Progress can be measured using edit distance—how much the revised code differs from the first draft—and error-catch rate, the percentage of bugs identified before release. For highly sensitive domains, such as authentication or encryption, human review must remain non-negotiable. By versioning code changes and storing test logs, organizations create accountability and compliance records that make the development process transparent. These practices ensure that rapid generation augments reliability rather than undermining it.

To make fast learning reliable, performance must be tracked with clear and transparent metrics. Time-to-first-draft is a simple but powerful measure of efficiency: it records how long it takes for a system to produce a usable first version of a task, whether that task is a student essay, a policy memo, or a block of code. Shorter times signal greater efficiency, but the metric also highlights where bottlenecks still exist in a workflow. Edit distance provides a complementary measure of quality by calculating how many changes are needed to transform the AI's draft into the final approved version (Levenshtein, 1966). A small edit distance suggests the system produced something close to the desired outcome, while a large one signals that human reviewers had to do heavy lifting. Pilot studies in education show that automated grading can speed up evaluation, but human moderation is still essential to ensure that feedback is fair and trusted. For analytical tasks, metrics might include numeric acceptance checks such as column totals or error margins, while creative tasks can be evaluated through win rates in head-to-head comparisons against baseline drafts. When models themselves are used as evaluators, a sample of results should always be reviewed by humans to monitor drift or subtle bias. Publishing metric definitions and targets ensures comparability across teams, while dashboards that track regressions over time turn one-off assessments into a culture of continuous evidence.

The impact of fast learning is uneven across roles and tasks. Randomized field experiments show that less experienced workers gain the largest boosts, often doubling productivity, while experts gain less speed but are freed to focus on higher-order tasks (Brynjolfsson et al., 2025). In professional writing, AI assistance speeds drafting and improves quality, especially in the early stages (Noy and Zhang, 2023). Creative writing research finds collaboration with AI can enhance originality scores, though outcomes depend heavily on how prompts are framed (Doshi et al., 2024). In coding, generative systems accelerate boilerplate work but leave complex debugging to human specialists (Jimenez et al., 2023). The implication is clear: organizations should pair junior staff with AI for drafting and rely on experts for critique and integration. Routine work can be triaged with lightweight tests, while high-risk tasks demand expert review. Role-specific metrics ensure gains are distributed fairly and risks remain contained. This division of labor mirrors the modular systems themselves—specialists working together toward resilient outcomes.

As such, a repeatable micro-workflow can turn rapid ideation into decision-ready artifacts. A short divergence sprint produces several variants under exploratory decoding, constrained by clear instructions. Pairwise evaluation against a rubric identifies the best option, which is then refined through self-critique. Analytical drafts should include citations, retrievals, and calculations, while code outputs should pass automated tests before moving forward. Every cycle should be documented, including prompts, decoding parameters, tool calls, and evaluation results. Human review provides the final sign-off, with notes on lessons learned feeding back into future prompts. Over time, this loop builds an evidence base that improves both governance and pedagogy. The result is a disciplined process where speed and accountability reinforce one another rather than compete.

The evidence across creative, analytical, and technical domains confirms that rapid generation is most effective when it is scaffolded, diversified, and rigorously evaluated. Scaffolds such as few-shot prompts and tool integration shape the "first mile" of drafting, while sampling strategies and decoding controls expand the idea space without losing coherence. External tools like retrieval engines, calculators, and interpreters convert plausibility into defensibility by grounding outputs in verifiable evidence. Self-critique frameworks and rubric-aligned evaluations further ensure that drafts improve iteratively rather than stagnate at first pass. In technical contexts like programming, versioning, automated testing, and error logs protect against hidden faults while maintaining velocity. Metrics such as time-to-first-draft and edit distance provide transparent ways to monitor progress and allocate resources. Studies consistently show that novice learners benefit most in speed and quality, while experts shift their effort toward higher-order critique and integration. Together, these practices demonstrate that fast learning is not reckless acceleration but structured divergence, guided by checks that transform quantity into quality.

The broader implication is that rapid content generation is not an endpoint but the opening act of a longer workflow. When properly orchestrated, fast divergence feeds into slower convergence phases where human judgment, structured evaluation, and iterative refinement dominate. This mirrors educational design studios, newsroom editing rooms, and agile software teams—contexts where multiple drafts are expected before final decisions are made. The interplay of machine-scale ideation with human-scale judgment creates a hybrid productivity model that is both efficient and accountable. Organizations and classrooms that adopt this approach gain the best of both worlds: more options in less time, paired with stronger evidence of quality and compliance. In turn, this cultivates a culture where experimentation is safe, evaluation is routine, and learning becomes visible at every step. Rapid generation is thus less about replacing human creativity than about amplifying it through disciplined orchestration. The takeaway is clear: speed is valuable only when it is paired with transparent processes that channel divergence into meaningful outcomes.

3.2 BRAINSTORMING TECHNIQUES ACROSS WEAK AND ADVANCED MODELS

"Weak" models can be defined as smaller, less instruction-tuned systems that require carefully designed scaffolds, while "advanced" models are larger, state-of-the-art systems trained to follow instructions more reliably and handle looser prompts (Table 3.2). Differences in capacity are well documented; both the scale of the model and the training regimen significantly shape what it can reliably produce (Kaplan et al., 2020; OpenAI, 2023; Liang et al., 2022). As a result, brainstorming strategies must match the system's capability. Weaker systems often need slot-filling templates, strict constraints, and retrieval augmentation to stay focused. Advanced models, by contrast, thrive with structured sampling, branching searches, and iterative critique loops that reward exploration. Studies emphasize that no universal "best" brainstormer exists across all tasks, making adaptation to context essential (Liang et al., 2022). For executives, the guiding principle is to select the lightest method that still preserves diversity without losing relevance. For educators, the priority is to clarify task expectations and pair brainstorming with rubrics that measure alignment to audience, purpose, and evidence quality. Transparent documentation of model versions and settings is essential to make comparisons meaningful.

Table 3.2 Brainstorming Techniques by Model Class

Model Class	***Scaffolds***	***Sampling***	***Tool Use***	***Evaluation***
Weak	Slot-fill prompts; simple exemplars	Greedy or low-temp sampling (temp≈0.2–0.3, top-p≈0.7)	Limited; basic calculator or lookup	Manual pairwise or rubric check
Mid	Least-to-most reasoning; structured decomposition	Self-consistency sampling (3–5 runs, temp≈0.5–0.7, top-p≈0.8–0.9)	Program-aided language models (PAL); retrieval-augmented generation (RAG) for context	Pairwise preference voting; lightweight metrics
Advanced	Complex multi-step scaffolds; role-play, chain-of-thought	Large self-consistency pools (10+ runs, temp≈0.7–0.9, top-p≈0.9–1.0)	Integrated PAL + RAG; API orchestration and external tools	Automated pairwise ranking; human-in-the-loop for edge cases

When working with weaker models, scaffolding is usually the most effective strategy. Scaffolding means building a structure around the task so the model has less room to drift into irrelevant or incorrect answers. A good starting point is to create a schema that explicitly defines purpose, audience, constraints, and outline, followed by two to four worked examples to anchor tone and format. This uses *in-context learning*—the model's ability to mimic demonstrated patterns without being retrained (Wei et al., 2022). For reasoning-heavy or multi-step problems, decomposition strategies are critical. *Least-to-most prompting* breaks a hard problem into easier steps, while *self-ask prompting* has the model generate sub-questions for itself, making reasoning clearer and more reliable (Zhou et al., 2022; Press et al., 2022). For example, instead of asking, *"Summarize U.S. Economic Policy Since 2008,"* a self-ask prompt might break it into: (1) "What were the key financial challenges in 2008?" (2) "How did the government respond?" (3) "What policies remained in place after recovery?" and then stitch those into a final answer. Parameters should stay conservative—low temperature to reduce randomness and short output lengths to keep focus. Fact-heavy work benefits from *retrieval augmentation*—attaching reference documents or curated excerpts—so the model builds from real sources. In classrooms, this resembles a studio protocol: define a template, generate small drafts, run a retrieval pass, and compare outputs. In professional contexts, the same approach could guide a policy memo or hypothesis generation exercise. The lesson is consistent: more structure up front yields stronger, more reliable results than uncontrolled expansion.

Advanced models, by contrast, can handle broader exploration if paired with guardrails. One method is *self-consistency checks*, which means generating several candidate answers and then converging on the one most often repeated across runs, filtering out outliers (Wang et al., 2024). Another is *Tree-of-Thoughts*, where the model branches reasoning paths and then selects among them, much like a debate team testing multiple arguments before deciding which stands strongest

(Yao et al., 2023). These techniques provide variety without chaos. Decoding strategies also matter: *temperature* controls how random the word choice is (low = predictable, high = more creative), while *nucleus sampling (top-p)* samples from the top percentage of likely words to maintain diversity without nonsense (Holtzman et al., 2019; Renze and Guven, 2024). Defaults tend to favor moderate creativity (temperature around 0.7 and top-p around 0.9) for brainstorming, while technical writing should stay conservative (temperature 0.2–0.3). Adding micro-rubrics—small reminders of purpose, audience, and evidence—helps keep variety useful rather than noisy. In classrooms, students might annotate each variant with "why this could work," strengthening metacognition. In teams, annotations can serve as records of assumptions, clarifying decision-making later. The principle is that diversity works best when structured, not when left to chance.

Another set of strategies uses *ensemble methods*, where more than one model or configuration is used together. Instead of trusting a single output, a team might sample from three decoding settings or different models and then use *pairwise selection*—comparing two options head-to-head—to pick the winner. Research shows pairwise comparison is easier and produces more agreement than scoring on a 1–10 scale (Liu et al., 2023; Gu et al., 2024; Watts et al., 2024). A more advanced ensemble is the *Mixture-of-Agents* approach, where one agent drafts, another critiques, and a third refines the result. For example, in writing a policy brief, Agent A might produce a draft, Agent B highlights weaknesses, and Agent C integrates the fixes. Ensembles should stay small (about three agents or settings) to keep evaluation manageable. In classrooms, this can be a round-robin where each "agent" (student + model) improves a draft using a rubric. In organizations, it provides diversity of options without hiring additional staff. Human oversight is still essential, as evaluators can bring biases and models can reinforce one another's mistakes. Archiving both winners and runner-ups ensures valuable alternatives aren't lost.

Established creativity frameworks also adapt well to AI brainstorming. One of the most practical is *SCAMPER*: Substitute, Combine, Adapt, Modify/Magnify/Minify, Put to other uses, Eliminate, and Reverse (Boonpracha et al., 2023). Each step asks the model to view the idea differently. For example, given a product like "a reusable water bottle," prompts could include: "What if we *substituted* the material for bamboo?" or "How might we *combine* this bottle with a filter?" Studies show SCAMPER improves fluency (number of ideas), flexibility (variety), and originality when paired with quick feedback (Wu and Wu, 2020; Xia et al., 2025). For weaker models, pre-filled examples guide the process. For advanced ones, SCAMPER can be extended: after producing a divergent set of ideas, ask it to choose the "top three with risks" for convergent refinement. In classrooms, SCAMPER can help students brainstorm creative writing plots or science experiments. In business, managers can link each SCAMPER step to product levers like pricing or features. To avoid unsafe ideas, compliance filters should screen steps like "eliminate" or "reverse." Evaluation should be guided by rubrics that measure novelty and usefulness.

Another structured approach is *morphological analysis*, ideal for problems with many possible combinations. The method starts by listing dimensions of the problem—say, audience, channel, message, and tone—and building a *morphological box* where each dimension has multiple options (Ritchey, 2002/2013). The model then fills in combinations. For example, a marketing team might build a grid: audience = "students, parents, professionals"; channel = "email, TikTok, print"; message = "cost-saving, eco-friendly, status"; tone = "formal, casual, humorous." The AI generates combinations (e.g., "parents + TikTok + eco-friendly + humorous"), and humans evaluate which are promising. Weaker models benefit from pre-populated grids, while advanced ones can cluster results into themes. In classrooms, students can define the dimensions and let the AI populate the box, practicing justification skills. Organizations can treat the box as an innovation backlog annotated with predicted impact and resource needs. Over time, dimensions can be refined to reflect evidence of what works. Morphological analysis generates systematic variety without repetition.

Breaking problems into smaller steps is another reliable tactic. *Self-ask* prompts encourage the model to generate its own sub-questions and answer them one by one. *Least-to-most* prompting solves easy sub-problems first, building momentum for harder ones (Press et al., 2022; Zhou et al., 2022). *ReAct* (Reason + Act) interleaves reasoning steps with actions, like calling a calculator or a search tool mid-process, so answers stay grounded (Yao et al., 2023). For example, a ReAct-style prompt for an economics question might be: *"Step 1: Plan how to solve. Step 2: Search for inflation rates. Step 3: Calculate percentage change. Step 4: Provide reasoning and final answer."* Retrieval-augmented generation can further improve factuality by injecting external sources (Lewis et al., 2020). For education, this shows students a transparent chain of reasoning. For professionals, it creates auditable records. Weaker models often need more retrieval and scaffolding, while advanced ones handle orchestration more smoothly. Adding an "assumptions" note to each idea creates a natural testing plan.

Another popular but mixed method is *role conditioning*, where the model is asked to "act as" a persona (e.g., a teacher, lawyer, or scientist). Some studies find role-play prompts improve performance on FAQs or explanations, while others show it can reduce reasoning quality or bias results (Chen et al., 2025; Han and Wang, 2024; Zhang et al., 2024). The safer practice is to use roles for tone and audience rather than for reasoning control. For example: *"Act as a supportive teacher. Provide feedback on this essay using the rubric below."* In this setup, the role sets style, but the rubric provides the real guardrails. In businesses, roles should always be combined with constitutional rules (hard-coded constraints) or rubric checks for compliance. Weaker models work best with short, clear roles, while advanced ones can sustain more elaborate "house style" prompts. Effectiveness must always be judged by results—if role conditioning adds noise or bias, it should be dropped.

Finally, decoding strategies shape how models sample text. *Temperature* controls randomness (low = predictable, high = creative), *top-p (nucleus sampling)* limits choices to the most probable words, *diverse beam search* creates non-redundant outputs, and *min-p sampling* filters out very unlikely words while preserving creativity (Holtzman et al., 2019; Nguyen et al., 2024). No one setting works universally, so systematic A/B testing is needed. In classrooms, students might generate drafts with three different settings and then annotate differences to build critical evaluation skills. Organizations should restrict experimentation to safe trials so production outputs remain stable. In high-stakes work like budgets or legal memos, decoding parameters should be fixed and logged for audit. The guiding principle is that decoding settings should expand useful variety, not substitute for clear prompting.

Selecting the best outputs requires careful evaluation. *Pairwise selection*—comparing two drafts side by side—is more reliable and less taxing than assigning scores to many outputs at once (Liu et al., 2023; Gu et al., 2024; Watts et al., 2024). For example, if a model produces five candidate marketing slogans, reviewers compare A vs. B, C vs. D, and then pit the winners against each other until a final choice emerges. In classrooms, this mirrors art or writing critiques. In workplaces, it can serve as the approval step before campaigns or proposals advance. Even when language models act as judges, a percentage of cases should be re-checked by humans to catch drift or bias. Reports should include win rates, confidence intervals, and rationales for decisions, creating transparency. This way, evaluation itself becomes part of the learning loop, reinforcing both efficiency and accountability.

The overall recommendation is to select the simplest method that reliably increases diversity without losing relevance (Table 3.3). For weaker models, this often means schema-driven prompts, decomposition, retrieval support, and conservative decoding. For advanced models, multi-sample strategies, branching searches, and pairwise selection with targeted rubrics are more effective. Across all contexts, rubric-based evaluation consistently outperforms persona conditioning, while decoding parameters should be treated as adjustable tools rather than strategic solutions. Educators can frame these approaches as structured studio protocols, while organizations can codify them into playbooks with explicit success metrics and rollback criteria. Monitoring should track time-to-shortlist, win rates, acceptance rates, and creativity scores. One widely used framework is the Consensual Assessment Technique (CAT), developed by Teresa Amabile (1982), which measures creativity based on the judgments of domain experts rather than fixed metrics—providing a more nuanced view of novelty and usefulness. Archiving prompts, parameters, and decision logs allows institutions to build an evidence base over time. In this way, brainstorming becomes a systematic capability for learning and governance, not just an informal exercise.

The main lesson from this section is that brainstorming with generative models is not a one-size-fits-all process—it depends heavily on the strength of the system and the context of use. Smaller, weaker models often need scaffolding: clearly defined templates, strict instructions, and examples that help them stay on track. They also benefit from decomposition methods, like breaking problems into sub-questions or solving simple parts first, and from retrieval augmentation, which grounds answers in real documents rather than guesswork. Advanced models, by contrast, can explore more widely, but they still need guardrails to keep variety from turning into noise. Techniques such as self-consistency (running multiple times and keeping the common results), Tree-of-Thoughts (branching reasoning paths), and careful decoding settings (temperature and top-p) provide structured diversity. Both model types benefit when evaluation is rigorous, whether through

Table 3.3 Brainstorming and Prompting Strategies for Weaker and Advanced Models

Method	*Plain Explanation*	*Example Prompt/Steps*
Scaffolding	Giving the model a structured template (purpose, audience, constraints, outline) plus examples so it knows exactly what to do.	"Write a policy memo. Purpose: persuade city council. Audience: local officials. Constraints: ≤500 words, formal tone. Outline: Introduction, Key Issue, Evidence, Recommendation."
In-Context Learning	The model learns from examples shown in the same prompt (without retraining).	Show 2–4 short examples of product reviews, then ask: "Now write a review for this laptop in the same style."
Least-to-Most Prompting	Breaking a complex task into smaller, easier steps, solving simple parts first.	Step 1: "List the key challenges in urban transport." Step 2: "Now suggest simple solutions for each challenge." Step 3: "Combine into a policy plan."
Self-Ask Prompting	Having the model generate its own sub-questions before answering.	"Question: What caused the fall of the Roman Empire? First, generate sub-questions you need to answer. Then answer them one by one before writing a final explanation."
Retrieval Augmentation (RAG)	Pulling in outside documents or facts so the model stays accurate.	Provide context: "Here are three news articles. Use them to summarize the key risks of climate change policy. Cite your sources."
Self-Consistency Checks	Running the model multiple times and keeping the most common or consistent answer.	Ask 5 times: "What are the key causes of inflation?" → Compare answers → Keep points repeated most often.
Tree-of-Thoughts	Exploring multiple reasoning paths like a decision tree, then picking the strongest.	"Solve this riddle: I'm taken from a mine… Step 1: Generate 3 reasoning paths. Step 2: Evaluate each. Step 3: Choose the most logical path."
Ensembles	Using several models or decoding settings and comparing outputs.	Generate a draft with Model A, one with Model B, and one with different parameters → compare side-by-side and choose.
Mixture-of-Agents	Different agents (e.g., drafter, critic, refiner) work together in sequence.	Agent A: Draft essay → Agent B: Critique flaws → Agent C: Revise based on critique.

SCAMPER	A creativity method: Substitute, Combine, Adapt, Modify, Put to use, Eliminate, Reverse.	"Take a smartphone. Substitute: new material. Combine: add wearable tech. Adapt: make child-friendly. Modify: mini size. Put to use: as classroom tool. Eliminate: remove camera. Reverse: charge other devices."
Morphological Box	Building a grid of dimensions (audience, channel, tone, message) and exploring combinations.	Dimensions: Audience = "students, parents." Channel = "TikTok, email." Tone = "formal, humorous." → AI fills in combinations, e.g., "Parents + TikTok + humorous safety campaign."
ReAct (Reason + Act)	Interleaving reasoning steps with actions like using tools, calculators, or searches.	"Step 1: Plan how to solve a budget. Step 2: Search for inflation rates. Step 3: Use calculator tool to find % change. Step 4: Write final answer with sources."
Role Conditioning	Asking the model to act in a role (teacher, reviewer, lawyer), usually for tone.	"Act as a supportive teacher. Provide feedback on this essay using the rubric below."
Decoding Strategies	Settings that shape randomness. Temperature (creativity), Top-p (sample from top % of likely words), Min-p (avoid very low probability words).	"Brainstorm marketing slogans. Use temperature 0.7, top-p 0.9 for variety. For technical reports, use temp 0.2, top-p 0.7 for stability."
Pairwise Selection	Comparing two drafts side-by-side instead of scoring them individually.	Generate 5 headlines → Compare A vs. B, C vs. D, then winners vs. each other until one remains.

rubrics, pairwise comparisons, or ensemble methods that combine multiple outputs. Creativity frameworks like SCAMPER and morphological boxes extend brainstorming by introducing systematic ways to push beyond obvious answers. In all cases, the goal is disciplined variety: letting models generate multiple options, but always paired with human-guided criteria that check for accuracy, usefulness, and fairness.

The significance of these findings is twofold. For educators, structured protocols—templates, micro-drafts, retrieval passes, and critique loops—turn brainstorming into a teachable skill rather than an unstructured gamble. Students not only see the process but also learn to evaluate assumptions and trade-offs. For professional settings, these methods scale ideation without losing rigor, allowing teams to broaden their creative options while still documenting reasoning, testing assumptions, and preventing drift into irrelevant or unsafe ideas. Future research should examine which combinations of scaffolds, sampling strategies, and evaluation methods work best in different domains—creative writing, technical drafting, or policy analysis. It should also track how these strategies impact outcomes across subgroups to ensure that variety does not reinforce bias. Ultimately, brainstorming techniques must evolve into evidence-based playbooks, where educators and organizations archive prompts, outputs, and evaluations. This will allow institutions to refine their methods over time, build institutional memory, and ensure that fast generation is always balanced by slow, careful evaluation.

3.3 WORKFLOW INTEGRATION AND HUMAN-IN-THE-LOOP REFINEMENT

Integrating rapid content generation into organizational workflows requires balancing automation with deliberate human oversight. Generative systems can accelerate drafting and ideation, but research consistently shows that the largest productivity gains occur when human expertise is layered into the process rather than removed from it (Brynjolfsson et al., 2021). The goal is not to replace human effort but to augment it: machines handle repetitive or generative subtasks, while humans provide contextualization, ethical judgment, and quality assurance (Figure 3.2). In practical terms, this means allowing an AI system to produce a draft but assigning human reviewers to check for tone, accuracy, and appropriateness before adoption. Studies in human–computer interaction further suggest that users are more likely to trust and adopt systems when they see themselves as co-authors, rather than passive approvers of machine work (Shneiderman, 2022). Effective integration therefore requires workflows that define when human intervention is mandatory, how outputs are validated, and which metrics determine acceptance. Without these structures, organizations risk producing content quickly but without accountability. With them, human-in-the-loop design turns automation into reliable collaboration.

Human-in-the-loop (HITL) refinement improves both accuracy and accountability across domains (Table 3.4). HITL refers to workflows where humans remain embedded at key decision points rather than only at the start or end. Empirical studies in applied machine learning show that adding human validation steps consistently outperforms fully automated processes on measures such as factual correctness and fairness (Cheng and Bernstein, 2021). This practice is especially critical in knowledge-intensive fields like healthcare, education, and law, where mistakes can have outsized consequences. By structuring checkpoints—draft generation, human evaluation, AI revision, and final approval—organizations reduce hallucinations (made-up facts) and decision errors. Human evaluators also calibrate confidence levels, deciding when to accept outputs or escalate them for further review. In other words, humans serve both as editors and as governors of system behavior. This dual role keeps generative systems aligned with institutional standards while ensuring that efficiency never overrides safety.

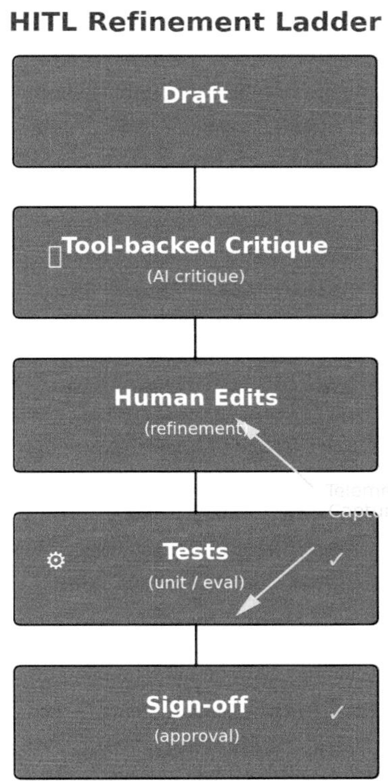

Figure 3.2 Human-in-the-Loop Refinement.

Effective workflow integration also depends on clear role definition. Responsibility-assignment frameworks, such as RACI matrices (which designate who is Responsible, Accountable, Consulted, and Informed), help clarify ownership in human–AI teams (Schmidt and Wiegand, 2021). When roles are structured—AI produces drafts, humans review, compliance teams audit—organizations reduce duplication and avoid gaps where accountability is unclear. Project management research shows that such governance frameworks also lower resistance to adoption because stakeholders know that legal, ethical, and professional standards remain protected (Dwivedi et al., 2021). In classrooms, this might mean clarifying whether

AI-generated drafts are raw input for peer review or finished work to be graded. In enterprises, it may involve specifying which departments sign off before public release. In both cases, accountability transforms generative systems from ad hoc helpers into structured collaborators. Without this codification, workflows risk either over-reliance on automation or paralysis by uncertainty.

The design challenge is deciding how much human oversight to include and at what points. Cognitive load theory shows that too many checkpoints create fatigue, reducing reviewers' accuracy and slowing workflows (Paas and van Merriënboer, 2020). Too few checkpoints, however, increase the chance of errors going unnoticed or content drifting away from organizational standards. Decision science research suggests that midstream evaluations—reviewing after the first draft but before final polishing—strike the best balance between efficiency and quality (Clark et al., 2020). This principle aligns with natural decision boundaries, such as moving from brainstorming to narrowing ideas, or from draft writing to editorial refinement. For example, in an educational context, reviewing AI-generated essay drafts after the brainstorming stage but before grading ensures students are learning rather than merely passing along machine output. In industry, reviewing product descriptions before public release but after internal drafting serves a similar role. Well-placed oversight allows workflows to remain fast without compromising judgment.

In educational contexts, HITL refinement doubles as pedagogy. Research shows that students who critique AI-generated drafts not only improve the final product but also strengthen their evaluative and metacognitive skills (Kasneci et al., 2023). Instructors can design classroom workflows where AI produces a starting draft, students critique it using rubrics, and teachers provide final guidance. This model maintains academic integrity while transforming generative AI into a learning catalyst rather than a shortcut. Students gain practice in identifying weaknesses, questioning assumptions, and applying disciplinary criteria. Such designs also allow instructors to track which skills students are practicing—critical thinking, argumentation, or evidence evaluation—during review. The broader takeaway is that human oversight in classrooms safeguards quality while reinforcing learning outcomes. Rather than reducing effort, it shifts student energy toward higher-order thinking.

In industry, human refinement builds trust and protects organizational reputation. Marketing research indicates that consumers respond more positively to AI-generated content when they know a human has reviewed it before publication (Longoni et al., 2019). The visible presence of human judgment mitigates fears about authenticity and reduces backlash from synthetic media. Companies that openly disclose hybrid workflows—using statements such as "AI-assisted, human-reviewed"—report higher acceptance from customers and fewer reputational risks (Mikalef et al., 2022). This transparency serves not only regulatory compliance but also strategic communication. It signals to stakeholders that speed and innovation are balanced with care and responsibility. For example, a healthcare provider posting AI-assisted patient education materials can reassure patients by emphasizing that clinicians reviewed the information before release. By making human roles explicit, organizations turn oversight into a competitive advantage.

Metrics are indispensable for embedding HITL refinement into daily practice. Time-to-first-draft measures efficiency, showing how quickly a usable draft is produced, while edit distance measures how much revision separates the AI's draft from the final approved version (Gregor et al., 2020). Error-catch rate quantifies the proportion of mistakes identified before deployment. Comparative evaluations show that hybrid workflows generally reduce edit distance and increase error detection when humans intervene earlier with rubrics (Dwivedi et al., 2021). Embedding these metrics into dashboards enables continuous monitoring and incremental improvement. Over time, this creates feedback loops where not only outputs but the workflows themselves evolve. In education, this might mean tracking how many AI-generated drafts required heavy revision, while in industry, dashboards could display cycle times and rejection rates across campaigns. Metrics thus move oversight from intuition to evidence, making HITL measurable and improvable.

Domain-specific needs further shape how HITL workflows are designed. In highly regulated sectors such as healthcare or finance, oversight often includes audit trails and versioning systems that log every human intervention for compliance (Esteva et al., 2019; Ghassemi et al., 2021). By contrast, in creative industries such as advertising or media, workflows prioritize originality and variety, but human editors still ensure tone and brand identity remain intact. This divergence highlights that workflow integration cannot be uniform: compliance-heavy contexts need documentation and traceability, while creative contexts require flexibility and aesthetic judgment. For example, a university's assessment system may log every use of AI in grading, while a design firm might focus on curating the most innovative outputs for presentation. In each case, workflows are adapted to the risks and goals of the domain. The principle remains the same: humans anchor generative systems to the standards of their field.

Workflow integration also benefits from continuous revision. Studies of sociotechnical systems show that human–AI workflows perform best when organizations treat them as living processes, updating prompts, evaluation rubrics, and checkpoints as models evolve (Sarker et al., 2022). Human oversight is not fixed; as systems improve in factual reliability, human attention can shift to higher-order concerns such as tone, framing, or ethics. For example, in early deployments, educators may spend time checking factual accuracy in AI-generated essays, but later they may focus on evaluating originality and argument structure. Similarly, in professional contexts, compliance officers may eventually move from basic correctness checks to strategic risk assessments. By embedding reflexivity into workflow design, organizations ensure that oversight remains efficient, targeted, and relevant. This adaptability keeps systems aligned with institutional priorities as both humans and models learn together.

HITL refinement also reinforces accountability and governance. Literature on responsible AI consistently emphasizes that oversight is a cornerstone of ethical deployment, ensuring that automated systems remain subordinate to human judgment and institutional norms (Floridi and Cowls, 2019). By mandating human sign-offs at key junctures, organizations create both procedural accountability and symbolic assurance that final responsibility rests with people. This protects against the illusion of autonomy in systems that are still fundamentally tools. The combination of speed, scale, and ethical anchoring turns AI from an experiment into an operational partner. In effect, human oversight is the guardrail that channels generative capability into socially acceptable and legally defensible outcomes. By embedding this principle into workflow design, institutions ensure that augmentation does not slip into abdication of responsibility.

Table 3.4 Human-in-the-Loop (HITL) Workflow Integration

Aspect	*Description*	*Example (Education)*	*Example (Industry)*
Purpose	Balance machine speed with human oversight for accuracy, ethics, and trust.	Students critique AI essay drafts before grading.	Marketing content labeled "AI-assisted, human-reviewed."
Role Definition	Clarify who drafts, who reviews, and who signs off to avoid gaps or duplication.	Instructor reviews AI draft, students provide peer critique.	Compliance officer approves reports before release.
Checkpoints	Place human reviews at natural decision boundaries (midstream is most effective).	Review essay drafts before submission for grading.	Review product descriptions before public release.
Metrics	Use measurable indicators such as time-to-first-draft, edit distance, error-catch rate.	Track how much student revision was needed on AI drafts.	Dashboard tracks revision cycles and customer complaint rates.
Context Variation	Oversight adapts to domain risk and goals.	Audit trail for academic integrity in grading.	Flexibility for creative tone in advertising campaigns.
Pedagogical Value	Students improve critical thinking and evaluative skills by critiquing drafts.	Students practice identifying weaknesses with rubric-based reviews.	Employees refine judgment on tone, brand, and compliance.
Governance Impact	Embeds accountability and protects against abdication of responsibility.	Instructor remains final authority on grading outcomes.	Executive sign-off ensures responsibility stays with people, not systems.
Adaptability	Workflows evolve as systems improve, shifting human focus to higher-order review.	Instructors move from fact-checking to judging originality.	Compliance shifts from correctness checks to strategic risk assessment.

The central insight from this section is that the most effective way to integrate generative systems into real work is through collaboration, not substitution. Machines are very good at producing quick drafts or summarizing large amounts of information, but humans are still needed to ensure that the results are accurate, appropriate, and aligned with organizational or educational goals. This model—often called human-in-the-loop—protects against errors while also building trust, since people know that a real person has reviewed and approved what the system produces. In education, this looks like students critiquing AI-generated drafts with rubrics so they practice critical thinking, while instructors retain authority over final grading. In industry, it can mean customer-facing content is labeled as "AI-assisted, human-reviewed," which reassures clients that speed has not replaced accountability.

The significance of this approach lies in its balance. With careful role definitions, such as who generates drafts, who reviews them, and who signs off, organizations avoid both over-reliance on automation and excessive bottlenecks. Well-placed checkpoints reduce risk without slowing workflows too much, and metrics like time-to-first-draft, edit distance, and error-catch rates make quality measurable rather than subjective. Importantly, these workflows adapt to context: in healthcare or finance, where stakes are high, detailed audit trails and versioning are critical, while in creative fields, oversight emphasizes originality and brand identity. Across all domains, the key principle is the same: humans remain the ultimate decision-makers, and their judgment gives legitimacy to the speed and scale that generative systems provide.

Looking ahead, future research and practice should focus on how human-in-the-loop methods evolve over time. As systems improve, human reviewers will likely shift their attention from catching simple mistakes to evaluating higher-level qualities such as ethics, tone, and fairness. Institutions will also need to explore how these workflows can be standardized across sectors without losing the flexibility that local contexts demand. Most of all, organizations must continue to see oversight as a strength rather than a cost—embedding accountability into their systems from the start. By doing so, they ensure that generative technology becomes a trusted partner rather than a source of unchecked risk.

3.4 CASE STUDIES: FAST UPSKILLING WORKFLOWS IN EDUCATION AND INDUSTRY

Building on the integration patterns and human-in-the-loop safeguards from the previous section, this discussion shows how fast-learning workflows play out in practice. Each case demonstrates a similar rhythm: deliberate divergence to generate options, rapid drafting with clear rubrics, and convergence guided by human accountability at defined decision points. Across settings, the role of intelligent systems is to accelerate the "first mile" of work, while educators and professionals anchor the process with contextual knowledge, ethical review, and final approval (Brynjolfsson et al., 2021; Floridi and Cowls, 2019). The cases illustrate that speed gains endure only when the workflow specifies who evaluates what, when, and under which criteria. Each example identifies the intervention, the coordination of human and machine roles, and the measurable outcomes. Attention to role clarity and auditability reduces friction in adoption, helping institutions avoid resistance while strengthening trust in hybrid workflows. The common theme is augmentation rather than automation: systems multiply draft options, while people provide judgment and legitimacy. This combination turns experimentation into repeatable, evidence-linked practice.

In higher education, one instructional design team used a generative system to draft parallel versions of interdisciplinary syllabi. They began with a 15-minute "divergence sprint," asking the system for five outlines per course. Faculty then ran pairwise comparisons—evaluating two drafts at a time—against a rubric emphasizing coverage, alignment with learning outcomes, and assessment integrity. This narrowed options to a winner that was further refined by human instructors. Compared with the prior manual process, time-to-first-draft dropped from six to eight weeks to just under two, a reduction of roughly 60% (Clark et al., 2020). Faculty noted that automation expanded the option set and freed them to focus on sequencing assignments and clarifying evidence of competency (Kasneci et al., 2023). To maintain governance, prompts, versions, and rationale notes were archived, and accreditation compliance remained a human responsibility. Reviews showed no decline in quality and in some cases clearer assessment criteria. The case demonstrates how structured divergence, paired with human gates, converts drafting speed into accredited curricular artifacts.

In K–12 settings, a district piloted lesson design to support mixed-ability classrooms. Teachers asked the system to generate three lesson variants per unit—standard, scaffolded for extra support, and extended for enrichment—then curated activities to match individualized education plans. Weekly reviews tracked teacher prep time, student engagement, and alignment to standards. The result was a four-hour reduction in weekly preparation time and improved participation, especially among students who struggled with grade-level content (Kasneci et al., 2023). Human checkpoints were required for content accuracy, age appropriateness, and cultural sensitivity. A standardized rubric kept lesson selection aligned with learning goals rather than novelty. Professional learning communities circulated effective prompts and examples, making the workflow replicable. By treating AI as a partner in option generation rather than a replacement, teachers preserved authority while scaling personalization.

Professional education shows similar benefits. A consulting firm incorporated fast-learning workflows into a policy analysis boot camp. Participants drafted briefs on regulatory topics, exchanged critiques using a rubric focused on clarity, evidence use, feasibility, and risk, and then revised drafts before instructor adjudication. This compressed the draft–critique–revise loop into a single day while maintaining evidence standards through citations and annotations. Evaluations found higher-quality briefs and increased learner confidence compared to prior cohorts without AI support (Dwivedi et al., 2021). Governance was built in: instructors retained approval authority, and all prompts, sources, and rationales were archived. Participants reported greater visibility into trade-offs and stronger argument discipline. Instructors noted that the human role shifted from correcting form to assessing assumptions and risks. The workflow was eventually embedded into onboarding, linking training to measurable outputs.

Industry cases underline the same orchestration principles. A technology company used generative systems to speed software engineer onboarding. New hires produced boilerplate code and documentation from specifications, then validated outputs with unit tests and code reviews. Automated checks came first, followed by mandatory senior review, especially for security-related code. Managers reported a 40% faster time-to-productivity, attributing gains to faster "first miles" and clearer correction cycles. Senior engineers emphasized that AI shifted their focus toward higher-value work—design, integration, and threat modeling—rather than replacing judgment. Post-mortems revealed fewer late-stage defects when tests were authored alongside generated code. Logs of code changes, test outcomes, and approvals created a reusable knowledge base. This illustrates how pairing rapid generation with structured review improves both throughput and long-term code quality.

Healthcare settings show how speed can coexist with safety. In one hospital network, clinicians used AI to generate first drafts of patient education materials tailored to literacy levels and cultural context. Staff then refined drafts to ensure medical accuracy and consistency with institutional style, citing authoritative sources for all claims. Production time dropped from four weeks to one, while readability scores improved. Patient surveys indicated greater clarity, and clinicians reported spending more time on personalization and communication rather than drafting (Esteva et al., 2019). Governance included mandatory clinician sign-offs and versioned storage for audit. A review committee sampled materials for bias, accessibility, and guideline compliance. Templates, prompts, and checklists were updated over time to capture organizational learning. The case demonstrates that rapid drafting can enhance—not endanger—cultural competence when human gates are enforced.

Creative industries highlight the importance of balancing innovation and governance. A consumer-goods company used AI to generate advertising copy variants under brand and legal constraints. Marketers applied pairwise comparisons and a rubric—clarity, resonance, and brand fit—to select finalists for A/B testing. Across campaigns, AI-assisted variants improved click-through rates while reducing time to launch (Cillo et al., 2024). Transparency that outputs were "human-reviewed" preserved trust and mitigated concerns about synthetic content (Longoni et al., 2019). Legal review remained a strict requirement, with substantiation records tied to claims. Post-campaign analyses linked performance back to prompt and decoding patterns, strengthening future workflows. This case shows how speed gains can be institutionalized without diluting compliance or brand safeguards.

In financial services, analysts used a rapid scenario-brief workflow to respond to regulatory changes. Generative systems produced alternative write-ups identifying impacted portfolios and controls, while analysts validated citations and added context. Internal advisories were produced in half the previous time, giving compliance and strategy teams earlier visibility. A risk committee reviewed high-impact outputs, ensuring accountability for critical decisions (Dwivedi et al., 2021). Analysts archived assumptions, sources, and decision logs to create an audit trail. Training emphasized when to escalate uncertainty rather than over-rely on drafts. Over time, last-minute rework declined, as alignment occurred earlier in the process. This illustrates how speed can coexist with a conservative risk posture when responsibilities and thresholds are explicit.

Media organizations face a different trust challenge. A national newsroom piloted AI-assisted briefings on corporate earnings and public data releases. Reporters generated initial summaries from filings, then performed verification, style edits, and headline tests. The newsroom adopted transparency notes acknowledging hybrid authorship, while editors retained full responsibility. Time-to-publish fell, with no measurable drop in perceived credibility—consistent with research showing that human oversight mitigates audience concerns (Diakopoulos, 2019; Longoni et al., 2019). A standards desk established rules for citation, embargo handling, and error correction. Periodic audits sampled articles for accuracy and tracked time savings. Training warned reporters against "anchoring bias"—over-relying on the first AI draft. The pilot shows that editorial gates and disclosure norms allow speed gains without eroding journalistic trust.

Across all these cases, the pattern is consistent: generative systems multiply credible first drafts, while human experts gate factuality, relevance, and ethics. Gains include shorter cycle times, higher personalization, and faster experimentation when workflows embed rubrics, audit trails, and assigned roles (Brynjolfsson et al., 2021). Institutions that treat prompts, parameters, and decisions as operational artifacts create reusable knowledge bases that improve with each iteration. In education, the same designs strengthen pedagogy by making AI a tool for practice, critique, and metacognition rather than a shortcut (Clark et al., 2020; Kasneci et al., 2023). Sector-specific differences matter, but the orchestration principles travel: divergence sprints, pairwise selection, tool-assisted verification, and explicit human sign-offs. These cases also surface the limits of fast workflows, including reviewer fatigue and over-trust in surface plausibility, which require cadence design and bias checks. What endures across contexts is the symbolic and procedural anchor of human judgment, ensuring that speed does not displace accountability. This alignment transforms rapid generation into durable institutional capability.

The central takeaway of this chapter is that the real value of rapid content generation comes from pairing speed with structure. Generative systems excel at multiplying first drafts, but without rubrics, templates, or checkpoints, speed quickly turns into noise. By embedding deliberate divergence—short sprints that produce multiple options—and concise rubrics for convergence, institutions can cut drafting time dramatically while still preserving relevance and quality. Smaller systems require tight scaffolding and retrieval support to stay useful, while advanced models thrive on multi-sample strategies and exploratory branching to surface better options. Yet across capacities, factual reliability still depends on tool-assisted verification: calculators for numbers, retrieval modules for sources, and audit logs for evidence. The lesson is clear: model sophistication is not a substitute for external checks.

A second insight is that human-in-the-loop refinement is the non-negotiable safeguard for reliability and trust. The most successful workflows put human judgment at defined decision gates—points where experts approve, revise, or reject outputs. These checkpoints are not just about catching errors; they are also about preserving ethical standards, institutional voice, and alignment with learning or business goals. Governance practices such as archiving prompts, logging citations, and defining rollback criteria give these workflows stability and accountability. Instead of viewing governance as bureaucracy, leading organizations and educators treat it as operating discipline: the set of practices that turns experimental drafting into durable, auditable processes. This ensures that rapid generation does not erode institutional standards but reinforces them.

Metrics emerged as another pillar of effective integration, transforming speed into stewardship. Tracking time-to-first-draft provides evidence of efficiency gains, while edit distance—the number of changes needed between an AI draft and the final version—reveals how much effort was saved or shifted. A/B win rates and error-catch rates offer additional lenses to evaluate which prompts, decoders, or workflows deliver better outcomes. By incorporating these metrics into retrospectives, instructors and managers can refine their processes in ways that systematically improve over time. Significantly, these workflows also build human capacity: when students and professionals critique and refine AI outputs, they sharpen evaluative judgment and domain reasoning. AI becomes a tool for practice and reflection rather than a shortcut around learning or expertise.

Another important theme is that external trust hinges on visible human accountability. Case studies showed that labeling outputs as "AI-assisted but human-reviewed" reassured students, patients, customers, and regulators that final responsibility still rested with people. Transparency in authorship and review proved essential in high-stakes fields such as education, journalism, healthcare, and finance. These disclosures are not only ethical but also strategic, protecting credibility while signaling responsibility. They underscore the broader pattern: generative systems accelerate the "first mile" of drafting, but humans remain indispensable for evaluation, integration, and sign-off.

Looking forward, the next steps are clear. Organizations and schools should codify their rapid-generation workflows into playbooks that specify roles, metrics, and gates. They should treat prompts, parameters, and decisions as operational artifacts, archived for audit and reuse. Training should emphasize critical review of AI drafts as a skill in its own right, cultivating evaluators who can separate useful novelty from surface plausibility. Finally, institutions should recognize that the combination of automation and human oversight is not a temporary compromise but a durable model. It is this hybrid discipline—speed guided by structure, and drafts anchored by human accountability—that turns generative systems from experiments into trusted, repeatable practices capable of meeting the standards of both classrooms and boardrooms.

REFERENCES

Amabile, T.M. 1982. Social psychology of creativity: A consensual assessment technique. Journal of Personality and Social Psychology. 43(5): 997–1013.

Boonpracha, J., Chaidaroon, S. and Sueblinvong, T. 2023. SCAMPER for creativity of students' creative idea creation in product design. Thinking Skills and Creativity. 48: 101313.

Brown, T., Mann, B., Ryder, N., Subbiah, M., Kaplan, J.D., Dhariwal, P., et al. 2020. Language models are few-shot learners. Advances in Neural Information Processing Systems. 33: 1877–1901.

Brynjolfsson, E., Rock, D. and Syverson, C. 2021. The productivity J-curve: How intangibles complement general purpose technologies. American Economic Journal: Macroeconomics. 13(1): 333–372. https://doi.org/10.1257/mac.20180386

Brynjolfsson, E., Li, D. and Raymond, L. 2025. Generative AI at work. The Quarterly Journal of Economics. 140(2): 889–939. https://doi.org/10.1093/qje/qjae005

Chen, Y.-C., Hsu, C.-C. and Wang, Y.-H. 2025. Enhancing responses from large language models with role-playing prompts. Humanities & Social Sciences Communications. 12: 210.

Cheng, J. and Bernstein, M.S. 2021. Flock: Hybrid crowd-machine learning classifiers. *In*: Proceedings of the ACM on Human-Computer Interaction, 5(CSCW1): pp. 1–20. https://doi.org/10.1145/3449096

Cillo, V., Rialti, R., Marzi, G., Dutot, V., Mlachila, C. and Rameshwar, S. 2024. Generative AI shaping innovation and marketing processes. Journal of the Academy of Marketing Science. 52(6): 1411–1435. https://doi.org/10.1007/s11747-024-00966-3

Clark, D., Luckin, R. and Holmes, W. 2020. Artificial intelligence in education: Promises and implications for teaching and learning. Computers and Education. 146: 103751. https://doi.org/10.1016/j.compedu.2019.103751

Diakopoulos, N. 2019. Automating the news: How algorithms are rewriting the media. Harvard University Press. https://doi.org/10.4159/9780674241602

Doshi, A.R., Agarwal, A., Hu, Y. and Rahwan, I. 2024. Generative AI enhances individual creativity but reduces collective variability. Science Advances. 10(28): eadn5290. https://doi.org/10.1126/sciadv.adn5290

Dwivedi, Y.K., Hughes, L., Kar, A.K., Baabdullah, A.M., Grover, P., Abbas, R., et al. 2021. Artificial intelligence (AI): Multidisciplinary perspectives on emerging challenges, opportunities, and agenda for research, practice and policy. International Journal of Information Management. 57: 101994. https://doi.org/10.1016/j.ijinfomgt.2019.101994

Esteva, A., Robicquet, A., Ramsundar, B., Kuleshov, V., DePristo, M., Chou, K., et al. 2019. A guide to deep learning in healthcare. Nature Medicine. 25(1): 24–29. https://doi.org/10.1038/s41591-018-0316-z

Floridi, L. and Cowls, J. 2019. A unified framework of five principles for AI in society. Harvard Data Science Review. 1(1). https://doi.org/10.1162/99608f92.8cd550d1

Fu, Y., Luo, Y., Wei, F., Liu, J. and Jiang, M. 2025. Min-p sampling: A family of samplers to trade off diversity and quality. ICLR 2025 (OpenReview).

Gao, L., Madaan, A., Zhou, Y., Liu, P., Alon, U., Schuurmans, D., et al. 2023. PAL: Program-aided language models. NeurIPS. 2023.

Ghassemi, M., Oakden-Rayner, L. and Beam, A.L. 2021. The false hope of current approaches to explainable artificial intelligence in health care. The Lancet Digital Health. 3(11): e745–e750. https://doi.org/10.1016/S2589-7500(21)00208-9

Gregor, S., Imran, A. and Turner, T. 2020. A "sweet spot" change strategy for a digital transformation. Information Systems Journal. 30(1): 96–124. https://doi.org/10.1111/isj.12233

Gu, J., Tang, X., He, J. and Zhang, T. 2024. A survey on LLM-as-a-Judge. arXiv:2411.15594.

Guu, K., Lee, K., Tung, Z., Pasupat, P. and Chang, M.-W. 2020. REALM: Retrieval-augmented language model pre-training. *In*: Proceedings of ICML, pp. 3677–3689.

Han, Z. and Wang, Z. 2024. Rethinking the role-play prompting in mathematical reasoning tasks. *In*: Proceedings of the 1st Workshop on Efficiency, Security, and Generalization of Multimedia Foundation Models, pp. 13–17.

Hartmann, J. and Heitmann, M. 2025. Superhuman visual marketing images. International Journal of Research in Marketing. https://doi.org/10.1016/j.ijresmar.2025.01.002

Holtzman, A., Buys, J., Du, L., Forbes, M. and Choi, Y. 2019. The curious case of neural text degeneration. arXiv:1904.09751.

Jimenez, C.E., Yang, J., Wettig, A., Yao, S., Pei, K., Press, O., et al. 2023. SWE-bench: Can language models resolve real-world GitHub issues? arXiv:2310.06770.

Kaplan, J., McCandlish, S., Henighan, T., Brown, T.B., Chess, B., Child, R., et al. 2020. Scaling laws for neural language models. arXiv:2001.08361.

Kasneci, E., Sessler, K., Küchemann, S., Bannert, M., Dementieva, D., Fischer, F., et al. 2023. ChatGPT for good? On opportunities and challenges of large language models for education. Learning and Individual Differences. 103: 102274. https://doi.org/10.1016/j.lindif.2023.102274

Le Bronnec, Y., Hendriksen, S. and Yeh, C. 2024. Precision is to recall what human preference is to factuality. ACL 2024 Findings.

Lee, G.G., Wang, G., Liao, C.H. and Chen, L.-H. 2024. Applying large language models and chain-of-thought for automated assessment. Discover Education. 3: 63. https://doi.org/10.1016/j.discedu.2024.100063

Levenshtein, V.I. 1966. Binary codes capable of correcting deletions, insertions, and reversals. Soviet Physics Doklady. 10(8): 707–710.

Lewis, P., Perez, E., Piktus, A., Petroni, F., Karpukhin, V., Goyal, N., et al. 2020. Retrieval-augmented generation for knowledge-intensive NLP tasks. Advances in Neural Information Processing Systems. 33: 9459–9474.

Liang, P., Bommasani, R., Lee, T., Tsipras, D., Soylu, D., Yasunaga, M., et al. 2022. Holistic evaluation of language models (HELM). arXiv:2211.09110.

Liu, Y., Iter, D., Xu, Y., Wang, S., Xu, R. and Zhu, C. 2023. G-eval: NLG evaluation using GPT-4 with better human alignment. arXiv preprint arXiv:2303.16634.

Longoni, C., Bonezzi, A. and Morewedge, C.K. 2019. Resistance to medical artificial intelligence. Journal of Consumer Research. 46(4): 629–650. https://doi.org/10.1093/jcr/ucz013

Lu, J., Li, Q. and Chen, X. 2024. Automated code review in practice. arXiv:2412.18531.

Madaan, A., Tandon, N., Gupta, P., Hallinan, S., Gao, L., Wiegreffe, S., et al. 2023. Self-Refine: Iterative refinement with self-feedback. NeurIPS 2023.

Mikalef, P., Conboy, K., Lundström, J.E. and Popovič, A. 2022. Thinking responsibly about responsible AI and 'the dark side'of AI. European Journal of Information Systems. 31(3): 257–268.

Nguyen, M.N., Minh, N.N. and Phan, A. 2024. Min-p sampling for creative and coherent LLM outputs. arXiv:2407.01082.

Noy, S. and Zhang, W. 2023. Experimental evidence on the productivity effects of generative AI. Science. 381(6654): 187–192. https://doi.org/10.1126/science.adh2586

OpenAI. 2023. GPT-4 technical report. arXiv:2303.08774.

Paas, F. and van Merriënboer, J.J. 2020. Cognitive-load theory: Methods to manage working memory load in the learning of complex tasks. Educational Psychology Review. 32(2): 401–423. https://doi.org/10.1007/s10648-019-09492-2

Press, O., Zhang, M., Min, S., Schmidt, L., Smith, N.A. and Lewis, M. 2022. Measuring and narrowing the compositionality gap in language models (self-ask). arXiv:2210.03350.

Renze, M. and Guven, E. 2024. The effect of sampling temperature on problem solving in large language models. Findings of EMNLP 2024. 7346–7356.

Ritchey, T. 2013. General Morphological Analysis. A General Method for Non-quantified Modelling. Swedish Morphological Society.

Sarker, I.H., Colman, A., Han, J. and Khan, A.I. 2022. Context-aware machine learning: A survey and framework for sustainable systems. ACM Computing Surveys. 54(5): 1–36. https://doi.org/10.1145/3447581

Schick, T., Dwivedi-Yu, J., Dessì, R., Raileanu, R., Lomeli, M., Zettlemoyer, L., et al. 2023. Toolformer: Language models can teach themselves to use tools. NeurIPS 2023.

Schmidt, R. and Wiegand, M. 2021. The role of governance in digital transformation. International Journal of Information Management. 57: 102229. https://doi.org/10.1016/j.ijinfomgt.2020.102229

Shneiderman, B. 2022. Human-centered AI. Oxford University Press. https://doi.org/10.1093/oso/9780192845290.001.0001

Wang, J., Wang, J., Athiwaratkun, B., Zhang, C. and Zou, J. 2024. Mixture-of-Agents enhances large language model capabilities. arXiv:2406.04692.

Wang, X., Wei, J., Schuurmans, D., Le, Q. and Zhou, D. 2023. Self-consistency improves chain-of-thought reasoning in language models. ICLR 2023 (workshop).

Watts, I., Gumma, V., Yadavalli, A., Seshadri, V., Swaminathan, M. and Sitaram, S. 2024. Pariksha: A large-scale investigation of human-LLM evaluator agreement on multilingual and multi-cultural data. arXiv preprint arXiv:2406.15053.

Watts, I., Hada, M. and Specia, L. 2024. A large-scale investigation of human–LLM evaluator agreement. EMNLP 2024.

Wei, J., Wang, X., Schuurmans, D., Bosma, M., Ichter, B., Xia, F., et al. 2022. Chain-of-thought prompting elicits reasoning in large language models. NeurIPS 2022.

Wu, T.-T. and Wu, Y.-T. 2020. Applying project-based learning and SCAMPER teaching strategies in engineering education. Thinking Skills and Creativity. 35: 100631.

Xia, N., Haron, S.H., Huang, Y. and Niu, R. 2025. The effectiveness of CPS+SCAMPER teaching mode and strategies on student creativity. Thinking Skills and Creativity. 56: 101758.

Yao, S., Yu, D., Zhao, J., Shafran, I., Griffiths, T., Cao, Y., et al. 2023. Tree of thoughts: Deliberate problem solving with large language models. Advances in Neural Information Processing Systems. 36: 11809–11822.

Yao, S., Zhao, J., Yu, D., Du, N., Shafran, I., Narasimhan, K., et al. 2023. ReAct: Synergizing reasoning and acting in language models. ICLR 2023.

Zhang, D.W., Zhang, Z. and Sun, X. 2024. Evaluating large language models for criterion-based grading. NPJ Science of Learning. 9: 20. https://doi.org/10.1038/s41539-024-00291-1

Zhou, D., Schärli, N., Hou, L., Wei, J., Scales, N., Wang, X., et al. 2022. Least-to-Most prompting enables complex reasoning in large language models. arXiv:2205.10625.

Chapter 4

Slow Learning and AI—Facilitating Reflective Critical Thinking

4.1 AI-ASSISTED DEEP ANALYSIS, CRITIQUE, AND METACOGNITIVE SCAFFOLDING

Building on the contrast between fast and slow learning established earlier, the focus here turns to how artificial intelligence can support deliberate, structured forms of reasoning. Slow learning emphasizes purposeful deliberation—evaluating evidence, interrogating assumptions, and making reasoning processes explicit. AI can assist in these processes by structuring analysis, surfacing counterarguments, and scaffolding metacognitive moves that otherwise remain tacit (Figure 4.1). The aim is not to produce verbosity but to generate "productive reflection," where explanations and evaluations are tied to clear criteria and sources. Research in cognitive psychology, particularly dual-process theory, highlights why deliberate reflection must be built into learning and decision-making. Fast, intuitive responses—what psychologists call *System 1 thinking*—are efficient and often useful, but they are also prone to shortcuts and bias (Evans, 2008; Stanovich and West, 2000). Slower, reflective responses—*System 2 thinking*—are more analytical and careful, yet they require prompts, structures, and supports to be sustained in practice. Tools such as templates, checklists, and evaluative gates can scaffold this process by organizing information and signaling where reflection is required, but humans must still make the final judgment. Feedback research reinforces this point: goal-referenced, criteria-based feedback—feedback that explicitly links performance to goals, identifies gaps, and recommends next steps—has been shown to be especially effective for improvement (Hattie and Timperley, 2007;

DOI: 10.1201/9781003688013-4

Shute, 2008). Similarly, research on self-regulated learning demonstrates that prompts encouraging learners to plan, monitor, and evaluate their own work strengthen knowledge transfer, particularly when these activities are grounded in authentic, real-world tasks (Azevedo and Hadwin, 2005; Winne and Hadwin, 1998). Taken together, these findings show that reflection is not a natural byproduct of slowing down; it must be deliberately supported through structures that make careful thinking visible and actionable.

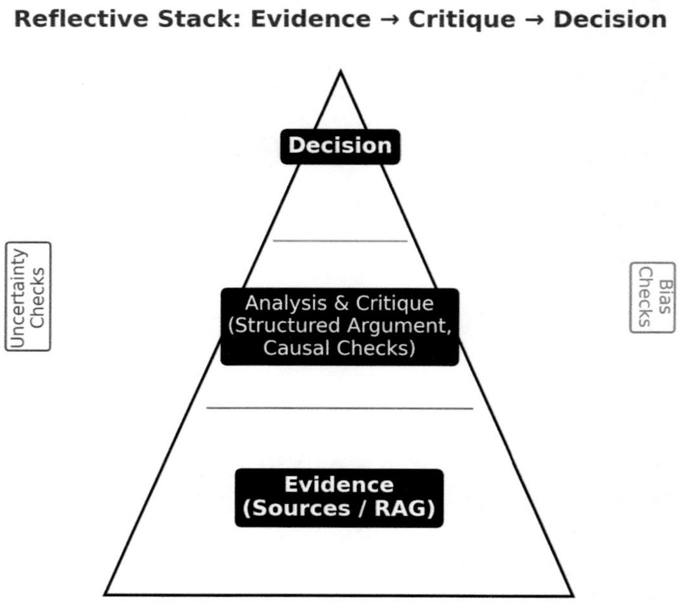

Figure 4.1 Reflective Stack: Evidence, Critique, Decision.

Extending this perspective, deep analysis requires evidence synthesis practices that are anchored in methodological rigor rather than intuition alone. Digital systems can be used to generate structured summaries aligned with established review frameworks such as PRISMA (*Preferred Reporting Items for Systematic Reviews and Meta-Analyses*), which provides a checklist and flow diagram to ensure that reviews are transparent and reproducible (Page et al., 2021). These summaries can also incorporate judgments from ROBIS (*Risk of Bias in Systematic Reviews*), a tool designed to assess whether a review has been influenced by design flaws or selective reporting (Whiting et al., 2016). Alongside these, GRADE (*Grading of Recommendations, Assessment, Development, and Evaluation*) offers a way to rate the certainty of evidence, making explicit whether conclusions rest on high, moderate, low, or very low confidence (Guyatt et al., 2008). Together, these frameworks guard against impressionistic interpretation by tying claims to evidence levels and explicit uncertainty. The *Cochrane Handbook* reinforces these practices by requiring steps such as pre-specifying outcomes, documenting analytic decisions, and justifying interpretations, all of which digital systems can support through structured checklists before human sign-off

(Higgins et al., 2019). Preregistration of analysis plans, where methods are declared before results are known, further reduces hindsight bias, and drafting assistance can make such preregistration documents more accessible (Nosek et al., 2018). Work in metascience underscores why these precautions matter, showing the fragility of many published findings when subjected to replication and bias checks (Ioannidis, 2005). Adapted for organizational contexts, the same discipline translates into linking judgments not just to statistical significance but also to effect sizes, risk profiles, and resource implications. The outcome is a reflective process that is both auditable and evidence-informed, where conclusions can be trusted because the reasoning behind them is transparent.

Turning from evidence synthesis to critique, structured argumentation provides a tested way to strengthen reflective thinking. Decades of research show that explicitly mapping the components of an argument—claims, supporting reasons, evidence, and counterarguments—enhances reasoning performance, particularly when learners are asked to revise their arguments over multiple rounds (Dwyer et al., 2012; Butchart et al., 2009). One widely used framework is the Toulmin model of argumentation, which breaks arguments into six elements: a claim (the main point), data (supporting evidence), a warrant (the principle connecting evidence to the claim), backing (additional support for the warrant), a qualifier (the degree of certainty), and possible rebuttals (counterarguments). This structure makes explicit both the strengths and vulnerabilities of reasoning. Language models can draft initial Toulmin-style maps, propose potential counterclaims, and even generate adversarial questions that probe weaker warrants or assumptions. Educational research confirms that dialogic engagement with counterarguments fosters deeper evaluative judgment, and this same principle applies in professional and policy contexts where contested reasoning is common (Kuhn, 2010). Reliability improves further when evaluators use rubrics that weight the validity, relevance, and clarity of warrants, ensuring that critiques focus on reasoning quality rather than style (Jonsson and Svingby, 2007; Panadero and Jonsson, 2013). In such workflows, automated tools serve as both generative aids and critical foils, while humans retain responsibility for final judgment. Over time, storing argument maps as shared repositories creates institutional memory, allowing educators and organizations to reduce redundancy and build cumulative reasoning capacity.

Complementing structured argumentation, adversarial testing serves to highlight weaknesses in reasoning and prevent complacency. In technical fields like machine learning, adversarial methods are used to expose brittle reasoning or "overfitting"—situations where a system appears accurate but fails under slightly altered conditions (Biggio and Roli, 2018; Yuan et al., 2019). Translated into deliberative or policy settings, this becomes a form of structured "red-teaming," where arguments are stress-tested by intentionally generating counterexamples, boundary cases, or stakeholder risks. A practical workflow involves two stages: first, an initial draft is produced with supporting citations, and second, adversarial questioning probes the draft for hidden assumptions and exceptions. This process often leads to revisions that qualify claims more carefully or highlight uncertainty where overconfidence once prevailed. Evidence synthesis frameworks, such as those used in Cochrane reviews, already emphasize the importance of sensitivity analyses and bias checks, which can be understood as forms of adversarial testing (Higgins et al., 2019; Whiting et al., 2016). Organizations can institutionalize this practice by assigning rotating "devil's advocate" roles, supported by structured prompts to ensure critique remains constructive rather than obstructive. The goal is not to tear arguments down but to make them more robust. When stakes are high, findings from adversarial passes should function as pause points, triggering either a re-examination of evidence or rollback of a premature decision.

Beyond critique, metacognitive scaffolding ensures that reflection becomes deliberate, systematic, and repeatable rather than incidental. Argument mapping plays an important role here: by visually laying out claims, evidence, warrants, and counterarguments, it makes reasoning transparent and easier to critique. Such maps also serve as external memory, helping individuals and groups revisit, refine, and extend prior reasoning rather than starting from scratch. Self-regulated learning research shows that prompts directing learners to plan their approach, monitor understanding, and evaluate progress significantly strengthen transfer to new tasks (Azevedo and Hadwin, 2005; Winne and Hadwin, 1998). Feedback research complements this by showing that progress is best supported by feedback that links performance directly to goals, identifies gaps, and suggests next steps (Hattie and Timperley, 2007; Shute, 2008). Digital tools can scaffold these processes by embedding consistent reflective prompts such as, *"What is the central claim?"*, *"What evidence supports it?"*, or *"What would change your conclusion?"* These prompts provide a portable framework that can be applied across projects and disciplines. Evidence from practice-testing and self-explanation research demonstrates that such retrieval and explanatory demands improve both monitoring accuracy and long-term retention (Chi et al., 1989; Roediger and Karpicke, 2006; Dunlosky et al., 2013). When implemented systematically, these scaffolds remain concise, striking a balance between encouraging reflection and avoiding cognitive overload. Over time, teams internalize these habits, with digital systems primarily serving to maintain consistency and prevent reflection from being overlooked.

Expanding on reflective methods, self-explanation and retrieval practice are two of the most robust strategies for strengthening durable learning and informed judgment. Self-explanation asks learners to articulate why a step makes sense, how evidence supports a claim, or how one concept connects to another. This act of "teaching oneself aloud" has been shown to deepen transfer of knowledge because it requires justification rather than passive acceptance (Chi et al., 1989). Digital systems can scaffold this by generating targeted prompts such as *"Why does this evidence support your claim?"* or *"What alternative explanation might exist?"*, and then collecting responses into structured summaries for later critique. Retrieval practice, sometimes called spaced testing, strengthens retention by asking learners to recall information or apply reasoning without immediate cues (Roediger and Karpicke, 2006; Dunlosky et al., 2013). Repeated recall not only improves memory but also helps individuals calibrate confidence, distinguishing what they truly know from what feels familiar. In organizational contexts, calibration is critical: probabilistic judgments—such as estimating the likelihood of a market shift or a clinical outcome—improve when individuals record their confidence levels and then receive structured feedback (Mellers et al., 2015). Systems can log probability estimates alongside the rationales behind them, producing datasets for retrospective analysis. Research shows that metacognitive monitoring improves when predictions are later compared to actual outcomes, reinforcing adaptive expertise (de Bruin and van Gog, 2012; Koriat, 1997). In this way, reflection becomes less an abstract exercise and more an evidence-driven routine, grounded in feedback loops between judgment, outcome, and revision.

Turning from individual reflection to evaluation, rubrics offer a systematic way to translate values into operational criteria. Analytic rubrics break performance into dimensions—such as clarity, evidence use, or ethical compliance—and assign criteria for each. Studies show that rubrics not only improve scoring reliability but also help students assess their own work and increase transparency in grading (Jonsson and Svingby, 2007; Panadero and Jonsson, 2013). Draft rubrics can be prepared quickly by systems that align proposed rows with stated goals, leaving human experts to refine them for local context. During reviews, outputs can be pre-annotated against rubric categories, flagging potential weaknesses and prompting reviewers with targeted questions. This accelerates evaluation without replacing expert judgment, while also generating logs that can inform rubric adjustments in future cycles. In professional contexts, rubrics can be extended beyond analytic quality to include compliance with legal standards, ethical norms, or reputational considerations. When used consistently, rubrics transform critique into a process that is not only reliable and transferable but also instructional, teaching evaluators and learners alike what quality looks like in practice.

Shifting from evaluation to synthesis, digital systems can support the demanding process of gathering, appraising, and integrating evidence. Systematic frameworks such as PRISMA, ROBIS, and GRADE provide established methods for structuring reviews and rating confidence in findings (Page et al., 2021; Whiting et al., 2016; Guyatt et al., 2008). A practical procedure is to begin with an evidence table that records study design, sample size, effect estimates, and risk-of-bias judgments, then build a narrative synthesis constrained to claims warranted by the data. Again, the *Cochrane Handbook* offers guidance on pre-specifying outcomes, documenting analytic choices, and justifying interpretations—steps that reduce common analytic errors and strengthen transparency (Higgins et al., 2019). Organizations can adapt these procedures by adding dimensions such as cost, feasibility, and time to implementation, linking evidence reviews directly to strategic decision-making. Preregistration of analytic plans remains important for reducing hindsight bias, and automated drafting can assist with preparing templates for human validation (Nosek et al., 2018). Where evidence is sparse or contradictory, reports should explicitly present uncertainty and qualify conclusions rather than overstate findings. This approach ensures that reflective synthesis balances ambition with caution and maintains credibility.

Addressing engagement, immersive reviews and studio-style critique practices extend the reach of slow learning into collaborative deliberation. Research in virtual reality (VR) and immersive environments shows that engagement and self-efficacy rise when experiences are well-aligned with learning goals and cognitive load is managed carefully (Radianti et al., 2020; Makransky and Petersen, 2021).

Applied to reflection, walkthroughs of complex systems—whether organizational processes, product prototypes, or policy scenarios—can be staged while participants annotate assumptions and comment on risks. Structured summaries produced afterward capture key tensions, alternatives, and unresolved questions. This mirrors the iterative critique central to studio pedagogy, but extends it into domains like business planning, engineering, or public policy. Teams can revisit annotated sessions to reconsider earlier decisions when new evidence emerges, creating a record of evolving reasoning. In these settings, digital systems play a supportive role: prompting questions linked to criteria, highlighting gaps, and ensuring evidence is referenced. Used strategically, immersive methods guard against premature closure by keeping deliberation open, visible, and reviewable.

Reproducibility provides the final anchor for slow learning, grounding reflective processes in rigor. Evidence synthesis research emphasizes pre-specified protocols, documentation of analytic deviations, and clear justification for interpretive decisions as essential practices (Higgins et al., 2019; Page et al., 2021). Replication concerns across the sciences demonstrate why these practices are critical for ensuring validity and public trust (Ioannidis, 2005). Multi-rater review procedures, in which multiple evaluators assess the same evidence independently, provide further protection against individual bias and increase reliability. Forecasting studies add a complementary lesson: calibration sessions—where predicted outcomes are compared against actual results—improve long-term accuracy and adaptive expertise (Mellers et al., 2015). Digital platforms can streamline these steps by collating predictions, outcomes, deviations, and reviewer notes into structured logs for later analysis. Crucially, however, interpretive authority must remain with human reviewers, ensuring that accountability and contextual judgment are preserved. The result is a reflective practice that is not only methodologically rigorous but also operationally sustainable across both academic and professional domains.

The discussion of deep analysis and reflective scaffolding makes one point very clear: slowing down is not about doing less, but about doing thinking better. Reflection is not something that naturally happens when we pause; it requires structures that make reasoning visible, testable, and accountable. Tools like templates, checklists, argument maps, rubrics, and evidence tables help learners and professionals alike surface assumptions, weigh evidence, and link claims to proofs. Systems such as PRISMA, ROBIS, and GRADE give concrete methods for tying conclusions to transparent levels of confidence, while frameworks like the Toulmin model organize arguments into their logical components. These practices create habits of "productive reflection" where evidence and reasoning move together, rather than relying on intuition or surface fluency.

The significance of these practices lies in their ability to turn abstract deliberation into repeatable routines. Self-explanation and retrieval practice make knowledge stick by requiring people to justify connections and recall facts without cues, while adversarial testing and devil's advocate roles strengthen claims by probing for hidden weaknesses. Rubrics and structured feedback turn evaluation into instruction, clarifying what counts as quality across domains. Immersive reviews and studio critiques extend this into collaborative spaces, making assumptions and alternatives explicit in ways that groups can revisit later. In professional and policy contexts, these same practices reduce bias, prevent premature closure, and anchor decision-making in auditable evidence.

Future work should focus on scaling these practices without losing nuance. Research must explore how argument mapping, adversarial testing, and evidence synthesis frameworks can be adapted across sectors with different levels of regulation and risk. There is also a need to study how digital scaffolds can maintain rigor without adding cognitive overload or reducing human agency. Finally, questions of equity and trust remain central: reflective systems must ensure that privacy is protected, outcomes are monitored across subgroups, and recourse remains simple when errors occur. The overarching lesson is straightforward but profound: slow learning is not a bottleneck, but a foundation, and with the right scaffolds it can transform both classrooms and workplaces into environments where reasoning is visible, contestable, and durable.

4.2 EMULATING REFLECTIVE PROCESSES ("DREAMING," STAGED REASONING, TOOL-USE)

Extending the slow-learning emphasis from the prior section, this discussion examines how digital systems can emulate reflection without replacing human judgment. Reflective cognition thrives when inference is slowed, assumptions are surfaced, and evaluation criteria are made explicit (Evans, 2008; Stanovich and West, 2000). Assistive tools can help by generating alternatives, counterexamples, and rationales that complement human deliberation. The aim is disciplined reflection rather than verbosity: outputs tied to specific purposes and grounded in standards of evidence (Kahneman, 2011). When structured properly, staged outputs separate what is truly known from what is merely plausible, allowing decision makers to focus their attention on boundaries and consequences rather than starting from a blank page. Over time, these practices encourage habits of inquiry and explanation that can be repeated and institutionalized. Reflection thus becomes less a matter of individual disposition and more a shared routine, reinforced by artifacts and templates.

One particularly valuable practice is "simulated dreaming", modeled on incubation effects in human cognition. In psychology, incubation describes the way stepping away from a problem or engaging in low-focus activity can lead to unexpected insights (Sio and Ormerod, 2009; Smallwood and Schooler, 2015). Simulated dreaming routines replicate this by generating low-constraint drafts or associations—analogies, distant cues, or loosely connected ideas—that are then set aside to "cool" before being re-examined. Research on sleep and creativity has shown that reorganizing information during rest, especially during rapid eye movement sleep, often yields nonobvious solutions (Cai et al., 2009). In practice, this can be operationalized as a two-phase cadence: first, a divergent pass produces wide-ranging drafts, then later passes apply tighter filters to retain only grounded and relevant ideas. This mirrors human mind-wandering but keeps outputs accountable to goals. The process guards against tunnel vision while preventing premature closure.

Staged reasoning makes thought processes transparent and improvable. Writing and design research shows that planning, drafting, and revising are distinct phases that benefit from explicit prompts and checkpoints (Flower and Hayes, 1981). Protocol analysis further demonstrates that structured verbalization exposes decision points and hidden gaps that would otherwise remain implicit (Ericsson and Simon, 1993). In applied problem solving, metareasoning frameworks recommend alternating between solving a task and reflecting on strategy, externalizing both steps into documented stages (Cox and Raja, 2011). Practical routines often follow a sequence: request a plan, generate a weak draft, critique it, and then refine the rationale. Reviewers can then compare each stage against rubrics for validity, clarity, and completeness. This converts reflection from a private act into a collective practice where reasoning is inspectable, auditable, and open to revision.

External representations extend reflective practice by serving as visible thinking aids that reduce cognitive load and make reasoning easier to inspect. Research on distributed cognition shows that cognitive processes are not confined to individual minds but are shared across people, tools, and environments; a pilot navigating with charts and instruments, for example, is reasoning jointly with artifacts as much as with memory alone (Hutchins, 1995). The extended-mind thesis builds on this idea by arguing that reliable external supports—such as notebooks, diagrams, or digital dashboards—effectively become part of our cognitive system, functioning as "mental prosthetics" that expand the boundaries of thought (Clark and Chalmers, 1998). Within this framework, epistemic actions are deliberate moves we make in the world to reduce mental effort and reveal hidden structure—such as sorting research articles into piles, rearranging sticky notes on a wall, or plotting data points to expose trends (Kirsh and Maglio, 1994). In organizational practice, these principles translate into the use of canvases, dashboards, or evidence maps that record claims, sources, assumptions, and risks in shared visual formats. By externalizing reasoning in this way, groups create representations that not only support immediate evaluation but also accumulate into durable knowledge bases over time. This reduces the burden on individual memory, stabilizes collective judgment, and frees mental resources for higher-order analysis and critique (Risko and Gilbert, 2016).

Evidence-heavy work requires scaffolds that enforce rigor rather than inflate citation volume. Reporting standards like PRISMA, appraisal tools such as ROBIS, and evidence-rating frameworks like GRADE provide templates for structuring review processes and appraising certainty (Page et al., 2021; Whiting et al., 2016; Guyatt et al., 2008). Procedure guides such as the *Cochrane Handbook* emphasize pre-specified outcomes, documentation of analytic deviations, and clear rationales for interpretive choices (Higgins et al., 2019). Preregistration of analytic plans adds further protection against hindsight bias (Nosek et al., 2018). Metascience highlights the fragility of published findings, underscoring why explicit weighting of evidence and transparent uncertainty statements should be required, not optional (Ioannidis, 2005). Organizations can adapt these principles by extending evidence tables with dimensions such as cost, risk, and feasibility.

Reviewers then judge whether a synthesized case meets sufficiency thresholds before action. In this way, deliberation privileges evidential quality over volume.

As critique deepens, adversarial checks function as devil's-advocate passes that probe for weaknesses. In computer security, adversarial testing reveals brittle spots in otherwise confident systems (Biggio and Roli, 2018; Yuan et al., 2019). In deliberative settings, analogous routines can search for exceptions, contradictions, and harms. Debiasing research shows that "consider-the-opposite" prompts reduce confirmation bias, while group decision studies highlight the importance of structured dissent (Larrick, 2004; Janis, 1972). A practical cadence runs one pass to build the best case, then another to identify harms and contradictions. Findings are reconciled by narrowing claims, adding qualifiers, or requesting more data. In high-stakes contexts, these adversarial passes may also trigger pause points or rollback criteria. Such rituals normalize skepticism while maintaining momentum toward well-grounded decisions.

For causal claims, reflective emulation depends on articulating assumptions and applying counterfactual discipline. Causal inference frameworks treat the task as identifying treatment–outcome relationships while acknowledging both testable and untestable assumptions (Morgan and Winship, 2015; Pearl, 2009). Practical guides recommend listing identifying assumptions, mapping potential confounders, and stress-testing results with sensitivity analyses (Hernán and Robins, 2020). Counterfactual thinking research shows that "what-if" prompts help clarify alternative pathways and outcomes (Roese, 1997). Draft causal diagrams, candidate adjustment sets, and robustness checks can be proposed in structured form, but analysts must evaluate whether they align with theory and data before sign-off. Where evidence is weak, outputs should explicitly present uncertainties and alternatives rather than overstate conclusions. This posture preserves progress while avoiding the dangers of overclaiming.

Ethical reflection also benefits from codification into operational checks. Reviews of global guidance converge on principles of beneficence, justice, and accountability, which can be translated into criteria for sign-off (Floridi and Cowls, 2019; Jobin et al., 2019). Legal scholarship on disparate impact stresses the importance of interrogating harms across protected groups and documenting justification for contested choices (Barocas and Selbst, 2016). In practice, reviewers apply short checklists that ask: Who is affected? What is the evidence of benefit? What mitigation plans are in place? Digital tools can surface candidate risks and precedents, but responsibility for ethical adjudication remains human. Where uncertainty persists, escalation to oversight committees balances prudence with timely decision-making. Embedding these steps ensures that ethical considerations are not afterthoughts but integral to reflection.

In both education and organizational practice, reflection becomes durable when embedded in iterative cycles of experience, critique, and revision. Experiential learning frameworks emphasize the sequence of concrete experience, reflective observation, conceptualization, and experimentation (Kolb, 1984). Professional practice studies highlight reflection-in-action (adjusting while doing) and reflection-on-action (reviewing afterward) as essential to expertise (Schön, 1983). Formative assessment research shows that clear criteria, actionable feedback, and opportunities for revision strengthen both performance and self-regulation (Black and Wiliam, 1998; Nicol and Macfarlane-Dick, 2006). Expertise research adds that targeted, feedback-rich practice accelerates skill acquisition (Ericsson et al., 1993). Applied in studios or professional teams, these cycles normalize the separation of generation from evaluation. Instructors and managers become facilitators of critique and coaching rather than sole arbiters of correctness. The culture that emerges treats reflection as a shared craft rather than a private habit.

Bringing these elements together, reflective emulation can be made routine and measurable. A typical cadence might begin with a focused question and inclusion criteria, proceed through a low-constraint "dreaming" pass, then narrow with staged reasoning and structured synthesis (Page et al., 2021; Whiting et al., 2016). An adversarial pass probes weaknesses, followed by causal and ethical checks before final review (Hernán and Robins, 2020; Jobin et al., 2019). Decision makers record rationales, alternatives considered, and follow-up plans. Metrics such as time-to-first-critique, revision distance, calibration accuracy, and post-implementation error rates translate reflection into organizational learning (Mellers et al., 2015). Over time, artifacts like maps, tables, and rubrics accumulate into reusable templates that reduce friction while raising standards. Governance becomes routine rather than exceptional, with final judgment anchored in human responsibility. The effect is to transform slow thinking from a perceived bottleneck into a reproducible institutional asset (Argyris and Schön, 1978).

This section shows that reflection does not have to be left to chance or personality; it can be systematically emulated, scaffolded, and reinforced through design. Practices like simulated dreaming, staged reasoning, external representations, and adversarial testing demonstrate how digital systems can complement human judgment without replacing it. The unifying goal is to slow cognition in ways that surface assumptions, make evidence visible, and structure critique—so that decisions are grounded, auditable, and transferable across contexts. When these methods are institutionalized, reflection shifts from being a private act to a shared routine supported by artifacts like checklists, rubrics, maps, and logs.

The significance of simulated dreaming lies in its ability to widen the search space while avoiding tunnel vision. By encouraging low-constraint drafts that are later refined under tighter scrutiny, organizations can harness the same incubation benefits humans experience in mind-wandering or rest. Staged reasoning adds transparency by externalizing planning, weak drafts, critiques, and refinements into discrete, inspectable phases. External representations—dashboards, canvases, or morphological boxes—extend human cognition by lowering memory load and stabilizing group judgment. These epistemic actions make thinking collective, durable, and easier to evaluate.

Critical rigor is further strengthened through adversarial passes and causal reasoning. Devil's advocate routines and "consider the opposite" prompts help reveal hidden risks, biases, or overconfidence, while causal inference frameworks and counterfactual thinking ensure claims are tied to explicit assumptions and alternative explanations. Ethical reflection, meanwhile, is operationalized through short, structured checklists that tie principles like fairness, beneficence, and accountability to concrete decisions and escalation paths. The outcome is that skepticism becomes constructive and normalized, protecting against premature closure while preserving momentum.

Thus, reflection only endures when embedded in cycles of experience, critique, and revision. Whether in classrooms, studios, or professional teams, iterative routines transform critique into a craft and reduce the fragility of decision-making under pressure. Metrics such as revision distance, calibration accuracy, or error rates convert reflection from an intangible value into an observable practice. Future research must investigate how to balance structured scaffolds with cognitive load, how to adapt reflective emulation across domains with different risk levels, and how to measure long-term benefits for equity and trust. The overall takeaway is simple: when emulated with rigor and humility, reflection becomes not a bottleneck but an asset—anchoring institutions in practices that are slower, clearer, and ultimately wiser.

4.3 EVALUATIVE CRITERIA FOR REFLECTIVE SYSTEMS IN CURRICULAR AND RESEARCH CONTEXTS

Building on the emulation mechanics described above, this section specifies the criteria that determine when reflective support can be considered educationally and scientifically sound. Evaluation cannot be reduced to a single dimension; it must instead consider validity, reliability, reproducibility, usability, equity, and decision impact (Shadish et al., 2002). The objective is not perfection across all categories, which is rarely achievable, but sufficiency relative to the risks and contexts of use. In curricular contexts, criteria should be tied directly to intended competencies, learning outcomes, and the assessment logic that governs whether students are achieving them (Table 4.1). In research contexts, evaluation must anchor claims to the soundness of methods, the quality of evidence, and the transparency of reasoning. Establishing a common language for these criteria reduces confusion in adoption debates, particularly when educators, researchers, and administrators approach the same tools from different perspectives. A shared vocabulary also enables fair comparisons across different implementations, avoiding the trap of "black box" claims about effectiveness. The result is a portfolio view of quality—a composite of multiple dimensions—rather than reliance on a single score or ranking.

Validity sits at the core of evaluation because it asks whether reflective support produces inferences that genuinely match the construct of interest. For example, does a system meant to encourage critical thinking actually elicit reasoned argument and evaluation of evidence, or does it reward superficial fluency and word count? Messick (1989) framed validity as a unified concept that integrates content, substantive, structural, and consequential facets into a single argument about the soundness of interpretations. Construct validity in this sense requires showing that the tasks, rubrics, and data capture methods genuinely represent the reasoning abilities being targeted. Kane's (2013) argument-based validation offers a practical stepwise approach: start with the quality of scoring, extend to the extrapolation of results, and finally evaluate whether decision uses are justified. In curricula, this means ensuring that reflective prompts and rubrics are aligned with standards and that the reasoning elicited is interpretable in terms of intended competencies. In research, it requires specification of constructs, explicit rival explanations, and transparent documentation of how evidence supports one interpretation over another. Without this grounding, reflection may appear robust but lack interpretive strength.

Table 4.1 Rubrics and Metrics for Reflective Work

Dimension	*Measures*	*Artifacts*	*Review Cadence*
Validity	Accuracy against trusted sources; coherence of argument	Annotated evidence briefs; source comparison logs	Per major deliverable; before decision release
Reliability	Consistency of outputs across runs or reviewers	Stability test reports; inter-rater agreement notes	Quarterly calibration sessions; system updates
Reproducibility	Ability to replicate findings with same data & method	Code notebooks; data provenance records	Every evaluation cycle; audit checkpoints
Equity	Fairness across subgroups; bias detection results	Bias audit logs; subgroup performance tables	At model retrain; annual fairness review
Usability	Clarity of explanations; accessibility of outputs	User feedback forms; design review notes	User studies bi-annually; design iteration cycles
Decision Impact	Downstream effects; cost/benefit analysis; risk outcomes	Impact assessment reports; risk registers	Before deployment; post-decision retrospectives

Turning to reliability, reflective outputs and ratings must be stable when subjected to reasonable variation. In practice, this means that two different evaluators, or the same evaluator at two different times, should arrive at similar judgments if they are using the same criteria. Inter-rater agreement statistics such as Krippendorff's alpha or Cohen's kappa provide ways of quantifying this consistency (Krippendorff, 2011). Procedural reliability matters just as much: prompts, timing, and scoring conditions should be consistent so that results reflect reasoning quality rather than environmental quirks. In classrooms, reliability can be strengthened through rater training and exemplar sets that show what good, fair, and poor performance looks like. In research, blinding reviewers to study hypotheses or having multiple coders independently analyze the same material reduces bias and strengthens confidence in results. Reliability does not guarantee that judgments are "true," but it does ensure that decisions are less noisy and less arbitrary. Reporting reliability alongside thresholds and confidence intervals allows educators and researchers to judge whether observed variation is tolerable given the stakes. The payoff is fewer disputes, less rework, and more stable evidence for learning and decision-making.

Beyond reliability lies the challenge of reproducibility and replicability, which make reflective work verifiable by others. In computational science, reproducibility means providing executable code, versioned datasets, and literate workflows so that results can be recreated exactly (Peng, 2011). More broadly, science distinguishes between three related terms: methods reproducibility (can the procedure be repeated?), results reproducibility (do the same analyses yield the same numbers?), and inferential replicability (do independent studies reach the same conclusions?) (Goodman et al., 2016). Open practices such as preregistration of hypotheses and sharing of research materials limit the flexibility researchers have after seeing results, reducing bias (Nosek et al., 2018). Data stewardship guided by the FAIR principles—that data should be Findable, Accessible, Interoperable, and Reusable—ensures that evidence is not only preserved but also usable by others across contexts (Wilkinson et al., 2016). In education, the same spirit applies: shareable task banks and rubrics allow instructors at different institutions to compare results more fairly. In research, registered reports and protocol archives stabilize inferences by tying claims to pre-specified methods. Together, these infrastructures turn reflection from an informal habit into an auditable practice, one that can be tested, verified, and built upon.

Turning to equity and ethics, reflective support must be designed so that it does not amplify harm or encode bias. In law and ethics, concepts such as disparate impact (policies that unintentionally disadvantage particular groups), proportionality (ensuring interventions are balanced against risks and benefits), and accountability (assigning responsibility for decisions) serve as anchors for responsible practice (Barocas and Selbst, 2016; Floridi and Cowls, 2019). Surveys of fairness in learning systems show that bias can emerge at many levels—within data collection, in the models built on that data, and in the evaluation criteria applied to outputs (Mehrabi et al., 2021). In education, accommodations for students with disabilities and adherence to accessibility standards guard against exclusion. In research, subgroup analyses (checking how results vary for different populations) and fairness audits (systematic reviews of potential inequities) can identify asymmetric errors before they cause harm. Documentation should explicitly record the trade-offs between accuracy, equity, and cost so that these are transparent rather than hidden. Governance processes should assign ownership for addressing fairness issues and clear procedures for escalation. Together, these measures protect stakeholders while ensuring reflective practices still deliver learning and performance gains.

Equity also connects directly to evidence quality. Claims must be weighted not only by their appeal but by the strength of the evidence behind them. Frameworks such as PRISMA (Preferred Reporting Items for Systematic Reviews and Meta-Analyses), ROBIS (Risk of Bias in Systematic Reviews), and GRADE (Grading of Recommendations, Assessment, Development, and Evaluation) provide scaffolds for reviewing evidence systematically and rating its certainty (Page et al., 2021; Whiting et al., 2016; Guyatt et al., 2008). For example, PRISMA ensures search and inclusion criteria are transparent; ROBIS helps identify bias at the review level; and GRADE translates certainty of evidence into actionable recommendations.

While these frameworks were developed for health and social sciences, their structure is useful across disciplines: local curriculum evaluations or pilot studies also benefit when evidence is appraised against standardized criteria. Weight-of-evidence approaches ensure that recommendations are calibrated to both certainty and effect size. This prevents over-claiming and ensures that action aligns with the strength of available data.

Turning to curricular alignment, reflective systems must make the logic of assessment explicit and teachable. Constructive alignment, a principle in instructional design, emphasizes that learning activities, assessments, and outcomes should fit together into a coherent whole (Biggs, 1996; Biggs and Tang, 2011). Formative assessment principles stress that feedback must be timely, specific, and actionable (Black and Wiliam, 1998; Nicol and Macfarlane-Dick, 2006). Rubrics, which operationalize performance criteria into measurable categories, support student self-assessment and make expectations transparent (Panadero and Jonsson, 2013). At the program level, curriculum maps show where competencies are introduced, developed, and ultimately mastered, allowing evidence to accumulate across courses toward credentialing decisions. Such coherence makes adoption defensible and ensures reflective systems do not operate as "bolt-on" tools but as part of the pedagogy itself.

Addressing usability and workload, reflective systems must be practical and sustainable. Human–computer interaction research stresses iterative evaluation methods such as think-aloud protocols (where users verbalize their thought processes), error logs, and task-time analyses to ensure systems are workable (Nielsen, 1994). The System Usability Scale (SUS) is a short, standardized survey that provides reliable benchmarking of usability across interventions (Brooke, 1996). Cognitive load theory warns that systems with too many steps, unclear instructions, or unnecessary complexity overwhelm learners and degrade judgment (Paas and van Merriënboer, 1994). In classrooms, this means reflective prompts must fit within realistic rhythms of teaching and assessment. In research, documentation must not consume so much time that analytic work suffers. Usability evaluations should drive adjustments that simplify workflows, reduce jargon, and cut visual clutter. These refinements ensure reflection becomes an embedded habit rather than an aspirational but impractical goal.

Considering decision quality, reflective systems must measurably improve choices, especially under uncertainty. Research on judgment and decision-making emphasizes criteria such as calibration (how well confidence matches reality), discrimination (the ability to separate likely from unlikely outcomes), and timeliness (acting before opportunities pass) (Hastie and Dawes, 2010). Forecasting studies show that training, structured feedback, and aggregation of multiple judgments improve probabilistic accuracy over time (Mellers et al., 2015). In education, scenario-based assessments can test whether students transfer reflection into action—for example, applying ethical reasoning to a new case. In research, pre-specified thresholds tie interpretations to clear decisions (e.g., proceeding with a trial only if effect sizes surpass a set level). Documentation should capture before-and-after comparisons on key metrics, while periodic reviews should revisit thresholds as stakes or contexts evolve. This ensures that reflective practice produces tangible improvements in decision-making quality.

When scaling reflective systems, evaluation must also consider context, fidelity, and reach. Program-evaluation frameworks such as CIPP (*Context, Input, Process, Product*) and RE-AIM (*Reach, Effectiveness, Adoption, Implementation, Maintenance*) provide structured ways to assess both design and impact (Stufflebeam, 2003; Glasgow et al., 1999). Fidelity checks verify that intended cadences and criteria are actually followed, while adaptation logs record pragmatic changes across sites. In education, professional development supports consistency across instructors, while in research, protocol deviations are logged and explained. Cost-effectiveness analyses document trade-offs between resources spent and outcomes gained. Stakeholders—whether faculty committees, ethics boards, or organizational leaders—then review results and decide whether to continue, adapt, or sunset an initiative. These cycles ensure reflective systems evolve responsibly rather than remaining frozen at the pilot stage.

Bringing the criteria together, portfolio dashboards can integrate indicators across validity, reliability, reproducibility, equity, usability, and decision impact. Visual summaries allow faculties or research boards to weigh trade-offs transparently, while weighting schemes can be tuned to reflect institutional mission, regulatory requirements, or risk appetite. Regular reviews ensure indicators remain relevant as contexts shift. Crucially, numbers are complemented by narrative justifications that preserve context and nuance. Over time, institutions develop norms for acceptable evidence and process quality, allowing adoption decisions to be made more quickly and confidently. The outcome is reflective practice that is not only cumulative and auditable but also accountable to the values and standards of the institution.

This section demonstrates that evaluating reflective systems—whether in classrooms or research environments—requires a portfolio of criteria rather than reliance on a single metric. The core message is that validity, reliability, reproducibility, usability, equity, and decision impact all matter, though the balance among them depends on the context and risks involved. For education, these criteria tie directly to competencies, outcomes, and assessment logic. For research, they ensure that claims rest on sound evidence, transparent reasoning, and reproducible methods. Together, they provide a shared vocabulary that allows stakeholders with different priorities—teachers, researchers, administrators—to evaluate reflective tools with common reference points rather than talking past one another.

Validity emerged as the anchor, asking whether systems truly elicit the reasoning they claim to measure rather than rewarding superficial fluency. Reliability ensures judgments remain consistent across raters and contexts, reducing noise and disputes. Reproducibility, supported by open data and the FAIR principles, makes results verifiable and comparable across sites. Equity foregrounds subgroup performance and fairness audits, ensuring reflective practices do not unintentionally privilege some learners or populations over others. Usability reminds us that systems must be learnable and practical within real-world constraints, or else reflection becomes burdensome rather than sustainable.

Decision impact ties reflection to actual improvements in judgment quality, calibration, and transfer into practice, making it clear that reflection must produce better choices, not just longer deliberations.

The broader significance lies in the shift from evaluating reflection as a vague ideal to evaluating it as an operational system. Using established frameworks like PRISMA, ROBIS, and GRADE to appraise evidence quality; CIPP and RE-AIM to assess implementation; and instruments such as rubrics, usability surveys, and calibration tests ensures that reflection is measurable and auditable. This transforms reflective practice from an aspirational virtue into something cumulative, comparable, and improvable. The portfolio view also enables trade-off decisions—for example, prioritizing validity and equity in high-stakes education while prioritizing reproducibility and decision impact in research.

Future work should build out cross-institutional dashboards that combine quantitative indicators with qualitative narratives, allowing faculties, ethics boards, and regulators to review reflective systems in a transparent and balanced way. Longitudinal studies are also needed to test how criteria like calibration accuracy or subgroup fairness evolve as systems mature. Ultimately, reflective practice gains legitimacy when it is not only deliberate but also governed by visible standards and evidence. In this framing, slow thinking becomes not a bottleneck but an accountable institutional asset.

4.4 CASE STUDIES: DEEP LEARNING VIA IMMERSIVE EXEMPLARS

Extending prior principles into concrete practice, this section presents immersive exemplars that cultivate durable judgment. Immersion here is not about spectacle or novelty; rather, it is a tool to surface constraints, trade-offs, and criteria under realistic conditions (Makransky and Petersen, 2021). When paired with structured critique, immersive environments foster deeper evaluation and more transferable skills. Meta-analyses and reviews consistently report that well-designed immersive experiences boost engagement and, when aligned with learning objectives, lead to measurable improvements in performance (Merchant et al., 2014; Radianti et al., 2020). The key is not the technology itself but the alignment between task demands and immersive affordances. Studio-style critique then converts these experiences into actionable learning through reflection and revision. Rubrics make evaluative criteria visible and teachable, helping learners internalize standards of quality. Across domains—from medicine and policy to journalism and industry—the same pattern holds, with adaptations tailored to local contexts.

In undergraduate anatomy, a medical school introduced headset-based dissection labs combined with weekly critique seminars. Students explored interactive, labeled 3D models of organs and structures, then wrote short method memos explaining what they observed and how they understood anatomical variants. Faculty used detailed rubrics to score these memos on accuracy, reasoning, and communication. Studies of immersive visualization confirm that such approaches improve spatial understanding and motivation when cognitive load is carefully managed (Moro et al., 2017; Makransky and Petersen, 2021). Compared with earlier cohorts, students performed better on spatial-rotation exam questions, a key test of anatomical reasoning. Reflection sessions highlighted recurring misidentifications, which faculty then used to refine both the models and the rubrics. This case demonstrates how immersion provides a scaffold for learning, while critique and revision transform raw engagement into durable understanding.

Building on these successes, surgical residency programs extended simulation into high-stakes training for laparoscopic procedures. Residents practiced on standardized modules in virtual environments, logging errors and reviewing their performance through checklists guided by faculty debriefs. Randomized trials confirm that such simulation-based practice improves operating-room performance and shortens learning curves compared to traditional observation methods (Seymour et al., 2002; Grantcharov et al., 2004). Importantly, progression was gated: residents had to meet performance thresholds before moving on to live patient procedures. Post-implementation audits showed reductions in intraoperative errors and faster completion times for common surgeries. Residents also reported stronger mental models of anatomy, instruments, and workflow. Faculty time was freed from repetitive demonstration and redirected toward individualized coaching. The result was a system that raised both patient safety and instructional efficiency by combining immersive practice with structured gating mechanisms.

Immersive critique has also been transformative in engineering education. An upper-division design studio blended collaborative walkthroughs with structured argument mapping. Students presented prototypes in an instrumented classroom while peers mapped claims, evidence, and risks on shared visual canvases. Instructors facilitated counterargument sessions and guided students through evidence checks using topic-specific rubrics. Iterative design cycles required teams to test revisions against prior critiques, reinforcing longitudinal learning. Over time, argument maps revealed improved clarity of warrants and tighter links to empirical data. Employers later reported that graduates from the program demonstrated stronger skills in design review and critical evaluation. This case illustrates how immersive collaboration and visual mapping co-develop technical competence and reflective judgment.

Policy education presents another context where immersion supports reflective practice. In a public-affairs program, a policy-lab course used crisis simulations structured around staged reasoning and ethical review. Students received evolving policy briefs, developed options under time pressure, and engaged in adversarial questioning sessions facilitated by faculty. Each group produced decision memos documenting claims, evidence quality, and feasibility risks, which were graded against rubrics emphasizing fairness, practicality, and ethical alignment. Post-mortem reviews compared predicted outcomes with simulated results, allowing students to calibrate their judgment under uncertainty. Surveys indicated that participants gained confidence in navigating ambiguous decision environments. Literature on formative assessment confirms that such cycles strengthen self-regulation and evaluative judgment (Black and Wiliam, 1998; Nicol and Macfarlane-Dick, 2006). This design showed how immersive policy simulations can prepare students for the complexity of real-world decision-making.

The principles of immersion and critique extend beyond higher education into K–12 environments. In one district, environmental science students conducted augmented-reality field studies, exploring local habitats and recording ecological observations. Their findings were structured into claims-and-evidence prompts, which they then debated in classroom "argumentation circles." Teachers facilitated these critiques using rubrics that emphasized warrant strength, acknowledgment of uncertainty, and multiple stakeholder perspectives. Research shows that carefully designed AR applications can enhance motivation and concept learning (Bacca et al., 2014; Dunleavy and Dede, 2014). Evaluations of the program showed that students transferred ecological reasoning from the field to classroom assessments more effectively. Teachers also noted improved norms of participation and collaborative reasoning. This case illustrates how immersive, place-based experiences coupled with critique can support both scientific literacy and civic-minded engagement.

Immersive critique also supports professional standards in journalism. A national newsroom developed interactive "data-room walkthroughs" for investigative projects, where reporters collaboratively explored large datasets. Leads, caveats, and verification plans were documented in real time. Editors then ran red-team sessions to challenge emerging narratives, while style desks applied rubrics focused on clarity, attribution, and proportionality. Scholarship on data literacy underscores the importance of triangulation and iterative questioning, particularly under deadline pressure (Bhargava et al., 2015). This process shortened publication cycles while lowering correction rates. Reporters reported stronger shared norms for evidential standards and due diligence. The newsroom case shows how immersion and critique can accelerate investigative rigor without compromising integrity.

Industry settings reveal similar gains. A manufacturing plant implemented immersive digital walkthroughs of assembly lines for safety and quality assurance. Cross-functional teams rehearsed responses to simulated incidents and scored performance against structured checklists. Post-exercise evaluations identified procedures most prone to errors, leading to targeted interventions. Over several quarters, near-miss incidents declined, compliance audit scores improved, and costs dropped due to reduced downtime. Industrial training literature affirms that simulation is especially effective for rare, hazardous, or high-stakes scenarios (Carvalho et al., 2021). Supervisors credited improvements to repeated simulation practice and the explicit use of evidence-based standards. The case demonstrates how immersive practice can yield measurable operational and financial benefits.

In nursing education, simulation and structured debriefing underpin clinical judgment. Students rotated through patient-care roles in scenario-based exercises and documented SBAR (Situation, Background, Assessment, Recommendation) handoffs for faculty review. Debriefs emphasized evidence quality, ethical considerations, and patient safety, supported by competency checklists that tracked progress across terms. Systematic reviews confirm that high-fidelity simulation improves clinical decision-making when paired with guided reflection (Cant and Cooper, 2017). Outcomes included modest gains in licensing-exam pass rates and significant improvements in the quality of clinical handoffs. Students reported that simulations created realistic stressors that prepared them for real-world practice. This design linked immersive experience to measurable improvements in professional readiness and identity formation.

Creative disciplines also benefit from immersive critique. In an architecture studio, students used virtual site visits and stakeholder walkthroughs to rehearse complex design trade-offs. Presence research shows that situated perspective-taking sharpens recognition of environmental and social constraints (Makransky and Petersen, 2021; Radianti et al., 2020). Students were required to defend design decisions against environmental, historical, and user-centered criteria. Argument maps and evidence tables anchored these claims to codes, precedents, and empirical data. Iterative cycles tested design features such as light, noise, and flow under different scenarios. External jurors consistently rated final presentations higher on clarity and constraint recognition. Graduates reported smoother transitions into professional roles where multi-criteria reasoning was essential. This case highlights how immersive perspective-taking fosters disciplined reasoning in design education.

The immersive exemplars discussed in this section demonstrate a clear throughline: technology by itself does not guarantee deeper learning, but when immersive experiences are paired with critique, structured reflection, and revision, they cultivate durable judgment and transferable skills. Across medicine, engineering, policy, journalism, manufacturing, and creative disciplines, immersion functions as a scaffold that exposes learners and practitioners to realistic constraints and trade-offs, while critique and rubrics transform engagement into measurable learning.

The significance of these cases lies in the consistent pattern: immersion accelerates experience, structured critique transforms that experience into insight, and revision secures long-term growth. The lesson is not domain-specific but systemic: immersive technologies yield durable value only when embedded in reflective ecosystems that make reasoning visible, hold learners accountable to standards, and link practice to performance. Looking forward, future research should compare immersive-critique cycles across fields to identify which scaffolds—argument mapping, adversarial questioning, rubric alignment—produce the strongest gains in transfer and professional readiness. Longitudinal studies could also track how immersive exemplars influence career trajectories, safety outcomes, and civic decision-making. By grounding immersive practice in evidence and reflection, institutions can move beyond novelty toward sustainable, trustworthy learning systems.

This chapter has emphasized the necessity of cultivating deliberation as a counterbalance to the acceleration made possible by generative and assistive technologies. While rapid tools can shorten cycle times and expand the range of options, durable judgment requires processes that deliberately slow thinking, surface assumptions, and weigh competing evidence. Structured methods such as staged reasoning, adversarial prompts, and systematic evidence synthesis prevent reflection from collapsing into verbosity or superficial elaboration. Instead, reflection becomes a disciplined and repeatable practice, one that anchors reliability in classrooms, laboratories, professional studios, and organizational decision rooms alike. The significance of this approach lies in its dual impact:

in education, slow learning nurtures metacognitive skills, critical thinking, and evaluative judgment; in research and enterprise, reflective scaffolds—argument maps, causal diagrams, and structured critiques—improve validity, reduce error, and guard against premature closure. Together, these strategies respond to widespread concerns about bias, reproducibility, and trust by embedding reflection into the structure of inquiry itself.

The cases presented across medicine, design, policy, journalism, and industry highlight the value of immersive exemplars and structured critique in cultivating habits of reflection. These practices show that slow learning does not mean passive delay; it means designing deliberate cadences where exploration and critique reinforce each other. When institutions routinize practices such as adversarial review, evidence weighting, and rubric-based evaluation, they transform reflection from an optional add-on into a cultural norm. Pedagogically, this results in learners who are trained not simply to produce answers but to interrogate reasoning, weigh alternatives, and recognize uncertainty. Organizationally, it produces decision environments where transparency and accountability are built in rather than retrofitted. In both settings, reflection becomes an institutional asset that improves quality and resilience.

Looking ahead, future research should examine how reflective scaffolds can be optimized for different domains and levels of expertise. Comparative studies could clarify which forms of staged reasoning or argument mapping are most effective for novice learners versus seasoned professionals. Longitudinal work is needed to trace whether immersive critique and metacognitive scaffolds lead to durable improvements in judgment and transfer across contexts. More attention is also required on equity: how reflective routines can be designed to include diverse voices, prevent exclusion, and counteract systemic biases. Finally, evaluation frameworks that integrate criteria such as validity, reproducibility, equity, and decision impact should be tested across disciplines to establish shared benchmarks.

Taken together, these insights position slow learning not as a drag on innovation but as the condition that makes innovation trustworthy. Institutions that design cadences where speed feeds reflection and reflection shapes action will be better prepared to navigate uncertainty in a rapidly evolving technological landscape. Reflection, when scaffolded by tools but authored and adjudicated by humans, will remain the cornerstone of rigorous education, credible research, and responsible leadership.

REFERENCES

Argyris, C. and Schön, D.A. 1978. Organizational Learning: A Theory of Action Perspective. Addison-Wesley.

Azevedo, R. and Hadwin, A.F. 2005. Scaffolding self-regulated learning and metacognition—Implications for the design of computer-based learning environments. Metacognition and Learning. 1(2): 95–111. https://doi.org/10.1007/s11409-006-9000-9

Bacca, J., Baldiris, S., Fabregat, R., Graf, S. and Kinshuk. 2014. Augmented reality trends in education: A systematic review of research and applications. Computers & Education. 72: 1–11. https://doi.org/10.1016/j.compedu.2013.10.018

Barocas, S. and Selbst, A.D. 2016. Big data's disparate impact. California Law Review. 104(3): 671–732.

Bhargava, R., Kadouaki, R., Bhargava, E., Castro, G., D'Ignazio, C., Zuckerman, E., et al. 2015. DataBasic: Design principles, tools and activities for data literacy learners. Journal of Community Informatics. 11(3): 1–22.

Biggio, B. and Roli, F. 2018. Wild patterns: Ten years after the rise of adversarial machine learning. Pattern Recognition. 84: 317–331. https://doi.org/10.1016/j.patcog.2018.07.023

Biggs, J. 1996. Enhancing teaching through constructive alignment. Higher Education. 32(3): 347–364. https://doi.org/10.1007/BF00138871

Biggs, J. and Tang, C. 2011. Teaching for Quality Learning at University, (4th Ed.). Open University Press.

Black, P. and Wiliam, D. 1998. Assessment and classroom learning. Assessment in Education: Principles, Policy & Practice. 5(1): 7–74. https://doi.org/10.1080/0969595980050102

Brooke, J. 1996. SUS: A "quick and dirty" usability scale. *In*: P.W. Jordan, B. Thomas, B.A. Weerdmeester and I.L. McClelland (eds). Usability Evaluation in Industry, pp. 189–194. Taylor & Francis.

Butchart, S., Forster, D., Gold, I., Bigelow, J., Korb, K.B., Oppy, G., et al. 2009. Improving critical thinking using web-based argument mapping exercises with automated feedback. Australasian Journal of Educational Technology. 25(2): 268–291. https://doi.org/10.14742/ajet.1149

Cai, D.J., Mednick, S.A., Harrison, E.M., Kanady, J.C. and Mednick, S.C. 2009. REM, not incubation, improves creativity by priming associative networks. *In*: Proceedings of the National Academy of Sciences. 106(25): 10130–10134. https://doi.org/10.1073/pnas.0900271106

Cant, R. and Cooper, S. 2017. Use of simulation-based learning in undergraduate nurse education: An umbrella systematic review. Nurse Education Today. 49: 63–71. https://doi.org/10.1016/j.nedt.2016.11.015

Carvalho, D.V., Pereira, E.M. and Cardoso, J.S. 2021. Machine learning interpretability and explainability in industrial training: A systematic review. Computers & Industrial Engineering. 153: 107078. Used to Evidence Industrial Training Practices.

Chi, M.T.H., Bassok, M., Lewis, M.W., Reimann, P. and Glaser, R. 1989. Self-explanations: How students study and use examples in learning to solve problems. Cognitive Science. 13(2): 145–182. https://doi.org/10.1207/s15516709cog1302_1

Clark, A. and Chalmers, D. 1998. The extended mind. Analysis. 58(1): 7–19. https://doi.org/10.1111/1467-8284.00096

Cox, M.T. and Raja, A. (eds). 2011. Metareasoning: Thinking about Thinking in Humans and Machines. MIT Press.

de Bruin, A.B.H. and van Gog, T. 2012. Improving self-monitoring and self-regulation: From cognitive psychology to the classroom. Learning and Instruction. 22(4): 245–252. https://doi.org/10.1016/j.learninstruc.2012.01.003

Dunleavy, M. and Dede, C. 2014. Augmented reality teaching and learning. *In*: M.J. Bishop and J. Elen (eds). Handbook of Research on Educational Communications and Technology, pp. 735–745. Springer.

Dunlosky, J., Rawson, K.A., Marsh, E.J., Nathan, M.J. and Willingham, D.T. 2013. Improving students' learning with effective learning techniques: Promising directions from cognitive and educational psychology. Psychological Science in the Public Interest. 14(1): 4–58. https://doi.org/10.1177/1529100612453266

Dwyer, C.P., Hogan, M.J. and Stewart, I. 2012. An evaluation of argument mapping as a method of enhancing critical thinking performance in e-learning environments. Metacognition and Learning. 7(3): 219–244. https://doi.org/10.1007/s11409-012-9092-1

Ericsson, K.A. and Simon, H.A. 1993. Protocol Analysis: Verbal Reports as Data (Rev. Ed.). MIT Press.

Ericsson, K.A., Krampe, R.T. and Tesch-Römer, C. 1993. The role of deliberate practice in the acquisition of expert performance. Psychological Review: 100(3): 363–406.

Evans, J. St. B.T. 2008. Dual-processing accounts of reasoning, judgment, and social cognition. Annual Review of Psychology. 59: 255–278. https://doi.org/10.1146/annurev.psych.59.103006.093629

Floridi, L. and Cowls, J. 2019. A unified framework of five principles for AI in society. Harvard Data Science Review. 1(1).

Flower, L. and Hayes, J.R. 1981. A cognitive process theory of writing. College Composition and Communication. 32(4): 365–387.

Glasgow, R.E., Vogt, T.M. and Boles, S.M. 1999. Evaluating the public health impact of health promotion interventions: The RE-AIM framework. American Journal of Public Health. 89(9): 1322–1327.

Goodman, S.N., Fanelli, D. and Ioannidis, J.P.A. 2016. What does research reproducibility mean? Science Translational Medicine. 8(341): 341ps12.

Grantcharov, T.P., Kristiansen, V.B., Bendix, J., Bardram, L., Rosenberg, J. and Funch-Jensen, P. 2004. Randomized clinical trial of virtual-reality simulation for laparoscopic skills. Annals of Surgery. 240(2): 205–209.

Guyatt, G.H., Oxman, A.D., Vist, G., Kunz, R., Falck-Ytter, Y., Alonso-Coello, P., et al. 2008. GRADE: An emerging consensus on rating quality of evidence and strength of recommendations. BMJ. 336(7650): 924–926. https://doi.org/10.1136/bmj.39489.470347.AD

Hastie, R. and Dawes, R. 2010. Rational Choice in an Uncertain World (2nd Ed.). Sage.

Hattie, J. and Timperley, H. 2007. The power of feedback. Review of Educational Research. 77(1): 81–112. https://doi.org/10.3102/003465430298487

Hernán, M.A. and Robins, J.M. 2020. Causal Inference: What if. Chapman & Hall/CRC.

Higgins, J.P.T., Thomas, J., Chandler, J., Cumpston, M., Li, T., Page, M.J., et al. (eds). 2019. Cochrane Handbook for Systematic Reviews of Interventions (2nd Ed.). Wiley. https://doi.org/10.1002/9781119536604

Hutchins, E. 1995. Cognition in the Wild. MIT Press.

Ioannidis, J.P.A. 2005. Why most published research findings are false. PLoS Medicine. 2(8): e124. https://doi.org/10.1371/journal.pmed.0020124

Janis, I.L. 1972. Victims of Groupthink. Houghton Mifflin.

Jobin, A., Ienca, M. and Vayena, E. 2019. The global landscape of AI ethics guidelines. Nature Machine Intelligence. 1(9): 389–399.

Jonsson, A. and Svingby, G. 2007. The use of scoring rubrics: Reliability, validity and educational consequences. Educational Research Review. 2(2): 130–144. https://doi.org/10.1016/j.edurev.2007.05.002

Kahneman, D. 2011. Thinking, Fast and Slow. Farrar, Straus and Giroux. Penguin.

Kane, M.T. 2013. Validating the interpretations and uses of test scores. Journal of Educational Measurement. 50(1): 1–73.

Kirsh, D. and Maglio, P. 1994. On distinguishing epistemic from pragmatic action. Cognitive Science. 18(4): 513–549.

Kolb, D.A. 1984. Experiential Learning. Prentice Hall.

Koriat, A. 1997. Monitoring one's own knowledge during study: A cue-utilization approach to judgments of learning. Journal of Experimental Psychology: General. 126(4): 349–370. https://doi.org/10.1037/0096-3445.126.4.349

Krippendorff, K. 2011. Content Analysis (3rd Ed.). Sage.

Kuhn, D. 2010. Teaching and learning science as argument. Science Education. 94(5): 810–824. https://doi.org/10.1002/sce.20395

Larrick, R.P. 2004. Debiasing. *In*: D.J. Koehler and N. Harvey (eds). Blackwell Handbook of Judgment and Decision Making, pp. 316–338. Blackwell.

Makransky, G. and Petersen, G.B. 2021. The cognitive affective model of immersive learning (CAMIL): A theoretical research-based model of learning in immersive virtual reality. Educational Psychology Review. 33(3): 937–958. https://doi.org/10.1007/s10648-020-09586-2

Mehrabi, N., Morstatter, F., Saxena, N., Lerman, K. and Galstyan, A. 2021. A survey on bias and fairness in AI. ACM Computing Surveys. 54(6): 1–35.

Mellers, B.A., Stone, E., Murray, T., Minster, A., Rohrbaugh, N., Bishop, M., et al. 2015. Identifying and cultivating superforecasters as a method of improving probabilistic predictions. *In*: Proceedings of the National Academy of Sciences. 112(12): 410–415. https://doi.org/10.1073/pnas.1418184114

Merchant, Z., Goetz, E.T., Cifuentes, L., Keeney-Kennicutt, W. and Davis, T.J. 2014. Effectiveness of virtual reality-based instruction: A meta-analysis. Computers & Education. 70: 29–40.

Messick, S. 1989. Validity. *In*: R.L. Linn (ed.). Educational Measurement, (3rd Ed.). pp. 13–103. American Council on Education/Macmillan.

Morgan, S.L. and Winship, C. 2015. Counterfactuals and Causal Inference (2nd Ed.). Cambridge University Press.

Moro, C., Štromberga, Z., Raikos, A. and Stirling, A. 2017. The effectiveness of virtual and augmented reality in health sciences education. Anatomical Sciences Education. 10(6): 549–559.

Nicol, D.J. and Macfarlane-Dick, D. 2006. Formative assessment and self-regulated learning. Studies in Higher Education. 31(2): 199–218.

Nielsen, J. 1994. Usability Engineering. Morgan Kaufmann.

Nosek, B.A., Ebersole, C.R., DeHaven, A.C. and Mellor, D.T. 2018. The preregistration revolution. Proceedings of the National Academy of Sciences. 115(11): 2600–2606. https://doi.org/10.1073/pnas.1708274114

Paas, F. and van Merriënboer, J.J.G. 1994. Instructional control of cognitive load in training complex cognitive tasks. Educational Psychology Review. 6(4): 351–371.

Page, M.J., Moher, D., Bossuyt, P.M., Boutron, I., Hoffmann, T.C., Mulrow, C.D., et al. 2021. PRISMA 2020 explanation and elaboration: Updated guidance and exemplars for reporting systematic reviews. BMJ, 372, n160. https://doi.org/10.1136/bmj.n160

Panadero, E. and Jonsson, A. 2013. The use of scoring rubrics for formative assessment purposes revisited: A review. Educational Research Review. 9: 129–144. https://doi.org/10.1016/j.edurev.2013.01.002

Pearl, J. 2009. Causality (2nd Ed.). Cambridge University Press.

Peng, R.D. 2011. Reproducible research in computational science. Science. 334(6060): 1226–1227.

Radianti, J., Majchrzak, T.A., Fromm, J. and Wohlgenannt, I. 2020. A systematic review of immersive virtual reality applications for higher education: Design elements, lessons learned, and research agenda. Computers & Education. 147: 103778. https://doi.org/10.1016/j.compedu.2019.103778

Risko, E.F. and Gilbert, S.J. 2016. Cognitive offloading. Journal of Applied Research in Memory and Cognition. 5(4): 318–324.

Roediger, H.L., III and Karpicke, J.D. 2006. Test-enhanced learning: Taking memory tests improves long-term retention. Psychological Science. 17(3): 249–255. https://doi.org/10.1111/j.1467-9280.2006.01693.x

Roese, N.J. 1997. Counterfactual thinking. Psychological Bulletin. 121(1): 133–148.

Schön, D.A. 1983. The reflective practitioner. Basic Books.

Seymour, N.E., Gallagher, A.G., Roman, S.A., O'Brien, M.K., Bansal, V.K., Andersen, D.K., et al. 2002. Virtual-reality training improves operating room performance. The New England Journal of Medicine. 346(23): 205–210.

Shadish, W.R., Cook, T.D. and Campbell, D.T. 2002. Experimental and Quasi-experimental Designs for Generalized Causal Inference. Houghton Mifflin.

Shute, V.J. 2008. Focus on formative feedback. Review of Educational Research. 78(1): 153–189. https://doi.org/10.3102/0034654307313795

Sio, U.N. and Ormerod, T.C. 2009. Does incubation enhance problem solving? Psychological Bulletin. 135(1): 94–120.

Smallwood, J. and Schooler, J.W. 2015. The science of mind wandering. Annual Review of Psychology. 66: 487–518.

Stanovich, K.E. and West, R.F. 2000. Individual differences in reasoning: Implications for the rationality debate? Behavioral and Brain Sciences. 23(5): 645–726. https://doi.org/10.1017/S0140525X00003435

Stufflebeam, D.L. 2003. The CIPP model for evaluation. Evaluation and Program Planning. 26(3): 341–347.

Whiting, P., Savović, J., Higgins, J.P.T., Caldwell, D.M., Reeves, B.C., Shea, B., et al. 2016. ROBIS: A new tool to assess risk of bias in systematic reviews was developed. Journal of Clinical Epidemiology. 69: 225–234. https://doi.org/10.1016/j.jclinepi.2015.06.005

Wilkinson, M.D., Dumontier, M., Aalbersberg, I.J., Appleton, G., Axton, M., Baak, A., et al. 2016. The FAIR Guiding Principles. Scientific Data. 3: 160018.

Winne, P.H. and Hadwin, A.F. 1998. Studying as self-regulated learning. *In*: D.J. Hacker, J. Dunlosky and A.C. Graesser (eds). Metacognition in Educational Theory and Practice, pp. 277–304. Lawrence Erlbaum.

Yuan, X., He, P., Zhu, Q. and Li, X. 2019. Adversarial examples: Attacks and defenses for deep learning. *In*: IEEE Transactions on Neural Networks and Learning Systems. 30(9): 2805–2824. https://doi.org/10.1109/TNNLS.2018.2886017

Chapter 5

Identity and Agency —AI-Enhanced Credentialing Systems

5.1 FROM STATIC CREDENTIALS TO DYNAMIC, EVIDENCE-LINKED IDENTITY REPRESENTATIONS

Across education and employment, the shift toward skills-first labor markets is accelerating, prompting a fundamental rethinking of credentials. Traditional degrees have long functioned as static signals: they summarize elapsed time in study and the successful completion of courses, but they capture little about performance in real contexts, adaptability, or growth over time (Varadarajan et al., 2023). In contrast, newer forms of recognition—such as micro-credentials and digital badges—highlight specific competencies, assessment criteria, and even linked artifacts. A digital badge in "data visualization," for example, can be tied to an actual dashboard a student built and the rubric used to assess it, offering a far more precise signal of capability. Reviews of higher education trends confirm that micro-credential ecosystems are expanding rapidly, though employers, accreditors, and learners alike want more clarity on how assessments are designed, whether credentials are interoperable, and how reliably they are recognized in the workplace (Varadarajan et al., 2023; Peters, 2025). At the same time, ePortfolios are becoming central because they link claims about learning to authentic work samples, reflections, and feedback that together tell a richer story of development (Yang, 2024; Zhang, 2024). Taken together, these innovations shift the landscape from declaring competence through degree titles to demonstrating competence through verifiable, portable evidence. In this model, identity in

DOI: 10.1201/9781003688013-5

education is not a static label but a dynamic narrative that evolves over time, anchored in evidence that can be verified across systems.

Learning and employment records (LERs) are emerging as one way to operationalize this new model. An LER acts like a persistent container that integrates learning across institutions, co-curricular settings, and the workplace, connecting each experience to verifiable claims. Studies of skills-based hiring suggest employers increasingly prioritize demonstrated skills over broad proxies like degree titles, even though adoption across industries remains uneven (Bone et al., 2025). Within these records, verifiable credentials (VCs) provide cryptographically secured attestations that can be trusted without contacting the issuing institution, improving reliability at scale (W3C VC Data Model 2.0). Importantly, holders control how these credentials are shared. Techniques such as selective disclosure allow someone to reveal only what is necessary for a given opportunity. For example, a paramedic applying for a new role could present proof of a "current pediatric life support certification" without revealing their full transcript, birthdate, or unrelated scores (Ramić et al., 2024). This balance between transparency and privacy improves both trust and proportionality in hiring and licensing. Over time, as LERs aggregate VCs and curated artifacts, they enable more accurate matching between individuals and roles, far beyond what a transcript alone can achieve. They also allow longitudinal analyses of progression, skill adjacency, and persistence, guiding individuals and institutions toward targeted upskilling. Put simply, LERs plus VCs transform identity from a fixed document into a continuously updated evidence graph.

ePortfolios provide another crucial layer by contextualizing credentials with narrative and reflection. A 2024 systematic review finds that ePortfolios enhance self-regulation, knowledge transfer, and integrative learning when they include explicit criteria and opportunities for feedback (Zhang, 2024). Other studies caution, however, that poorly designed portfolios risk devolving into unstructured "file dumps" unless templates, prompts, and alignment to competencies are clear (Yang, 2024). When implemented well, portfolios serve as living dossiers. For instance, a computer science program might ask students to include code reviews, usability tests, and project post-mortems, each tagged to competencies such as "requirements analysis" or "ethical reasoning." Supervisors during internships could add commentary or artifacts, which the learner could later route to employers through selective disclosure. Post-pandemic studies even suggest that ePortfolios support student well-being by making progress visible and connecting personal purpose with tangible evidence of growth (McCarthy et al., 2025). In this sense, portfolios deepen the narrative dimension of identity, adding reflection and context to the cryptographic trust layer provided by VCs.

Micro-credentials and digital badges complement this narrative by making competency claims modular and portable. Research shows that well-designed badges—those with explicit assessment rubrics and transparent issuer information—can promote goal setting, self-efficacy, and persistence in learning programs (DeMarco et al., 2024). In some universities, badges are being used in place of grades, shifting course design toward formative feedback and mastery learning (Goulding et al., 2024). Foundational work situates badges within broader recognition systems that include both formal and informal learning, making them "stackable" toward larger awards. For example, a teacher-education program might issue badges for discrete skills like "instructional adaptation for multilingual learners." These can then stack into a "Differentiated Instruction" micro-credential verified by multiple assessors, showing a cumulative record of skill acquisition (Goulding et al., 2024). Employer interest appears strongest when badges are granular and evidence-linked rather than symbolic. When bound as verifiable credentials, badges can be checked for integrity and authenticity, while learners maintain control over what they disclose (Ramić et al., 2024). In this ecosystem, badges provide the atomic units of capability, while portfolios and VCs supply the narrative and trust layers that make those units legible across contexts.

Because dynamic identity depends on trust, privacy-preserving infrastructure is essential for both social acceptance and regulatory compliance. Reviews in healthcare and computing show that techniques such as federated learning (training models collaboratively without moving sensitive data) and edge processing (running algorithms directly on a user's device) reduce risks associated with centralizing personal information (Ahmed et al., 2025; Wang et al., 2022). In credentialing, selective disclosure and zero-knowledge proofs allow individuals to verify attributes—such as "this credential is active and valid"—without revealing the raw certificate or unrelated personal data (Ramić et al., 2024). For instance, a licensed nurse could demonstrate that a certification is up to date without disclosing other records irrelevant to the role being sought. Educational pilots might therefore pair LER wallets with local, on-device matching systems that calculate skill fit privately and release only minimal, scoped attestations to employers. These layered defenses protect against data leakage and unauthorized profiling, ensuring that identity systems remain trustworthy.

Equally important are provenance and accountability practices that explain how evidence enters and flows through the identity record. Tools such as model cards (summaries of an algorithm's intended use, performance, and limits), datasheets for datasets (documentation of dataset composition and collection), and internal auditing frameworks clarify how assessments were produced and under what conditions (Mitchell et al., 2019; Gebru et al., 2021; Raji et al., 2020). Applied to credentialing, this might mean documenting how rubric scores were generated, by whom, and with what inter-rater reliability. When LER platforms log verification events and consent transactions, they create an auditable trail that allows learners to understand and, if necessary, contest how their data is used. Research on tamper-evident ledgers suggests that such systems can track status changes—such as suspension or revocation of a credential—without undermining governance by human institutions (Akbarfam and Maleki, 2024). In practice, this means a university could attach model cards to automated classifiers used in portfolio evaluation, publish assessor calibration procedures, and make audit reports available to external reviewers. These transparency measures are not ornamental—they are essential for sustaining multi-party trust in evidence-linked identity systems.

Interoperability ensures that dynamic identity does not fragment across sectors and jurisdictions. Studies show that mapping curricular outcomes to frameworks like SFIA (Skills Framework for the Information Age) helps higher education institutions align program outcomes with employer language (Bowers et al., 2022). Technical "crosswalks" between systems like ESCO (*European Skills, Competences, and Occupations*) and ONET (the U.S. occupational database) demonstrate that machine-assisted mappings can preserve granularity while making skills legible across labor markets. Ontology research now integrates credentials, occupations, and skills into shared graphs that allow reasoning about adjacency and progression (Baker et al., 2024). For example, a badge in "data wrangling" aligned to ESCO could automatically be interpreted as related to ONET skills for U.S. recruiters, reducing barriers to cross-border hiring. Courses can embed SFIA-linked rubrics so that LER wallets can tag artifacts in ways that improve automated role matching. Over time, interoperable graphs reduce duplication and confusion, ensuring that learners' records travel with them smoothly from classroom to workplace.

Concrete institutional pilots demonstrate how dynamic identity can be implemented responsibly. Work-integrated learning research emphasizes authentic assessment—tasks with real-world relevance, calibrated mentors, and iterative feedback—as the foundation for valid performance evidence (Luk and Chan, 2024). For instance, a college of business might issue verifiable badges for "client discovery interviews" and "unit economics modeling," each tied to actual artifacts, reflection prompts, and assessor notes. Employer partners could then verify completion with signed comments, visible only to the learner and designated verifiers. Similarly, a nursing school might bind simulation outcomes and SBAR (Situation, Background, Assessment, Recommendation) handoff artifacts into the learner's LER, with performance thresholds gating clinical placements. These examples show that dynamic identity is not just a technical layer but also a curricular design and governance intervention. Studies confirm that portfolio-based authentic assessment strengthens employability when frameworks, evidence, and feedback are closely linked (Vlachopoulos, 2024; Yang, 2024).

At the individual level, dynamic identity systems empower learners to articulate skills, plan development, and negotiate value in skills-based labor markets. Research in learning analytics highlights the importance of dashboards that connect self-efficacy, skill awareness, and career planning. Personal agents that ingest portfolio artifacts, course outcomes, and workplace tasks could suggest next steps, such as completing a supervised A/B testing project to strengthen experimental design. Selective disclosure allows applicants to tailor evidence bundles for specific contexts, whether licensure audits, equity-focused hiring, or promotion reviews. For instance, a mid-career educator applying for a district-level position might choose to disclose only micro-credentials in "validated assessment design" and "multilingual pedagogy" while keeping other data private. Over time, such agentic curation moves beyond generic resumes and enables more precise, fairer matching between individuals and opportunities. Studies suggest that granular, evidence-linked credentials paired with high-quality feedback improve employability signals and confidence (Vlachopoulos, 2024; Liu et al., 2025b).

Because identity systems evolve, robust mechanisms for status and revocation are crucial for maintaining trust. Emerging research explores privacy-preserving credential status lists and revocation schemes that avoid unnecessary data exposure

(Mikroyannidis et al., 2025). In practice, issuers must be able to suspend or revoke credentials when necessary, while holders must be able to prove that a credential remains valid without revealing its full contents. Governance frameworks for verifiable credentials outline issuer obligations, dispute resolution procedures, and audit requirements to ensure integrity over time. Combined with transparency tools such as model cards, datasheets, and audit trails, these mechanisms sustain reliability as records accumulate across a career (Figure 5.1) (Mitchell et al., 2019; Raji et al., 2020). As learners acquire new competencies, older claims remain traceable to their provenance, while outdated or erroneous items can be retired transparently. In this way, credibility becomes a matter of ongoing stewardship rather than a one-time ceremony. Dynamic identity is achieved when evidence is portable, privacy-preserving, and governable across time and context.

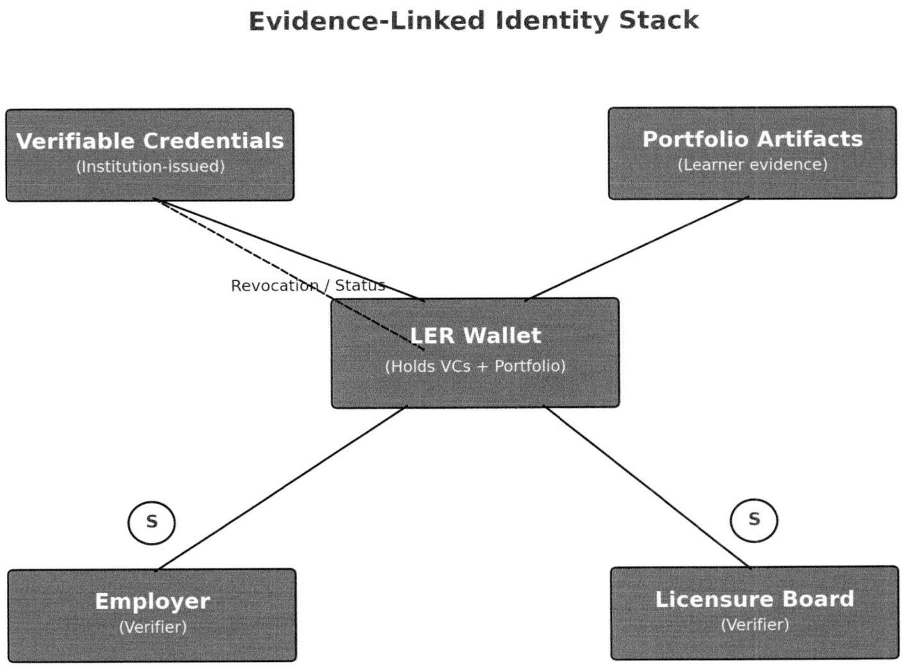

Figure 5.1 Evidence-Linked Identity Stack (VCs + LER + Portfolio + Selective Disclosure).

This section highlights the shift from traditional, static credentials like degrees—which signal time spent in education but reveal little about actual skills or growth—to dynamic, evidence-linked identities that are portable, verifiable, and continuously updated. Static transcripts or diplomas are increasingly insufficient in a skills-first labor market that values demonstrated capabilities. In their place, micro-credentials, digital badges, and ePortfolios are gaining traction. These newer forms of recognition emphasize competencies, assessment criteria, and linked artifacts—for example, a badge in “data visualization” tied directly to a dashboard a learner built and the rubric that assessed it. The growing demand for clarity and interoperability underscores the need for systems that show not just what learners have done, but how that learning was evaluated and why it can be trusted.

LERs are emerging as a backbone of this new model. They aggregate experiences across institutions, extracurriculars, and workplaces into a persistent record that integrates VCs. VCs provide cryptographic proof of skills or statuses, allowing employers or licensing bodies to trust claims without repeatedly contacting issuers. Crucially, selective disclosure and privacy-preserving proofs allow individuals to share only the evidence relevant to a particular opportunity—such as showing proof of an active certification without disclosing unrelated personal or academic data. This proportional approach builds both efficiency and trust while protecting privacy.

ePortfolios add a narrative and reflective layer that credentials alone cannot provide. They contextualize skills with artifacts, self-reflection, and feedback, ensuring that identity is represented as an evolving story rather than a flat label. Well-designed portfolios connect to competencies and frameworks, include supervisor input, and show progression over time. They can even support well-being by making growth visible and aligning learning with purpose. Micro-credentials and badges complement portfolios by breaking down skills into modular, stackable units, which can accumulate into broader credentials or micro-degrees. Employers increasingly value these when they are evidence-linked, granular, and verifiable. Together, badges act as "atoms of capability," portfolios serve as the narrative container, and VCs provide the cryptographic trust layer.

Trust in dynamic identity systems depends on privacy-preserving infrastructures such as federated learning and edge processing, which reduce risks from centralizing sensitive data. Selective disclosure and zero-knowledge proofs strengthen proportionality, while provenance tools like model cards, datasheets, and audit trails create transparency about how assessments were produced and used. This transparency is vital for sustaining trust across students, institutions, employers, and regulators. Similarly, interoperability—through frameworks like SFIA, ESCO, and ONET—ensures that credentials map cleanly to labor markets and can be read across borders and industries. Without interoperability, dynamic identity risks fragmenting into siloed systems that reduce portability.

Case studies of institutional pilots demonstrate how this vision works in practice: business schools issuing verifiable badges tied to real client interviews, nursing schools binding clinical simulations into LERs, and teacher-training programs stacking badges into meaningful micro-credentials. At the individual level, learners gain agency through dashboards and personal agents that help them plan next steps, curate portfolios, and negotiate value in the labor market. Employers benefit from more precise matches between demonstrated skills and role requirements, while learners maintain privacy and control.

Credentials must be revocable, updateable, and transparently managed to remain credible over time. Privacy-preserving revocation schemes and audit trails ensure ongoing trust. As new skills are acquired, older credentials remain linked to provenance but can be retired or replaced. In this way, identity becomes a dynamic, stewarded construct—anchored in evidence, portable across contexts, and accountable to evolving standards. The key takeaway is that the future of credentials lies in moving from declarations to demonstrations: identity is not what a degree says you are, but what your evidence shows you can do, and that evidence must be portable, verifiable, and governed responsibly.

5.2 PERSONAL AI AGENTS FOR SKILL ARTICULATION, PORTFOLIO CURATION, AND CAREER NAVIGATION

Extending the shift to evidence-linked identity, personal agents can be positioned as supervised co-authors of an individual's public competence narrative. Rather than expecting students or professionals to constantly compile and format their own records, agents can summarize artifacts, extract claims and warrants, and link proofs to machine-readable skills so that evidence can travel across different contexts without losing meaning. Reviews of LLM-driven tutors and assistants show that such systems are particularly useful in scaffolding reflection, explanation, and planning when human oversight remains in place (Córdova-Esparza et al., 2025; Sharma et al., 2025). This supervision matters because unguided autonomy risks well-documented problems such as hallucination, over-claiming, or equity harms. For trust to hold, agent outputs must therefore be inspectable, versioned, and traceable back to original sources and rubrics. In practical terms, a student's agent might draft a "capability card" for each learning outcome, citing GitHub commits or lesson plans and highlighting gaps still to be addressed. These short, source-anchored drafts give mentors or instructors an efficient basis for review before anything is published or disclosed more broadly. Taken together, agentic drafting plus human critique accelerates clarity without ceding final judgment to the machine (Figure 5.2).

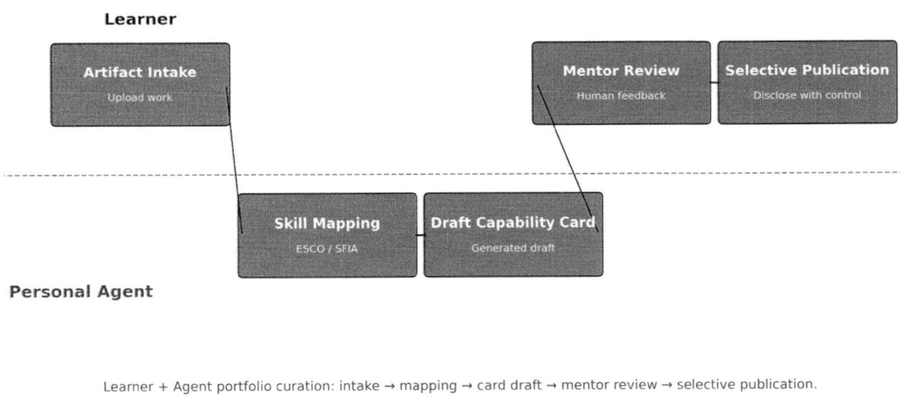

Figure 5.2 Agent-Assisted Portfolio Curation.

Another important consideration and option is to make student-trained personal agents a core, credit-bearing practice—not a side project. Learners should iteratively build and refine a custom agent ("knowledge clone") across their program to surface identity, strengthen metacognition, and rehearse workforce-ready collaboration with agents. Practically, institutions can stage this as a four-term (or four-year) sequence: (1) identity and onboarding (self-assessment, values inventory, reflective journaling), (2) academic integration and agent tuning (domain prompts, study planning, bias tests), (3) professional simulation (résumé/cover-letter drafting, interview rehearsal, stakeholder messaging), and (4) capstone and lifelong-learning launch (version history, ethical guardrails, post-graduation update plan). Each stage should culminate in a verifiable artifact—a capability card, agent log, or micro-credential—that ties claims to evidence and rubric-based feedback. This turns the agent from a novelty into a durable learning partner and a portable signal of capability to employers.

A way to frame this approach is to adopt a tripartite learning model: identity mirror, professional clone, and metacognitive engine. Three mutually reinforcing uses for personal agents are recommended. First, as an identity mirror, the agent compels learners to articulate values, ethical rules, and decision heuristics, then test them in simulated dilemmas (e.g., privacy vs. transparency). Second, as a professional clone, it rehearses real tasks—literature scans, code generation, data visualization—and produces reusable knowledge artifacts that persist beyond a single course. Third, as a metacognitive engine, the agent makes planning, monitoring, and evaluation explicit, training students to diagnose hallucinations, tune instructions, and justify revisions—habits that transfer to new tools and domains. Programs can grade these dimensions through paired artifacts: agent behavior + reflective narrative (what changed and why).

At the same time, one should staff the work with clear roles and guardrails: AI literacy coach, reflective mentor, and technical liaison. Successful implementation relies on defined responsibilities. An AI literacy coach curates evolving tools and prompt patterns; a reflective mentor scaffolds identity work and ethics; and a technical liaison aligns platforms with FERPA/GDPR, IP, and accessibility requirements. Together, these roles keep agent development safe, inclusive, and aligned to policy—especially when combined with consent logging, version control, and mandatory human override. Institutions should codify these expectations in course shells (intended-use statements, escalation paths, model-card requirements) and in program-level playbooks (incident response, supplier updates, rollback rights).

Another very important consideration is to embed heutagogy: treat learners as designers of their own learning tools. Agent-building should be deeply linked to heutagogical practice—self-determined learning that privileges capability (knowing how, when, and why to adapt) over static competence. Recommended moves include reflective journaling tied to agent behavior changes, scenario testing that elicits pluralistic reasoning, and "push-back" rules where the agent challenges users to consider alternatives. Instructors can assess capability by asking, "When did you *not* use the agent, and why?" or "How did you change your agent after this ethical dilemma?" The meta-lesson is that learners should leave with the methods to steer, critique, and evolve their agents—not simply operate them.

Sequence assessment and credentialing to recognize agentic literacy. Offer micro-credentials for metacognitive agent design, prompt transparency, and ethical implementation. Formative assessment can score explainability (e.g., confidence statements, source display), bias audits, and improvement over time; summative assessment can combine an agent demo with a reflective essay on identity, judgment, and transfer. Programs should store these outputs in LER/VC-compatible formats so graduates can disclose "just enough" to a licensure board or recruiter without oversharing. Tightly coupling credentials to artifacts (e.g., code commits, SBAR handoffs, scenario logs) raises employer trust while preserving privacy.

Plan infrastructure with privacy-by-design and equitable access. Include local/edge processing for sensitive content, federated learning for cross-party collaboration, and selective disclosure/zero-knowledge proofs for status checks. Equity requires multilingual interfaces, low-bandwidth options, bias testing of agent outputs, and faculty development so guidance is consistent across courses. Governance should mandate consent logs, revocation/status lists, and auditable trails for who verified what, when, and why—backed by model cards and datasheets for any automated classifiers used in credentialing.

Mitigate risks explicitly: metacognitive laziness, over-automation, and bias. To avoid over-reliance, encourage "productive friction": assignments where students must justify when *not* to accept an agent's answer, compare agent suggestions to human norms, and rewrite prompts after finding errors. Programs should publish negative test libraries (common failure modes) and require agent abstention or escalation in ambiguous cases. Regular "drift huddles" can review telemetry (override rates, error patterns, equity deltas) and drive targeted redesigns of prompts, datasets, or guardrails. These moves keep agency with the learner while strengthening trust in the overall system.

Lastly, adopt a longitudinal model so agents and learners co-evolve. A four-year arc is recommended—from identity onboarding to professional simulation to lifelong-learning launch—so the agent grows with the student. By graduation, each learner carries not only VC-backed micro-credentials but also a versioned, auditable agent that records strategies for studying, ethical decision-making, and domain tasks. Alumni follow-ups can measure real-world utility for upskilling and adaptation, closing the loop between curriculum and career. This longitudinal approach turns the agent into a living extension of self-authorship, not a disposable class deliverable.

From that foundation, one of the most important technical tasks is mapping artifacts to shared skills taxonomies so that stakeholders can agree on meaning. Education and labor markets already rely on frameworks such as ESCO in Europe, ONET in the United States, and SFIA for digital skills. Crosswalks between these frameworks allow evidence generated in one system to be translated into another, reducing friction in hiring and credential evaluation. For example, an agent might tag a "data wrangling" project to ESCO skills and then infer related ONET categories recognizable to an American recruiter (European Commission, 2023). Similarly, a nursing student's clinical SBAR handoff could be aligned with SFIA responsibility levels, making competencies legible to healthcare employers (Bowers et al., 2022; Kitto, 2024). Without such translation, two institutions could describe the same skill differently, leading to confusion or under-recognition of competence. Taxonomy-aware agents solve this by preparing evidence bundles that maintain semantic fidelity while allowing for selective disclosure when only certain competencies are relevant. In this way, identity records become portable across borders and sectors rather than trapped in institutional silos.

Curation is another key function because portfolios quickly become bloated and unwieldy if every artifact is included without discrimination. Scholarship on portfolios consistently shows that quality hinges on alignment to outcomes, structured templates, and mentor prompts rather than raw file storage (Yang, 2024; Zhang, 2024). Personal agents can assist by scoring "evidence tightness" against rubrics, flagging weak or duplicative items, and suggesting reflection prompts that make transfer across contexts more visible. For instance, a computing student's agent might link a pull request, the peer review it received, and a performance benchmark to support the outcome "systems optimization." In teacher education, an agent could pair lesson plans with classroom observation notes and student work tagged to inclusive teaching competencies. These curatorial suggestions are only recommendations; learners must approve or annotate them to maintain authorship and integrity. Logging these acceptances ensures accountability and demonstrates that agency remains human-centered. By supporting curation in this way, agents help portfolios evolve as meaningful narratives rather than degenerating into static archives.

Agents also orchestrate connections between portfolios, badges, and micro-credentials, which increasingly serve as modular building blocks of identity. Research on digital badges shows that they are most effective when they include explicit criteria, transparent evidence, and feedback from assessors (DeMarco et al., 2024; Goulding et al., 2024). A personal agent can streamline this process by auto-assembling a badge application from tagged artifacts, surfacing missing elements, and drafting an assessor-facing rationale. In health sciences, for example, the agent could bundle a simulation video, checklist data, and a reflective memo into an application for a "Team Handoff Quality" badge. In a teacher-education course, it could assemble classroom artifacts and supervisor notes into a claim for a badge in "Differentiated Instruction for Multilingual Learners." When bound as verifiable credentials, badges gain cryptographic trust that assures authenticity, while the portfolio preserves the narrative context of how skills were applied. This layered design makes badges credible to employers and accreditors because they are backed by both technical assurance and authentic artifacts. Over time, these connections allow identity to be expressed flexibly, from granular competencies to larger qualifications.

Beyond documentation, personal agents can help individuals navigate careers by combining learning analytics with labor-market intelligence. Studies of AI-enhanced analytics and career guidance highlight benefits when systems remain grounded in pedagogy and present their reasoning transparently (Gedrimiene et al., 2024; Masiello et al., 2024). Dashboards that emphasize self-efficacy, progress toward goals, and metacognitive reflection are more actionable than raw scores or opaque predictions. An agent might suggest completing a supervised A/B testing project to strengthen experimental design skills, explicitly linking the recommendation to both current artifacts and target roles. It could also simulate "what-if" reskilling paths, such as estimating the time required for a finance professional to pivot into data analytics. Crucially, these recommendations must show the evidence chain and express uncertainty to avoid misleading precision. Human advisors then critique and contextualize the plan, ensuring it accounts for equity, feasibility, and personal goals. This collaborative model aligns technological utility with learner agency, keeping individuals in control of their trajectories. In effect, the agent offers guidance, but humans retain the authority to decide.

Since learners present themselves to diverse audiences, translation becomes a vital function of personal agents. Graduate admissions officers may want to see growth trajectories and alignment with program outcomes, while employers care more about demonstrated role-ready competencies. Licensure boards, in contrast, require evidence tied directly to standards and assessor attestations. Agents can prepare these audience-specific translations while preserving the integrity of underlying artifacts. For example, a mid-career nurse might disclose proof of active certification to a licensing body while highlighting clinical performance notes only to supervisors. Version control and diff views allow reviewers to audit how evidence is reframed, ensuring that presentation layers do not distort substance (Yang, 2024; Varadarajan et al., 2023). This separation of content from presentation reduces cognitive load for each stakeholder without fragmenting the record. In practice, translation layers make identity both honest and portable, allowing individuals to adapt presentation without compromising authenticity.

Because disclosure is always context-dependent, privacy-preserving credential exchange is fundamental to trust. Techniques such as selective disclosure and zero-knowledge proofs allow holders to prove specific attributes without revealing unrelated data (Ramić et al., 2024; W3C, 2025). For example, a paramedic could present evidence of "active pediatric life support certification" and "unrevoked status" without disclosing personal identifiers or unrelated credentials. For transitions from campus to employer, agents might prepare minimal claims aligned to the exact job description, reducing the risk of unnecessary data exposure. In inter-institutional transfers, they could disclose outcomes and evidence links rather than full coursework histories. These practices align with data minimization principles that regulators increasingly emphasize. Cryptographic verification provides technical assurance of authenticity but complements, rather than replaces, trust in the institutions and assessors behind the evidence. Privacy-by-design, therefore, must be a foundational principle of agentic credentialing if adoption is to gain social legitimacy.

External validation further strengthens credibility, and agents can coordinate this process efficiently. Research consistently shows that authentic assessment and calibrated supervision increase both employability and the validity of credentials (Luk and Chan, 2024; Vlachopoulos, 2024). For example, a business school might issue a verifiable badge in "Client Discovery Interviews" only after an employer partner signs off on task completion and quality. In nursing, simulation metrics and supervisor notes can be bound to a credential that gates entry into clinical placements. Personal agents can manage these workflows by coordinating submissions, scheduling debriefs, and reconciling mismatches between learner claims and assessor comments. These practices deter résumé inflation by ensuring that external validators confirm performance. They also reveal gaps in program design when evidence is consistently weak or missing. Over time, credentials accumulate credibility through repeated cycles of validation, giving both learners and employers greater confidence in their accuracy.

Because professional development is ongoing, agents should help turn portfolio analytics into actionable learning plans. Studies of agent-supported reflection link structured prompts and portfolio assessment to improvements in emotion regulation, persistence, and long-term achievement (Khasawneh et al., 2025; Gedrimiene et al., 2024). An agent might recommend a "stretch task," suggest potential mentors, and sequence practice windows with built-in feedback opportunities. It could also monitor the "freshness" of evidence, flagging outdated claims and prompting learners to seek re-validation. For example, a software engineer might be reminded that a credential in a rapidly evolving framework, such as TensorFlow, needs updating to stay relevant. Learners remain in control by accepting, rejecting, or annotating suggestions, leaving an auditable trail for advisors. Human advisors then review the plan against constraints such as licensing requirements or visa regulations. Through this cycle, reflection and growth become routine, with agents supporting continuity and humans anchoring judgment.

Moreover, extending agency also expands risks, which makes governance essential. Personal agents increase the surface area for potential harms such as privacy leakage, provenance confusion, or bias in recommendations. Governance frameworks must therefore bind agents to accountable workflows, auditable logs, and guaranteed human override. Documentation instruments like model cards and datasheets for datasets should accompany any automated classifiers used in the pipeline to clarify intended use and limitations (Raji et al., 2020; Al-Zahrani, 2024). Algorithmic auditing practices need to be adapted specifically for educational and hiring contexts, ensuring that equity, accuracy, and transparency are continuously monitored. Privacy protections must be layered, combining local processing, selective disclosure, and institutional oversight rather than relying on a single safeguard. When these guardrails are in place, personal agents can extend capacity without undermining trust. They function best as co-authors of competence narratives: accelerating clarity, supporting navigation, and preserving accountability in dynamic credentialing ecosystems.

5.3 ETHICAL, PRIVACY, AND OPERATIONAL CHALLENGES OF AGENTIC CREDENTIALING

Having outlined the capabilities of personal agents and dynamic credentialing systems, it is essential to pause and address the risks they introduce. These risks can be situated along four axes: privacy, consent, provenance, and bias. Each axis reflects recurring challenges documented in reviews of AI in education, where issues of data protection, transparency, and access equity remain unresolved (Al-Zahrani, 2024). Credentialing magnifies these risks because identity records are durable: they shape access to jobs, training, and licensure, and they are often reused across multiple contexts without the learner's direct involvement. For example, a clinical simulation video used to verify competency in nursing could later be requested by employers, raising questions about who controls access and how long such evidence should persist. Consent must therefore be granular, allowing learners to decide what evidence is disclosed for each use, and revocable, so that permissions can be withdrawn over time. Provenance—the ability to trace how evidence was created, transformed, and certified—must be visible from artifact to credential. Bias must be scoped broadly, covering not only training data and algorithms but also user interfaces and governance processes. Operationally, addressing these risks requires more than statements of principle; it requires concrete controls, procedures, and technologies that embed safeguards directly into credentialing workflows.

Privacy is often the first axis to surface in these discussions, because identity records by design involve sensitive personal data. A promising response is the use of federated learning and edge inference, both of which reduce exposure by keeping computation close to where the data originates (Table 5.1) (Eden et al., 2025; Liu et al., 2025a). In federated learning, models are trained across distributed devices or institutions without moving raw data into a central repository, lowering the chance of large-scale leakage. This approach is already being explored in healthcare, where patient records must remain local but aggregate insights are needed for diagnostic improvement. Edge inference complements this by performing computation directly on the learner's device—such as a phone, laptop, or institutional portal—so that sensitive artifacts like youth work samples or clinical videos never leave local storage. For example, an agent might calculate a "job fit score" on the learner's device, disclosing only a minimal proof such as "competency verified" rather than uploading the underlying work to a server. This keeps leakage surfaces smaller and easier to explain to stakeholders, including parents, regulators, or employers. However, both approaches raise new governance questions about heterogeneity, fairness, and performance when devices or institutions have unequal resources. Documenting and revisiting privacy–utility trade-offs therefore becomes an ongoing responsibility rather than a one-time design choice. In this sense, privacy is not contractual—it is architectural, embedded into how systems are built and maintained.

Moving to identity proofs, personal records must balance verification with privacy, allowing individuals to prove qualifications without revealing unnecessary information. Selective disclosure refers to cryptographic techniques that let credential holders share only the attributes required in a specific situation. Zero-knowledge proofs (ZKPs) allow someone to prove a claim—such as holding an active license—without exposing the credential itself. In credentialing, this means an applicant could prove a certificate is "active and unrevoked" without revealing unrelated coursework, grades, or demographic details (Ramić et al., 2024; Podda et al., 2025). Practical deployments use protocols such as SD-JWT (Selective Disclosure–JSON Web Tokens) and ZK schemes to implement scoped sharing and status checks. However, designers must guard against correlatability, where repeated disclosures can be linked back to an individual, and verifier overreach, where institutions request more data than necessary. Wallets should default to least-privilege bundles and warn holders when verifiers request excess scope. Institutions, in turn, should publish acceptable-use policies, enforce rate limits, and deny over-broad requests. Clear user experience design is critical so holders know exactly what is being shared. Privacy is not a default guarantee but a practice that must be embedded in tools and policies.

Table 5.1 Privacy-by-Design: Minimum Disclosure by Scenario

Scenario	***Claim Proved***	***Proof Method***	***Data Withheld***	***Revocation/Status Check***
Hiring	Degree completion; skill certifications	Verifiable credential with selective disclosure	Full transcript; unrelated personal identifiers	Employer queries credential registry for validity
Licensure Renewal	Current licensure; required continuing education credits	Verifiable credential updated by licensing board	Full course history; unrelated certifications	Licensure authority checks active registry and revocation lists
Internal Promotion	Performance ratings; completed training modules	Employer-issued credential or internal HR record	Peer reviews; non-relevant feedback	HR system maintains validity and status updates
Cross-Institution Transfer	Completed courses and credits eligible for transfer	Learning and Employment Record (LER) with selective disclosure	Grades for unrelated courses; non-academic records	Receiving institution validates via issuing institution's registry

Turning to provenance and accountability, transparency is necessary to avoid "black box" credentialing pipelines. Documentation artifacts such as model cards summarize the intended use of algorithms, subgroup performance, and known failure modes (Mitchell et al., 2019). Datasheets for datasets track where data originated, how it was processed, and what limitations apply (Gebru et al., 2021). In educational contexts, this means attaching a model card to any classifier used to tag portfolio artifacts or predict mastery. Audit trails should capture when rubrics were applied, how assessors calibrated their scoring, and when badges or credentials were issued. Some systems use tamper-evident ledgers to store these logs, ensuring they cannot be quietly altered, but such ledgers should supplement rather than replace human governance (Alkemade et al., 2023). Public summaries of audits and corrective actions can foster trust between institutions, employers, and learners. Without such documentation, calls for "explainability" remain rhetorical rather than operational. Provenance practices keep credentialing ecosystems accountable, legible, and contestable.

Bias is perhaps the most complex axis because it enters at multiple levels and rarely has a single solution. Multidisciplinary studies of algorithmic hiring highlight how bias can enter through proxies in text, uneven training labels, or feedback loops where biased outcomes reinforce themselves (Raghavan et al., 2020). Bias also arises from interface design—how options are presented—and from institutional incentives that may privilege efficiency over fairness. In education, additional challenges come from distributional shifts, where learners' skills evolve but credentialing models lag behind, or from selective disclosure where only certain artifacts are uploaded. Mitigation requires layered approaches: representative sampling in training data, counterfactual testing to check how outcomes change if sensitive attributes are varied, subgroup error reporting to monitor disparities, and human red-teaming of outputs to spot harms missed by metrics. Documentation must clearly explain trade-offs and known limitations for each use case so stakeholders can make informed decisions. Contestability mechanisms should be visible and easy to access, giving learners straightforward ways to challenge outcomes. Fairness is not a single test passed once; it is a continuous practice embedded in design, auditing, and governance.

Because accountability requires leverage points, systems must be designed so that audits are both possible and routine. Assurance audit frameworks define verifiable claims, the evidence needed to support them, and the validation steps auditors must follow. In the learning analytics domain, audit models often emphasize autonomy for learners, limitations on purpose, and risk-based criteria for evaluation. Education-specific proposals stress that auditability must be designed from the outset, not retrofitted after deployment (Lam et al., 2024; Simbeck, 2024). Institutions should therefore plan for periodic audits of wallet transactions, assessor calibration processes, and revocation workflows. Importantly, audits must lead to action: findings should trigger remediation, and results should be shared with communities of practice to strengthen standards. A consistent cadence of audits builds organizational muscle memory, making accountability a lived routine rather than an occasional response to crisis. Systems are only auditable when they are intentionally designed to be.

Another challenge is gaming and adversarial behavior, which predictably rise as credentials become more modular and portable. Literature on authentic assessment warns that shallow proxies encourage learners to optimize for the badge rather than the skill, creating incentives for boilerplate submissions or inflated self-claims (Vlachopoulos, 2024; Fawns et al., 2025). Personal agents must therefore detect near-duplicate files, repeated templates, or implausible self-reports and route them for human review. Programs can raise the cost of gaming by incorporating controlled simulations, employer-verified tasks, or oral defenses that demonstrate situated performance. Rubrics should explicitly document the warrants required for claims, and assessor rationales should be archived for audit. Periodic proficiency checks can reaffirm time-sensitive claims, such as certifications in emergency response or data security. When evidence quality is tightly specified and validated, credentials become much harder to spoof. Integrity in credentialing is ultimately a design decision, not an accident of enforcement.

Because careers are dynamic, revocation and status checks must preserve both reliability and privacy. Emerging mechanisms propose privacy-preserving status lists that allow verifiers to confirm whether a credential is valid without exposing additional details about issuer behavior (Hoops et al., 2025; Germenia et al., 2025). Wallets should present holders with clear views of suspension notices, expiration dates, and appeal options. Verifiers, by contrast, should receive only yes/no responses bound to specific purposes and time frames, not entire credential histories. Issuers need well-defined playbooks for re-issuing credentials after remediation, ensuring that learners who address deficiencies are not permanently penalized. Cross-institution agreements should harmonize reasons and notifications for revocation to reduce confusion for both learners and employers. These lifecycle controls maintain trust by ensuring credentials are reliable over time while respecting privacy. Status is not a side feature but a core requirement of a trustworthy credentialing ecosystem.

Operational governance ties all these safeguards together by defining roles, escalation paths, and consent defaults across the institution-to-employer boundary. Reviews of AI in higher education emphasize that integrations must remain pedagogy-first, with staff trained to supervise and interpret system outputs (Wang and Wang, 2024). Policies should clearly state what personal agents can pre-process, when human advisors must review evidence, and how learners can restrict or revoke downstream use. Training for staff and assessors should include bias awareness, red-teaming exercises, and portfolio forensics to detect manipulation. Vendor contracts must include clauses for audit rights, full model documentation, and guarantees of portability to prevent lock-in. Program reviews should add "evidence ecology" checks to confirm that credentials remain aligned with learning outcomes and authentic artifacts. Clear governance frameworks keep innovation bounded by ethical practice while allowing scale. Guardrails are not constraints that slow development; they are enablers that make sustainable adoption possible.

With these guardrails articulated, the discussion can now shift to the system-level effects of agentic credentialing. The central claim is that granular, verifiable evidence has the potential to accelerate reskilling and clarify value in skills-based markets. Yet the outcomes depend heavily on how programs are designed, how employers receive and recognize new forms of evidence, and how policy frameworks evolve to support or constrain their use. The next section synthesizes emerging evidence on learning gains, pathway clarity, and career transitions, while also considering equity, variation in return on investment, and unintended consequences. Throughout, the emphasis remains on augmentation rather than displacement of traditional degrees. Dynamic identity does not replace existing systems of recognition but deepens and personalizes them. As such, agentic credentialing should be seen not as a disruption to be resisted, but as an evolution to be governed with care.

5.4 IMPACTS ON PROFESSIONAL DEVELOPMENT, LIFELONG LEARNING, AND CAREER TRAJECTORIES

To connect governance to lived outcomes, we begin with lifelong learning and micro-credentials as the scaffolds for agent-supported growth. Research argues that micro-credentials offer a flexible way to target emergent skills while embedding learners in a culture of continuous development rather than one-off certifications (Peters, 2025). Education programs show particular value when these micro-credentials align with authentic assessments and outcomes that employers already recognize. Personal agents amplify uptake by translating portfolio evidence into ready-to-submit applications, highlighting what is missing, and proposing "plan-next" actions. For instance, a student with several coding projects could have an agent bundle the evidence into a micro-credential application for "full-stack development," flagging gaps in testing or documentation. However, the impact of such credentials is shaped heavily by program quality and employer recognition, underscoring the importance of metadata, assessment rubrics, and verification. Learners benefit most when badges are evidence-rich, criteria-transparent, and stackable toward larger awards. For institutions, analytics from these portfolios not only support individuals but also inform curriculum design, turning lifelong learning into a continuous and data-driven process (Varadarajan et al., 2023).

From a pathway perspective, stacking credentials enables learners to assemble role-ready combinations over time. Stacks are effective when they map to established frameworks and culminate in recognitions that employers understand (Digital Promise, 2024; Bowers et al., 2022). For example, a computing student might progress from "Data Wrangling" to "Experiment Design" to "Causal Inference," creating a clear trajectory toward an analyst role. In teaching, a stack of "Universal Design for Learning," "Multilingual Pedagogy," and "Assessment Design" can point to inclusion-focused career paths. Agents help by sequencing badges logically, surfacing adjacent skills, and prompting refresh cycles when technologies or practices change. Without clear mappings or crosswalks, stacks risk opacity or duplication, leaving learners unsure how skills connect to job roles. With transparent taxonomies and frameworks in place, portfolios tell a coherent story of progression rather than a patchwork of disconnected claims. Stacking therefore operationalizes lifelong learning in visible, evidence-based ways that both learners and employers can interpret.

Because career transitions are often disruptive, evidence-linked identities can de-risk mobility by clarifying what transfers and what does not. Longitudinal reviews of career change highlight the importance of clear cues, self-efficacy, and visible opportunity structures in making transitions successful (Akkermans et al., 2024). Skills taxonomies and ESCO-to-O*NET crosswalks make claims of transferability testable rather than aspirational (European Commission, 2023; Kitto, 2024). A mid-career worker seeking to move from journalism to communications, for instance, could use an agent to identify overlapping skills such as audience analysis and evidence synthesis, while flagging gaps in digital marketing that require new training. Agents can also simulate role matches, showing where an individual is closest to meeting requirements and recommending targeted projects to close remaining gaps. This reduces reliance on degrees as blunt proxies for capability and improves match quality between workers and roles. Non-linear career histories—common in today's labor markets—become coherent when presented as graphs of competencies and experiences. With clarity and evidence, mobility increases without erasing prior expertise, turning transitions into design challenges rather than leaps of faith.

At the market level, early evidence on skills-based hiring remains mixed, highlighting both potential and limitations. Studies in technology sectors suggest employers are paying more attention to skills-based signals, but broader adoption across industries is still uneven (Bone et al., 2025). Agent-supported portfolios may narrow this gap by making skills auditable, portable, and easier to compare across candidates. Where degree filters remain, high-quality micro-credentials combined with work samples can still influence internal mobility and promotion decisions. For older or non-traditional workers, presenting skills through verifiable credentials may help counter stigma if evidence is strong and contextualized. Nonetheless, institutions should temper their claims, as outcomes vary significantly by sector and employer culture. Some industries with clear regulatory standards adopt skills-based evidence more readily, while others still privilege traditional degrees. Nuance in evaluation is not a weakness but a feature of responsible adoption, reminding stakeholders that design, culture, and context ultimately shape results.

Within programs, authentic assessment, work-integrated learning (WIL), and calibrated mentorship consistently show employability gains. Reviews of assessment practice emphasize explicit criteria, iterative feedback, and employer co-assessment as keys to validity (Vlachopoulos, 2024). Personal agents can strengthen this by scheduling debriefs, collating assessor notes, and ensuring each portfolio claim links to a rated performance. For example, a nursing student's agent could pair simulation scores with supervisor comments and track progress toward licensing requirements. Agents can also flag "evidence rot," prompting re-demonstration of time-sensitive skills like CPR or data security. Program dashboards that aggregate these analytics highlight systemic gaps for curriculum designers and external partners. This shifts the focus from seat time or credit hours to situated performance that can be observed and verified. Graduates thus present proof, not just proxies, making employability a function of demonstrated capability rather than assumed readiness (Luk and Chan, 2024).

Equity remains a critical concern, hinging on both access and measurement. Reviews of AI in education warn that without safeguards, benefits are likely to accrue inequitably, reinforcing rather than reducing disparities (Al-Zahrani, 2024). Agentic systems must therefore default to local processing and selective disclosure, ensuring that learners in lower-resource environments retain control over data while still participating fully. Programs must also budget for mentoring, connectivity, and device access so that reflective and credentialing practices do not widen digital divides. Assessment policies should explicitly incorporate accommodations that preserve rigor while recognizing diverse ways of demonstrating competence. For example, a learner with accessibility needs might submit video reflections instead of written ones, supported by the same rubric. Contestability and appeal processes must be easy to find and simple to use, giving all learners the chance to challenge decisions. Finally, audit results related to fairness should be shared with communities of practice, creating collective accountability and trust. Equity is not delivered by any single tool; it is built through a web of design decisions that accumulate over time.

Sector specificity also shapes outcomes: some micro-credentials generate strong returns while others falter. Health and safety-critical domains, such as nursing or aviation, show consistent value because they align with established standards and authentic practice opportunities (Zdunek et al., 2024). In these cases, portfolios tied to supervised tasks and regular status checks reassure employers of validity. Conversely, in more fluid domains like digital marketing or entrepreneurship, badges may carry less weight unless they foreground artifacts and clear impact metrics. Institutions should publish outcome studies by field and cohort rather than rely on broad averages that obscure these differences. Employers, for their part, should share performance data tied to skill profiles, allowing evidence-driven iteration of programs. Over time, these feedback loops improve return on investment and ensure that micro-credentials remain credible. In short, sober evaluation and transparency beat hype.

For infrastructure, interoperability is the linchpin of portability at scale. Cross-institution wallets, verifiable records, and privacy-preserving revocation protocols ensure that learners can carry their credentials across programs and employers without losing trust (W3C, 2025; Germenia et al., 2025). Standards bodies are actively defining data formats and integrity models for verifiable credentials, while higher education coalitions pilot integration of CLRs (Comprehensive Learner Records), Open Badges, and LERs (Learning and Employment Records). Personal agents sit atop these infrastructures, preparing minimal proof bundles and routing disclosures only when learners consent. Governance frameworks must ensure that learners can export their data if they switch institutions or jobs, avoiding vendor lock-in. Public transparency artifacts such as model cards, audit summaries, and mapping tables give third parties confidence in what they see. Infrastructure is valuable only if it underwrites mobility, not if it traps learners in proprietary silos. The core point is that portability is not an afterthought but the purpose of dynamic credentialing.

At the level of individual agency, playbooks help learners and workers translate evidence into value. Best practices include STAR-style (Situation, Task, Action, Result) narratives linked directly to rubrics, targeted bundles of proof tailored for each audience, and refresh cycles to ensure claims remain current. Agents can propose drafts of these bundles, but individuals must retain ownership of voice, consent, and boundaries. Advisors play an important role in coaching learners on how to negotiate roles and compensation by interpreting capability graphs as wage or promotion arguments. Alumni networks and employer partners can further verify tasks, strengthening the credibility of portfolios. Over time, analytics from these negotiations feed back into program design, showing which skills carry the most weight in real-world contexts. This makes agency less about improvisation and more about informed, repeatable practice. Negotiation of value, in short, rides on verifiable proof, not just aspiration (Gedrimiene et al., 2024; Khasawneh et al., 2025).

Bringing these strands together, agentic credentialing augments rather than replaces degrees by layering granular, portable evidence on top of formal recognition. Institutions gain diagnostic insights that guide curriculum design and partnership strategy. Learners gain clarity and leverage in navigating careers, presenting authentic evidence of growth rather than static proxies. Employers gain verifiable, comparable signals that reduce uncertainty in hiring and promotion.

Risks remain—around privacy, equity, and provenance—but they are governable through design choices such as privacy-by-design, transparent documentation, auditing, and human oversight. Impact scales when credentials are interoperable, assessments are authentic, and feedback is formative. Evaluation must remain uncompromising, measuring real outcomes rather than adoption rates. Above all, identity must remain human-centered, with agents amplifying rather than substituting individual agency. In this model, capability not only deepens but also remains visible and portable across a lifetime (Peters, 2025; Bone et al., 2025; Varadarajan et al., 2023).

Taken together, therefore, this chapter reframes academic and professional identity as something dynamic and continuously updated, rather than a one-time certificate or degree. Instead of a transcript that lists courses and grades, identity becomes a portfolio of evidence: work samples, badges, and curated reflections that demonstrate how skills are applied and how they grow over time. This reframing matters because it communicates situated performance, adaptability, and progression in ways static records never could. The division of labor also becomes clearer: personal agents can draft summaries, map skills to frameworks, and prepare translations, while educators and employers provide evaluation and ethical oversight. The result is an identity system that feels more like a living narrative than a static label, with credibility built through authentic tasks, transparent criteria, and links between claims and evidence. Shared taxonomies ensure that skills described in one country or sector can be recognized in another, reducing confusion and “lost in translation” moments. In practical terms, this means learners can more easily explore career pathways while employers can discover talent using the same evidence base. At its core, this shift moves us from assertion—“I have this degree”—to demonstration—“Here is the evidence of what I can do.”

Personal agents are most valuable when they operate as supervised editors of evidence rather than independent judges of merit. In this role, agents can pull skills from artifacts, align them with frameworks like ESCO in Europe, O*NET in the United States, or SFIA in technology fields, and suggest development plans. Instructors or advisors then refine these drafts, ensuring they remain accurate and contextually appropriate. Because translations for different audiences—universities, employers, or licensing boards—risk distorting meaning, the chapter emphasizes the importance of version control, provenance, and human review. When this scaffolding is present, portfolios remain lean, badges stay tied to evidence rather than symbolism, and credentials retain both cryptographic trust and narrative context. The practical gain is a faster feedback loop: learners see gaps sooner, can respond with new evidence, and gain recognition more quickly in fast-changing markets. Pedagogically, it aligns assessments with outcomes more precisely because the gaps are visible in the evidence, not hidden behind a single grade. For employers, it reduces the burden of reviewing bloated dossiers by delivering only the proofs they need, cutting down on wasted time and unnecessary exposure of private data. In short, supervised agents help make capability legible without stripping learners of agency.

At the operational level, the most consequential claim is that trust emerges from architecture and governance, not slogans. Privacy-by-design means keeping processing local where possible, sharing only what is necessary, and defaulting to minimal disclosure. Accountability-by-design means every classifier or decision support tool is documented with model cards, audit trails, and clear processes for suspension or re-issuance of credentials. Interoperability-by-design means shared schemas and mappings so that evidence keeps its meaning as it moves across institutions and borders. These controls are not optional—they are the conditions that allow systems to scale responsibly and equitably. Without them, risks shift onto those least able to absorb harm: learners with limited resources, workers in precarious positions, or applicants from marginalized groups. Institutions that treat auditability, consent logging, and revocation as core features will build durable legitimacy in recognition practices. Those that treat them as afterthoughts will face crises of confidence when stakeholders inevitably question fairness and accuracy. Reliable credential systems, in short, must be governed systems first and technological systems second.

Equity threads through every part of the design. Modular evidence can expand opportunity, but only if mentoring, access, and contestability are built in from the start. Micro-credentials deliver the most value when criteria are clear, feedback is timely, and learners have supervision and support to reach them. Work-integrated learning, employer-verified tasks, and oral defenses raise the cost of "gaming" the system and provide credible routes for non-traditional learners to demonstrate skills. At the same time, systems must avoid privileging those who already know how to market themselves. Agents can help by prompting reflection, surfacing exemplars, and ensuring all learners receive advisor feedback on curation decisions. Bias audits that track subgroup errors and visible appeals processes are critical safeguards, not optional extras. Selective disclosure and privacy-preserving checks reduce the risks of repeated overexposure, which disproportionately harms those with fewer opportunities. Done well, equity becomes a property of the entire evidence ecosystem—from task design to user interfaces—rather than a band-aid applied after harm occurs.

Looking forward, dynamic and governed identity systems offer a hedge against market volatility and a foundation for lifelong learning. For learners, portable evidence lowers the costs of switching careers, clarifies adjacent opportunities, and allows them to negotiate based on proven skills rather than prestige alone. For employers, minimally sufficient proofs accelerate trust in candidates and broaden the pool of qualified applicants, particularly where degree filters previously excluded capable workers. For institutions, analytics from portfolios highlight under-evidenced outcomes and prompt redesigns that focus on authentic tasks and meaningful rubrics. For regulators, transparent pipelines and clear revocation processes make it easier to protect the public without stifling innovation. For vendors, guarantees of exportability and interoperability shift competition toward quality rather than lock-in. For researchers, longitudinal studies tracing evidence patterns to outcomes can move debates beyond anecdotes toward cumulative knowledge. In short, credible, portable evidence reduces friction across the entire education–work–licensure continuum, making identity not a static record of the past but a dynamic signal of growth and capability.

REFERENCES

Ahmed, S.T., Kaladevi, A.C., Shankar, A. and Alqahtani, F. 2025. Privacy enhanced edge-AI healthcare devices authentication: A federated learning approach. *In*: IEEE Transactions on Consumer Electronics, vol. 71, no. 2, pp. 5676–5682. doi: 10.1109/TCE.2025.3542955.

Akbarfam, A.J. and Maleki, H. 2024. SOK: Blockchain for Provenance. arXiv preprint arXiv:2407.17699.

Akkermans, J., da Motta Veiga, S.P., Hirschi, A. and Marciniak, J. 2024. Career transitions across the lifespan: A review and research agenda. Journal of Vocational Behavior. 148: 103957.

Al-Zahrani, A.M. 2024. Unveiling the shadows: Beyond the hype of AI in education. Education and Information Technologies. 29: 1–24.

Alkemade, H., Claeyssens, S., Colavizza, G., Freire, N., Lehmann, J., Neudecker, C., et al. 2023. Datasheets for digital cultural heritage datasets. Journal of Open Humanities Data. 9(1): 124.

Baker, S., Gunn Watkinson, M., Honeyman, F., Mowll, J. and Tyulkina, S. 2024. Rethinking student engagement for 'hyflex'teaching and learning in post-compulsory settings: Acknowledging flexibility and agency needed for unplanned events. International Journal of Lifelong Education. 43(4): 432–447.

Bowers, D.S., Sabin, M., Raj, R.K. and Impagliazzo, J. 2022. Computing competencies: Mapping cc2020 dispositions to sfia responsibility characteristics. *In*: 2022 IEEE Global Engineering Education Conference (EDUCON), pp. 428–437. IEEE.

Bone, M., Brunswicker, S. and Rayna, T. 2025. Skills or degree? The rise of skills-based hiring. Technological Forecasting & Social Change. 210: 122728.

Córdova-Esparza, D.M. 2025. AI-powered educational agents: Opportunities and challenges. Information. 16(6): 469.

DeMarco, B., Ebanks, Y. and Tafuto, B. 2024. Digital badges in academia: An educational tool for the clinical research coordinator. Journal of Clinical and Translational Science. 8(1): e51.

Digital Promise. 2024. The role of micro-credentials in lifelong learning. digitalpromise.dspacedirect.org

Eden, R., Chukwudi, I., Bain, C., Barbieri, S., Callaway, L., de Jersey, S., et al. 2025. Governance of federated learning: A scoping review. NPJ Digital Medicine. 8: 1–15.

European Commission. 2023. ESCO↔O*NET crosswalk. https://esco.ec.europa.eu/en/about-esco/data-science-and-esco/crosswalk-between-esco-and-onet

Fawns, T., Bearman, M., Dawson, P., Nieminen, J.H., Ashford-Rowe, K., Willey, K., et al. 2025. Authentic assessment: from panacea to criticality. Assessment & Evaluation in Higher Education. 50(3): 396–408.

Gebru, T., Morgenstern, J., Vecchione, B., Vaughan, J.W., Wallach, H., Iii, H.D., et al. 2021. Datasheets for Datasets. Communications of the ACM. 64(12): 86–92.

Hoops, F., Gebele, J. and Matthes, F. 2025. CRSet: Private non-interactive verifiable credential revocation. arXiv preprint arXiv:2501.17089.

Gedrimiene, E., Celik, I., Kaasila, A., Mäkitalo, K. and Muukkonen, H. 2024. Artificial intelligence (AI)-enhanced learning analytics (LA) for supporting career decisions: Advantages and challenges from user perspective. Education and Information Technologies. 29(1): 297–322.

Germenia, R., Manfredi, S., Sciarretta, G., Scuro, M. and Tomasi, A. 2025. Comparison of credential status mechanisms for the digital wallet ecosystem. *In*: Proceedings of the 22nd International Conference on Security and Cryptography, SECRYPT 2025.

Goulding, J., Sharp, H. and Twining, P. 2024. Awarding digital badges: Research from a first-year university course. Higher Education Research & Development. 43(3): 640–656.

Khasawneh, M.A.S., Aladini, A., Assi, S.A. and Ajanil, B. 2025. Portfolio assessment in AI-enhanced learning environments: A pathway to emotion regulation, mindfulness, and language learning attitudes. Language Testing in Asia. 15(1): 5.

Kitto, K. 2024. Will a Skills Passport ever get me through the lifelong learning border?: Two critical challenges facing personalised user models for lifelong learning. *In*: Proceedings of the 32nd ACM Conference on User Modeling, Adaptation and Personalization, pp. 132–142.

Lam, K., Lange, B., Blili-Hamelin, B., Davidovic, J., Brown, S. and Hasan, A. 2024. A framework for assurance audits of algorithmic systems. *In*: Proceedings of the 2024 ACM Conference on Fairness, Accountability, and Transparency, pp. 1078–1092.

Liu, X., Li, B., Chen, S. and Xu, Z. 2025a. A survey on multi-user privacy issues in edge intelligence: State of the art, challenges, and future directions. Electronics. 14(12): 2401.

Liu, Y., Hu, X., Ng, J.T.D., Ma, Z. and Lai, X. 2025b. Ready or not? Investigating in-service teachers' integration of learning analytics dashboard for assessing students' collaborative problem solving in K–12 classrooms. Education and Information Technologies. 30(2): 1745–1776.

Luk, L.Y.Y. and Chan, C. 2024. Assessing student learning in work-integrated learning. Studies in Educational Evaluation. 80: 101314.

Masiello, I., Mohseni, Z., Palma, F., Nordmark, S., Augustsson, H. and Rundquist, R. 2024. A current overview of the use of learning analytics dashboards. Education Sciences. 14(1): 82.

McCarthy, A., Mitchell, K. and McNally, C. 2025. ePortfolio practice for student well-being in higher education: A scoping review. Journal of University Teaching and Learning Practice. 22(3): 1–19.

Mikroyannidis, A., Third, A. and Domingue, J. 2025. Blockchain-based decentralised micro-accreditation for lifelong learning. Interactive Learning Environments. 33(3): 2201–2215.

Mitchell, M., Wu, S., Zaldivar, A., Barnes, P., Vasserman, L., Hutchinson, B., et al. 2019. Model cards for model reporting. *In*: FAT '19: Proceedings of the Conference on Fairness, Accountability, and Transparency, pp. 220–229, GA, Atlanta, USA.

Peters, M. 2025. Micro-credentials and lifelong learning. Distance Education. 46(2): 96–112.

Podda, E., Hölzmer, P., Amard, A., Sedlmeir, J. and Fridgen, G. 2025. The impact of zero-knowledge proofs on data minimisation compliance of digital identity wallets. Internet Policy Review. 14(3).

Raghavan, M., Barocas, S., Kleinberg, J. and Levy, K. 2020. Mitigating bias in algorithmic hiring: Evaluating claims and practices. *In*: Proceedings of the 2020 Conference on Fairness, Accountability, and Transparency, pp. 469–481.

Ramić, Š.B., Cogo, E., Prazina, I., Cogo, E., Turkanović, M., Mulahasanović, R.T., et al. 2024. Selective disclosure in digital credentials: A review. ICT Express. 10(4): 916–934.

Raji, I.D., Smart, A., White, R.N., Mitchell, M., Gebru, T., Hutchinson, B., et al. 2020. Closing the AI accountability gap: Defining an end-to-end framework for internal algorithmic auditing. *In*: Proceedings of the 2020 Conference on Fairness, Accountability, and Transparency, pp. 33–44.

Sharma, S., Mittal, P., Kumar, M. and Bhardwaj, V. 2025. The role of large language models in personalized learning: A systematic review of educational impact. Discover Sustainability. 6(1): 1–24.

Simbeck, K. 2024. They shall be fair, transparent, and robust: Auditing AI in learning analytics. AI and Ethics. 4: 1–22.

Varadarajan, S., Koh, J.H.L. and Daniel, B.K. 2023. Micro-credentials in higher education: A systematic review. International Journal of Educational Technology in Higher Education. 20: 77.

Vlachopoulos, D. 2024. Authentic assessment: A systematic review. Studies in Educational Evaluation. 80: 101306.

W3C. 2025. Verifiable Credentials Data Integrity 1.0 and VC Data Model 2.0.

Wang, R., Lai, J., Zhang, Z., Li, X., Vijayakumar, P. and Karuppiah, M. 2022. Privacy-preserving federated learning for internet of medical things under edge computing. IEEE Journal of Biomedical and Health Informatics. 27(2): 854–865.

Wang, X.H. and Wang, Y.Z. 2024. Research on the evaluation system of higher education teaching quality based on artificial intelligence. *In*: Proceedings of the 2024 7th International Conference on Big Data and Education, pp. 42–48.

Yang, H. 2024. An in-depth literature review of e-portfolio implementation in higher education. Impacting Teaching and Learning Today.

Zdunek, K., Dobrowolska, B., Dziurka, M., Galazzi, A., Chiappinotto, S., Palese, A., et al., 2024. Challenges and opportunities of micro-credentials as a new form of certification in health science education—A discussion paper. BMC Medical Education. 24(1): 1169.

Zhang, P. 2024. e-Portfolio use during the pandemic: A systematic review. Open Praxis. 16(3): 289–305.

Chapter 6

Building AI-Ready Organizational Cultures

6.1 INSTITUTIONAL READINESS AND CULTURE-BUILDING FOR AI ADOPTION

The first step in building an AI-ready organization is not a technology purchase but a cultural one. The real question is whether an institution treats new tools as passing gadgets or as part of its shared way of working. Culture determines who feels empowered to experiment, who gets credit when projects succeed, and how risk is shared when outcomes are uncertain (Schein and Schein, 2016). A practical way to make culture visible is to draft a short culture charter. This charter should do more than talk about "innovation" or "trust." It should list specific, observable behaviors—experiment in the open, evaluate rigorously, disclose limits—and tie them to incentives, recognition, and recurring rituals so that values become routines rather than slogans (Kotter, 1996). Leaders must also ensure psychological safety, meaning that teams feel free to raise concerns about models, data, or procedures without fear of embarrassment or punishment (Edmondson, 1999). In AI contexts, this is reinforced by reproducible experiments, shared baselines, and blameless post-incident reviews that emphasize learning rather than blame (Edmondson, 2019). Organizations that codify these practices reduce variance in delivery and accelerate learning cycles across projects (Argyris and Schön, 1978). In short, readiness is not a one-time procurement decision but an institutional habit of aligning curiosity with controls (NIST, 2023).

Role clarity is the anchor that makes this culture real. Without clear ownership, responsibilities diffuse and risks are missed. A handful of roles should be defined explicitly, spanning problem framing, workflow design, evaluation, and data stewardship (Papagiannidis et al., 2025). The product owner carries responsibility

DOI: 10.1201/9781003688013-6

for hypotheses, value metrics, red lines, and the business context that defines acceptable risk (Amershi et al., 2019). The orchestrator translates intentions into workflows, designing human-in-the-loop checkpoints, guardrails, and escalation paths (Breck et al., 2017). The evaluator maintains gold standard datasets, scenario rubrics, fairness analyses, and drift monitors, turning quality into evidence (Raji et al., 2020). The data steward manages lineage, consent, retention, minimization, supplier clauses, and documentation artifacts such as datasheets for datasets (Gebru et al., 2021). In small teams, one person may wear multiple hats, but responsibilities should remain separable on paper and auditable in practice (Sculley et al., 2015). Clear charters not only reduce diffusion of responsibility but also speed incident response when model behavior shifts unexpectedly (ISO/IEC, 2023a). Culture clarity, in practice, is enacted through role clarity—not aspirational memos (Papagiannidis et al., 2025).

Governance rituals then convert these role charters into reliable, repeatable practices that outlive personnel turnover. Model update councils, for example, should log version changes, acceptance tests, rollback triggers, and sign-offs so that change control is legible (Breck et al., 2017). Drift huddles allow teams to review monitoring signals, examine upstream data shifts, and decide whether to retrain or pause deployment (Lu et al., 2018). Incident reviews should be blameless, evidence-rich, and time-boxed, producing actionable items that update playbooks, model cards, and runbooks (Edmondson, 2019). Quarterly portfolio reviews should check high-risk systems against management standards such as ISO/IEC 42001, making oversight systematic rather than episodic (ISO/IEC, 2023a). Publishing short summaries of these rituals internally builds trust and spreads effective patterns across teams (Kotter, 1996). These small, repeated investments reduce variance and make quality auditable by executives, auditors, and regulators (NIST, 2023). Rituals embed culture by putting "how we decide" directly on the organizational calendar (Schein and Schein, 2016).

A maturity ladder can help institutions see where they are and where they need to go. The first rung tolerates isolated wins but documents lessons and risks (Figure 6.1) (Kotter, 1996). The second standardizes gold datasets, acceptance criteria, and issue triage to reduce dependence on individual heroics (Breck et al., 2017). The third introduces common observability, model registries, data contracts, and change-management gates across business units (NIST, 2023). The fourth aligns culture with policy through management systems like ISO/IEC 42001 and risk frameworks like ISO/IEC 23894 (ISO/IEC, 2023a). The fifth optimizes for reusable agents, cross-team workflows, external audits, and continuous improvement tied directly to outcomes (Schein and Schein, 2016). Progression depends not on hype but on demonstrating safe value and being able to answer, at any time, "who changed what, when, and with which tests" (NIST, 2023). The ladder calibrates ambition to control maturity, ensuring institutions do not outpace their guardrails (Papagiannidis et al., 2025).

Strategy, to be effective, must be framed as a series of reversible bets rather than irreversible leaps. Reversibility lowers the psychological and political cost of learning under uncertainty (Edmondson, 2019). Teams should predeclare success metrics, guardrails, and rollback triggers so that canceling a pilot becomes evidence of governance, not failure (Kotter, 1996). Reversible bets are essential in sensitive domains such as health, finance, and safety, where risks are not fully understood (ISO/IEC, 2023b). Bounded sandboxes with shadow evaluations allow side-by-side comparisons against human baselines before real decisions are affected (NIST, 2023). Documenting these experiments reduces rationalization after the fact and lowers status threat among experts who fear replacement (Edmondson, 1999). Decision logs should record the evidence, dissent, and rationale for acting under uncertainty (Argyris and Schön, 1978). Transparency about canceled pilots demonstrates that safety is valued over showmanship (Raji et al., 2020). Reversibility enables bold experimentation without recklessness in AI adoption (Edmondson, 2019).

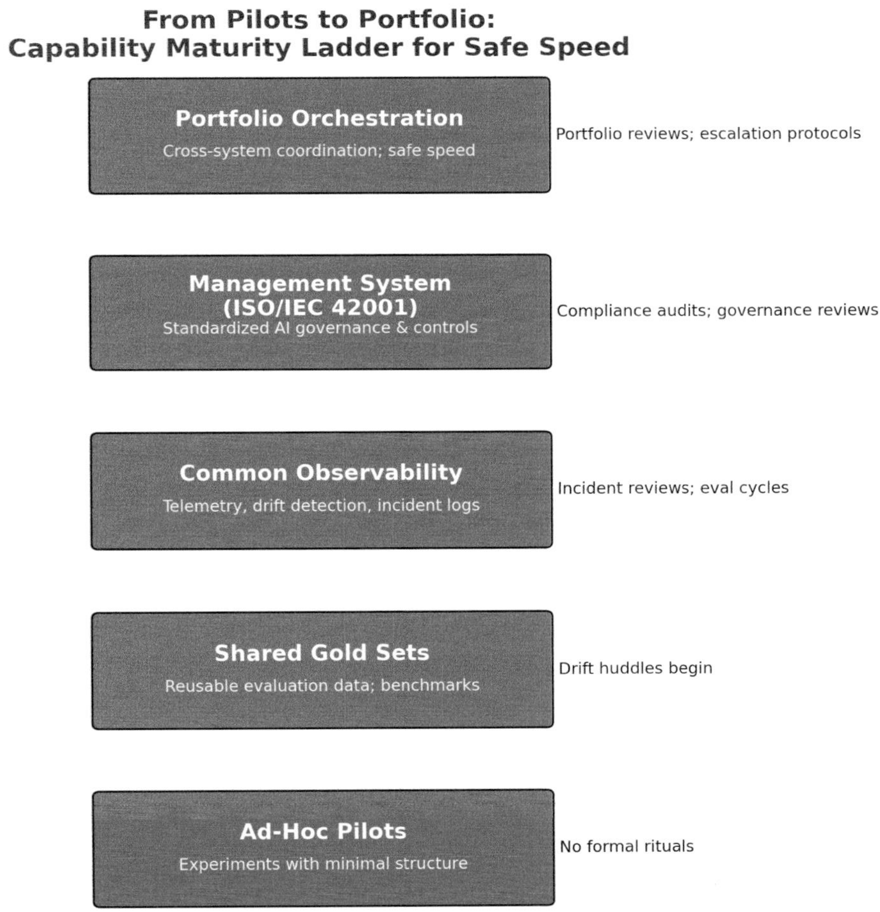

Figure 6.1 Capability Maturity Ladder for Safe Speed.

Shared language is another cornerstone of readiness. Without agreed-upon definitions, debates about fairness, privacy, and quality quickly devolve into gridlock. Model cards, written in accessible language, should describe intended uses, subgroup performance, and known failure modes (Mitchell et al., 2019). Datasheets for datasets should record sources, consent, preprocessing, and limitations so downstream teams inherit context (Gebru et al., 2021). Fairness reviews should identify risks of harm—allocation issues, quality of service disparities, or underrepresentation—and propose proportionate mitigations (Suresh and Guttag, 2021). Security reviews should check for vulnerabilities such as prompt injection, data leakage, or misuse of tool-calling in multi-agent systems (Amodei et al., 2016). Privacy reviews should minimize collection, prioritize local computation, and align disclosures with necessity and proportionality principles (NIST, 2023). When these artifacts are mandatory, teams quickly converge on shared definitions and can focus energy on problem-solving rather than terminology debates (Kotter, 1996). Shared language, in practice, is one of the lowest-cost accelerators of culture change (Schein and Schein, 2016).

Scaling beyond early wins requires an organizational structure that balances experimentation with stewardship. A hub-and-spoke model does this effectively. The central hub provides shared services such as model registries, observability stacks, red-team playbooks, procurement standards, and legal templates so domain teams do not reinvent the wheel (ISO/IEC, 2023a). Spokes—domain teams—bring expertise, test data, and pilot opportunities that ensure real-world outcomes (Amershi et al., 2019). The hub convenes quarterly communities of practice for orchestrators, evaluators, and stewards to exchange patterns and anti-patterns (NIST, 2023). This design keeps innovation close to the problem while ensuring compliance and security practices remain uniform. A chargeback model can make shared services sustainable by pricing their use, clarifying the total cost of ownership, and encouraging responsible consumption (Schein and Schein, 2016). Publishing internal case notes accelerates learning and reduces the likelihood of repeating mistakes (Edmondson, 2019). Hub-and-spoke governance balances speed and control in complex organizations (Papagiannidis et al., 2025).

Additionally, readiness requires attention to people and careers. Evaluators and stewards—often seen as back-office constraints—must be elevated to visible, respected career tracks (Kotter, 1996). Compensation, promotion, and recognition should reward those who improve signal quality, reduce variance, and strengthen guardrails (Table 6.1) (Schein and Schein, 2016). Rotations through evaluation and data stewardship roles should be standard so that product owners and orchestrators internalize risk and documentation practices (Edmondson, 2019). Internal certification programs can validate competencies in acceptance testing, fairness analysis, and incident response through rigorous scenario-based assessments (NIST, 2023). External credentials aligned to management standards like ISO/IEC 42001 or risk frameworks like ISO/IEC 23894 can signal institutional maturity to regulators and partners. Talent reviews should track the depth of the bench in these roles as carefully as in development and design (Argyris and Schön, 1978). Without these incentives, organizations risk reverting to hero-centric delivery that does not scale or withstand scrutiny (Raji et al., 2020). Culture shifts decisively when evaluators and stewards share prestige with builders and sellers.

Table 6.1 RACI for Product Owner, Orchestrator, Evaluator, Data Steward

Lifecycle Phase	***Product Owner***	***Orchestrator***	***Evaluator***	***Data Steward***
Scope & Requirements	A/R	C	C	I
Data Sourcing & Governance	I	C	C	A/R
Build/Integrate (Models & Tools)	A	R	C	C
Evaluate (Gold sets, metrics, safety)	I	C	A/R	C
Release Planning & Risk Review	A/R	C	C	I
Deploy	A	R	C	I
Monitor & Drift Management	I	A/R	C	C
Incident Response	C	A/R	C	C
Retire/Refactor	A/R	C	C	I

Artifacts referenced across phases include: model cards, datasheets, and evidence briefs. Legend: R = Responsible, A = Accountable, C = Consulted, I = Informed. Where "A/R" appears, the role is both Accountable and Responsible.

Metrics must capture value, quality, safety, and learning so that teams are not rewarded for speed alone (Figure 6.2). If an organization only measures throughput—how many tasks or projects are completed—teams will naturally optimize for volume rather than meaningful outcomes. Value metrics, by contrast, focus on whether the work actually delivers benefits, such as shorter cycle times for approvals, reduced decision latency, higher win rates on proposals, or improved patient throughput in healthcare settings without raising costs (Kotter, 1996). Quality metrics matter just as much, assessing task accuracy, calibration of outputs, and robustness when conditions change, all tested against carefully curated gold-standard datasets (Lu et al., 2018). Safety metrics ensure systems are not just effective but also fair and trustworthy, tracking fairness deltas across sensitive groups, recording privacy or security incidents, and monitoring how risks evolve over time (Suresh and Guttag, 2021). Learning metrics measure whether organizations adapt when things go wrong: how quickly corrective actions close after an incident, how complete documentation is, and how often proven solutions are reused across teams (Edmondson, 2019). Dashboards displaying these metrics should include confidence intervals and clearly stated limitations, reminding decision-makers that no metric is perfect and avoiding the trap of false certainty (Breck et al., 2017). Executives must review these metrics with the same seriousness and cadence as financial statements to make accountability routine, not exceptional. The principle is simple: what gets measured drives behavior, so measurement must encompass the entire system—not just the output numbers (Schein and Schein, 2016).

Readiness also depends on supplier governance, since many AI capabilities rely on external vendors for models, data, or services. These external dependencies extend both the organization's attack surface and its risk envelope, which means procurement must move beyond cost negotiations to include risk management (ISO/IEC, 2023b). Contracts should require vendors to provide clear documentation artifacts, security attestations, and options for data localization so that sensitive information does not leave required jurisdictions. Audit rights should be built into agreements, proportional to the level of risk carried by the vendor's product. Vendor models must also be tested against internal gold datasets before deployment, and periodic re-tests should be scheduled whenever models are updated or when data distribution shifts in practice. Procurement teams should work closely with privacy and security officers to enforce data minimization and retention standards for all third-party integrations, ensuring external services do not quietly expand the organization's risk exposure (Gebru et al., 2021). To avoid dependency traps, exit and portability clauses must be non-negotiable, guaranteeing that services and data can be transferred to alternatives if needed (ISO/IEC, 2023a). Supplier-related incidents should flow into the same incident review and learning loops used for internal failures, ensuring that institutional memory captures lessons no matter where the issue originated (Edmondson, 2019). Maintaining a living supplier register that includes risk tiers, required controls, and direct contact paths shortens time-to-mitigation when problems arise. Strong supplier governance completes the readiness picture by aligning external dependencies with internal standards, ensuring consistency and resilience across the organizational ecosystem (ISO/IEC, 2023a).

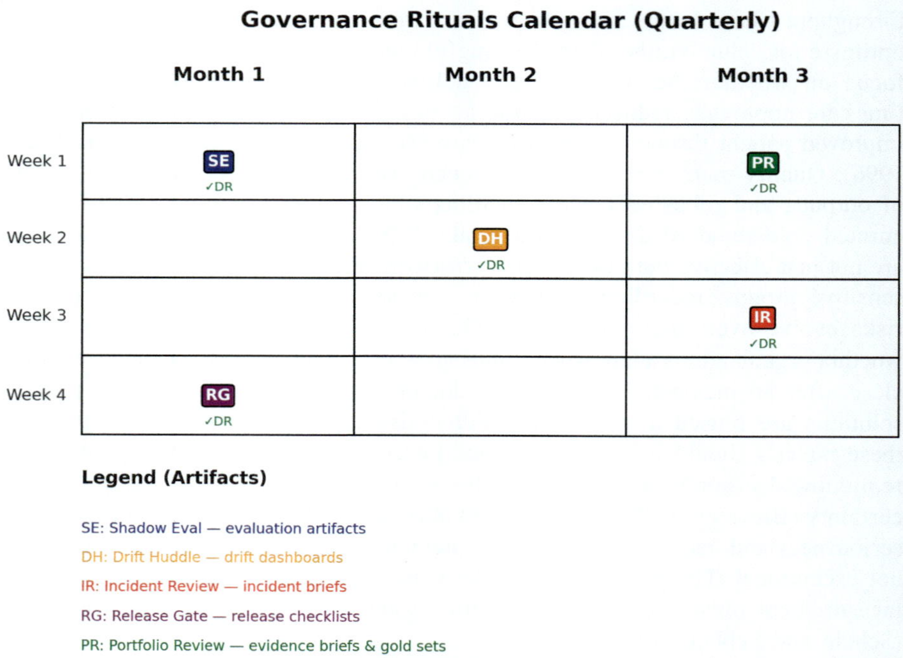

Figure 6.2 Governance Rituals Calendar.

The lessons of this section point to a simple but often overlooked truth: organizational readiness is less about technology and more about culture. Tools may change every quarter, but culture determines who feels safe to experiment, how risk is shared, and whether lessons are captured or lost. By distinguishing between "tools in use" and "tools in culture," institutions can move from one-off wins to habits of learning that compound over time. Culture becomes visible when values are tied to behaviors—experiment visibly, evaluate rigorously, disclose limits—and reinforced by rituals like blameless incident reviews and portfolio-level audits. These practices create the psychological safety needed for people to speak openly about failures, drift, or bias without fear of blame.

Clarity of roles transforms these cultural aspirations into daily reality. When product owners, orchestrators, evaluators, and data stewards each know their lane—and when their responsibilities are documented and auditable—accountability becomes a strength rather than a vulnerability. Governance rituals then stitch those roles together into a living system of practice. Metrics broaden the definition of success, reminding teams that value, quality, safety, and learning all matter as much as throughput. Dashboards that combine accuracy with fairness, decision latency with privacy incidents, cycle time with post-incident learning rates make it impossible to hide behind shallow productivity measures. Executives reviewing these indicators with the same cadence as financials normalize accountability as part of leadership.

Supplier governance closes the loop by extending these standards to external dependencies. Just as internal systems are tested, logged, and audited, so too must vendor-provided models, data, and services be subject to transparency requirements, gold-set evaluations, and exit clauses that preserve reversibility. A living supplier register that categorizes risks and defines escalation paths prevents surprises and speeds response. In effect, governance is not an overhead but the connective tissue that makes innovation trustworthy.

The overarching takeaway is that readiness is not a destination but an ongoing practice: codifying cultural behaviors, clarifying roles, institutionalizing rituals, measuring what matters, and holding vendors to the same standards as internal teams. Leaders who approach readiness this way shift AI adoption from risky heroics to durable, organization-wide competence. They build not just projects, but institutions capable of learning at scale.

6.2 TRAINING PROGRAMS AND COMPETENCY DEVELOPMENT (PROMPTING, EVALUATION, MODULAR FLUENCY)

Training for AI adoption should feel less like a crash course in clever prompting tricks and more like a structured journey from tool fluency to organizational orchestration. Early exposure may begin with simple prompts and "aha" moments, but true readiness demands deeper competencies in evaluation, modular design, and governance. A tiered curriculum helps individuals move step by step from isolated interactions to end-to-end system design and oversight (Amershi et al., 2019). The first tier introduces responsible prompting, documentation habits, and interpreting results against clear baselines, so users can see when a system is genuinely helpful and when it drifts (Clark et al., 2012). The second tier builds technical depth by teaching data preparation, using pattern libraries, and practicing retrieval augmentation, ensuring outputs remain grounded in authoritative sources (Lewis et al., 2020). The third tier focuses on evaluation literacy: learners practice setting acceptance criteria, performing ablation studies, and conducting fairness checks tied to decision risk (Raji et al., 2020). The fourth tier advances to orchestration, where students design workflows that combine multiple agents, human-in-the-loop review, monitoring systems, and rollback plans. Each tier should end with a mentored pilot—small, supervised projects that let learners apply what they know in a real but bounded environment. Debriefs after each pilot capture where theory clashed with practice and turn lessons into reusable playbook entries. The endpoint is not a handful of clever prompts but repeatable decision quality under monitoring.

Evaluation literacy is the foundation because, without evidence, improvements collapse under scrutiny. Learners should learn to construct gold-standard datasets and define "must-not-fail" scenarios, such as compliance-related outputs or safety-critical recommendations (Breck et al., 2017). They should practice sensitivity analyses to see how fragile models become when inputs shift slightly, surfacing brittleness before it causes damage. Fairness diagnostics are essential: learners test for allocation harms, service disparities, and representation gaps across groups (Suresh and Guttag, 2021). Red-teaming exercises push systems to failure on purpose—eliciting unsafe completions, leakage, or jailbreak behaviors—to understand risks before deployment (Amodei et al., 2016). Writing evidence briefs is another key practice: short, executive-ready summaries that explain performance, limits, mitigations, and what remains unknown. Evaluation also means learning to set thresholds tied to decision risk and designing graceful degradation paths when thresholds aren't met. Finally, learners should connect their findings to artifacts like model cards and datasheets so that documentation and evidence stay in sync. When evaluation becomes a shared language, disagreement becomes less about opinion and more about evidence, improving psychological safety across teams.

Modular fluency is just as important because organizations cannot afford to reinvent the wheel every time they adapt a system. Practitioners should master patterns like retrieval-augmented generation, tool-using agents, review queues, and decision buffers—design choices that create space for human oversight in high-risk settings (Lewis et al., 2020). Pattern libraries should include not only "how it works" notes but also "how it fails," outlining common weaknesses such as prompt injection attacks, hallucination risks, or brittle dependencies (Amodei et al., 2016). Exercises should involve swapping components—such as trying different retrievers, rerankers, or model versions—and measuring effects on latency, cost, and accuracy. Documentation discipline matters too: each module should be accompanied by model cards, datasheets, and change logs to make it trustworthy across teams. Continuous integration and deployment should extend beyond code to include data pipelines and evaluation artifacts, ensuring quality checks happen continuously, not just at launch. Shared observability lets teams detect drift, regressions, or abuse before harm spreads (Allam, 2024). Mastering modularity builds both technical competence and cultural resilience, supporting safe speed under changing conditions.

Role-aligned learning paths reduce friction at handoffs by giving each group the skills and questions it needs. Product owners should focus on framing hypotheses, defining value capture, and identifying red lines, particularly in regulated contexts where risk tolerance is low (Papagiannidis et al., 2025). Orchestrators need to practice workflow design, adding guardrails, coordinating agents, and mapping escalation under real latency and cost constraints. Evaluators learn to design metrics, curate golden sets, detect drift, and conduct fairness audits tied to decision risk. Data stewards focus on lineage, consent, retention, and vendor clauses, ensuring provenance and privacy remain intact (Acev et al., 2025). Cross-training strengthens empathy: when orchestrators spend time as evaluators or stewards, they internalize different perspectives and learn shared vocabulary (Lancaster et al., 2025). Capstone projects should require cross-role collaboration on live pilots with executive reviews, simulating the governance pressures of real deployments. This approach builds interlocking competence rather than isolated pockets of expertise, preparing organizations for scalable adoption.

Pedagogy matters as much as content, and research shows that minimal-guidance discovery learning is less effective for complex cognitive tasks (Clark et al., 2012). Instead, guided practice accelerates mastery: worked examples, faded scaffolds, and deliberate practice help learners transfer skills to production environments (Ericsson et al., 1993). The ICAP framework—Interactive, Constructive, Active, Passive—reminds us that interactive and constructive activities lead to deeper learning than passive tasks (Chi and Wylie, 2014). In practice, AI training should involve code-along labs with embedded evaluation checks, fairness prompts, and decision logs that learners must complete and defend. Reflection prompts should ask learners when they would override a system's output and how they would communicate uncertainty to stakeholders. Feedback should be criterion-based, timely, and specific, much like real-world acceptance tests and dashboard reviews. Assessments should include oral defenses and scenario walkthroughs, making it difficult to hide superficial understanding. Pedagogical rigor ensures that operational rigor carries into delivery teams.

Mentored pilots translate classroom learning into operational culture. Learners should be paired with experienced orchestrators and evaluators on bounded projects, such as automating a reporting workflow or testing a retrieval-augmented search tool (Canales et al., 2024). Each pilot defines users, tasks, baselines, acceptance tests, and rollback criteria before work begins, mirroring governance in real deployments. Mid-sprint reviews allow learners to surface risks early, making changes reversible while costs are low. Final demos should include evidence briefs and updated model cards, preparing learners to communicate with executives and compliance officers (Mitchell et al., 2019). Postmortems should be blameless, focusing on systemic lessons rather than individual mistakes, with findings added to the pattern library for reuse. Graduates of these pilots can then serve as mentors for the next cohorts, creating a sustainable cycle of capacity building. Over time, mentored practice becomes a flywheel: training produces mentors, mentors create reusable patterns, and patterns reduce risk and time-to-value.

Domain-specific tracks ensure that training is relevant, because safety, evidence, and governance requirements vary by sector. Health cohorts need deeper content on explainability, documentation, and clinical escalation because mistakes can cause immediate harm (ISO/IEC, 2023b). Public-sector cohorts must focus on transparency, accessibility, and procurement literacy, aligning with obligations for equity and accountability (NIST, 2023). Legal and finance professionals need higher standards for model documentation, version control, and audit readiness, given their exposure to regulatory scrutiny (Mitchell et al., 2019). Creative and marketing teams face different challenges: brand safety, attribution, and privacy controls when using generative tools for public-facing content. Technical cohorts require advanced training in MLOps, CI/CD for data, and observability practices to prevent brittle deployments (Vadde and Munagandla, 2024). All cohorts, regardless of domain, need fairness and privacy content scaled to the level of risk and audience vulnerability (Suresh and Guttag, 2021). Tailored training avoids the pitfall of generic content that collapses under real-world constraints.

Assessment and credentialing must also reward the right behaviors. If training only measures speed or output, it will create perverse incentives that ignore safety and governance. Practical exams should include tasks like building a small retrieval-augmented generation (RAG) system, evaluating it against golden sets, running fairness diagnostics, and planning a rollback procedure (Lewis et al., 2020). Grading rubrics should award points for clarity of acceptance criteria, monitoring design, and post-incident responses, not just accuracy. Portfolios should include evidence briefs, model cards, and datasheets linked to artifacts and baselines, demonstrating traceability from design to evaluation (Zmitrowicz, 2024). Oral defenses should test judgment under uncertainty and communication of risk to executives and frontline staff. Renewal requirements should keep credentials fresh, requiring periodic refreshers on new risks, standards, and sector regulations (ISO/IEC, 2023a). These practices align individual incentives with institutional risk postures, ensuring that training scales into governance. Credentials should signal safe speed, not reckless output.

Change navigation deserves explicit attention because resistance often stems from human concerns rather than technical ones. Micro-modules can teach teams to frame pilots as reversible bets, publish transparent metrics, and run blameless reviews so learning feels safe (Kotter, 1996). Communication drills should give staff practice in explaining system limits, uncertainty, and escalation paths in plain language to build trust. Negotiation exercises should help teams secure data access, compute budgets, and evaluation time in resource-constrained environments (Schein and Schein, 2016). Role-play scenarios can simulate regulator questions, media inquiries, or internal audits, preparing teams for external scrutiny. Leaders should model vulnerability by showcasing canceled pilots with documented rationale, normalizing prudence rather than overconfidence. Teams can maintain a living FAQ that addresses recurring concerns about quality, privacy, fairness, and security in concrete terms (Suresh and Guttag, 2021). Change skills stabilize culture when technology shifts faster than policy.

Supplier literacy must also be part of training because many risks come from outside. Learners should practice evaluating vendors by testing their models against internal golden sets, reviewing security questionnaires, and negotiating privacy addenda that align with institutional requirements (ISO/IEC, 2023b). Exercises can include simulating model upgrades or rollbacks when vendors change terms or telemetry policies. Teams should verify that exit and portability clauses are in place to protect autonomy and user rights (ISO/IEC, 2023a). Joint incident drills should include vendor contacts and service-level agreements so that evidence requirements are clear during crises. Supplier registers that categorize risks and define review cadences can be practiced in the classroom, helping learners anticipate future responsibilities. Training that spans institutional boundaries ensures internal excellence does not collapse when external dependencies fail. Supplier-aware training prepares organizations for safe scale in AI adoption.

The core lesson from this section is that training cannot stop at prompt tricks or isolated technical skills—it must prepare people to design, evaluate, and govern systems as part of an organizational culture. A readiness mindset means teaching not just how to use a tool, but how to judge its value, recognize its limits, and know when to pull the plug. Tiered learning pathways give individuals a gradual progression, from basic prompting to orchestration and governance, ensuring no one is left with half-formed skills that don't scale to production. Mentored pilots, role-specific curricula, and domain-sensitive tracks make training authentic and applicable, helping learners see how their decisions fit into broader organizational outcomes.

Equally important, evaluation literacy shifts the conversation from "what looks good" to "what holds up under scrutiny." By building comfort with fairness checks, drift detection, and graceful degradation plans, teams learn to disagree constructively using evidence rather than status or intuition. Modular fluency reinforces this by treating systems as building blocks that can be swapped, tested, and reused safely under pressure. When these practices are ingrained, organizations avoid brittle one-off solutions and instead develop reusable patterns that shorten time-to-value.

The larger takeaway is that training is not a classroom event but an engine of culture. Guided practice, evidence-based feedback, and realistic assessments instill habits that later become governance rituals. When stewards, evaluators, orchestrators, and product owners are trained to understand each other's responsibilities, handoffs become smoother and accountability becomes shared rather than avoided. Supplier literacy ensures external dependencies are held to the same standards, keeping risks visible even when they come from outside the organization.

In the end, competency development is less about filling a skills gap and more about shaping a mindset: curiosity anchored by controls, innovation balanced by reversibility, and speed tempered by evidence. Training that follows this path produces not just technically fluent staff but culturally aligned professionals who know how to navigate uncertainty, protect trust, and turn lessons into playbooks for others. It is this flywheel of learning, mentoring, and pattern reuse that transforms isolated adoption experiments into durable, organization-wide readiness.

6.3 OVERCOMING RESISTANCE AND RAISING AI LITERACY ACROSS ROLES

Resistance must be named before it can be navigated. Many culture-level fears—loss of status, worries about quality, or anxieties about compliance—often show up as technical objections, slowing experimentation that could be managed safely (Gruenewald and Mueller, 2025). Status threat emerges when experts worry their judgment or prestige will be diminished. Quality concerns arise when acceptance criteria are unclear, and compliance anxiety spikes when privacy, security, or fairness duties feel undefined or constantly shifting (Hutson, 2025). A practical way forward is to create a shared risk taxonomy that ties every proposed use case to decision criticality, possible harm pathways, and proportional controls. Teams should spotlight allocation harms, service disparities, and representational harms early, since these can be measured and mitigated rather than left abstract (Suresh and Guttag, 2021). Supplier and model dependencies should also be mapped to show where external change could create internal vulnerabilities (ISO/IEC, 2023b). Documentation then grounds these conversations by making intended use, limitations, and subgroup performance part of everyday vocabulary rather than rarefied audit jargon. When disagreements shift from opinion to evidence, organizations can bound experiments without suffocating them (Schein and Schein, 2016).

Transparent metrics and reversible experiments are effective antidotes to quality concerns. Each pilot should begin with baseline performance, acceptance thresholds, and must-not-fail cases written down before any claims of success are made. Run-time monitors and rollback triggers should be designed upfront so reversals are seen as governance working, not as embarrassing failures. Decision logs—capturing who changed what, when, and with which tests—turn organizational memory into an asset, helping shorten the learning curve for future projects (Mezzina et al., 2025). Executives should review these artifacts with the same seriousness as financial reports, signaling that quality and safety are first-class performance goals. Teams then learn to argue from shared evidence rather than hierarchy, which increases psychological safety for dissenting perspectives. Reversibility lowers the political cost of caution while raising the standard of scientific rigor (Edmondson, 2019).

Frontline staff play a decisive role in adoption, so co-design with practitioners is critical. Workshops should bring out tacit knowledge, exception handling, and "known bads" that often never make it into documentation but shape real practice (Amershi et al., 2019). Interfaces should be designed to show system confidence scores, links to provenance, and quick ways to correct outputs so humans supervise actively rather than rubber-stamp results. Fairness and error trade-offs should be framed as selectable policies so that accountability for value choices rests with domain experts, not hidden in the code (Suresh and Guttag, 2021). Early pilots must constrain scope to reversible, bounded tasks while guaranteeing human override rights. Trust accumulates through lived experience rather than promises, so debriefs should reward surfacing failure modes as much as celebrating wins.

When frontline staff see their practical constraints encoded in workflows, they reciprocate with higher-quality data and operational care (Malik et al., 2025).

Communication also determines whether literacy gaps harden into resistance. Plain-language "evidence briefs" can summarize task scope, baselines, acceptance criteria, fairness checks, and known limitations for executives, compliance teams, and practitioners alike (NIST, 2023). Model cards and datasheets should accompany production components so information about intended use, data provenance, and subgroup performance is accessible without needing an audit. Visual examples of good and bad outputs, archived with context on why errors matter, transform quality from an abstract concept into shared craft knowledge. Leaders should narrate canceled pilots with the same visibility as successful ones to normalize prudence as a professional virtue (Edmondson, 2019). FAQs tied to specific use cases, where every answer points to a test, a policy, or a documented limit, reduce rumors and folk theories (NIST, 2023). When uncertainty is made speakable and evidence visible, people can engage without pretense or fear (Schein and Schein, 2016).

Incidents will happen, and how they are handled can either erode trust or strengthen it. Escalation trees should specify who receives alerts, what evidence must be captured, and when compliance or external stakeholders must be notified, making responses predictable under stress (NIST, 2023). Monitoring should track drift in both inputs and outcomes so distribution shifts are caught before harm accumulates (Lu et al., 2018). Post-incident reviews should focus on system factors, test coverage, and thresholds, producing updates to playbooks and documentation instead of individual blame (Breck et al., 2017). Near-misses should also be logged and shared, since "no harm today" may reflect luck rather than robustness (Argyris and Schön, 1978). Regular portfolio-level summaries promote cross-team learning and discourage repeating mistakes in parallel. De-identified lessons can be published internally or externally, fostering legitimacy with both staff and regulators. This cadence reinforces a culture that values candor over concealment (Edmondson, 2019).

Resistance often concentrates at role boundaries, where misunderstandings about accountability slow progress. Role-aligned literacy reduces friction by clarifying the questions each group must ask and answer. Product owners learn how to frame hypotheses, capture value, and define red lines for acceptable risk (Kotter, 1996). Orchestrators practice workflow design, guardrails, and escalation mapping to ensure human oversight lands where it matters most (Amershi et al., 2019). Evaluators focus on metric design, golden-set curation, drift detection, and fairness auditing so claims remain testable and comparable (Raji et al., 2020). Data stewards gain expertise in lineage, consent, retention, and vendor clauses so provenance and privacy are built into systems from the start (Gebru et al., 2021). Cross-training across adjacent roles fosters empathy and shared vocabulary, helping prevent bottlenecks at handoffs (Edmondson, 2019). Capstone projects that require cross-role collaboration on live pilots with executive review simulate real governance rhythms and build trust before scale (NIST, 2023).

Job design also shapes resistance. Adoption reads as threatening when framed as displacement, but it becomes an opportunity when framed as enrichment and skill growth. Redistribution of labor should emphasize that machines handle drafting and summarizing while humans focus on judgment, negotiation, and explanation (Edmondson, 2019). Progression rubrics should explicitly reward time spent on evaluation, mentoring, and supervision so these activities are visible and promotable rather than hidden toil (Schein and Schein, 2016). Career paths should elevate evaluator and steward roles to parity with engineering and product roles, reducing perceptions that governance is "second-class" work (Kotter, 1996). Leadership should highlight promotions and awards for those who improved quality or canceled unsafe pilots, making governance visible as achievement (NIST, 2023). Tracking time returned to higher-value work as systems stabilize counters narratives of job loss with evidence of enrichment (Argyris and Schön, 1978). Where genuine displacement occurs, retraining and internal mobility should come before external cuts to preserve trust (Edmondson, 2019).

Compliance anxiety is real, especially in regulated domains, and it must be addressed proactively. Embedding policy pathways into system design makes conformance a natural by-product of engineering rather than paperwork after the fact. Management-system controls should set expectations for risk assessments, acceptance tests, monitoring, incident logs, and status checks so teams know what "good" looks like before they begin (ISO/IEC, 2023a). Privacy reviews should minimize data collection, localize computation where possible, and align disclosures with necessity and proportionality principles (NIST, 2023). Security reviews should test for injection, leakage, and over-broad tool permissions to preempt misuse (Amodei et al., 2016). Fairness reviews should select metrics and mitigations proportional to the level of harm at stake, with documented trade-offs approved by leadership (Suresh and Guttag, 2021). Procurement teams should enforce requirements for exportability, audit rights, and supplier cooperation so external risk is managed with the same rigor as internal risk (ISO/IEC, 2023a). When policy is engineered in, compliance stops being a blocker and becomes an enabler of safe scale (NIST, 2023).

Equity concerns require attention because risks compound quietly when they are not measured. Subgroup performance reporting should be routine for high-impact systems so disparities are visible instead of buried in averages (Suresh and Guttag, 2021). Appeals should be easy to find, simple to file, and time-bound so ordinary users can trigger review without specialist knowledge or social capital (Edmondson, 1999). Interfaces must avoid dark patterns that pressure users into over-disclosure or hide dissent options, aligning with the spirit of fairness rather than its formalities (Selbst et al., 2019). Outreach should explain what data is collected, how it is used, and how redress works to build trust. Community advisory input should be built into systems that affect rights or entitlements, with meeting notes and actions published for accountability (Schein and Schein, 2016). Equity becomes real when measurement, recourse, and participation are engineered as core features, not afterthoughts (Raji et al., 2020).

Incentives close the loop by ensuring safe practices are rewarded the same way revenue is rewarded. Quarterly reviews should incorporate value, quality, safety, and learning metrics so teams cannot game one dimension at the expense of others (NIST, 2023). Leadership stories should highlight people who improved data quality, tightened guardrails, or canceled unsafe pilots, making these visible achievements rather than invisible sacrifices (Edmondson, 2019). Communities of practice can curate patterns and anti-patterns with credited authorship, spreading wisdom while elevating the prestige of stewardship work (Schein and Schein, 2016). Budgeting processes must protect evaluator and steward roles so governance capacity is not cut under pressure (ISO/IEC, 2023a). Performance targets should match maturity stage so pilot teams are not punished for failing to meet portfolio-level expectations (Papagiannidis et al., 2025). When incentives, recognition, and structures align, curiosity thrives under control, and resistance gives way to responsible participation.

6.4 CASE STUDIES: SUCCESSFUL STRATEGIES FOR INSTITUTIONAL ADOPTION

Safety-critical environments offer some of the clearest lessons for adoption done responsibly. A regional health network piloted a triage summarization assistant that drafted risk-flagged notes for nurses, but it was never allowed to make a diagnosis on its own (NIST, 2023). The product owner deliberately limited scope to intake narratives and required that any "must-not-fail" cases be escalated to human-only review whenever confidence dropped below pre-declared thresholds. Evaluators built gold test sets that included patients from across age, gender, and demographic groups to detect service disparities and tuned thresholds to emphasize sensitivity—better to raise a few extra false alarms than to miss a serious condition (Suresh and Guttag, 2021). Drift monitors tracked seasonal changes, such as spikes in respiratory illness, and triggered conservative modes until retraining was completed (Lu et al., 2018). Datasheets and model cards documented exactly what the assistant could and could not do, allowing clinicians and compliance teams to inspect claims easily (Mitchell et al., 2019). Importantly, deployment was reversible: early weeks included rollback gates so that turning the system off was seen as governance, not failure (Argyris and Schön, 1978). The end result was faster triage decisions, reduced back-and-forth in documentation, and stronger clinician trust because override authority always remained with humans (Edmondson, 2019).

Education offers a different but equally revealing example. One university introduced a feedback assistant that suggested rubric-aligned comments for instructors but required human acceptance and logged all edits (Amershi et al., 2019). The orchestrator constrained the tool to comment templates linked to course outcomes and banned grade assignment entirely, avoiding the conflation of formative guidance with summative judgment (NIST, 2023). Evaluators tested outputs against gold sets of exemplar feedback to ensure tone, relevance, and actionability across diverse student groups (Breck et al., 2017). Model cards and datasheets documented intended use and training data provenance so faculty governance had oversight (Mitchell et al., 2019). Each term ended with debrief sessions where instructors reported where the assistant saved time and where it caused friction, leading to updates in templates and policies (Argyris and Schön, 1978). Crucially, override was expected and dissent fed reform rather than punishment, which improved psychological safety (Edmondson, 2019). Within two terms, the turnaround time for actionable feedback dropped while student complaints about opacity decreased, showing that speed can be safely paired with transparency.

Public agencies demonstrate how careful scoping can avoid political backlash. A city benefits office piloted a triage assistant that flagged applications for manual review based on completeness and risk of deadline breach, but never predicted eligibility for entitlements (NIST, 2023). Product owners deliberately tied metrics to service levels—such as reducing backlog and preventing missed deadlines—rather than to high-stakes eligibility outcomes (ISO/IEC, 2023b). Evaluators added fairness checks to monitor whether wait times differed across neighborhoods or language groups, aligning directly with equity obligations (Suresh and Guttag, 2021). Drift detection flagged surges after policy changes, giving the agency a chance to reallocate staff before queues ballooned (Lu et al., 2018). Documentation artifacts were published for council oversight and included clear complaint channels (Mitchell et al., 2019). When a near-miss highlighted weaknesses in escalation rules, the team revised procedures in a blameless review rather than punishing the staff who reported it (Edmondson, 2019). By separating assistance from adjudication and designing reversibility into the workflow, the agency improved throughput without undermining procedural justice.

Manufacturing plants provide a more operational perspective. One facility deployed predictive maintenance with human-in-the-loop review to cut downtime on critical production lines (Breck et al., 2017). The orchestrators inserted the assistant before maintenance scheduling, ensuring humans cross-checked alerts with vibration and thermal sensor data to avoid complacency (Sculley et al., 2015). Evaluators created scenario tests to measure both false alarms and missed detections, tracking how cost, latency, and accuracy traded off under different models (Breck et al., 2017). Drift monitors tracked changes in sensor quality and seasonal environment shifts, prompting recalibration after summer heat waves or layout changes on the floor (Lu et al., 2018). Documentation captured updated thresholds and rationales, so audits could reconstruct why decisions were made. Reversible experiments compared competing pipelines with shadow traffic for two months before a final decision, avoiding lock-in (Argyris and Schön, 1978). Results showed less unplanned downtime and greater supervisor confidence, precisely because authority remained visibly human (Edmondson, 2019).

Legal operations illustrate how constraints can protect reputation while enabling efficiency. An in-house legal team adopted a contract-support assistant that drafted clause suggestions and flagged deviations from playbooks but left all edits and sign-offs to attorneys (Mitchell et al., 2019). The product owner confined use to low-risk vendor agreements in early stages and prohibited any client-facing drafts (ISO/IEC, 2023a). Evaluators built gold sets from prior negotiations to measure precision and recall on deviations and tracked how many suggestions lawyers accepted as a quality signal (Breck et al., 2017). Datasheets documented the sources of clause libraries and licensing terms to protect IP hygiene (Gebru et al., 2021). Ambiguous suggestions were analyzed in incident reviews and then used to update prompts and playbooks (Argyris and Schön, 1978). Attorneys trained in plain-language uncertainty communication so they could explain that drafts were advisory, not authoritative (Edmondson, 2019). Over several quarters, turnaround time fell without harming quality, supporting gradual expansion to higher-value contract classes under tighter controls (ISO/IEC, 2023a).

Customer service adoption highlights how visibility builds trust. A support organization deployed a retrieval-augmented summarizer that pulled case histories and suggested responses with citations (Lewis et al., 2020). Orchestrators required that every reply include source links so human agents could verify before sending (Amershi et al., 2019). Evaluators tracked first-contact resolution, handle time, and escalation rates while randomly auditing for hallucinations (NIST, 2023). Fairness checks monitored performance across languages and accessibility needs (Suresh and Guttag, 2021). Datasheets documented update schedules for the knowledge base and flagged repeated failures on certain topics (Gebru et al., 2021). Reversible experiments compared agent-assist versus auto-draft variants, rolling back whenever guardrail violations spiked (Argyris and Schön, 1978). Results showed quicker resolution and fewer copy-paste errors, with agents reporting higher trust because provenance was visible and override was expected (Edmondson, 2019).

Hiring offers another instructive case. An HR team piloted a screening assistant that bundled applicant evidence by skills but left all selection decisions to humans working with structured rubrics (Raji et al., 2020). Product owners explicitly banned automated rejection and required justification fields tied to rubric criteria for every decision (NIST, 2023). Evaluators monitored subgroup error rates and adverse impact ratios to detect disparities early (Suresh and Guttag, 2021). Datasheets documented the provenance of embeddings and feature extraction models, allowing targeted remediation if bias crept in (Gebru et al., 2021). User interfaces emphasized consent and selective disclosure for sensitive attributes (ISO/IEC, 2023b). Appeals were made visible and time-bound, providing recourse for candidates and feedback for policy updates (Edmondson, 1999). Over two hiring cycles, managers reported clearer evidence bundles and fewer résumé fabrications, showing that fairness and efficiency can reinforce one another when governance is embedded (Raji et al., 2020).

Financial services underline the importance of external dependencies. A risk group piloted an analyst-assist workflow that generated structured memos for know-your-customer reviews, complete with cited sources and confidence bands (NIST, 2023). Orchestrators required that external data stay in read-only sandboxes and prohibited personal data from being stored in prompt histories (ISO/IEC, 2023b). Evaluators ran red-team prompts to elicit over-confident claims and tracked refusal rates for risky requests (Amodei et al., 2016). Monitoring flagged when supplier models were updated, triggering re-tests against gold sets before production resumed (Breck et al., 2017). Documentation artifacts were audited quarterly, and incident drills rehearsed regulator questions (NIST, 2023). The reversible-bet strategy allowed fast rollback when a supplier changed telemetry terms, preserving compliance posture (ISO/IEC, 2023a). Over time, memos became more reliable while review latency dropped, demonstrating value without diminishing accountability (Edmondson, 2019).

Municipal services show how adoption can build public trust. A planning office introduced a document-routing assistant that classified submissions and assembled checklists for human review but left all approval authority intact (NIST, 2023). Orchestrators limited scope to intake tasks to avoid premature automation of contested decisions (ISO/IEC, 2023b). Evaluators stress-tested the system with edge-case documents and tracked false-routing rates across neighborhoods (Breck et al., 2017). Public model cards and briefs documented intended use, evaluation results, and complaint channels (Mitchell et al., 2019). Drift monitors flagged seasonal spikes in certain project types, prompting retraining (Lu et al., 2018). Executive reviews tied budgets to artifact completeness and incident close-outs, aligning incentives with governance rather than throughput. Cycle time improved while appeal rates held steady, showing that efficiency gains did not come at the expense of fairness (Edmondson, 2019).

Research institutions provide another perspective, focusing on institutional memory. One organization deployed a retrieval-augmented assistant to surface prior studies, decisions, and post-mortems for new proposals (Lewis et al., 2020). Orchestrators required source links and date stamps in every answer and added a "show counter-evidence" button to combat confirmation bias (Amershi et al., 2019). Evaluators tracked citation accuracy and proposal cycle time, while datasheets documented corpus coverage and gaps (Gebru et al., 2021). Change-control procedures paused the assistant whenever upstream model versions changed until re-tests passed (Sculley et al., 2015). Incident reviews after misleading summaries created new negative tests and user warnings (NIST, 2023). The assistant improved decision quality by making institutional memory accessible while preserving human judgment about next steps (Edmondson, 2019).

Across all of these examples, the most important finding is that success came not from novelty alone but from embedding cultural and governance practices into each step. Health networks thrived by enforcing human oversight and reversibility. Universities built trust by clarifying boundaries between formative and summative tasks. Public agencies managed compliance anxiety with transparency and procedural fairness. Manufacturing plants and financial firms hardened safety and accountability by testing rigorously and documenting decisions. Legal and HR teams strengthened legitimacy by restricting early use and aligning outputs to established playbooks and rubrics. In each case, the common denominator was safe speed: governance rituals, role clarity, and reversible bets that allowed organizations to learn quickly without gambling on legitimacy.

Upon reflection then, the central claim of this chapter is that organizational culture, far more than technical horsepower, determines whether emerging technologies generate lasting value or fade into novelty. Culture comes alive not through lofty statements but through the everyday work of roles, rituals, and artifacts that normalize safe experimentation. Product owners, orchestrators, evaluators, and stewards together form the minimal governance quorum that converts scattered trials into auditable practice. Their efforts are sustained by routines such as drift huddles, incident reviews, and portfolio audits, all of which anchor institutional memory. Readiness is not outsourced to tools; it is enacted through decision logs, model cards, datasheets, and post-incident reviews that preserve why and how choices were made.

A useful practitioner summary for this approach is as follows:

Practitioner Summary: Building Technology-Ready Organizational Cultures

Core Message

Culture—not tools—determines whether technology adoption creates lasting value or erodes trust. Readiness comes from roles, rituals, and routines that make safe experimentation normal and auditable.

1. Culture First, Tools Second

- Draft a *culture charter* that spells out expected behaviors: experiment visibly, evaluate rigorously, and disclose limits.
- Make culture observable through rituals—incident reviews, drift huddles, and portfolio audits—that repeat regardless of staff turnover.
- Treat reversibility as a strength: canceling or rolling back a pilot signals governance, not failure.

2. Role Clarity Anchors Accountability

- Assign four core roles to every project:
  - Product Owner – defines hypotheses, value, and red lines.
  - Orchestrator – designs workflows and guardrails.
  - Evaluator – builds gold sets, metrics, and monitors for drift.
  - Data Steward – manages lineage, consent, retention, and provenance.
- One person may hold multiple hats in small teams, but responsibilities must remain visible and auditable.

3. Metrics Beyond Speed

- Track **value** (cycle time, decision latency), **quality** (accuracy, robustness), **safety** (fairness, privacy, security), and **learning** (incident closure, reuse of playbooks).
- Show confidence intervals and known limitations to prevent false certainty.
- Review these indicators with the same seriousness as financial metrics.

4. Training as a Flywheel

- Design tiered training: start with responsible prompting, then progress to evaluation, orchestration, and governance.
- Pair classroom content with *mentored pilots* that turn theory into lived practice.
- Role-specific curricula (owners, orchestrators, evaluators, stewards) create interlocking competence.
- Graduates of pilots become mentors, spreading practice sustainably.

5. Managing Resistance

- **Status threat** → Frame adoption as skill enrichment, not replacement.
- **Quality fears** → Use transparent baselines and reversible experiments.
- **Compliance anxiety** → Build policy into design so oversight is routine, not retrofitted.
- Psychological safety grows when dissent is tied to evidence artifacts instead of hierarchy.

6. Governance of Suppliers

- Require vendors to provide documentation, security attestations, and audit rights.
- Re-test vendor models against internal gold sets after each update.
- Insist on portability and exit clauses to avoid lock-in.
- Maintain a *living supplier register* with risk tiers and escalation paths.

7. Lessons from Case Studies

- **Healthcare**—trust rose when assistants flagged risks but nurses retained authority.
- **Education**—feedback tools saved time while instructors kept grading control.
- **Public services**—triage assistants improved throughput without deciding eligibility.
- **Manufacturing**—predictive maintenance reduced downtime with human cross-checks.
- **Legal & HR**—contract and hiring assistants worked only when outputs stayed advisory and governance was explicit.

Furthermore, training programs carry this cultural DNA into the future by teaching learners to move beyond tactical tool use toward orchestration and governance. The shift from simple prompting to workflow design shows participants not just how to produce outputs, but how to evaluate them, monitor for drift, and prepare fallback strategies. Curricula tailored to roles and sectors ensure that questions are asked at the right level of depth, while mentored pilots turn classroom theory into lived competence. Over time, this training creates a flywheel: learners become mentors, mentors create playbooks, and playbooks embed muscle memory across leadership transitions and technology cycles.

Resistance, while unavoidable, can be harnessed when treated as a rational response rather than obstruction. Status concerns ease when adoption is framed as skill enrichment rather than replacement. Quality fears diminish when metrics and reversible experiments make learning under uncertainty safe. Compliance anxiety recedes when policy pathways are embedded into design rather than bolted on afterward. Psychological safety grows as dissent is channeled through evidence briefs, test sets, and documentation so that debate is about systems, not individuals. In this way, skepticism becomes a safeguard and resistance turns into constructive participation.

Case studies from healthcare, education, public services, manufacturing, law, finance, and municipal planning show that cycle time and decision quality can improve without compromising equity or accountability. Success hinged not on novelty but on bounded pilots, transparent artifacts, and reversible deployments. Incidents were treated as learning opportunities rather than crises, fairness was made measurable, and governance was reframed as a shared service rather than a compliance tax. The diversity of examples demonstrates that readiness is not confined to a single sector—it is a transferable institutional capability once codified.

The significance of these findings is that scaling intelligent systems responsibly requires sociotechnical design, where incentives, training, and governance align curiosity with control. Without culture, adoption fragments into isolated wins that erode trust; with culture, adoption compounds into reusable practices that accelerate both value and safety. The maturity ladder provides a roadmap from one-off pilots to orchestrated portfolios, but its rungs are climbed only when leadership, staff, and governance act in concert. Future research should examine how different organizational structures affect progression along this ladder, how metrics can best balance efficiency with fairness, and how training can scale sustainably without creating new inequities.

In the end, building technology-ready cultures means designing for augmentation: humans supported rather than displaced, judgment strengthened rather than diminished, and equity safeguarded rather than assumed. When evidence, transparency, and learning become habitual, institutions shift from experimenting with new tools to embedding them as trusted components of organizational life. The promise is not simply faster outcomes but more resilient, accountable, and equitable ones—hallmarks of cultures prepared to thrive amid continual change.

REFERENCES

Acev, D., Biyani, S., Rieder, F., Aldenhoff, T.T., Blazevic, M., Riehle, D.M., et al. 2025. Systematic analysis of data governance frameworks and their relevance to data trusts. Management Review Quarterly. 1–56.

Allam, H. 2024. Shift-left observability: Embedding insights from code to production. International Journal of AI, BigData, Computational and Management Studies. 5(2): 58–69.

Amershi, S., Weld, D., Vorvoreanu, M., Fourney, A., Nushi, B., Collisson, P., et al. 2019. Guidelines for human-AI interaction. *In*: Proceedings of the 2019 CHI Conference on Human Factors in Computing Systems. 1–13. https://doi.org/10.1145/3290605.3300233

Amodei, D., Olah, C., Steinhardt, J., Christiano, P., Schulman, J. and Mané, D. 2016. Concrete problems in AI safety. arXiv preprint arXiv:1606.06565. https://arxiv.org/abs/1606.06565

Argyris, C. and Schön, D.A. 1978. Organizational Learning: A Theory of Action Perspective. Addison-Wesley.

Breck, E., Cai, S., Nielsen, E., Salib, M. and Sculley, D. 2017. The ML test score: A rubric for ML production readiness and technical debt reduction. *In*: 2017 IEEE International Conference on Big Data, pp. 1123–1132. https://doi.org/10.1109/BigData.2017.8258038

Canales, R., Bradbury, M., Sheldon, A. and Cannon, C. 2024. Evidence in practice: How structural and programmatic scaffolds enable collaboration in international development. Administrative Science Quarterly. 69(3): 655–710.

Chi, M.T.H. and Wylie, R. 2014. The ICAP framework: Linking cognitive engagement to active learning outcomes. Educational Psychologist. 49(4): 219–243. https://doi.org/10.1080/00461520.2014.965823

Clark, R.E., Kirschner, P.A. and Sweller, J. 2012. Putting students on the path to learning: The case for fully guided instruction. American Educator. 36(1): 6–11.

Edmondson, A.C. 1999. Psychological safety and learning behavior in work teams. Administrative Science Quarterly. 44(2): 350–383. https://doi.org/10.2307/2666999

Edmondson, A.C. 2019. The Fearless Organization: Creating Psychological Safety in the Workplace for Learning, Innovation, and Growth. Wiley.

Ericsson, K.A., Krampe, R.T. and Tesch-Römer, C. 1993. The role of deliberate practice in the acquisition of expert performance. Psychological Review. 100(3): 363–406. https://doi.org/10.1037/0033-295X.100.3.363

Gebru, T., Morgenstern, J., Vecchione, B., Vaughan, J.W., Wallach, H., Daumé III, H., et al. 2021. Datasheets for datasets. Communications of the ACM. 64(12): 86–92. https://doi.org/10.1145/3458723

Gruenewald, H. and Mueller, M. 2025. Leadership and corporate culture in the context of reskilling and upskilling. *In*: Reskilling and Upskilling in a Globalized Economy: Essential Strategies for Workforce Transformation, pp. 135–165. Wiesbaden: Springer Fachmedien Wiesbaden.

Hutson, J. 2025. The Adoption of Artificial Intelligence and Inertia in Higher Education: Exploring Complex Resistance to Technological Change. Taylor & Francis.

ISO/IEC. 2023a. ISO/IEC 42001:2023 Artificial intelligence—Management system. International Organization for Standardization and International Electrotechnical Commission.

ISO/IEC. 2023b. ISO/IEC 23894:2023 Information technology—Artificial intelligence—Risk management. International Organization for Standardization and International Electrotechnical Commission.

Kotter, J.P. 1996. Leading Change. Harvard Business School Press.

Lancaster, C.M., Duan, W., Mallick, R. and McNeese, N.J. 2025. Human-Centered Team Training for Human-AI Teams: From Training with AI Tools to Training for AI Teammates. Proceedings of the ACM on Human-Computer Interaction. 9(2): 1–38.

Lewis, P., Perez, E., Piktus, A., Petroni, F., Karpukhin, V., Goyal, N., et al. 2020. Retrieval-augmented generation for knowledge-intensive NLP. Advances in Neural Information Processing Systems. 33: 9459–9474.

Lu, J., Liu, A., Li, J. and Zhang, G. 2018. Learning under concept drift: A review. *In*: IEEE Transactions on Knowledge and Data Engineering. 31(12): 2346–2363. https://doi.org/10.1109/TKDE.2018.2876857

Malik, A., Wankhade, P., Patnaik, S. and Budhwar, P. 2025. Renegotiating HRM Practices and Delivering Service Transformation of Frontline Workers: Insights from the UK's NHS Ambulance Trust During a Significant Disruption. Human Resource Management.

Mezzina, C.A., Tiezzi, F. and Yoshida, N. 2025. Checkpoint-based rollback recovery in session programming. Logical Methods in Computer Science. 21.

Mitchell, M., Wu, S., Zaldivar, A., Barnes, P., Vasserman, L., Hutchinson, B., et al. 2019. Model cards for model reporting. *In*: Proceedings of the Conference on Fairness, Accountability, and Transparency, 220–229. https://doi.org/10.1145/3287560.3287596

National Institute of Standards and Technology (NIST). 2023. Artificial Intelligence Risk Management Framework (AI RMF 1.0. U.S. Department of Commerce). https://doi.org/10.6028/NIST.AI.100-1

Papagiannidis, S., Mikalef, P. and Conboy, K. 2025. Developing AI readiness in organizations: A socio-technical perspective. European Journal of Information Systems. 34(1): 1–19.

Raji, I.D., Smart, A., White, R.N., Kleinberg, B., Hutchinson, B., Mitchell, M., et al. 2020. Closing the AI accountability gap: Defining auditing and supporting evidence. *In*: Proceedings of the 2020 Conference on Fairness, Accountability, and Transparency, 33–44. https://doi.org/10.1145/3351095.3372873

Schein, E.H. and Schein, P.A. 2016. Organizational Culture and Leadership (5th Ed). Wiley.

Sculley, D., Holt, G., Golovin, D., Davydov, E., Phillips, T., Ebner, D., et al. 2015. Hidden technical debt in machine learning systems. Advances in Neural Information Processing Systems. 28: 2503–2511.

Selbst, A.D., Boyd, D., Friedler, S.A., Venkatasubramanian, S. and Vertesi, J. 2019. Fairness and abstraction in sociotechnical systems. Communications of the ACM. 61(6): 36–43. https://doi.org/10.1145/3287560

Suresh, H. and Guttag, J.V. 2021. A framework for understanding unintended consequences of machine learning. *In*: Proceedings of the 2021 ACM Conference on Fairness, Accountability, and Transparency, 695–706. https://doi.org/10.1145/3287560.3287571

Vadde, B.C. and Munagandla, V.B. 2024. DevOps in the age of machine learning: Bridging the gap between development and data science. International Journal of Machine Learning Research in Cybersecurity and Artificial Intelligence. 15(1): 530–544.

Zmitrowicz, K. 2024. Requirements engineering. *In*: Business Analysis Done Right: Lessons Learned and Pitfalls Avoided. pp. 197–302. Cham: Springer Nature Switzerland.

Chapter 7

Custom AI Solutions—Practical Applications Across Domains

7.1 SECTOR-SPECIFIC SOLUTIONS: HEALTHCARE, EDUCATION, PUBLIC SECTOR, AND CREATIVE INDUSTRIES

Designing sector-specific solutions begins by translating general architecture patterns into domain outcomes. The same building block—retrieval-augmented generation—may reduce hallucinations across fields, but the way it is deployed in a hospital differs from its use in classrooms or city offices (Yang et al., 2025). In healthcare, retrieval supports assistive counsel, summarizing clinical guidelines without overstepping into diagnosis. In education, solutions emphasize formative feedback linked to rubrics, ensuring students receive guidance without compromising grading integrity (Amershi et al., 2019). Public-sector systems lean on document triage that prioritizes workloads without making eligibility decisions, which protects procedural justice. Creative industries prioritize multi-tool co-creation, enabling human–machine collaboration in design, media, and storytelling with attribution logs to safeguard authorship (Labkoff et al., 2024). Governance in these contexts shifts from abstract policy to operational guardrails such as acceptance thresholds, drift monitors, and appeal paths that make quality auditable (Labkoff et al., 2024). Table 7.1 summarizes these emphases, highlighting the different ways architecture is adapted to context while retaining the same foundational principles.

Across all four domains, the operational logic converges: retrieval reduces error, guardrails structure accountability, and user experience ensures humans

DOI: 10.1201/9781003688013-7

remain in charge. Healthcare assistants demonstrate value when they reduce back-and-forth in triage notes while leaving final judgment to clinicians (NIST, 2023). Educational systems succeed when they accelerate instructor feedback without reducing transparency or fairness for students). Government agencies find efficiency in workload triage but must prioritize equity, ensuring that backlog reduction does not create hidden biases across neighborhoods or language groups. Creative studios thrive when systems help with iterative drafts but provide attribution logs and rollback options so ownership disputes are minimized (Jiang et al., 2024). User experience principles—clear explanations, transparent affordances, and one-click recovery—are the connective tissue across contexts. These practices turn adoption into support rather than burden, strengthening trust in the process. Return on investment is thus framed not as raw speed but as balanced improvement across error reduction, fairness, and total cost of ownership (NIST, 2023). As Table 7.1 makes clear, the pattern is consistent: domain-specific tuning converts modular building blocks into trustworthy, context-sensitive outcomes.

Table 7.1 Assistive, Predictive, Constrained-Autonomous Patterns by Sector

Sector	***Assistive Pattern***	***Predictive Triage***	***Constrained Autonomy***	***Primary Guardrails***	***UX Safety (Explain/Afford/ Recover)***
Healthcare	Clinical decision support; summarization of patient notes	Risk scoring; early warning alerts	Dose calculation; protocol-driven order sets	Regulatory compliance; clinician override	Explain rationale with citations; afford user override; recover with rollback to manual mode
Education	Lesson planning aid; grading rubric suggestions	Identify at-risk learners; recommend interventions	Adaptive quiz sequencing; pacing adjustments	Transparency in scoring; teacher-in-the-loop	Explain recommendations; afford teacher choice; recover to baseline curriculum
Public Sector	Policy brief drafting; case intake summarization	Fraud detection; service eligibility flagging	Form pre-population; workflow routing	Equity audits; appeals processes	Explain decision factors; afford citizen appeal; recover with human review
Creative	Idea generation; mood boards; text-to-image drafts	Audience trend prediction; performance forecasting	Automated layout suggestions; draft edits	IP boundaries; attribution requirements	Explain creative sources; afford designer edit; recover to original design

Within healthcare, the most reliable pattern is retrieval-augmented counsel—often called RAG—that drafts guideline-linked notes for clinician review rather than making decisions on its own (Yang et al., 2025). In practice, this looks like a triage assistant that can summarize a patient's complaint, retrieve relevant local care pathways, and surface citations with confidence indicators. Importantly, it includes "must-not-fail" gates, meaning that if the system is uncertain it automatically escalates to human-only handling (Labkoff et al., 2024). Equity improves when the knowledge base includes multilingual sources and population-specific guidance, not just English-language evidence (Yang et al., 2025). Ethical frameworks stress proportionality and transparency, so interfaces must clearly show where information came from and allow one-click overrides (Ong et al., 2024). Tools like model cards—short documents explaining a system's intended use and limits—shift trust from personality to documentation, giving compliance teams evidence they can audit (Labkoff et al., 2024). Early studies in surgical fitness checks and pre-op instructions suggest measurable gains in accuracy when retrieval is carefully curated (Ke et al., 2025). The real return on investment, however, only counts when error bars and subgroup performance are reported alongside efficiency metrics, ensuring safety keeps pace with speed (NIST, 2023).

Healthcare also benefits from predictive triage, where systems flag risk levels or prioritize reviews, as long as thresholds are carefully calibrated and can be reversed when conditions shift (Labkoff et al., 2024). Continuous monitoring should track both the inputs—like patient complaints—and the outcomes—like diagnoses—to catch silent degradations when seasonal illnesses or policy changes occur (NIST, 2023). Evaluators must design golden sets, or high-quality reference datasets, that include rare but catastrophic cases; otherwise average accuracy can be misleading (Labkoff et al., 2024). Interfaces should display "why this case was flagged" with evidence links, preserving clinician authority and agency (Jiang et al., 2024). Ethical reviews recommend keeping data collection proportional to the task and allowing selective disclosure so unnecessary personal details are not exposed (Ong et al., 2024). Clinicians report higher trust when predictive scores are paired with explanations retrieved from trusted guidelines, rather than opaque black-box numbers (Yang et al., 2025). Measuring ROI in this pattern means pairing time-to-decision and override rates with adverse-event tracking and fairness checks, not just queue throughput (NIST, 2023). Predictive systems, in short, complement retrieval when guardrails and explanations are consistently visible to users.

A third healthcare pattern is constrained autonomy for narrow tasks such as generating discharge instructions or checking vaccine contraindications, always with human sign-off (Labkoff et al., 2024). Autonomy here is tightly bounded: outputs are limited by templates, whitelists, and rollback rules, avoiding free-form responses (NIST, 2023). Retrieval once again adds value by providing citations and links to local policy, giving clinicians quick review targets instead of long prose to rewrite (Yang et al., 2025). Ethical guidance stresses that intended use and subgroup performance should be published openly as living documents, not hidden in internal memos (Ong et al., 2024). Safety improves when counter-examples from incident reviews—cases where things nearly went wrong—are converted into negative tests that block similar failures in the future (NIST, 2023). Institutions that publish thresholds and summaries of near-misses make adoption easier, since teams can reuse judgment rather than reinvent safeguards (Labkoff et al., 2024). Return on investment shows up as fewer rewrites, clearer patient instructions, and lower correction costs because evidence is transparent at the point of care (Yang et al., 2025). In practice, constrained autonomy works when the system feels like a checklist assistant, not a replacement clinician.

In education, a high-impact pattern is evidence-linked tutoring, where interactive dialogue is combined with retrieval of course-approved materials, worked examples, and cited explanations (Li et al., 2025). Randomized trials show that students learn faster and retain more when tutors scaffold reflection and show their sources, rather than handing over answers (Kestin et al., 2025). Academic integrity is reinforced when tutors clearly mark uncertainty and restrict retrieval to vetted course texts, which reduces confident but incorrect answers (Wang et al., 2024). Faculty-assist tools that generate draft comments aligned with rubrics must always require human acceptance and log edits to support calibration and appeals (Peláez-Sánchez et al., 2024). User experience should emphasize "why this hint," "from which section," and "try another approach," encouraging students to think critically instead of copying answers (Li et al., 2025). At the program level, ROI should measure teaching-assistant hours saved, time-to-feedback, and student transfer performance, not just satisfaction ratings (Kestin et al., 2025). Departments can publish acceptance tests and common failure cases, helping tutors remain aligned with outcomes across courses (Wang et al., 2024). Evidence-linked tutors raise quality without displacing instructor authority when explanations and guardrails are made central.

Education also profits from document triage systems that organize drafts, route them to rubrics, and flag gaps in structure or evidence—without assigning grades (Peláez-Sánchez et al., 2024). This setup accelerates formative feedback by highlighting weak arguments or missing sources while leaving final evaluation to instructors (Li et al., 2025). Teachers need to see what sources were used and where the system is uncertain, preventing misplaced trust or over-correction (Wang et al., 2024). Department dashboards can then track feedback cycles, showing metrics like average time-to-feedback and rubric alignment, helping administrators spot where materials or prompts need updating (Kestin et al., 2025). Fairness checks are vital, ensuring that feedback quality does not vary unfairly across student groups or formats, with mitigations elevated to policy when needed (Wang et al., 2024). Retrieval boundaries also reduce risks of content leakage, keeping advice tied to the curriculum rather than stray internet sources (Li et al., 2025). ROI comes from shortening cycles without increasing appeals or integrity incidents, proving value beyond speed alone (Kestin et al., 2025). Document triage earns trust when it functions as a supportive aid and cites its sources transparently.

In the public sector, early adoption wins often come from citizen-service chat and document triage that answer common "how-to" questions, track application status, and route requests to staff (Larsen et al., 2024). Agencies typically start with intake and status updates, delaying eligibility decisions until audit and appeal pathways are more robust (Hjaltalín et al., 2024). Interfaces that show provenance, provide escalation links, and always include a "talk to a person" option reduce frustration and uphold procedural justice (Larsen et al., 2024). Success often depends less on algorithms than on data cleaning and monitoring infrastructure, so roadmaps must budget for logging and observability rather than just licenses (Hjaltalín et al., 2024). Metrics should cover first-contact resolution, wait-time equity by neighborhood or language, and the number of rollbacks during early trials (Larsen et al., 2024). Privacy-by-design principles—necessity, proportionality, and minimization—help maintain public trust in how data is handled (Hjaltalín et al., 2024). When assistants stay within scope and provide plain-language explanations, citizen complaints drop and throughput rises. Public value grows not just from efficiency but from visibly accountable service.

Public agencies also see gains from case-prioritization tools that flag applications at risk of missing deadlines or missing documentation, provided entitlement decisions remain human-made (Hjaltalín et al., 2024). Fairness reviews must check wait-time disparities across geography and language to catch inequity before it compounds (Larsen et al., 2024). Drift monitors can alert teams to surges caused by new policies, giving leaders time to shift resources before queues become unmanageable (NIST, 2023). Documentation should be public, with briefs outlining intended use, evaluation results, and open complaint channels (Larsen et al., 2024). Interfaces must avoid manipulative design patterns that coerce disclosure, instead making appeal rights and data-use policies clear (Hjaltalín et al., 2024). Retrieval constraints help answers stay aligned to current law and policy, minimizing mismatches between guidance and practice (Larsen et al., 2024). ROI is best measured by reduced backlog and steady appeal rates, not raw query volume (Hjaltalín et al., 2024). Case-aware triage proves its worth as a service-level management tool, not an adjudication engine.

In creative industries, the leading pattern is a multi-tool studio that combines research copilots, outline assistants, storyboard generators, and brand-safety validators rather than relying on a single model (Long et al., 2024). Human–computer interaction (HCI) studies show creators thrive when they can set the "initiative level"—choosing intermittent support for brainstorming, continuous drafting, or proactive versioning—rather than being confined to editing outputs (Van Berkel et al., 2024). Co-creation has been shown to increase originality and self-confidence compared to passive editing, reducing risks of homogenized content (McGuire et al., 2024). Interfaces should reveal source lineage, display variation grids, and allow one-click recovery to maintain both accountability and creative freedom (Van Berkel et al., 2024). Versioned prompt libraries and peer critiques encourage reuse of strong practices and make knowledge transferable across teams (Long et al., 2024). ROI metrics should include time-to-concept, revision cycles, and brand or legal correction costs rather than just throughput of assets (Mastrianni et al., 2024). Studios that adopt attribution logs and version control also protect against supplier instability, since outputs remain auditable across updates (Subramonyam et al., 2025). Creative success emerges from governed co-creation, not unchecked automation.

Across all these sectors, modular solutions—retrieval-augmented counsel, predictive triage, and constrained autonomy—consistently outperform one-size-fits-all deployments. The common thread is an evidence spine: users must be able to interrogate sources, see uncertainty, and recover gracefully from errors (Figure 7.1) (Jiang et al., 2024). Governance artifacts such as model cards, test suites, and incident logs convert improvements into reusable knowledge across teams. Healthcare shows that safety grows with citations and thresholds; education shows that quality grows with formative, source-linked feedback; public agencies show that legitimacy grows with transparency and appeal rights; and creative industries show that originality grows with co-creative controls (Larsen et al., 2024). ROI increases when learning loops—red-teaming, monitoring, retraining—are budgeted as core costs rather than afterthoughts (NIST, 2023). Anti-patterns like silent failures, hidden data flows, and brittle prompts shrink when retrieval, documentation, and recovery options are non-negotiable (Labkoff et al., 2024). While details differ by sector, the architecture of trustworthy practice repeats in recognizable ways (ISO/IEC 42001, 2023). Practical success follows when curiosity is aligned with controls and adoption is tuned to domain realities.

Figure 7.1 UX Safety Triad: Explain, Afford, Recover.

The lesson across healthcare, education, public services, and creative industries is that the same technical building blocks must be tuned to very different realities. In hospitals, retrieval-augmented counsel and predictive triage improve documentation and prioritization, but trust comes only when citations, thresholds, and override rights are built in. In classrooms, evidence-linked tutoring and feedback triage accelerate learning and save instructor time, yet adoption succeeds only when human authority and transparency remain central. In government agencies, citizen-service assistants and case-prioritization tools reduce backlogs and wait times, but legitimacy hinges on procedural fairness, public documentation, and visible appeal channels. In creative studios, multi-tool co-creation accelerates iteration and originality, though attribution logs and version control are non-negotiable safeguards for ownership and accountability.

What these sectors share is the value of modular composition over monolithic systems. Retrieval reduces hallucinations, guardrails translate policy into practice, and user experience principles—like clear explanations and one-click recovery—keep judgment in human hands. Return on investment is reframed from speed alone to a broader balance: fewer errors, fairer outcomes, and sustainable maintenance. When organizations embed these practices, sector-specific solutions become more than proofs of concept; they mature into durable components of institutional workflows. The common thread is not autonomy for its own sake but assistance with accountability—systems that amplify human capacity while preserving oversight.

7.2 INTEGRATING ASSISTIVE, PREDICTIVE, AND AUTONOMOUS TOOLS INTO EXISTING SYSTEMS

Successful integration begins with the idea that not all tools should be given the same level of independence. Every use case should be placed on an autonomy spectrum before development starts, which means specifying whether the system is assistive (supporting a human), predictive (flagging or ranking cases), or constrained-autonomous (carrying out narrow, rule-bound tasks with oversight) (NIST, 2023). Assistive copilots work best when they emphasize *explainability* (showing how they reached a suggestion), *editability* (making it easy for humans to adjust outputs), and *provenance* (clear records of what sources were used). Predictive triage systems must balance sensitivity (catching true positives) against specificity (avoiding false alarms), while also checking for fairness across groups so accuracy does not come at the expense of equity (Wang et al., 2024). Constrained autonomy requires strict boundaries: narrow scope, easy reversibility, and human override so that failures degrade safely rather than creating hidden risks (Acharya et al., 2025). RAG, which grounds outputs in trusted sources instead of a model's memory, should be used across all three patterns to reduce hallucination risk (Yang et al., 2025). Governance mechanisms like change-control tie prompts, models, and data into versioned releases so updates are traceable (Akheel, 2025). Rollbacks must be rehearsed ahead of time, with predeclared triggers, so that reversing a deployment is routine rather than improvised during a crisis. This "spectrum-first design" ensures that exploration is paired with controls, making governance part of the system's architecture instead of an afterthought.

Integration also requires a practical stack—a layered approach that defines responsibilities at each stage. A four-layer model is often recommended: data products, retrieval and tools, orchestration, and evaluation (Klesel and Wittmann, 2025). Data products include curated datasets, vector indexes (specialized databases that support semantic search), and access policies. These must publish versions, permissions, and lineage so downstream teams know exactly what they are using. Retrieval and tools should expose deterministic functions—such as calculators, validation checks, or database queries—so that the model calls reliable operations instead of improvising under pressure (Sporsem and Ulfsnes, 2025). Orchestration manages the flow of work: coordinating when the system calls agents, setting timeouts, enforcing guardrails around cost and latency, and preventing malicious content from breaking workflows (NIST, 2024). Evaluation ties everything back together with golden sets (reference test cases), fairness audits, and drift monitors that detect when input data shifts. Dashboards should report confidence intervals, abstention rates (times when the system declines to answer), and known limitations to help decision-makers calibrate trust (Yuan et al., 2025). Model registries and sealed prompts enforce version control and log changes, preventing silent behavior drift between releases. This stack favors composability—reusing standard building blocks—over bespoke, one-off solutions, since reusability concentrates assurance and reduces redundant risk.

Data paths must be privacy-preserving from the outset. Privacy is guided by the principles of *necessity* (only collect what is needed) and *proportionality* (limit collection to what the task requires), which are emphasized by European data regulators such as the EDPB (European Data Protection Board, 2024). Techniques like local processing (keeping computation on the user's device) and selective disclosure (revealing only necessary attributes at verification) help minimize exposure (EDPB, 2025). Logging should track who accessed what, with what purpose, and under what consent conditions, creating an audit trail across teams and suppliers (Solove, 2025). De-identification (removing identifying details) and retention limits (deleting old data) further reduce risk (Ye et al., 2024). Transparency also matters: organizations should publish plain explanations of what is processed, where, and why, so stakeholders can judge proportionality without guesswork. For cross-party collaboration, approaches like federated learning—training models across multiple institutions without moving raw data—allow shared improvement under governance (Pati et al., 2024). Privacy, in this view, becomes architectural: it is built into data products, workflows, and contracts rather than left to policy statements.

User experience (UX) is just as critical as data and governance because it is the layer where humans actually interact with outputs. Embedding assistance directly into host platforms reduces context switching and errors. In electronic health records (EHRs), clinicians need linked evidence, displays of uncertainty, and one-click escalation to human-only review (Zhao and Li, 2025). In learning management systems (LMSs), instructors need rationales tied to rubrics and quick re-prompting tools to ensure that feedback remains formative and transparent. In case-management systems, frontline staff need clear status displays, appeal options, and a visible "talk to a person" button to preserve procedural fairness (Gómez et al., 2025). In creative studios, makers need lineage views, variation grids, and undo features so experimentation is recoverable and attributable (Van Berkel et al., 2024). Across contexts, micro-explanations should answer simple questions like "why this output," "what source was used," "how confident is the system," and "what should I do if it's wrong" (Jiang et al., 2024). Corrections provided by users should feed back into improvement loops, teaching the system under supervision. In this way, UX becomes part of the safety system, governing calibration, control, and recovery.

Evaluation must be continuous, not a one-time event. Golden sets must reflect domain-specific harms: for example, must-not-fail medical cases or sensitive legal contexts, not just generic benchmarks (NIST, 2024). Scenario tests should exercise unusual conditions and policy exceptions so brittleness is exposed before deployment (AVF, 2024). Subgroup reports must check for disparities in service quality, prompting mitigations proportional to risk. Drift monitors should track both inputs (like demographic shifts) and outcomes (like diagnostic accuracy) so that systems adapt safely when conditions change. Post-incident reviews must translate surprises into new tests and updated playbooks so teams learn across deployments, not just locally. Portfolio-level reviews should verify that documentation is current, risks are closed, and maturity matches organizational stage. Most importantly, evaluation literacy turns opinion into evidence: thresholds, tests, and documented limits become part of daily delivery, not reserved for audits (Yuan et al., 2025).

Predictive components require calibration—adjusting thresholds so alerts balance risks of false positives and false negatives—and explanation, so reviewers know why a case was flagged. Sensitivity and specificity must be tied to actual harms and costs, not arbitrary targets. Explanations should link directly to policies, pathway logic, or retrieved sources rather than relying only on abstract "feature importance" graphs that are difficult to interpret (Schneider, 2024). Interfaces must allow easy deferral and escalation, ensuring humans retain authority over borderline or urgent cases (Jiang et al., 2024). Monitors should alert when calibration drifts, so safety margins are not silently lost over time (NIST, 2024). Adverse events should feed into formal reviews with authority to pause systems until fixes are in place (AVF, 2024). Importantly, human overrides should be seen as healthy supervision, not counted as "system errors," to avoid incentives against vigilance (Labkoff et al., 2024). Predictive tools earn trust when alerts come with reasons and clear exits, turning them into accountable recommendations instead of opaque alarms (Benkirane, 2025).

Constrained autonomy works best when applied to narrow, predictable routines with strong oversight. For example, discharge-instruction templates or routine compliance checks can be automated so long as humans approve the final output. Whitelists restrict what tools can do, limiting them to predictable operations (OWASP, 2025). Templates standardize form and content, making review faster and safer. Guardrails impose limits on rate, cost, and context to prevent systems from running unchecked under stress (Chen et al., 2024). Rollback rehearsals and shadow modes (running new systems alongside human baselines without exposure) reduce risk during transitions (Agarwal et al., 2024). Documentation must clarify intended use, subgroup limits, and failure cases so expectations remain aligned as systems evolve. Constrained autonomy, when governed this way, feels like a checklist assistant—helpful, bounded, and always subordinate to human judgment.

Integration also depends on vendor governance, since many organizations rely on third-party models or services. Contracts must require transparency artifacts like model cards and datasheets, guarantee exportability, and include audit cooperation. Supplier updates must trigger re-testing against internal golden sets before production resumes (NIST, 2024). Telemetry terms should prevent raw sensitive data from being stored unnecessarily, enforcing proportionality (EDPB, 2024). Certification under a formal AI management system (such as ISO/IEC 42001) can harmonize processes across organizations, reducing friction. Incident playbooks must include vendor contacts and evidence requirements for joint responses. Portability clauses should allow graceful exits if risk or economics change, avoiding lock-in. In short, external changes become manageable when tests, obligations, and exit strategies are defined upfront.

Security and robustness depend heavily on the "plumbing" of integrations, not just model accuracy. Prompt injection attacks, where malicious inputs manipulate system behavior, must be countered in retrieval and tool layers with measurable reductions under red-team tests (Liu et al., 2024). Sandboxes and strict permissions limit damage from risky tool use or external calls (Agarwal et al., 2024). Rate limits and cost ceilings prevent runaway expenses or denial-of-service risks (OWASP, 2025). Input validation and content filters block obvious abuse, while detailed logs support investigations when failures occur (NIST, 2024). Observability—tracking every step in a workflow—ensures incidents can be diagnosed quickly. Red-teaming should focus on seams where permissions and state transitions can be exploited (Ferrag et al., 2025). A unified threat model helps teams think holistically about how agents, tools, and hosts interact, identifying vulnerabilities before attackers do (Alothman, 2025).

7.3 BENEFITS AND ROI: WORKFLOW OPTIMIZATION AND USER EXPERIENCE

Integration is sustainable only when ROI is measured honestly. Metrics should balance value, quality, safety, and learning rather than rewarding speed alone (BCG, 2024). Teams should provide evidence briefs that tie improvements to baselines, error rates, and costs, making results auditable (NIST, 2024). Executives should treat rollbacks as signs of maturity, celebrating reversibility rather than punishing it. Communities of practice should share success patterns and anti-patterns, allowing lessons to spread. Evaluators and stewards must be recognized and rewarded to keep governance visible. Training should progress from prompt use to orchestration so staff can design, evaluate, and operate responsibly. Culture, not code, is what makes reliability scale (Covin, 2025).

Moreover, ROI must be calculated across the full lifecycle. It includes not just licenses but also costs for monitoring, retraining, and vendor re-testing (Ziegler et al., 2024). Field studies show productivity gains, especially in routine coding or drafting, but effects vary by complexity (Noy and Zhang, 2023). Predeclared acceptance tests make benefits auditable. Rollbacks protect credibility when drift undermines gains. Total cost of ownership is real—without pricing evaluation and documentation, ROI is overstated (BCG, 2024). Finance leaders support what is predictable and auditable, so governance rigor translates into budget continuity (McKinsey, 2023). Evidence shows ROI and governance maturity rise together, as disciplined controls stabilize returns.

The central lesson of this section is that integration is not about adding a model to a workflow, but about designing a layered system where curiosity is always matched with controls. Tools must be placed on an autonomy spectrum—assistive, predictive, or narrowly autonomous—before deployment so that thresholds, overrides, and rollback rules are clear from the start. Retrieval-augmented generation acts as the connective tissue across all three, grounding outputs in vetted evidence to reduce hallucination and make reasoning traceable. A four-layer integration stack—data, retrieval and tools, orchestration, and evaluation—keeps responsibilities explicit, with contracts at each seam so no component becomes a black box. Privacy becomes structural when necessity and proportionality guide data flows, local processing reduces exposure, and federated learning supports collaboration without surrendering sensitive records. User experience then emerges as a safety system: explanations, affordances, and one-click recovery lower cognitive load while keeping humans firmly in charge of judgment. Continuous evaluation ensures systems adapt safely under drift, converting surprises into new tests and playbook entries instead of repeating mistakes.

What emerges is a picture of integration as governance in action. Predictive components only earn trust when scores travel with explanations and override options. Constrained autonomy is reliable only when it looks like a checklist assistant—bounded, reversible, and signed off by humans. Vendor dependencies must be governed with the same rigor as internal systems, with contracts mandating transparency, re-tests, and graceful exits. Security and robustness hinge less on algorithmic novelty than on defending the seams of orchestration—where permissions, state, and trust boundaries often break down. Above all, return on investment is not measured in throughput alone but in stability: fewer errors, equitable performance across groups, and predictable costs that survive supplier updates and audits. Integration, when designed this way, transforms technical potential into institutional reliability, making adoption sustainable, auditable, and worthy of trust.

7.4 CASE STUDIES: SUCCESSFUL DEPLOYMENT OF CUSTOM AI ACROSS SECTORS

A clinic network deployed a retrieval-augmented counsel tool to help with vaccination contraindication checks. In this case, nurses used the assistant to draft notes, while strict "must-not-fail" gates routed ambiguous cases directly to human review (Labkoff et al., 2024). Product owners deliberately scoped the tool for drafting only, avoiding any autonomous diagnoses to preserve clinical authority. Evaluators designed "golden sets"—reference datasets with known outcomes—that included rare but serious edge cases, while subgroup audits checked for quality differences across populations. Data stewards tracked consent and lineage in the electronic health record (EHR) snippets so provenance could be reconstructed in audits. Drift huddles, which are regular monitoring sessions, tightened thresholds during seasonal spikes such as flu season. Templates and linked citations reduced documentation time, but uncertainty remained visible so nurses could make informed calls. By treating explanations and override paths as core features, not add-ons, the network preserved safety and trust (Ong et al., 2024).

A hospital introduced predictive triage for sepsis alerts, a time-sensitive condition where rapid intervention is critical. Each alert came with a retrieval-linked explanation that clinicians could either defer or escalate in one click (NIST, 2024). Thresholds were tuned to reflect real harm trade-offs—for instance, prioritizing catching more true sepsis cases even if it meant more false alarms—rather than arbitrary accuracy scores. Weekly subgroup reports exposed disparities that aggregate numbers might hide, while missed cases and false alarms were converted into new negative tests that blocked future regressions. Drift detection caught shifts in patient data distributions, pausing system expansion until recalibration. Overrides were logged as healthy supervision rather than errors, with patterns feeding improvements in clarity. Incident reviews updated playbooks and documentation, reducing reliance on informal memory. Trust grew because alerts carried reasons and exits, transforming them from opaque warnings into accountable recommendations (Tun et al., 2025).

In higher education, a university rolled out evidence-linked tutoring systems. These tutors retrieved course-approved materials, offered step-by-step hints, and required instructor approval for final capstone feedback (Peláez-Sánchez et al., 2024). Direct-answer modes were disabled, instead prompting students to reflect on reasoning that instructors could inspect. Logs supported an ethics-approved study comparing outcomes to prior semesters, showing stronger learning gains and fewer integrity violations (Li et al., 2025). Faculty saved time because rubric-aligned drafts cut down repetitive phrasing. Department-level exemplars clarified expectations and reduced grading disputes. Hallucinations—outputs that sounded confident but were wrong—declined once retrieval was restricted to vetted sources, which also boosted transfer of knowledge across assignments. The gains came from transparency and formative feedback, not from replacing instructors in grading.

A college tested document triage systems that routed student drafts through rubrics and highlighted gaps without assigning grades. This separation preserved the integrity of summative grading while speeding formative feedback (Peláez-Sánchez et al., 2024). Teachers saw evidence links and uncertainty scores before choosing to accept suggestions. Dashboards revealed hidden prompt or material gaps that were hurting feedback quality. Feedback turnaround time dropped without raising appeal rates, thanks to version histories that made edits auditable. Each term, fairness checks ran across modalities and demographics, ensuring consistent service quality. Students reported clearer expectations when exemplars and rationales were attached to comments. Teachers adopted the system broadly because grading authority remained human, while retrieval kept advice on-syllabus (Li et al., 2025).

A city benefits agency deployed intake chat and case triage tools to prioritize deadline risks while keeping "talk to a person" visible. Eligibility decisions remained human to avoid contested automation (Larsen et al., 2024). Equity metrics tracked wait times by neighborhood and language to ensure fairness. Drift monitors caught surges after policy changes, prompting conservative operation modes. Public briefs and complaint links built legitimacy and educated residents on the system's limited scope. Queue times improved without a rise in appeal rates, and staff focused on complex cases needing discretion. Citizens appreciated transparent escalation paths, which lowered frustration even when responses were correct. The agency aligned its practices with guidance on explainability, recourse, and minimal data use in public services (Cabinet Office et al., 2024).

A permitting office used document routing assistants to classify submissions and assemble checklists for human confirmation. The system was deliberately scoped to intake and triage, not final approvals (U.S. General Services Administration, 2024). Evaluators designed scenario tests to cover edge cases that often produced errors in classification. Public performance briefs and appeal channels gave applicants a way to contest mistakes. Misroutes generated new negative tests, improving recall while maintaining precision. Seasonal changes in project submissions triggered retraining cycles. Executive release gates were tied to artifact completeness—such as model cards and incident logs—rather than speed alone. Results showed faster cycle times with no increase in appeals, and reusable templates accelerated adoption across departments (U.S. Department of Energy, 2024).

In the creative sector, a media studio adopted a multi-tool pipeline combining research copilots, outline assistants, storyboard generators, and brand-safety validators. This modular design avoided the brittleness of relying on a single model (Long et al., 2024). Creators adjusted tool initiative by project stage: brainstorming with intermittent suggestions, drafting with continuous help, and versioning with proactive outputs. Variation grids generated diverse drafts before narrowing choices, countering homogenization. Lineage views and one-click recovery made exploration safe by lowering the cost of "branch and revert." Shared prompt libraries and peer critiques turned personal tricks into institutional assets. Guardrails were updated after incidents, reducing repeated errors. Throughput improved, but more importantly, teams reported higher creative agency. Modular composition outperformed monolithic pipelines, absorbing supplier model updates without halting production (Van Berkel et al., 2024).

A newsroom deployed a retrieval-first assistant for background briefs that cited sources and flagged "what changed since last update." Editors required source verification before publication so no unvetted text slipped into news copy (AP, 2023). Confidence bands were shown in the interface, encouraging calibration rather than blind acceptance. For the first month, the system ran in "shadow mode" alongside human baselines. Supplier model updates triggered pause-and-retest cycles before resuming production. As sourcing improved, correction rates dropped, and staff developed stronger shared standards for evidence. Reporters and editors credited transparency choices with improving pitch and review discussions. This aligned with research showing that disclosure about AI use increases audience trust in newsrooms (Reuters Institute, 2024).

In finance, a bank piloted a Know-Your-Customer (KYC) memo assistant that generated structured summaries with citations and confidence intervals. All external data remained sandboxed and read-only, preventing sensitive data from leaking into prompts (BIS, 2025). Prompts themselves were treated as regulated records. Red-team prompts tested over-confidence and refusal behavior on out-of-policy requests. Supplier updates paused production until internal golden sets confirmed safety. Compliance teams rehearsed regulator questions using evidence briefs and logs, cutting response times. Memo clarity improved while review latency fell, reducing back-and-forth between analysts and reviewers. Governance practices matched emerging supervisory expectations for supplier oversight, strengthening risk culture (EBA, 2024).

A customer-support center deployed a RAG summarizer to assemble case histories and propose replies with mandatory source links. Human agents always confirmed responses, raising first-contact resolution while reducing handle time (Jiang et al., 2024). Random audits tracked hallucination rates and directed content remediation. Equity checks ensured quality remained consistent across languages. Failures triggered knowledge-base updates rather than manual patches. Auto-draft modes were rolled back after breaches, proving reversibility was built into the process. Staff trusted the tool because provenance and correction paths were visible. Managers credited these features for enabling safe scaling (NIST, 2024).

Across these deployments, a consistent theme emerges: success comes not from autonomy alone but from retrieval, supervision, and reversibility. Healthcare systems emphasized evidence-linked counsel and safe triage; education prioritized formative feedback and academic integrity; public agencies built legitimacy through transparency and appeal rights; and creative professionals flourished when co-creation remained recoverable and attributable. In every case, governance artifacts—model cards, datasheets, golden sets, and incident logs—turned experimentation into repeatable practice. ROI was framed not simply as time saved but as reduced error rates, fairer subgroup outcomes, and sustainable maintenance. User experience—explanations, editability, and recovery—proved to be a safety mechanism as much as a usability feature. Most importantly, modular composition consistently outperformed monolithic deployments by making systems more resilient to drift, supplier updates, and real-world surprises. The lesson is clear: institutional value arises when technology is paired with transparent governance, turning custom solutions into durable capabilities.

The core argument of this chapter is that custom solutions succeed when they are designed not as abstract demonstrations of capability but as domain-tuned systems that respect local risks, workflows, and values. Across healthcare, education, public services, and creative industries, the same building blocks—retrieval for grounding, orchestration for coordination, evaluation for accountability, and guardrails for safety—were shown to behave differently depending on the context. The lesson is that architecture does not deliver value in the abstract; it delivers value when adapted to sector-specific demands, whether those are clinical safety, academic integrity, procedural justice, or creative attribution.

Integration principles anchored these examples. Placing every use case on an autonomy spectrum, from assistive to predictive to constrained-autonomous, ensures that curiosity is matched with controls before deployment. Retrieval-augmented generation emerged as a universal stabilizer, reducing hallucinations and making reasoning inspectable. User experience—through explanations, editability, and recovery—proved to be more than a usability feature; it was a governance mechanism that made oversight possible in real time. Evaluation and monitoring reinforced this design by keeping systems aligned to baselines, subgroup fairness, and must-not-fail cases even as conditions drifted. As such a practitioner summary is as follows:

Practitioner Summary: Cross-Sector Lessons from Custom Deployments

Core Message

Custom deployments succeed not by replacing human judgment but by combining **retrieval, supervision, and reversibility**. The most durable value comes from modular, evidence-linked solutions with clear governance artifacts.

Healthcare

- **Pattern**: Retrieval-augmented counsel & predictive triage.
- **Practice**: Nurses and clinicians remained decision-makers; "must-not-fail" gates escalated risky cases.
- **Artifacts**: Golden sets, subgroup audits, model cards, drift huddles.
- **Outcomes**: Faster documentation, safer triage, reduced hallucinations, stronger clinician trust.
- **Lesson**: Evidence-linked notes and clear override paths protect both speed and safety.

Education

- **Pattern**: Evidence-linked tutoring & document triage.
- **Practice**: Systems retrieved course materials, offered hints, and required faculty approval for grading-related outputs.
- **Artifacts**: Reflection prompts, ethics-approved logs, fairness checks, dashboards.
- **Outcomes**: Higher learning gains, reduced integrity incidents, faster feedback without grade automation.
- **Lesson**: Formative transparency—not automated grading—earns adoption and preserves integrity.

Public Sector

- **Pattern**: Citizen-service intake & document routing.
- **Practice**: Tools triaged cases and prioritized risks, while eligibility and approvals stayed human.
- **Artifacts**: Intended-use briefs, complaint channels, public performance reports.
- **Outcomes**: Reduced backlogs, stable appeal rates, legitimacy through transparency and recourse.
- **Lesson**: Procedural justice (explainability, recourse, equity) is as valuable as efficiency.

Creative Industries

- **Pattern**: Multi-tool studios for co-creation.
- **Practice**: Pipelines included research copilots, outline tools, storyboard generators, and brand-safety validators.
- **Artifacts**: Variation grids, lineage views, peer-critique libraries.
- **Outcomes**: Faster ideation, resilience to supplier updates, preserved originality and attribution.
- **Lesson**: Modular composition outperforms monolithic pipelines in creative work.

Journalism & Finance

- **Pattern**: Retrieval-first backgrounders & KYC memo assistants.
- **Practice**: Source-linked outputs, shadow-mode pilots, pause-and-retest with supplier changes.
- **Artifacts**: Confidence bands, red-team prompts, golden sets, regulator rehearsal.
- **Outcomes**: Improved credibility, reduced corrections, faster compliance reporting.
- **Lesson**: Transparency and governance artifacts build legitimacy under scrutiny.

Customer Service

- **Pattern**: RAG summarizers with human verification.
- **Practice**: Agents confirmed outputs with source links; auto-draft modes rolled back after breaches.
- **Artifacts**: Random audits, equity checks, knowledge-base updates.
- **Outcomes**: Higher first-contact resolution, reduced handle time, sustained trust during scale-up.
- **Lesson**: Provenance and recovery affordances make adoption safe at scale.

Cross-Sector Lessons

- **Retrieval is non-negotiable**—grounding outputs in vetted sources reduces risk across domains.
- **Supervision is strength**—overrides are safeguards, not failures.
- **Reversibility is maturity**—rollbacks and shadow modes normalize safe learning.
- **Governance artifacts**—model cards, datasheets, incident logs, and golden sets turn pilots into reusable practice.
- **ROI must be holistic**—count fairness, subgroup performance, and maintenance costs, not just speed.

- **UX is governance**—explanations, editability, and recovery are safety systems, not just usability features.
- **Modularity wins**—multi-tool approaches absorb change better than single-model pipelines.

Moreover, return on investment was reframed throughout the chapter as a multidimensional calculation. Time saved mattered, but only alongside error profiles, fairness outcomes, and the total cost of ownership that includes red-teaming, retraining, supplier governance, and documentation. Case studies showed that when ROI was measured narrowly, systems faltered; when it was measured holistically, adoption created durable improvements in both trust and performance. Modularity and composability consistently outperformed monolithic deployments, not only because they were more efficient but because they made resilience and reversibility part of the design.

The significance of these lessons lies in demonstrating that successful deployments depend as much on organizational habits as on technical features. Institutions that treated documentation, transparency, and reversibility as first-class design elements scaled more safely and earned broader legitimacy. Those that paired retrieval with governance reduced variance and gained trust across users. The broader insight is that custom solutions are not just technical artifacts but sociotechnical arrangements where supervision, appeal rights, and traceable evidence are as important as code.

Looking forward, future research must examine how these sector-specific practices can be codified into portable playbooks without erasing the nuances of local context. Comparative studies across industries could reveal which integration rituals travel well and which require tailoring. Longitudinal work is also needed to measure how continuous evaluation and supplier governance shape long-term ROI, especially as external models evolve faster than internal oversight cycles. Perhaps most crucially, more evidence is needed on how user experience features—explanations, affordances, and recovery—directly affect trust, adoption, and error mitigation.

Therefore, the promise of custom solutions lies not in replacing human judgment but in amplifying it through architectures that embed governance into their very design. When retrieval, supervision, and reversibility are treated as non-negotiables, sector-specific deployments transform from fragile pilots into durable components of institutional practice. The lesson of this chapter is simple but profound: custom solutions succeed when they make governance visible, evidence traceable, and human oversight easy. That is how organizations align curiosity with control and turn experimentation into lasting value.

REFERENCES

Acharya, D.B., Kuppan, K. and Divya, B. 2025. Agentic AI: Autonomous intelligence for complex goals – A comprehensive survey. IEEE Access.

Agarwal, D., Kumar, S., Subramani, K. and Saha, A. 2024. Prompt leakage effect and defense strategies for multi-turn LLM interactions. *In*: Proceedings of the 2024

Conference on Empirical Methods in Natural Language Processing: Industry Track, pp. 1177–1189. Association for Computational Linguistics.

AI Verify Foundation (AVF). 2024. Model AI Governance Framework for Generative AI (June 19, 2024). https://aiverifyfoundation.sg/wp-content/uploads/2024/06/Model-AI-Governance-Framework-for-Generative-AI-19-June-2024.pdf

Akheel, S. 2025. Guardrails for large language models: A review of techniques and challenges. Journal of Artificial Intelligence, Machine Learning & Data Science. 3(1): 2504–2512.

Alothman, N. 2025. From prompt injections to protocol exploits: Threats in LLM-powered agent workflows. arXiv preprint arXiv:2506.23260. https://arxiv.org/abs/2506.23260

Amershi, S., Begel, A., Bird, C., DeLine, R., Gall, H., Kamar, E., et al. 2019. Software engineering for machine learning: A case study. *In*: 2019 IEEE/ACM 41st International Conference on Software Engineering: Software Engineering in Practice (ICSE-SEIP), pp. 291–300. IEEE.

Associated Press (AP). 2023. Standards around generative AI. https://www.ap.org/the-definitive-source/behind-the-news/standards-around-generative-ai/

Bank for International Settlements (BIS). 2025. Governance of AI adoption in central banks (Other publications no. 90). https://www.bis.org/publ/othp90.pdf

Benkirane, K. 2025. How can we diagnose and treat bias in large language models for clinical decision-making? *In*: Proceedings of the 2025 Conference of the North American Chapter of the Association for Computational Linguistics (NAACL 2025). Association for Computational Linguistics.

Boston Consulting Group (BCG). 2024. GenAI can't scale without responsible AI. https://www.bcg.com/publications/2024/genai-cant-scale-without-responsible-ai

Cabinet Office & Central Digital and Data Office (COCDD). 2024. Generative AI framework for HM Government. https://www.gov.uk/government/publications/generative-ai-framework-for-hmg

Chen, S., Song, R., Zou, J., Li, B. and Xu, K. 2024. A comprehensive study of prompt injection attacks against LLM-integrated applications. arXiv preprint arXiv:2402.06363. https://arxiv.org/pdf/2402.06363

Covin, C.K. 2025. Unified AI Ops: How to scale AgentOps, MLOps, DataOps, and LLMOps together (May 30, 2025). https://blog.dataiku.com/unified-ai-ops

European Banking Authority (EBA). 2024. Special topic—Artificial intelligence. https://www.eba.europa.eu/publications-and-media/publications/special-topic-artificial-intelligence

European Data Protection Board (EDPB). 2024. Opinion 28/2024 on certain data protection aspects related to the use of AI models. https://www.edpb.europa.eu/system/files/2024-12/edpb_opinion_202428_ai-models_en.pdf

European Data Protection Supervisor (EDPS). 2025. TechDispatch #1/2025—Federated Learning. https://www.edps.europa.eu/data-protection/our-work/publications/techdispatch/2025-06-10-techdispatch-12025-federated-learning_en

Ferrag, M.A., Shu, L., Ahmadian, A. and Choo, K.-K.R. 2025. Generative AI in cybersecurity: A comprehensive review of risks, attacks, and defenses. Journal of Information Security and Applications. 82: 103676. https://doi.org/10.1016/j.jisa.2025.103676

Gómez, C., Fernández, J. and de la Torre, J. 2025. A taxonomy of interaction patterns in AI-assisted decision making. Frontiers in Computer Science. 7: 1521066. https://doi.org/10.3389/fcomp.2024.1521066

Hjaltalín, I.T., Mergel, I. and Loukis, E. 2024. The strategic use of AI in the public sector: A public values perspective. Government Information Quarterly. 41(2): 101924. https://doi.org/10.1016/j.giq.2024.101924

International Organization for Standardization & International Electrotechnical Commission. 2023. ISO/IEC 42001:2023 Artificial intelligence—Management system. https://www.iso.org/standard/42001

Jiang, T., Yin, G., Ye, X. and Li, Z. 2024. Human–AI interaction: A user-centered research agenda. Patterns. 5(5): 100845. https://doi.org/10.1016/j.patter.2024.100845

Ke, Y.H., Jin, L., Elangovan, K., Abdullah, H.R., Liu, N., Sia, A.T.H., et al. 2025. Retrieval augmented generation for large language models in healthcare: Accuracy, consistency, and safety in surgical fitness and preoperative instructions. NPJ Digital Medicine. 8: 1519. https://www.nature.com/articles/s41746-025-01519-z

Kestin, G., Laski, E., Browne, W., Kim, J., Farmer, R. and O'Shea, B. 2025. AI tutoring outperforms in-class active learning. Scientific Reports. 15: 97652. https://doi.org/10.1038/s41598-025-97652-6

Klesel, M. and Wittmann, H.F. 2025. Retrieval-augmented generation (RAG). Business & Information Systems Engineering. 67: 7–30. https://doi.org/10.1007/s12599-025-00945-3

Labkoff, S., Oladimeji, B., Kannry, J., Lee, E., Ford, L.A., Nair, K., et al. 2024. Toward a responsible future: Recommendations for AI-enabled clinical decision support. Journal of the American Medical Informatics Association. 31(11): 2730–2739. https://doi.org/10.1093/jamia/ocae209

Larsen, A.G., Enli, G. and Karlsen, R. 2024. The impact of chatbots on public service provision: A qualitative interview study with citizens and providers. Government Information Quarterly. 41(2): 101933. https://doi.org/10.1016/j.giq.2024.101933

Li, Z., Chen, Q. and Zhang, H. 2025. Retrieval-augmented generation for educational applications: A survey. Patterns. 6(2): 100567. https://doi.org/10.1016/j.patter.2025.100567

Liu, X., Wang, K., Wang, H. and Liu, Y. 2024. Automatic and universal prompt injection attacks against large language models. arXiv preprint arXiv:2403.04957. https://arxiv.org/abs/2403.04957

Long, T., Chilton, L.B., Hartmann, B. and Bernstein, M.S. 2024. Not just novelty: A longitudinal study on utility and customization of an AI tool for science communication. *In*: DIS '24: Designing Interactive Systems Conference, pp. 1–15. https://doi.org/10.1145/3652577.3658342

Mastrianni, A., Liu, S. and Nichols, J. 2024. Exploring the design of a generative AI-based assistant to support domain experts in knowledge work. *In*: Proceedings of the ACM on Human-Computer Interaction, 8(CSCW1): 1–27. https://doi.org/10.1145/3756326

McGuire, J., Muthukrishnan, A. and Shankar, K. 2024. Establishing the importance of co-creation and self-efficacy in human–AI creativity. Scientific Reports. 14: 18525. https://doi.org/10.1038/s41598-024-69423-2

McKinsey Global Institute. 2023. The economic potential of generative AI: The next productivity frontier. https://www.mckinsey.com/capabilities/mckinsey-digital/our-insights/the-economic-potential-of-generative-ai-the-next-productivity-frontier

National Institute of Standards and Technology (NIST). 2023. Artificial Intelligence Risk Management Framework (AI RMF 1.0) (NIST AI 100-1). https://doi.org/10.6028/NIST.AI.100-1

National Institute of Standards and Technology (NIST). 2024. Artificial Intelligence Risk Management Framework: Generative AI Profile (NIST AI 600-1). https://doi.org/10.6028/NIST.AI.600-1

Noy, S. and Zhang, W. 2023. Experimental evidence on the productivity effects of generative artificial intelligence. Science. 381(6654): 187–192. https://doi.org/10.1126/science.adh2586

Ong, J.C.L., Chang, S.Y.-H., Wasswa, W., Butte, A., Chan, K.-S., Viswanath, V., et al. 2024. Medical ethics of large language models in medicine. NEJM AI. 1(7): e2400038. https://doi.org/10.1056/AIra2400038

OWASP Foundation. 2025. OWASP Top 10 for LLM applications: LLM01—Prompt Injection. https://genai.owasp.org/llmrisk/llm01-prompt-injection/

Pati, S., Gupta, S., Sharma, A. and Chatterjee, J. 2024. Privacy preservation for federated learning in health care: A practical guide. Patterns. 5(10): 100774. https://doi.org/10.1016/j.patter.2024.100774

Peláez-Sánchez, I.C., Ortega-Rodríguez, J.M. and García-Peñalvo, F.J. 2024. The impact of large language models on higher education: A systematic literature review. Frontiers in Education. 9: 1392091. https://doi.org/10.3389/feduc.2024.1392091

Reuters Institute for the Study of Journalism. 2024. Public attitudes towards the use of AI and journalism. https://reutersinstitute.politics.ox.ac.uk/digital-news-report/2024/public-attitudes-towards-use-ai-and-journalism

Schneider, J. 2024. Explainable generative AI (GenXAI): A survey, conceptualization, and research agenda. Artificial Intelligence Review. 57(11): 24253–24298. https://doi.org/10.1007/s10462-024-10916-x

Solove, D.J. 2025. Artificial intelligence and privacy. Florida Law Review. 76: 1–69. https://www.floridalawreview.com/api/v1/articles/129976-artificial-intelligence-and-privacy.pdf

Sporsem, T. and Ulfsnes, R. 2025. Towards requirements engineering for RAG systems. arXiv preprint arXiv:2505.07553. https://arxiv.org/abs/2505.07553

Subramonyam, H., Panganiban, J.P., Dey, A. and Oulasvirta, A. 2025. Emerging approaches and challenges in generative AI prototyping. Interactions. 32(1): 34–47. https://doi.org/10.1145/3706598.3713166

Tun, H.M., Rahman, H.A., Naing, L. and Malik, O. A. 2025. Trust in artificial intelligence–based clinical decision support systems among health care workers: Systematic review. Journal of Medical Internet Research. 27: e69678. https://www.jmir.org/2025/1/e69678

U.S. Department of Energy. 2024. Generative AI reference guide v2 (DOE/OCIO. https://www.energy.gov/sites/default/files/2024-12/Generative%20AI%20Reference%20Guide%20v2%206-14-24.pdf

U.S. General Services Administration. 2024. GSA releases generative AI acquisition resource guide for agencies [Press release]. https://www.gsa.gov/about-us/newsroom/news-releases/gsa-releases-generative-ai-acquisition-resource-gu-04292024

Van Berkel, N., Gammelgård-Larsen, A., Skov, M.B. and Kjeldskov, J. 2024. Designing for human-AI interaction: Comparing intermittent, continuous, and proactive interactions. *In*: CHI '24 Late-Breaking Work, pp. 1–7. Association for Computing Machinery. https://doi.org/10.1145/3613904.3642793

Wang, A., Kapoor, S., Barocas, S. and Narayanan, A. 2024. Against predictive optimization: On the legitimacy of decision-making algorithms that optimize predictive accuracy. ACM Journal on Responsible Computing. 1(1): 1–45.

Wang, S., Luo, H., Liu, B. and Feng, S. 2024. Large language models for education: A survey and outlook. arXiv preprint arXiv:2403.18105. https://arxiv.org/abs/2403.18105

Yang, R., Ning, Y., Keppo, E., Liu, M., Hong, C., Bitterman, D.S., et al. 2025. Retrieval-augmented generation for generative AI in health care. NPJ Health Systems. 2(2): Article 2. https://doi.org/10.1038/s44401-024-00004-1

Ye, X., Tang, Y., Liu, J. and Wu, J. 2024. Privacy and personal data risk governance for generative AI. Telecommunications Policy. 48(9): 102768. https://doi.org/10.1016/j.telpol.2024.102768

Yuan, J., Zhang, J., Wen, A. and Hu, X. 2025. The science of evaluating foundation models. arXiv preprint arXiv:2502.09670. https://arxiv.org/abs/2502.09670

Zhao, C. and Li, H. 2025. Human-AI interaction design standards: A comparative synthesis. arXiv preprint arXiv:2503.16472. https://arxiv.org/abs/2503.16472

Ziegler, A., Kalliamvakou, E., Li, X.A., Rice, A., Rifkin, D., Simister, S., et al. 2024. Measuring GitHub Copilot's impact on productivity. Communications of the ACM. 67(3): 62–71. https://cacm.acm.org/research/measuring-github-copilots-impact-on-productivity/

Chapter 8

Training and Deploying AI Agents for Personal and Professional Use

8.1 METHODOLOGIES FOR DEVELOPING, REFINING, AND MAINTAINING PERSONAL/TEAM AGENTS

The move from experimental prototypes to production-ready agents marks a turning point for organizations. Early pilots often succeed on novelty or narrow scope, but scaling requires more than clever prompting or ad hoc integrations. Without clear methodologies, agents risk becoming brittle, opaque, or unsafe as conditions change. The challenge is not simply technical performance, but institutional reliability: can the system explain its decisions, recover from errors, and evolve under governance? Addressing these questions demands structured processes that align with established standards, combine human oversight with automation, and embed accountability at every stage. In this sense, developing agents is less about coding behaviors and more about engineering life cycles—frameworks that define how agents are scoped, built, evaluated, and maintained. By treating agents as managed products rather than experiments, organizations build resilience and trust while reducing the cost of mistakes.

Likewise, organizations that want to move beyond one-off experiments with agents toward durable, reliable use need a rigorous and repeatable methodology (Table 8.1). The goal is not simply to create an agent that "works" in a demo, but to build systems that can be trusted, monitored, and improved over time. As shown in Figure 8.1, this process resembles a life cycle: beginning with scoping and data access, moving through tool selection, skill decomposition, and evaluation design, and extending into deployment, maintenance, and eventual retirement or

DOI: 10.1201/9781003688013-8

Table 8.1 Agent Development and Maintenance Lifecycle

Lifecycle Stage	*Purpose*	*Key Practices & Artifacts*	*Practical Examples*
Scoping	Define objectives, risks, and boundaries	Capability cards (task, inputs, metrics, autonomy limits, HITL checkpoints); acceptance tests; downgrade modes	Vaccination agent scoped only to draft notes; must-not-fail case: never recommend unsafe drug combo
Data Access	Ensure privacy and proportionality	Least-privilege permissions; redaction; audit logging; federated learning; local processing	Personal agents restricted to device-level data; team agents with intended-use briefs for stakeholders
Tool Selection & Orchestration	Structure workflows and tool use	Four-layer stack (data, tools, orchestration, evaluation); deterministic tools for compute; versioned prompts/configs	AutoGen multi-agent design (researcher, critic, planner); DSPy declarative pipelines with metrics
Skill Decomposition	Break tasks into manageable, testable units	Skill cards (inputs/outputs/tests); scoped memory; pre/post-conditions for tool calls; reflection modules	Agent decomposes "write report" into plan → retrieval → draft → critique → finalize, with memory checkpoints
Evaluation Design	Establish reliability and accountability	Golden sets for must-not-fail cases; synthetic evals for coverage; human spot-checks; shadow-mode baselines	RAGAS metrics (context relevance, groundedness, answer relevance); AgentBench stress tests
Telemetry	Make evaluation continuous and visible	Logging outcome quality, latency, cost, satisfaction; per-stage metrics; evidence briefs for executives	RAG triad signals tracked in dashboards; early-exit triggers if thresholds drop below safety margins
Guardrails & HITL	Scale safety with routine oversight	Allow-lists; refusal logic; input validation; cost/time ceilings; one-click escalation; updated playbooks	AutoGen agents debate and critique outputs before escalation to a human; escalation logs captured for audits
Maintenance	Adapt to drift and supplier updates	Drift huddles; supplier registers; re-tests for every update; synchronous documentation	Pause-and-retest gates after supplier model update; runbooks updated with near-miss learnings
Portfolio Management	Sustain value and prevent "zombie agents"	Retire/fix/scale decisions tied to evidence briefs; sunset dates; pattern libraries for reuse	Agent triaged out if fails fairness audits; successful modules refactored into new portfolio patterns

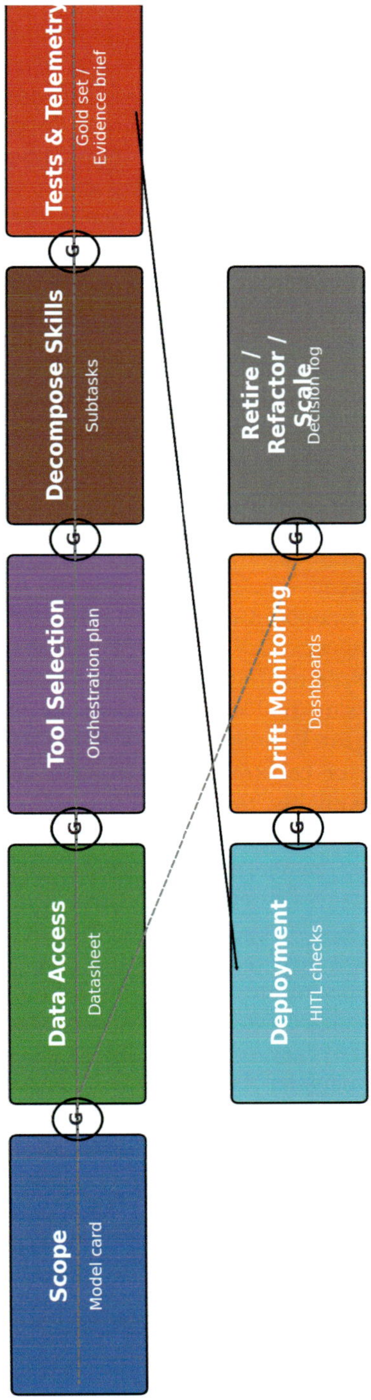

Figure 8.1 Agent Lifecycle with Gates.

scaling. Each stage introduces its own risks and responsibilities. Standards bodies like NIST (2024) stress that the key to reliable practice is tying every objective to explicit risk and measurement profiles, not just aspirational goals that can drift under pressure. ISO/IEC (2023) 42001 complements this by treating agent development as a management system, which means documenting roles, artifacts, and audits across the life cycle. In pragmatic terms, this translates into writing short "capability cards" before coding—small documents that specify the task, inputs, success metrics, autonomy limits, and human checkpoints. It also means agreeing on test suites and rollback triggers that are reviewed during **go/no-go meetings** instead of after incidents. As OWASP (2025) notes, agent applications introduce new attack surfaces, so security controls should be built in from the start rather than patched later. When observability—measures like accuracy, latency, safety, and satisfaction—is anticipated early, telemetry in production can enforce standards instead of being a dashboard promise. With this scaffolding in place, agents become governable systems rather than clever but fragile experiments.

Scoping is the stage where most downstream failures can be prevented, because it defines the boundaries of what an agent is allowed to do, how it will operate, and under what conditions humans must intervene. To scope an agent is essentially to answer the question: *what exactly is this agent for, and under what limits?* A poorly scoped agent—one given vague goals or excessive autonomy—creates brittleness that no amount of clever prompting can repair. As Wang et al. (2023) emphasize, LLM agents vary widely in capability and in the types of errors they produce, so scoping requires teams to categorize tasks carefully by interaction type, necessary tool use, and tolerance for error. The autonomy spectrum—whether an agent is assistive (supporting human work), predictive (flagging or prioritizing), or constrained-autonomous (executing narrow, rule-based tasks)—must be explicitly tied to human-in-the-loop checkpoints, not to aspirational trust statements. OWASP's LLM Top 10 warns that risks like prompt injection (malicious manipulation of inputs), data leakage, and supply-chain vulnerabilities increase when agents call tools or execute multi-step flows, making it vital to document adversary models during scoping.

In practice, good scoping involves writing acceptance tests for "must-not-fail" cases—such as ensuring a healthcare triage agent never recommends a dangerous drug interaction—and defining downgrade modes so that if conditions shift, the agent can fail safely instead of catastrophically. ISO/IEC (2023) 42001 stresses that these decisions should be captured in controlled documents, not transient chats, because accountability attaches to formal artifacts. Teams must also define data-use boundaries—what the agent is allowed to read, write, or store—since ambiguity at this stage often produces security or compliance incidents once systems go live. In short, scoping is less about enthusiasm for what agents *could* do and more about evidence-based constraints that ensure the environment keeps them honest.

Once an agent's scope is defined, the next step is ensuring that it has the right access to the right data under the right conditions. Data access is often where hidden risks emerge, because even well-scoped agents can create vulnerabilities if their data pathways are poorly designed. Privacy-preserving data design must be structural, not rhetorical; it is not enough to promise compliance—controls must be embedded in the system itself. The European Data Protection Board (2024) emphasizes the principles of necessity (collect only what is required) and proportionality (share only what is appropriate for the task), which means an agent should process only the data it needs and reveal only the attributes a verifier must see. For cross-organization collaborations, the board recommends approaches like federated learning—where models are trained across multiple institutions without moving raw data—and local processing, which keeps sensitive information on-device. In practice, this requires binding data products to explicit policies covering identity, permissions, and retention, while logging every access event with purpose and consent so that audits can reconstruct exactly how data was used. For personal agents inside enterprises, least-privilege access and strong redaction policies prevent personal context from leaking into team-level systems. NIST (2024) stresses that disclosure minimization and detailed audit logs turn vague promises about privacy into measurable, testable controls. For team or enterprise agents, publishing intended-use briefs that describe what data is processed, where, and why provides visibility into proportionality for all stakeholders. In short, secure and transparent data pathways are not just a prelude to agent design—they are the foundation that determines whether an agent is legitimate and trustworthy.

With scope and data access in place, the next challenge is deciding how the agent will actually perform its tasks—what tools it can call and how its actions are orchestrated into reliable workflows. Tool selection and orchestration determine whether agents remain understandable as they scale or collapse into opaque, brittle systems. As Khattab et al. (2023) note, frameworks such as DSPy replace fragile chains of prompts with declarative modules that can self-optimize toward defined metrics, making systems more robust and transparent. Wu et al. (2023) highlight multi-agent systems like AutoGen, where specialized roles—a researcher, a critic, and a planner—collaborate with one another and with humans, ensuring that complexity is distributed but still manageable.

In practice, organizations should think in terms of a four-layer stack: data products, retrieval and tools, orchestration, and evaluation. Each layer serves as a boundary where contracts, tests, and accountability must be explicit. At the tool layer, deterministic functions—such as calculators, search engines, or API lookups—should handle raw computing or fact retrieval, while the model focuses on reasoning and routing. This separation reduces the risk of hallucinated logic and makes debugging significantly easier. Orchestration adds another layer of discipline by defining timeouts, cost ceilings, and escalation paths, as well as clarifying "who owns the next move" when workflows face uncertainty or stress. Next, prompts and configurations should never be left to chance; they must be version-controlled in registries with digital signatures so silent drift cannot bypass governance. When tool selection is careful and orchestration is explicit, teams can reuse proven components, reduce redundancy, and concentrate assurance where it delivers the greatest value. The result is not only technical reliability but also institutional accountability, since every decision path is documented, testable, and reversible.

Once tools and orchestration are in place, the next consideration is how to structure an agent's abilities so they remain understandable and adaptable as tasks become more complex. Skill decomposition is the process of breaking large tasks into smaller, testable components, making agents both teachable and maintainable over time. Huang et al. (2024) show that dividing tasks into explicit plans, sub-skills, memory functions, and reflection modules makes systems easier to debug and extend, since each piece can be improved or replaced without rewriting the whole agent. Shinn et al. (2023) demonstrate that reflective agents—systems that critique their own reasoning traces in natural language—can improve accuracy significantly without retraining underlying models. In practice, this involves creating skill cards: modular documents that define each capability, its inputs and outputs, associated tests, and negative examples to avoid repeated errors. Memory design is equally important; it should be scoped into short-term memory for traces of ongoing interactions and long-term memory for reusable lessons, since endless context windows often confuse models rather than guide them. When agents call tools, developers should enforce pre-conditions and post-conditions that validate inputs and outputs, preventing "garbage in, garbage out" scenarios from cascading into failures. Finally, ambiguous states should always be escalated to humans through quick decision huddles that present concise evidence for review. Over time, careful decomposition and reflective design yield agents that not only perform better but are also easier to maintain, audit, and extend across use cases.

After skills are decomposed into manageable parts, the next question becomes how to ensure those skills perform reliably in real environments. Evaluation design is the backbone of reliability because it provides the evidence that agents are safe, accurate, and aligned with expectations before they are trusted in production. Liu et al. (2023) propose AgentBench, a benchmark that tests agents across interactive environments and exposes weaknesses in reasoning, instruction-following, and decision-making that may not surface in static evaluations. Es et al. (2024) developed RAGAS metrics—measuring context relevance, groundedness, and answer relevance—that are specifically designed to test retrieval pipelines, an area where errors often arise. Liu et al. (2023) also show that LLM-as-a-Judge systems like G-Eval can align with human judgments, but only if they are carefully designed with bias checks and meta-evaluation to prevent drift. Gu et al. (2024) emphasize that evaluators themselves must be monitored because automated scoring can degrade in quality just as models do. A robust evaluation strategy therefore combines golden sets for must-not-fail cases, synthetic tests to expand coverage, and human spot-checks to calibrate the results. To build accountability, launches should be gated to explicit thresholds with rollback triggers defined in advance, and new systems should first run in shadow mode against baselines before being exposed to real users. Embedding evaluation into the codebase—so every deployment automatically includes its tests, traces, and dashboards—ensures that reliability is not a one-time certification but a continuous practice.

After evaluation establishes whether an agent is ready for deployment, the next step is to ensure that its performance can be monitored continuously in real-world use. Telemetry extends evaluation into everyday practice by turning performance measurement into an ongoing feedback loop rather than a one-time certification. NIST (2024) emphasizes that production agents should log outcome quality, latency, cost, safety incidents, and user satisfaction on a regular basis to provide a comprehensive view of behavior. TruLens (2025) adds specificity for retrieval-based systems by operationalizing three key RAG signals—context relevance, groundedness, and answer relevance—so teams can pinpoint exactly which pipeline stage is failing. In practice, spans should be attached to every retrieval, tool call, and agent decision, and metrics should be calculated with confidence intervals rather than single averages to avoid misleading conclusions. User satisfaction should be collected with lightweight prompts and triangulated against observable behavior such as edits, overrides, or escalations, since survey-only feedback often drifts. Telemetry also enables early exits, meaning agents can gracefully degrade or hand off to humans when thresholds are crossed instead of failing silently. To support learning, anonymized traces should be stored for red-teaming and evaluation rather than mined indiscriminately. Finally, internal "evidence briefs" should be published each release cycle so executives see a balanced account of successes and limitations, preventing cherry-picking and ensuring accountability.

Once telemetry makes performance visible, the next concern is ensuring that agents operate safely even under stress or attack. Guardrails and HITL controls are critical because they embed boundaries and oversight into the system architecture, enabling safe scale. OWASP (2025) warns that risks like prompt injection, information disclosure, and supply-chain vulnerabilities are particularly acute in tool-using agents, which means defenses must be embedded directly in the pipeline. Wu et al. (2023) highlight a productive pattern in AutoGen, where agents critique or debate each other's outputs before handing them off, with a human providing the final judgment. Practical guardrails include tool allow-lists, strict input validation, cost and time ceilings, refusal logic for unsafe prompts, and one-click escalation so humans can intervene easily. Interfaces should make uncertainty and rationale visible so that human supervisors understand why an output was produced, which prevents blind trust. NIST (2024) emphasizes that incident reviews should generate new negative test cases and updated playbooks, ensuring that mitigations persist beyond a single crisis. Logs must capture decisions and supporting evidence to allow auditors to reconstruct events and identify accountability if something goes wrong. Ultimately, oversight is most effective when it is routine, inexpensive, and well-documented rather than sporadic and heroic.

Even with guardrails, agents will inevitably face changes in data, tasks, or external dependencies, making maintenance a permanent requirement. Maintenance is the phase where organizational trust is either strengthened or lost, because drift in inputs, user expectations, or supplier updates can erode reliability if not managed carefully. NIST (2024) advises that organizations use continuous monitoring linked to pause-and-retest gates, ensuring systems can be temporarily halted and validated whenever anomalies appear. ISO/IEC 42001 (2023) stresses that change control and documented roles should govern updates so accountability remains clear during adjustments. OWASP (2025) adds that supply-chain risks are especially dangerous in LLM-based applications, meaning teams must map dependencies and rerun tests whenever upstream models change. In practice, every upstream modification should be treated as a new release, with golden sets, fairness audits, and scenario tests rerun before resuming production use. A living supplier register with contacts, obligations, and incident service-level agreements (SLAs) shortens the time to mitigate external risks. Regular drift huddles should review telemetry and near-misses, deciding whether retraining, threshold adjustments, or feature flags are needed. Finally, documentation must evolve alongside the system, keeping model cards, datasheets, and runbooks synchronous with reality rather than lagging behind.

As agents accumulate within an organization, the focus shifts from individual deployments to overall program sustainability. Portfolio management ensures that agent investments compound value instead of stagnating, by systematically deciding which systems to retire, refactor, or scale. Khattab et al. (2023) argue that programmatic pipelines make it possible to manage these decisions consistently rather than leaving them to ad hoc judgments. Agents that repeatedly fail cost, quality, or safety gates should be retired, while those with identifiable but fixable weaknesses should be refactored. High-performing agents that meet thresholds consistently can then be scaled responsibly. NIST (2024) recommends tying these portfolio decisions to evidence briefs rather than charisma or internal politics, so that resources follow reliability. Pilots should be given sunset dates to prevent "zombie agents" that linger without purpose but still consume resources. Pattern libraries of successful practices and known anti-patterns should be maintained so new teams can build on accumulated knowledge rather than repeating old mistakes. Huang et al. (2024) highlight that emerging research in planning modules and memory abstractions can be integrated into portfolios over time, allowing organizations to upgrade capabilities without wholesale rewrites. In short, agents must be managed like evolving products with defined life cycles, not like demos with indefinite tenure.

The central message of this section is that moving from experimental agents to durable, governable systems requires treating them as managed products with life cycles rather than as ad hoc prototypes. Reliability is achieved when organizations embed standards, guardrails, and accountability artifacts at every stage—from scoping and data access to evaluation, deployment, and eventual retirement or scaling. Scoping emerges as the first line of defense, since most downstream failures can be traced to unclear objectives, undefined autonomy boundaries, or neglected human-in-the-loop checkpoints. Data access decisions establish legitimacy, with privacy-preserving pathways, proportional disclosure, and audit logging transforming policy promises into enforceable controls. Tool selection and orchestration keep systems explainable, with deterministic functions handling computation and orchestration layers managing workflows, costs, and escalation under stress.

Skill decomposition and reflective design make agents teachable and debuggable, while evaluation strategies—combining golden sets, synthetic tests, and human spot-checks—ensure that must-not-fail cases remain visible. Telemetry turns evaluation into habit, creating continuous evidence streams on accuracy, latency, cost, safety incidents, and user satisfaction. Guardrails and human oversight are not barriers but enablers, scaling safety by making escalation and supervision routine rather than exceptional. Maintenance practices, including drift huddles, supplier registers, and synchronous documentation, keep agents resilient as environments and models evolve and portfolio management allows organizations to retire, refactor, or scale agents based on evidence briefs, preventing "zombie agents" and compounding value through reusable patterns. Taken together, these methodologies align with guidance from NIST, ISO/IEC, and OWASP, reinforcing the principle that governance is not external to agent design but intrinsic to it. Agents that are scoped carefully, evaluated continuously, and maintained with discipline can evolve alongside organizational needs while preserving safety, trust, and legitimacy.

8.2 APPLICATIONS IN EXPERIENTIAL LEARNING AND PRODUCTIVITY AUGMENTATION

Experiential learning with AI agents merges authentic tasks, immediate feedback, and safe reversibility, transforming isolated "demos" into sustained practice. As NIST frames it, reliable augmentation depends on pairing assistance with explicit measurement, escalation, and rollback—not just clever prompting. In practical terms, this means instrumenting tutors, copilots, and workflow agents with the same telemetry one would apply to production software. It also means aligning agent affordances—explain, edit, escalate—with the user's moment-to-moment goals. As Tsiakas (2024) argues, interaction primitives such as propose, critique, confirm, and defer let teams compose agent behaviors that fit real work. When these primitives are mapped to outcomes and risks, agents support practice rather than distract from it. The result is experiential learning that feels like work, not a lab exercise, because evidence, recovery, and ownership are always at hand. Culture learns as quickly as individuals when artifacts, tests, and traces persist beyond a single session.

AI tutors are the clearest example of experiential augmentation when they couple dialogue with retrieval of course-vetted resources and reflections. As Kestin et al. (2025) show in a randomized field study, a carefully designed tutor produced stronger learning in less time than in-class active learning while sustaining engagement. Létourneau et al. (2025) argues that gains are largest when tutors scaffold metacognition—progress monitoring, self-explanation, and regulation—rather than answer delivery. A RAG-based tutor makes sources visible, constrains hallucination, and fine-tunes hints to local syllabi so students practice with the same evidence they will be assessed on (Li et al., 2025). In this design, formative transparency discourages shortcuts because students can interrogate citations and ask for alternative routes. Instructors retain authority by accepting or revising AI-proposed feedback before release, which calibrates expectations and protects integrity. Telemetry closes the loop by tracking time-to-feedback, transfer performance, and dispute rates across cohorts. Experiential learning becomes a supervised conversation grounded in evidence rather than an opaque oracle (Kestin et al., 2025).

Simulation-anchored experiences likewise benefit when agents ground counsel in current standards and expose uncertainty transparently. As Yang et al. (2025) argue, retrieval-augmented counsel can attach guideline links and local policy to each suggestion, making debriefs concrete rather than rhetorical. In clinical training or safety drills, this turns "why" into inspectable evidence that educators can question. Malik et al. (2025) emphasize that trust rises when explanations and human control remain visible, especially in safety-critical contexts. Students and staff can then escalate borderline cases, note subgroup caveats, and update checklists with new negative tests from near-misses. These practices allow instructors to evaluate judgment, not just accuracy, because rationale and recovery are part of the artifact. Over time, scenario libraries accumulate as shared institutional memory for both learning and risk management. The same pattern applies to finance, law, or compliance simulations when provenance, debrief rituals, and pause-and-retest gates are first-class (Yang et al., 2025).

For professional writing and knowledge work, assistive agents compress drafting while preserving editorial control and auditability. As Noy and Zhang (2023) show, generative assistance can raise throughput on mid-level writing tasks, with the caveat that variance by task type and user skill is large. Zhao and Li (2025) argue that human-AI design standards should foreground explanation and recovery so speed does not become silent risk. In practice, experiential workflows pair "explain this change" with "show sources," letting reviewers accept, edit, or escalate in one motion. Teams that log changes and rationale can later analyze where the agent helps or harms under deadline pressure. Post-hoc learning is accelerated when common edits become pattern rules or prompt libraries. Because drafts, evidence, and decisions are instrumented, performance reviews speak in data rather than anecdotes. Productivity gains thus accrue without degrading attribution, quality, or professional judgment (Noy and Zhang, 2023).

Coding copilots provide a parallel case in technical work, where much of the learning and productivity comes directly from doing the work. Tools such as GitHub Copilot generate code suggestions as developers type, helping with routine tasks like boilerplate code (e.g., writing standard functions or repetitive configurations) and code search (e.g., recalling library syntax). Ziegler et al. (2024) report that developers perceive meaningful productivity gains from copilots in these areas, but they emphasize that real benefits depend on verification and team norms. In other words, a suggested snippet may save time, but it still needs to pass tests and code review before it can be trusted. NIST (2024) recommends binding copilots to acceptance tests, review queues, and rollback triggers so that speed never outpaces safety. A practical way to think about this is "test-first assistance": the agent proposes code, automated tests validate it, and humans decide on design trade-offs. Teams can also use agent-suggested diffs—the proposed changes to code—as learning material during reviews, transforming assistance into a form of pedagogy. For example, a junior developer might learn why a copilot's suggestion was accepted or rejected during review, reinforcing best practices. Onboarding also improves when teams document clear playbooks: when to route a task to the copilot, when to decline its output, and how to escalate uncertainties. Over time, repositories of good and bad prompts create a shared library of craft knowledge, much like a workshop where apprentices study exemplars. The result is a studio model for engineering where humans and copilots co-create under the governance of tests and peer review, balancing efficiency with safety (Ziegler et al., 2024).

Team knowledge assistants extend this model of experiential learning beyond code and into enterprise problem-solving by grounding their guidance in an organization's own history and resources. As Li et al. (2025) argue, the same RAG principles developed for education—curating high-quality sources, measuring groundedness, and constraining generation to vetted content—generalize well to enterprises. A complementary 2025 survey stresses that knowledge-oriented RAG only works when retrieval scope, ranking, and fusion are aligned with the user's task; otherwise, answers risk being misgrounded, meaning they sound correct but are based on irrelevant or incomplete evidence (Zhang et al., 2025). In practice, this means exposing internal resources such as policies, playbooks, and post-mortems as versioned data products that agents can cite directly. For example, if a manager asks about past decisions on a failed project, the assistant can pull directly from the relevant post-mortem instead of improvising an answer. Experiential improvement happens when user edits and escalations feed back into the corpus, gradually raising the system's accuracy over time. Dashboards help by showing where the assistant saves time (e.g., quickly locating a policy) and where it creates confusion (e.g., surfacing outdated procedures), which guides ongoing curation. Because both the sources and their limits are visible, teams learn the institution itself, not just the interface, strengthening organizational literacy. In this way, knowledge work becomes a repeatable exercise in asking better questions of a transparent institutional memory rather than relying on opaque model guesses.

Public-sector services demonstrate how experiential augmentation can improve civic-scale interactions while simultaneously training staff. Larsen et al. (2024) show that well-scoped government chatbots reduce citizen frustration when three features are prioritized: clear provenance of answers, visible escalation paths, and easy "talk to a person" options. NIST advises that intake and status queries—such as "Was my application received?" or "What is my current case status?"—are the safest early use cases, while more complex eligibility decisions should wait until stronger evaluations are in place. Staff learn through the process as their escalations and corrections become new test cases and feed directly into updated documentation, building legitimacy by showing that human oversight drives system improvement. Citizen-facing explanations in plain language double as micro-lessons, reducing repeat calls by teaching individuals how the process works. Drift monitors tied to policy updates ensure answers remain current, essentially turning the system into a learner as well. Agencies can then measure value with fairness-oriented metrics such as wait-time equity across neighborhoods and appeal rates, instead of raw chatbot usage counts. This creates a feedback loop where transparency and recourse are non-negotiable, reshaping service delivery and staff development simultaneously (Guo, 2024).

Creative work illustrates a different application of experiential augmentation, where the goal is not automation but support for ideation and critique. Long et al. (2024) find that value is sustained when creators adjust the initiative level of agents—intermittent assistance for brainstorming, continuous support for drafting, and proactive outputs for versioning tasks. McGuire et al. (2024) argue that co-creation and self-confidence grow when tools expose lineage—the history of prompts and outputs—and make branching new drafts inexpensive.

In practice, variation grids that present multiple creative options side by side and one-click recovery to revert to earlier drafts turn experimentation into a safe habit rather than a risky investment of time. Ethical and brand-safety validators can run in parallel, flagging issues like policy violations or offensive content without stifling creativity. Teams can formalize successful creative flows into reusable patterns, ensuring that lessons from one project feed into future work. Because all sources, prompts, and choices are visible, creative studios become places where style and judgment are taught through artifacts rather than informal word-of-mouth. This approach privileges directed exploration, ensuring that creativity is amplified without being reduced to generic speed (Long et al., 2024).

Telemetry-driven feedback loops show how one-off experiments can become cumulative organizational learning. Telemetry refers to the automated collection of performance data, and NIST (2024) stresses that outcome quality, latency, cost, safety incidents, and user satisfaction should all be logged continuously to detect regressions. Zhao and Li (2025) caution that UX standards must require explanations and recovery features so telemetry can be interpreted meaningfully rather than just stored. In education, for example, tutors can track which hints students accept, which sources they view, and how well they transfer skills across assignments (Li et al., 2025). In engineering contexts, diffs paired with failing tests identify fragile prompts that need to be re-engineered. In public services, high escalation rates in particular topics highlight knowledge-base gaps that require content updates. Aggregated "evidence briefs" published each sprint keep executives focused not only on successes but also on system limitations and areas for improvement. Over time, telemetry transforms feedback into a pedagogy for the organization itself, teaching teams how to refine both processes and tools in tandem (National Institute of Standards and Technology, 2024).

Equity and privacy considerations ensure that experiential augmentation broadens opportunities instead of reinforcing inequality. The European Data Protection Board (2024) emphasizes the principles of necessity and proportionality, which require that only essential data is collected and disclosed so practice does not slip into surveillance. It also recommends federated learning and local processing whenever possible, approaches that align well with personal agents used in classrooms or workplaces. Tun et al. (2025) remind system designers that explainability and training build trust, particularly in settings where power imbalances—such as between governments and citizens—could amplify skepticism. Kestin et al. (2025) demonstrate that AI tutors can quickly improve outcomes, but institutions should publish acceptance tests, failure cases, and accessibility plans to prevent uneven distribution of benefits. In creative and public-sector contexts, provenance and clear appeal channels prevent silent exclusion and allow individuals to challenge errors. Workforce development programs should also teach orchestration and evaluation as transferable skills, enabling people to carry these competencies across different industries. Future research should measure not only short-term productivity metrics but also long-term impacts on social mobility. Thus, experiential augmentation has its greatest value when it equips people to adapt, explain, and improve together rather than concentrating advantage in the hands of a few.

Taken together, these cases illustrate how experiential augmentation reshapes learning, work, and governance across very different domains. In the public sector, carefully scoped assistants show that transparency, escalation, and plain-language explanations can build trust while teaching both citizens and staff how processes function. In creative industries, augmentation fosters exploration rather than automation, with variation grids, lineage, and recovery tools making experimentation safe and repeatable. Telemetry then provides the connective tissue, converting isolated experiments into cumulative organizational learning by capturing outcome quality, fairness, costs, and satisfaction in ways that can be acted upon. Finally, equity and privacy concerns remind us that experiential systems succeed only when their benefits are broadly distributed and grounded in clear principles of necessity, proportionality, and recourse.

Experiential Augmentation Across Domains

Public-Sector Services

- Start with intake and status queries; defer eligibility decisions until systems are proven (NIST, 2024).
- Ensure provenance, escalation paths, and "talk to a person" options are visible (Larsen et al., 2024).
- Staff corrections should feed back as new tests and documentation, making oversight visible.
- Measure legitimacy with fairness metrics like wait-time equity and appeal rates, not raw chatbot volumes.

Creative Industries

- Use augmentation for ideation, variation, and critique—not end-to-end automation (Long et al., 2024).
- Support safe exploration with variation grids, lineage, and one-click recovery (McGuire et al., 2024).
- Pair creativity with validators (brand-safety, ethics) that catch problems early without stifling experimentation.
- Archive prompts, sources, and outputs so studios can teach style and judgment through artifacts rather than folklore.

Telemetry and Feedback Loops

- Collect continuous data on quality, latency, cost, satisfaction, and fairness (NIST, 2024).
- Require explainability and recovery features so telemetry can be interpreted by humans (Zhao and Li, 2025).
- In education, track hint acceptance, source use, and transfer performance to refine tutors (Li et al., 2025).
- Convert telemetry into **evidence briefs** each sprint to highlight both limits and opportunities.

Equity and Privacy

- Follow principles of necessity and proportionality in data collection (EDPB, 2024).
- Favor local processing and federated learning to minimize exposure (EDPS, 2025).
- Publish acceptance tests, failure cases, and accessibility plans to prevent uneven benefits (Kestin et al., 2025).
- Provide provenance and appeal channels so users can contest errors and avoid silent exclusion.

The overarching lesson is that augmentation is not about speed for its own sake but about embedding feedback loops that teach both people and systems how to improve. Well-designed agents turn escalations into new tests, prompts into shared craft knowledge, and telemetry into organizational memory. When paired with strong privacy and fairness safeguards, these loops amplify human capability without eroding trust. Institutions that treat experiential augmentation as a practice of co-learning—between citizens and agencies, creators and studios, students and tutors—will be best positioned to translate novelty into durable capability. In this sense, experiential agents are not replacements for human judgment but instruments for cultivating resilience, equity, and continuous improvement at scale.

8.3 WORKFORCE PREPAREDNESS: ADAPTABILITY, TRANSFER, AND POWER SKILLS

Preparing a workforce to thrive with agents demands capabilities that travel across roles, tools, and domains rather than mastery of a single platform. As the World Economic Forum (2025) argues, the skills that compound value are analytical thinking, creative thinking, resilience, and curiosity—capacities that support adaptation as tasks and models change. Employers also continue to prize communication, teamwork, and leadership, which are increasingly exercised through human–AI collaboration rather than only human–human interaction (National Association of Colleges and Employers, 2024). In this chapter's frame, these "power skills" become the glue for transfer, allowing people to move their orchestration and evaluation habits from one workflow to another. Adaptability is not improvisation; it is a repeatable method of scoping decisions, testing claims, and recovering safely when assumptions fail. Transfer is likewise a design choice, achieved by teaching people to generalize patterns such as retrieval, tool use, guardrails, and telemetry. Power skills ensure that such patterns remain legible to teammates and stakeholders who must trust the results. Workforce preparedness thus becomes a coherent system of adaptability, transfer, and communication-enabled judgment.

Defining adaptability first clarifies what training must cultivate and how progress should be assessed. As the Organisation for Economic Co-operation and Development (2023) argues, adaptive expertise rests on two pillars—efficient routine performance and flexible innovation—so programs should alternate between stability and stretch. The National Academies (2024) add that foundational skills like digital literacy, reasoning, and communication provide the substrate for "learn-how-to-learn," which predicts long-run mobility. Practically, this means mixing familiar tools with novel tasks, pairing quick wins with deliberate struggle in safe sandboxes, and foregrounding reflection about strategy choice. Adaptability training should also make uncertainty explicit by asking learners to name risks, trade-offs, and "must-not-fail" thresholds before touching a model. Assessment then rewards calibrated decision-making, not only speed, by scoring how well people bound scope and select appropriate controls. By treating adaptability as a method rather than a trait, organizations transform anxiety into craft. Over time, the habit of structured adaptation compounds into credible leadership under change.

Transfer requires mapping skills to reusable patterns so people can move competence across contexts without starting over. As NIST's Generative AI Profile suggests, orchestration and evaluation are domain-agnostic disciplines that can be taught as portable patterns—retrieve, reason, tool, review, and roll back (National Institute of Standards and Technology, 2024). ISO/IEC 42001 complements this view by embedding those patterns in a management system—roles, artifacts, audits—so practice survives team turnover. Instructionally, this implies teaching "design once, use many": document playbooks, acceptance tests, and escalation paths that travel from marketing to operations to compliance. Teams should practice rewriting the same use case for different risk classes to make transfer visible and discussable. Learners then see that the choreography, not the specific model, is what endures as vendors evolve. Transfer thus becomes a measurable outcome rather than an accidental by-product. Graduates of such programs speak the same operational language even when their tools diverge.

Curricula that build these capacities must blend short concept blocks with mentored, bounded pilots so knowledge crosses the classroom–work boundary. As EDUCAUSE (2024) argues, experiential learning with generative systems accelerates only when guardrails, data provenance, and clear assessment are present. The LinkedIn Workplace Learning Report (2024) also finds that organizations invest most in communication and leadership, which underwrite the collaboration patterns needed for human–AI teams. Practical course design therefore stages learning in sprints: scope and risk rating, retrieval and tool use, evaluation and rollback, and communication of limits. Each sprint culminates in a "readiness brief" that executives could actually read—metrics, failures, mitigations, and next bets. Faculty or coaches serve as orchestrators rather than lecturers, modeling escalation and trade-off language in real time. Because artifacts persist, each cohort inherits a living library of successes and anti-patterns. Over time, these portfolios become the institution's transferable memory of safe speed.

Assessing adaptability and transfer credibly requires authentic evidence rather than quiz scores alone. As W3C's verifiable credentials work shows, portable attestations with issuer, criteria, and proof links can make capabilities inspectable outside the issuing program (WWWC, 2024). Donelson et al. (2025) further argue that selective disclosure allows individuals to share "just enough" evidence for a role or audit without oversharing sensitive details. In practice, learners submit performance artifacts—scoping cards, evidence briefs, failure postmortems—tied to explicit rubrics and signed by mentors or employers. Programs publish their criteria and negative test libraries so reviewers can understand what "good" means in context. As careers progress, holders refresh claims by linking new deployments and incident reviews, not just course completions. This evidence spine turns "soft" skills into auditable practice. The result is transfer that others can see, verify, and reward.

Preparing for productivity augmentation requires honest calibration of what current tools actually change. As Ziegler et al. (2024) show, developer copilots can raise throughput on certain categories while leaving complex design work variable. Noy and Zhang (2023) similarly find that generative assistants improve mid-level writing tasks for many users, with benefits moderated by verification habits and task type. Training should therefore teach "where to aim the agent": boilerplate and search first, structured transformation next, and only then higher-variance synthesis under strong review. Learners practice test-first assistance so acceptance gates—not vibes—decide when suggestions stick. Teams also rehearse rollbacks and incident responses so speed does not erode safety during crunch times. Managers evaluate uplift alongside rework cost and error containment, not just raw time saved. By making augmentation accountable, organizations avoid productivity illusions.

Power skills must be recast as the operating system of human–AI work, not a "soft" afterthought. As Deloitte argues, communication, critical thinking, and collaboration become "power skills" precisely because they determine whether technical capabilities translate into outcomes others can trust (Deloitte, 2024). The World Economic Forum echoes this by ranking analytical and creative thinking, resilience, and curiosity among the most rising skills in the workplace. Instructionally, this means practicing explanation, negotiation, and boundary-setting with agents as often as with people. Learners should role-play stakeholder conversations about limits, fairness, and escalation—core acts in any governed deployment. Review sessions should grade the clarity of uncertainty statements and the quality of trade-off reasoning, not only the technical artifact. Teams that normalize these conversations ship faster because controversy is anticipated and structured. Power skills thus become the throttle that converts capability into legitimate change.

Equity and privacy are not parallel goals to be "balanced" after the fact; they are conditions for participation at scale. As the European Data Protection Board (2024) contends, necessity and proportionality should govern collection and disclosure in AI-mediated work, which is best achieved with local processing and selective disclosure by default. UNESCO likewise recommends that generative uses in learning contexts be transparent, accessible, and paired with human review so power asymmetries do not deepen (UNESCO, 2023). Workforce programs should therefore evaluate subgroup outcomes and provide recourse pathways that are visible and easy to use. Assignments should include accessible alternatives and explicit accommodations that preserve rigor without exclusion. Managers should publish intended-use briefs for internal agents so staff understand scope, rights, and complaint channels. When these norms are routine, adoption compounds rather than stalls on trust concerns. Equity becomes a property of the system, not a promise.

Organizations must also invest in the social infrastructure that sustains adaptability and transfer once courses end. As NIST stresses, communities of practice, incident reviews, and portfolio-level audits are the rituals that keep lessons fresh and visible beyond individual teams. Boston Consulting Group (2024) adds that scaling generative tools or agents stalls without responsible scaffolding—metrics, governance, and empowered stewards—who can say "not yet" when evidence is thin. Practically, this means staffing evaluators and data stewards as first-class roles with career paths and recognition. It also means budgeting for continuous testing and supplier retests as recurring operating costs, not emergencies. Leaders should celebrate correct rollbacks as evidence of maturity, thereby lowering the political cost of caution. Public artifacts—tests, briefs, incident summaries—should be shared internally to reduce duplicated mistakes. With this scaffolding, cultures learn faster than any one tool can change.

Power skills and transfer also hinge on credentialing that keeps up with the pace of change. As LinkedIn Learning (2024) reports, organizations are shifting toward skills-first hiring internally, but credibility rests on evidence that survives manager turnover. Verifiable records and portfolio-based attestations allow hiring managers to inspect scope, metrics, and mitigations rather than infer competence from job titles (WWWC, 2024). Programs can then align micro-credentials to orchestration and evaluation milestones—e.g., "designed shadow-mode pilot with acceptance tests and rollback plan." Alumni refresh credentials with new deployments, negative tests, and incident reviews that broaden their evidence base. Employers reciprocate by co-signing task verifications and sharing outcome metrics that help programs improve. This ecosystem rewards the teachable parts of performance rather than the most charismatic demos. In the long run, trust follows proof, not just promise.

Noteworthy, workforce preparedness should include a research agenda that tracks adaptation and transfer over time rather than snapshots at launch. As the AI Index suggests, measurement must evolve with tasks, models, and institutions, which requires more longitudinal studies linking capabilities to outcomes and governance (Stanford HAI, 2024). Future work should compare modular versus monolithic agent curricula on transfer and safety across sectors with different risk appetites. Researchers should also quantify the ROI of power-skills training when paired with orchestration and evaluation, not in isolation. Additional priorities include studying recourse usability, subgroup error dynamics under drift, and credential validity in skills-based mobility. National Academies-style syntheses can distill evidence for policymakers who set funding and reporting incentives (National Academies of Sciences, Engineering, and Medicine, 2024). In practice, programs should publish open rubrics, tests, and anonymized artifacts to accelerate cumulative knowledge. Preparedness, in short, is a public project that grows with shared evidence.

Therefore, the central insight from this section is that workforce preparedness in an era of intelligent agents is less about mastering a particular tool and more about cultivating capacities that travel across contexts. Adaptability, transfer, and power skills operate as a mutually reinforcing system: adaptability provides the method for managing uncertainty, transfer encodes practices into reusable patterns, and power skills ensure those practices remain legible, explainable, and trustworthy to colleagues and stakeholders. Together, they transform anxiety about change into structured capability, turning improvisation into evidence-based craft.

Examples from coding copilots, tutoring systems, and public-sector chatbots show that agents deliver value only when humans can scope tasks, test results, and escalate appropriately. This reinforces the argument that adaptability is not innate flexibility but a skill that can be deliberately taught and evaluated. Transfer emerges when these orchestration and evaluation practices are documented, shared, and applied across domains, ensuring that lessons learned in marketing, compliance, or education can travel with workers into new contexts. Power skills—communication, teamwork, leadership—function as the social operating system that makes technical performance meaningful and auditable in organizational life.

Equity and privacy remain non-negotiable conditions for preparedness, shaping not just who benefits from augmentation but whether adoption is legitimate at scale. Verifiable credentials and portfolio-based attestations provide the evidentiary backbone for demonstrating these skills, while selective disclosure and accessible recourse protect individuals from overexposure or exclusion. Organizations that pair credentialing with continuous communities of practice, incident reviews, and portfolio audits create the infrastructure needed to sustain these habits over time.

In sum, preparedness for agent-rich work is a project of building people who can adapt, transfer, and explain under pressure, not just operators of a single model. Institutions that invest in these capacities will not only ship safer and more effective systems, but also cultivate workforces that thrive across technological shifts. This is the promise of power skills recast for the age of agents: not "soft" add-ons, but the throttle that converts technical possibility into sustainable and equitable change.

8.4 EVALUATIVE CRITERIA AND BEST PRACTICES FOR LONG-TERM AI STRATEGY INTEGRATION

Long-term AI strategy becomes durable when evaluation is treated as a management system rather than a one-time checklist, binding goals, risks, and evidence into a repeatable cadence (Table 8.2; Figure 8.2). As ISO/IEC 42001 emphasizes, organizations should encode roles, artifacts, and audits across the full lifecycle so oversight survives personnel changes and vendor shifts. NIST frames the same idea in operational terms: define context, map risks, select controls, and measure outcomes with thresholds that trigger rollbacks, not debates. Practically, that means every initiative ships with acceptance tests, negative tests, model cards, datasheets, and incident runbooks. It also means that leaders review value, quality, safety, and learning on the same drumbeat as finances. As AI Verify argues, governance should be task-proportional, scaling documentation and evaluation to the potential for harm rather than applying the same burden to all uses (AI Verify Foundation, 2024). OMB's federal guidance adds a public-sector lens: publish inventories, designate officials, and require impact assessments and waivers for high-risk uses (OMB, 2024). Strategy integration, in short, is the institutionalization of evaluation as a living practice.

Table 8.2 Telemetry Scorecard Template

Week	*Outcome Quality*	*Groundedness/ Citations*	*Latency*	*Cost*	*Safety Incidents*	*Abstention/ Override*	*Subgroup Deltas*	*Drift Signals*
Week 1								
Week 2								
Week 3								
Week 4								

The first evaluative criterion is strategic fit, which asks whether an agent proposal meaningfully advances organizational objectives within explicit boundaries of risk, resources, and governance. Too often, new projects are launched on the basis of novelty or executive pressure to "do something with AI," rather than a sober analysis of alignment to measurable goals. The AI Index (SIHCAI, 2024) stresses that leaders should tie initiatives to outcomes that can be tracked over time, publishing before-and-after baselines so claims remain falsifiable rather than anecdotal. NIST recommends classifying agents along an autonomy spectrum—assistive, predictive, or constrained-autonomous—so that expectations about oversight, escalation, and monitoring are specified up front. Strategic fit also forces trade-offs: boards should routinely ask "What will we stop doing if this system is adopted?" This ensures new capacity is freed for retraining, evaluation, or supplier re-tests, rather than layering novelty on top of existing burdens. Portfolio councils must be empowered to reject technically "impressive" ideas that dilute focus or add surface area for governance without corresponding business value. BCG (2024) emphasizes that scaffolding—evaluation metrics, governance gates, shared services—is not a tax on innovation but an enabling condition for scaling responsibly. Over time, treating strategic fit as a scored gate rather than a "gut feel" reduces governance debt and keeps investment portfolios coherent. For example, a healthcare system might decline a proposal for a diagnostic chatbot—even if technically accurate—because it adds malpractice exposure and distracts from investments in retrieval systems that improve clinician efficiency.

The second criterion is governance maturity, which evaluates whether oversight practices are real, recurring, and documented—or whether they exist only in slide decks. ISO/IEC 42001 conceptualizes governance as a management system, spanning policy, planning, support, operation, performance evaluation, and continuous improvement. In practical terms, maturity means that teams don't just have policies but also predictable operating rhythms. NIST translates this into rituals such as shadow evaluation (testing against human baselines before exposure), drift huddles (reviewing data distribution shifts), incident reviews (time-boxed, blameless analyses of failures), and release gates (structured checklists before deployments). These rituals embed accountability into calendars rather than leaving it to chance. OMB's 2024 memo operationalizes maturity for U.S.

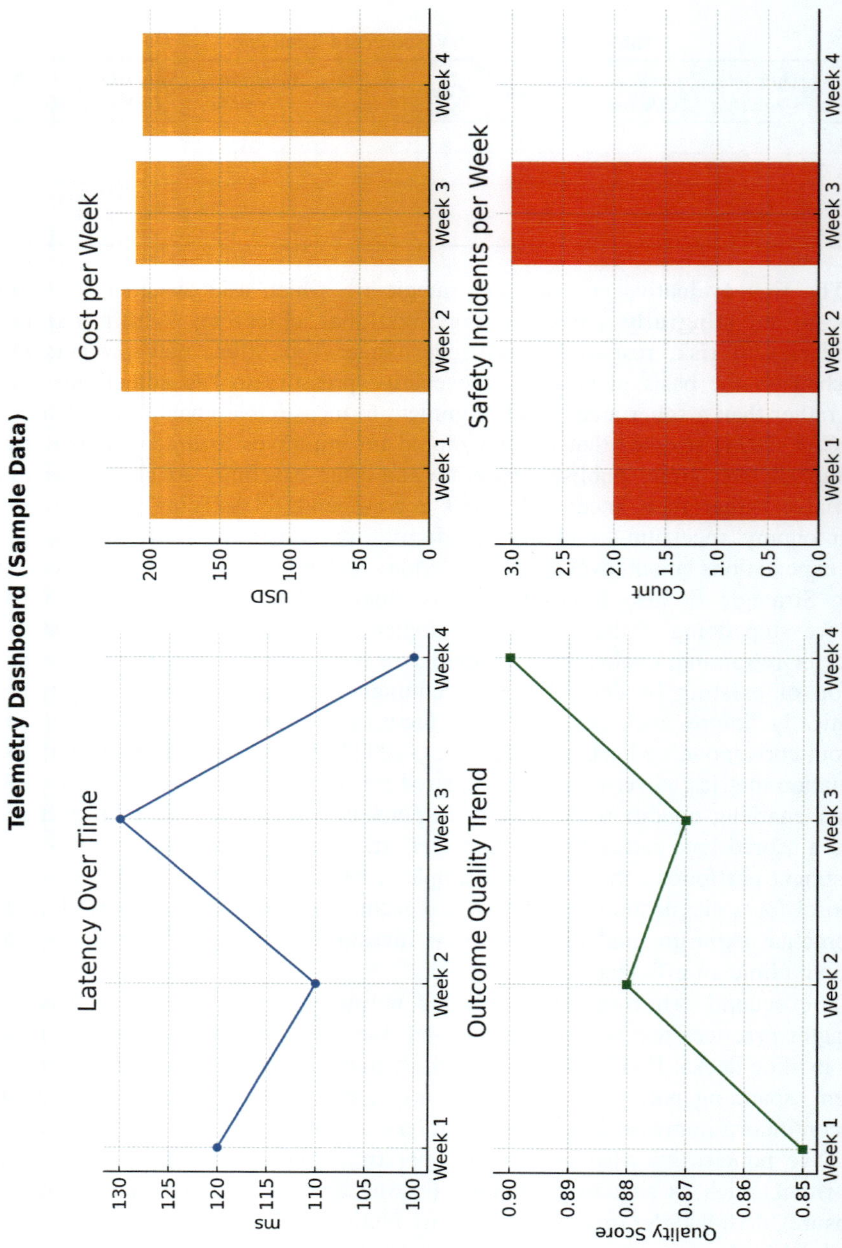

Figure 8.2 Sample Telemetry Dashboard.

federal agencies by requiring system inventories, risk tiers, and public reporting—mechanisms private firms can mirror to gain legitimacy with regulators and customers. A best practice is to audit a sample of systems every quarter to verify artifact completeness (model cards, data sheets, acceptance tests) and decision traceability. Mature programs ensure that red-team findings do not disappear into reports but become negative test cases that prevent regressions across the portfolio. AI Verify (2024) encourages publishing summaries of audit results and mitigations, which both socialize lessons internally and build external trust. Governance maturity is evidenced not by slogans or compliance theater, but by the cadence of real, documented action.

The third criterion is risk and harm management, which demands that proportional controls are visible, testable, and reversible. ISO/IEC 23894 (2023) places risk management in a loop: identification, analysis, evaluation, and treatment, each evidenced with artifacts and measurable outcomes. NIST translates this into control families—valid use, design and development, deployment—each with example actions (like sandboxing high-risk modules) and acceptance measures tailored for generative system. OWASP's LLM Top-10 contributes an attack-surface perspective: prompt injection (malicious manipulation of prompts), insecure plug-in use, or hidden data leakage should be explicitly modeled in threat scenarios and acceptance tests. Leaders should require "must-not-fail" cases: for instance, an intake assistant for unemployment claims must always escalate certain categories of urgent hardship applications. These gates should be coupled with impact-weighted thresholds and fallback pathways that degrade safely under drift. Post-incident reviews should not end with memos but with updated playbooks and new blocking test cases. Suppliers, too, must face identical risk gates when shipping updated models or changing telemetry terms. Risk programs that normalize reversibility—routine rollbacks, phased releases, feature flags—scale more quickly because caution is institutionalized rather than stigmatized. An example is a municipal permitting office: when a new policy shifts zoning categories, the agent must degrade gracefully to "manual review" rather than producing invalid classifications.

The fourth criterion is evidence quality, which determines whether claims of value would persuade skeptics with different incentives. Organizations are often tempted to overstate pilot results in dashboards that highlight speed but neglect quality or safety. The AI Index stresses the need to distinguish perceived speed (users feel faster) from verified outcomes (measured error reduction, reduced rework) and to report confidence intervals, not cherry-picked averages (SIHCAI, 2024). NIST recommends instrumenting outcome quality, latency, cost, and safety incidents, tying each metric to acceptance gates and rollback triggers. For retrieval-grounded systems, specialized metrics like context relevance, groundedness, and answer relevance help localize failure rather than mystify it. A robust evaluation program combines golden sets for must-not-fail cases, synthetic tests for broad coverage, and targeted human audits for calibration. Evidence must also surface subgroup disparities, so hidden inequities are not masked by global averages. Executives should receive evidence briefs that pair successes with limits and trade-offs, not only marketing claims. For example, an educational tutor might report 20% faster homework completion times, but evidence briefs should also show whether English-language learners benefited equally. Evidence quality transforms evaluation into a persuasive practice, ensuring that scaling decisions rest on shared credibility.

The fifth criterion is portfolio health, which shifts focus from isolated wins to whether the entire ecosystem of agents is sustainable. Many organizations stall because they scale pilots without scaling evaluation literacy, shared services, or steward capacity. BCG (2024) highlights that a strong portfolio is characterized not by dozens of flashy pilots but by compounding capability—pattern libraries, telemetry dashboards, and governance staff—that make judgment reusable across contexts. ISO/IEC 42001 suggests treating portfolio reviews as part of continuous improvement, ensuring that weak systems are retired, promising ones refactored, and reliable ones scaled. NIST identifies practical triggers for portfolio triage: recurring drift incidents, supplier updates, or clusters of similar failures should move projects onto a retire/refactor/scale Kanban. Leaders should see heat maps of artifact completeness, red-team coverage, and incident density, which help prioritize scarce evaluation resources. Sunset dates on pilots prevent "zombie systems" from consuming attention without delivering trust. Shared pattern libraries allow a win in one unit—say, customer service escalation templates—to become a standard asset across divisions. In effect, portfolio health creates a strategic asset: the ability to learn once and reuse everywhere.

The sixth criterion is data and privacy posture, which evaluates whether systems achieve value without undermining public trust or regulatory compliance. The European Data Protection Board argues for necessity and proportionality by design: collect only the data required for the task, and disclose only the attributes that verifiers must see. The European Data Protection Supervisor recommends federated learning (training models across multiple parties without centralizing raw data) and local processing (keeping sensitive information on-device), both of which reduce cross-party exposure while maintaining learning. NIST complements these principles with logging requirements—purpose, consent, access events—so audits can reconstruct boundaries. Evaluators should score systems not just on access controls but also on de-identification practices, retention schedules, and selective-disclosure mechanisms. Intended-use briefs should clearly explain "what is processed, where, and why" in plain language, accessible to staff and external reviewers. Privacy posture must be proven by artifacts—tests, contracts, and logs—rather than aspirational statements. Programs that embed privacy controls well often reduce regulatory delays and gain faster adoption approvals, as in the case of banks that implement zero-knowledge proofs to verify compliance attributes without exposing full transaction histories.

The seventh criterion is security and supply-chain assurance, which recognizes that most failures occur at interfaces—between prompts, tools, and suppliers—rather than inside models themselves. OWASP highlights that risks like prompt injection (maliciously altering instructions) and insecure tool use are primary attack surfaces for agentic systems, requiring defenses at points where untrusted content enters. NIST recommends sandboxing, rate limits, budget guards, and cross-agent observability so incident response can target failures at the correct seam. OMB's requirements for agency supplier inventories and standardized control language provide a template that enterprises can adapt in contracts and service agreements. Assurance programs should trigger mandatory re-tests whenever vendors update models, telemetry, or policies. Organizations should maintain supplier registers with risk tiers, escalation contacts, and incident SLAs, enabling faster joint remediation. Red-team findings must become blocking tests in CI/CD pipelines so both internal and third-party changes are subjected to scrutiny. Security maturity is proven not by claiming invulnerability but by showing resilience: the ability to survive inevitable supplier or adversarial changes. For example, an enterprise might rerun all regression tests when OpenAI or Anthropic updates APIs, treating supplier change as a routine event rather than an unpredictable shock.

The eighth criterion is financial realism, which insists that budgets account for the recurring costs of safety and stewardship. BCG (2024) warns that many "AI ROI" cases collapse because financial models count only license fees while ignoring the costs of red-teaming, drift monitoring, retraining, supplier audits, and compliance reporting. NIST suggests reviewing value, quality, safety, and learning metrics together so throughput gains are not purchased at the expense of hidden risk. OMB demonstrates how agencies budget explicitly for evaluation staff, reporting requirements, and monitoring infrastructure—cost centers that private firms often neglect but can adapt. Finance leaders should view evaluation and stewardship as first-class operating costs, not overhead to be cut during downturns. Leaders should demand ROI analyses that show margin after controls, not before, preventing illusions of productivity. Scenario analysis should test for supplier price shocks, regulatory changes, or sudden retraining costs. Strategic patience requires acknowledging that some percentage of budget will always flow to governance. Financial realism is the antidote to hype-driven fiscal planning.

The ninth criterion is human factors and power skills, which recognize that adoption is not sustained by technical capacity alone but by people's ability to supervise, explain, and negotiate. The World Economic Forum highlights analytical and creative thinking, resilience, and curiosity as the fastest-rising skills (WEF, 2025). NACE (2024) reports that employers continue to prize communication, teamwork, and leadership—capabilities that govern how staff escalate issues, interpret uncertainty, and manage consent in hybrid human–agent workflows. NIST recommends UX affordances such as one-click recovery, visible escalation paths, and user-facing explanations to keep trust calibrated. Training programs should grade not only technical artifacts but also the clarity of uncertainty statements and trade-off reasoning. Communities of practice should share patterns and anti-patterns with credited authorship so institutional judgment becomes portable. Power skills should be deliberately paired with orchestration and evaluation practices, making transfer visible across contexts. Human factors are not a footnote—they are the criterion that determines whether adoption sticks once hype fades.

The tenth criterion is transparency and legitimacy, which determine whether organizations earn the permission to scale. AI Verify (2024) encourages publishing audit summaries, model-card snapshots, and mitigations proportional to risk, which builds credibility with regulators and customers. OMB's policy requiring system inventories and impact assessments for significant uses provides a governance model that private firms can emulate. The AI Index (SIHCAI, 2024) suggests that openness about limits, failures, and incident histories improves both external oversight and internal learning. Organizations should adopt quarterly evidence briefs that combine wins with known limits in plain language. Public-facing FAQs should describe system scope, user rights, and complaint channels in accessible terms. Vendor contracts should stipulate audit cooperation and documentation obligations as non-negotiables. Transparency, when routine rather than performative, becomes a competitive moat: customers, regulators, and staff are more likely to trust systems whose builders are candid about risks.

This chapter set out to establish that the adoption of intelligent agents is not a matter of raw technical capability or organizational enthusiasm, but of disciplined evaluation across multiple, interlocking criteria. Strategic fit, governance maturity, risk and harm management, evidence quality, portfolio health, data and privacy posture, security and supply-chain assurance, financial realism, human factors, and transparency were identified as the essential gates that transform experiments into durable practice. The central point is that agents are not trustworthy simply because they "work" in a pilot; they are trustworthy when their design, deployment, and oversight can withstand scrutiny, reversibility, and change.

Key points can be summarized as follows: Strategic fit ensures that deployments serve declared goals rather than diffuse focus or add unmanaged complexity. Governance maturity anchors oversight in rhythms, audits, and artifacts, moving from policy rhetoric to operational discipline. Risk and harm management emphasizes proportionality and reversibility, designing for safe failure rather than brittle optimism. Evidence quality raises the standard of proof so that claims persuade skeptics as well as advocates, while portfolio health shifts attention from isolated wins to reusable judgment across contexts. Data and privacy posture clarifies necessity and proportionality, protecting legitimacy with selective disclosure and architectural safeguards. Security and supply-chain assurance address the reality that most failures occur at interfaces, not inside models, demanding resilience in the face of supplier updates and adversarial probes. Financial realism prevents illusions of productivity by pricing learning loops—red-teaming, monitoring, retraining—into business cases. Human factors and power skills acknowledge that adoption depends on people's ability to supervise, explain, and negotiate, while transparency extends credibility outward to regulators, customers, and the public.

The significance of this framework is twofold. First, it redefines governance as an enabling practice rather than a brake on innovation. By making evaluation a structured habit, organizations reduce governance debt and compound capability, converting one-off lessons into institutional assets. Second, it positions transparency, privacy, and human oversight not as afterthoughts but as preconditions for legitimacy. In an environment where regulators, employees, and citizens all scrutinize the use of generative and agentic systems, organizations that embed evaluative rigor earn permission to scale, while those that shortcut these disciplines risk backlash, stalled adoption, and credibility loss. Governance becomes a strategic differentiator, separating institutions that can adapt responsibly from those caught in cycles of hype and retreat.

Future research should deepen and extend this evaluative model. Longitudinal studies are needed to test which criteria predict sustained adoption and resilience across industries. Comparative work can explore how governance maturity scales differently in regulated sectors such as healthcare and finance versus creative or educational domains. More evidence is also required on the return on investment of evaluation itself: what combinations of red-teaming, telemetry, and stewardship deliver the best balance of safety and efficiency? Further investigation into human factors—how power skills like negotiation and explanation mediate trust in agentic systems—will clarify how to integrate technical and organizational training. Finally, cross-national studies of transparency and legitimacy can reveal how cultural, legal, and regulatory environments shape the success of evaluative frameworks.

Ergo, the chapter demonstrates that the future of agent adoption lies not in unbounded experimentation but in disciplined governance. By embedding evaluation across strategy, process, and culture, organizations can transform curiosity into compounding capability, building portfolios of systems that are auditable, reversible, and aligned with purpose. The research frontier is to move beyond frameworks into empirical validation—showing, with cumulative evidence, how evaluative criteria make the difference between fragile novelty and sustainable impact.

REFERENCES

AI Verify Foundation (AVF). 2024. Model AI Governance Framework for Generative AI (June 19, 2024). https://aiverifyfoundation.sg/wp-content/uploads/2024/06/Model-AI-Governance-Framework-for-Generative-AI-19-June-2024.pdf

Boston Consulting Group (BCG). 2024. GenAI can't scale without responsible AI. https://www.bcg.com/publications/2024/genai-cant-scale-without-responsible-ai

Deloitte. 2024. Power skills in the age of AI. Deloitte Insights. https://www2.deloitte.com/insights

Donelson, D.C., Kim, M.J., Kim, S. and Yip, M.A. 2025. Strategic AI disclosures: Determinants and consequences of obfuscated and overstated AI investments. Available at SSRN 5265257.

EDUCAUSE. 2024. Horizon Report: Teaching and Learning Edition. EDUCAUSE. https://library.educause.edu

Es, S., James, J., Espinosa-Anke, L. and Schockaert, S. 2024. RAGAS: Automated evaluation of retrieval-augmented generation. *In*: Proceedings of EACL 2024 (Demos): 154–165. https://aclanthology.org/2024.eacl-demo.16/

European Data Protection Board (EDPB). 2024. Opinion 28/2024 on certain data protection aspects related to the use of AI models. https://www.edpb.europa.eu/system/files/2024-12/edpb_opinion_202428_ai-models_en.pdf

European Data Protection Supervisor (EDPS). 2025. TechDispatch #1/2025—Federated learning. https://www.edps.europa.eu/data-protection/our-work/publications/techdispatch/2025-06-10-techdispatch-12025-federated-learning_en

Gu, J., Jiang, X., Shi, Z., Tan, H., Zhai, X., Xu, C., et al. 2024. A survey on LLM-as-a-Judge. arXiv. https://arxiv.org/abs/2411.15594

Guo, Y. (ed.). 2024. Digital Government and Public Interaction: Platforms, Chatbots, and Public Satisfaction: Platforms, Chatbots, and Public Satisfaction. IGI Global.

Huang, X., Liu, W., Chen, X., Wang, X., Wang, H., Lian, D., et al. 2024. Understanding the planning of LLM agents: A survey. arXiv. https://arxiv.org/abs/2402.02716

International Organization for Standardization & International Electrotechnical Commission (ISO/IEC). 2023. ISO/IEC 23894:2023 Information technology—Artificial intelligence—Risk management. https://www.iso.org/standard/77304.html

International Organization for Standardization & International Electrotechnical Commission (ISO/IEC). 2023. ISO/IEC 42001:2023 Artificial intelligence—Management system. https://www.iso.org/standard/42001

Khattab, O., Singhvi, A., Maheshwari, P., Zhang, Z., Santhanam, K., Vardhamanan, S., et al. 2023. DSPy: Compiling declarative language model calls into self-improving pipelines. arXiv. https://arxiv.org/abs/2310.03714

Kestin, G., Laski, E., Browne, W., Kim, J., Farmer, R. and O'Shea, B. 2025. AI tutoring outperforms in-class active learning. Scientific Reports. 15: 17458. https://doi.org/10.1038/s41598-025-97652-6

Létourneau, A., O'Neil, K., Dastin, C. and Chen, H. 2025. A systematic review of AI-driven intelligent tutoring systems in K-12 education. NPJ Science of Learning. https://www.nature.com/articles/s41539-025-00320-7

Li, Z., Chen, Q. and Zhang, H. 2025. Retrieval-augmented generation for educational applications: A survey. Patterns. 6(2): 100567. https://doi.org/10.1016/j.patter.2025.100567

Liu, X., Yu, H., Zhang, H., Xu, Y., Lei, X., Lai, H., et al. 2023a. AgentBench: Evaluating LLMs as agents. arXiv. https://arxiv.org/abs/2308.03688

Long, T., Chilton, L.B., Hartmann, B. and Bernstein, M.S. 2024. Not just novelty: A longitudinal study on utility and customization of an AI tool for science communication. *In*: DIS '24: Designing Interactive Systems Conference, pp. 1–15. https://doi.org/10.1145/3652577.3658342

Malik, O.A., Tun, H.M., Rahman, H.A. and Naing, L. 2025. Trust in AI-based clinical decision support systems among health care workers: Systematic review. Journal of Medical Internet Research. 27: e69678. https://doi.org/10.2196/69678

National Academies of Sciences, Engineering, and Medicine (NASEM). 2024. Foundational Skills for the U.S. Workforce. The National Academies Press. https://doi.org/10.17226/27591

National Association of Colleges and Employers (NACE). 2024. Job outlook 2024: Career readiness competencies. NACE. https://www.naceweb.org

National Institute of Standards and Technology (NIST). 2024. Artificial Intelligence Risk Management Framework: Generative AI Profile (NIST AI 600-1). https://doi.org/10.6028/NIST.AI.600-1

Noy, S. and Zhang, W. 2023. Experimental evidence on the productivity effects of generative artificial intelligence. Science. 381(6654): 187–192. https://doi.org/10.1126/science.adh2586

Office of Management and Budget (OMB). 2024. Advancing governance, innovation, and risk management for agency use of artificial intelligence (M-24-10). https://www.whitehouse.gov/omb

OWASP Foundation. 2025. OWASP Top 10 for LLM applications: LLM01—Prompt injection (v2025). https://owasp.org/www-project-top-10-for-large-language-model-applications/assets/PDF/OWASP-Top-10-for-LLMs-v2025.pdf

Shinn, N., Cassano, F., Berman, E., Gopinath, A., Narasimhan, K. and Yao, S. 2023. Reflexion: Language agents with verbal reinforcement learning. arXiv. https://arxiv.org/abs/2303.11366

Stanford Institute for Human-Centered Artificial Intelligence (SIHCAI). 2024. AI Index Report 2024. Stanford University. https://aiindex.stanford.edu

TruLens. 2025. The RAG triad: Context relevance, groundedness, answer relevance. https://www.trulens.org/getting_started/core_concepts/rag_triad/

Tsiakas, K., Kocielnik, R., Rapp, A. and Grgić-Hlača, N. 2024. Unpacking human-AI interactions: A design space of interaction primitives and patterns. arXiv preprint arXiv:2401.05115. https://arxiv.org/abs/2401.05115

Tun, H.M., Rahman, H.A., Naing, L. and Malik, O.A. 2025. Trust in artificial intelligence–based clinical decision support systems among health care workers: systematic review. Journal of Medical Internet Research. 27: e69678.

United Nations Educational, Scientific and Cultural Organization (UNESCO). 2023. Guidance for generative AI in education and research. UNESCO. https://unesdoc.unesco.org

Wang, L., Ma, C., Feng, X., Zhang, Z., Yang, H., Zhang, J., et al. 2023. A survey on large language model–based autonomous agents. arXiv. https://arxiv.org/abs/2308.11432

World Economic Forum (WEF). 2025. The future of jobs report 2023. World Economic Forum. https://www.weforum.org/reports/future-of-jobs-2023

World Wide Web Consortium (WWWC). 2024. Verifiable Credentials Data Model 2.0. W3C. https://www.w3.org/TR/vc-data-model-2.0/

Wu, Q., Bansal, G., Zhang, J., Wu, Y., Li, B., Jiang, L., et al. 2023. AutoGen: Enabling next-gen LLM applications via multi-agent conversation. arXiv. https://arxiv.org/abs/2308.08155

Yang, R., Ning, Y., Keppo, E., Liu, M., Hong, C., Bitterman, D.S., et al. 2025. Retrieval-augmented generation for generative AI in health care. NPJ Health Systems. 2(2): Article 2. https://doi.org/10.1038/s44401-024-00004-1

Zhang, Z., Chen, T., Sun, S., Wang, Y. and Tang, J. 2025. A survey on knowledge-oriented retrieval-augmented generation. arXiv preprint arXiv:2503.10677. https://arxiv.org/abs/2503.10677

Zhao, C. and Li, H. 2025. Human-AI interaction design standards: A comparative synthesis. arXiv preprint arXiv:2503.16472. https://arxiv.org/abs/2503.16472

Ziegler, A., Kalliamvakou, E., Li, X.A., Rice, A., Rifkin, D., Simister, S., et al. 2024. Measuring GitHub Copilot's impact on productivity. Communications of the ACM. 67(3): 62–71. https://cacm.acm.org/research/measuring-github-copilots-impact-on-productivity/

Chapter 9

Conclusion—Toward a New Paradigm in AI-Enhanced Learning and Work

9.1 SYNTHESIZING FAST/SLOW LEARNING WITHIN MODULAR AND AGENTIC CONTEXTS

Across the book, fast learning (rapid generation, exploration, and option-surfacing) was treated as a catalyst, and slow learning (evaluation, critique, testing, and reflection) as the governor that channels speed into trustworthy outcomes. The concluding synthesis frames these modes not as psychological metaphors alone but as design requirements for modular, agentic systems that separate—and instrument—planning, retrieval, synthesis, testing, critique, and verification. In classrooms and boardrooms, the choreography that works is divergence first, convergence next, with human judgment positioned at named checkpoints and clear criteria for escalation and rollback. What follows distills that choreography into operational patterns, governance moves, and a research agenda for the next wave of AI-enhanced learning and work.

Consider a classroom where students are drafting essays with the aid of a generative writing assistant. The "fast" move is to have the system propose multiple possible outlines or thesis statements in minutes, saving the student from staring at a blank page. The "slow" move is for the instructor to step in with a rubric that asks the student to justify why one outline is stronger than the others, linking claims back to evidence from assigned readings. Instead of choosing quickly, the student must explain their reasoning and defend their choice,

DOI: 10.1201/9781003688013-9

embedding reflection into the process. Over time, students internalize that speed is useful for surfacing options but not for making commitments. In this way, the system acts as a brainstorming partner, while the teacher and student ensure rigor through critique. This choreography, divergence first then convergence, transforms writing from a private struggle into an inspectable, teachable process. The same sequence applies to organizations brainstorming policy proposals or marketing campaigns: rapid option generation, followed by structured evaluation before adoption.

The dual-process literature explains why fast ideation and slow evaluation must be deliberately interleaved, not left to chance (Kahneman, 2011; Evans, 2008). Modular and agentic architectures make that interleaving concrete by assigning roles—planner, retriever, solver, critic, verifier—with explicit handoffs and termination conditions (Wu et al., 2023). In this design, fast components propose multiple candidate plans or drafts, while slow components test claims against evidence, constraints, and risk posture (Yao et al., 2023; Wang et al., 2023). The benefit is cognitive and operational: teams externalize tacit judgment into inspectable steps that can be audited, tuned, and taught. Retrieval-augmented generation grounds fast proposals in current context, shrinking the space where slow checks must work hardest (Lewis et al., 2020). Human-in-the-loop gates then decide when to accept "good enough" and when to push for deeper analysis, matching cost to consequence (Amershi et al., 2019). This alignment turns "thinking fast and slow" into "building fast and slow," with speed reserved for exploration and rigor reserved for commitment (Kahneman, 2011). Having established why the principle matters, the next step is to consider how divergence and convergence unfold in practice.

Imagine a hospital using an agentic decision-support system. A "planner" module quickly assembles three possible treatment pathways based on the patient's history and current symptoms. A "retriever" module pulls recent guidelines from trusted medical sources, while a "solver" ranks the options based on probable outcomes. At that point, the "critic" checks for contraindications—say, potential allergic reactions—and the "verifier" ensures that the proposed plan passes all compliance requirements. The human physician acts as the final gate, reviewing the outputs and making the ultimate decision. This division of labor mirrors the fast/slow model: speed to generate possible solutions, deliberate checks to safeguard against error. Because each role is explicit, accountability is clear—if something goes wrong, teams can trace which module or checkpoint failed. The physician's authority is preserved, but the system accelerates option generation while embedding trust in the process.

Operationally, the fast phase should be time-boxed and plural: generate several small alternatives, each tagged with assumptions and success criteria. The slow phase should be evidence-anchored: require sources, calculations, or tests, and record decisions with rationales that survive audit (NIST, 2024). RAG pipelines make this practical by separating "fetch" from "frame," so slow evaluators can inspect citations and retrieval coverage rather than guess at hidden parametric memory (Lewis et al., 2020). Human checkpoints should be placed at natural decision boundaries—before policy claims, irreversible actions, or public release—so reflection is efficient, not performative (Amershi et al., 2019). Pairwise comparison reliably accelerates convergence while preserving quality, especially when rubrics make trade-offs explicit (Watts et al., 2024). Tool-use patterns such as ReAct preserve inspectability by interleaving reasoning traces with actions, enabling slow verification without freezing fast exploration (Yao et al., 2023). Teams should log time-to-first-draft and edit distance to track speed, alongside error-catch rate and escalation frequency to track safety (NIST, 2024). Building from this operational choreography, modular design provides a framework to sustain reliability across contexts.

Picture a design team at a technology company developing slogans for a new product. In the fast phase, an AI system generates ten short slogans in under two minutes, each labeled with its target audience and assumptions about tone. The team knows not to pick immediately; instead, they use a slow phase rubric that asks: Which slogan aligns best with brand values? Which could be misinterpreted? Which requires revision to be culturally sensitive? Each decision is logged, along with the rationale, so that future teams can learn from this cycle. To speed convergence, team members use pairwise comparisons, voting between two slogans at a time rather than ranking all ten. The AI's reasoning traces show why it suggested particular words, making its logic inspectable. Leaders track how quickly the team reaches a final slogan and how many required significant revisions, giving both speed and quality metrics. By staging the workflow explicitly, creativity is balanced with rigor.

Separation of concerns—plan, retrieve, synthesize, test, critique, verify—translates fast/slow into components that can be versioned and measured. Deterministic interfaces (schemas, grammars, typed tools) constrain surface forms so many classes of failure disappear by construction during slow checks (Tuccio et al., 2025; Park et al., 2025). Programmatic structuring of outputs (e.g., JSON that validates) shifts oversight from prose inspection to contract compliance, which is faster and safer in production (Wang, 2025). Diagnostic frameworks like RAGAS and RAGChecker localize errors to the retrieval or generation stage, allowing slow evaluators to fix the right thing without generalizing from symptoms (Es et al., 2024; Ru et al., 2024). Management-system scaffolds (ISO/IEC 42001; NIST AI RMF) make these controls routine by demanding roles, artifacts, and auditable gates across the system life cycle (ISO/IEC, 2023; NIST, 2023). In regulated contexts, selective-prediction and abstention policies formalize "slow down" as a first-class outcome when uncertainty is high (Swaminathan et al., 2024). Conformal wrappers supply coverage guarantees that convert probabilistic outputs into deterministic go/no-go rules aligned to risk (Sreenivasan et al., 2025). Once reliability is modularized, attention shifts to reasoning and reflection as mechanisms for continual self-improvement.

Take an online banking app designed to approve small loans. The "fast" system proposes an approval or denial within seconds based on user input, but its output must be formatted in a strict JSON schema. If the data does not meet validation rules, the request is flagged automatically, preventing hidden errors. The "slow" evaluators then review the flagged cases, with diagnostic tools indicating whether the issue came from the retrieval of financial history or the generation of risk scores. Regulators require that every decision can be explained, so abstention policies allow the system to decline to decide when data is ambiguous. This prevents hasty approvals that could lead to defaults. Coverage guarantees from conformal wrappers ensure that confidence intervals around risk predictions are explicit. By structuring outputs and embedding diagnostics, the bank transforms decision-making into a modular system that combines speed with accountability.

Fast idea generation often benefits from plural reasoning paths; slow evaluation benefits from legible traces that can be critiqued. Techniques such as self-consistency and Tree-of-Thoughts diversify candidate chains of thought before selection, raising accuracy on reasoning tasks (Wang et al., 2023; Yao et al., 2023). Reflective agents that critique and revise their own outputs further reduce error without retraining, provided slow evaluators retain veto authority (Shinn et al., 2023). In multi-agent settings, critic and verifier roles operationalize slow cognition as standing services rather than ad-hoc prompts (Wu et al., 2023). Evaluation must keep pace: AgentBench-style stressors and capability-specific probes surface where the choreography fails—long-horizon planning, instruction following, or tool orchestration (Liu et al., 2023). Telemetry should quantify both speed (latency, cost, time-to-draft) and safety (groundedness, abstention rate, override patterns) so improvements are not illusory (NIST, 2024; Es et al., 2024). When reflection becomes a module—backed by tests, traces, and thresholds—teams learn where to invest next, not just that something went wrong. With reflection embedded, the next challenge is linking outputs to evidence and identity for trust.

Picture a law school moot court exercise. Students use an assistant to draft opening arguments on a legal case, but the system generates three different reasoning paths, each with citations. Instead of accepting the first, students must compare the alternatives, critique weaknesses, and choose the most defensible version. An "AI critic" suggests counterarguments, forcing the student to anticipate opposition. The instructor then evaluates whether the student's reasoning traces demonstrate genuine legal understanding. Logs capture latency (time to draft), edit distance (changes between draft and final), and error catch rate (how many flaws were identified). This turns reflection into a tangible skill rather than vague advice. Over time, students learn that speed provides options, but careful critique makes arguments credible and defensible.

The identity layer connects fast production to slow accountability by preserving provenance, criteria, and proofs. Verifiable credentials and learning/employment records allow institutions to issue portable, tamper-evident attestations anchored to artifacts and rubrics (W3C, 2025; Varadarajan et al., 2023). Selective disclosure enables "just-enough" verification—e.g., active certification status—without oversharing personal data, aligning fast transactions with slow privacy norms (Ramić et al., 2024). Portfolios and e-portfolios supply the narrative context that credentials compress, making slow review teachable and auditable rather than folkloric (Yang, 2024). Agentic curation can draft capability cards, link artifacts to frameworks, and propose next steps, but human reviewers must control publication and scope (Córdova-Esparza et al., 2025). In classrooms, evidence-linked assessment rewards visible reasoning and revision, not only answers, harmonizing fast drafts with slow critique (Panadero and Jonsson, 2013). In workplaces, employer-verified tasks and status checks prevent résumé inflation and keep recognition current, preserving trust at scale (Luk and Chan, 2024; W3C, 2025). Having addressed identity as slow governance, the discussion now turns to pedagogical and workplace practices that institutionalize this cadence.

Imagine a young engineer applying for a new job. Instead of sending a résumé filled with unverifiable claims, she provides a portfolio with verifiable credentials: a "System Optimization" badge tied to code commits and supervisor comments, and a "Safety Protocol Certification" signed by her former employer. Selective disclosure allows her to prove the certification is still active without revealing personal data such as her full work history. A hiring manager can inspect the linked artifacts, see the context in which the skills were demonstrated, and trust that the claims are accurate. The engineer's personal agent has curated capability cards that summarize her competencies, but she remains in control of what gets disclosed. In this way, her fast productivity with generative tools is anchored by slow accountability through verifiable evidence. Trust emerges not from her words alone but from transparent, portable records. This is how identity shifts from static degrees to dynamic, evidence-linked profiles.

Evidence-linked tutors deliver fast hints grounded in course materials while instructors retain slow acceptance and calibration authority (Li et al., 2025; Kestin et al., 2025). Draft-critique-revise loops make student reasoning inspectable, improving transfer and reducing integrity incidents without dampening speed (Kasneci et al., 2023). In industry, RAG-first copilot patterns speed documentation, analysis, and response drafting while human gates protect tone, risk, and policy alignment (Lewis et al., 2020; Amershi et al., 2019). Clinical and public-sector deployments demonstrate "assist, don't decide" early, with slow escalation paths and published intended-use briefs to protect procedural justice (Labkoff et al., 2024; NIST, 2024). In creative studios, multi-tool workflows pair intermittent fast exploration with proactive versioning and one-click recovery, preserving originality and accountability (Long et al., 2024). Across contexts, the choreography is the same: explore broadly, filter with evidence, and commit under guardrails. Institutions should teach this choreography explicitly through studios, capstones, and mentored pilots. To make these practices sustainable, culture must embed the fast/slow balance as a collective norm.

Consider a university biology course. Students use a tutoring agent to get quick clarifications on genetic processes, but the agent always cites passages from the textbook and requires students to explain the logic back in their own words. Instructors then step in to grade the reasoning, not just the answer. This mirrors industry practices, where an AI might draft a compliance report but managers must review it against policies before submission. In healthcare, a triage tool might suggest a patient pathway but always escalate uncertain cases for human approval. In design studios, artists generate multiple drafts but keep recovery tools handy to preserve originality. Whether in school, hospital, or business, the pattern is consistent: speed to surface ideas, governance to ensure quality. The pedagogy reinforces habits that graduates carry into the workplace, bridging learning and professional judgment.

Fast/slow only scales when encoded in roles, rituals, and artifacts rather than in slogans. Management-system scaffolds (ISO/IEC 42001) and risk frameworks (NIST AI RMF, Generative AI Profile) turn gates—shadow evals, drift huddles, incident reviews—into calendar-anchored habits (ISO/IEC, 2023; NIST, 2023, 2024). Reversibility lowers the political cost of caution: predeclared rollback triggers make "not yet" a mark of maturity, not failure (Edmondson, 2019; BCG, 2024). Role clarity—product owner, orchestrator, evaluator, data steward—binds accountability to the right questions at the right time (Amershi et al., 2019). Supplier governance mirrors internal standards so external model updates cannot silently break the choreography (ISO/IEC, 2023; NIST, 2024). Documentation artifacts—model cards, datasheets, evidence briefs—keep slow reasoning visible to decision-makers who must defend outcomes later (Mitchell et al., 2019; Gebru et al., 2021). Communities of practice spread patterns and anti-patterns so judgment compounds beyond single teams. With governance in place, institutions require metrics that can balance speed with safety and fairness.

Think of a municipal government rolling out an AI-powered benefits portal. The culture is reinforced through rituals: weekly drift huddles to see if input data has shifted, monthly incident reviews to refine playbooks, and predeclared rollback triggers in case the system starts failing. Roles are crystal clear: the product owner defines the scope, the orchestrator manages workflows, evaluators test fairness and accuracy, and data stewards oversee privacy and provenance. If a supplier updates their model, it cannot be deployed until all local acceptance tests pass again. Citizens are informed of limits through intended-use briefs and can escalate concerns to a human official. The system's legitimacy rests on documentation and repeatable rituals, not just technical performance. By embedding fast/slow thinking into culture and roles, the city creates an environment where innovation proceeds with accountability.

The synthesis of fast and slow learning within modular and agentic contexts demonstrates that speed and rigor are not opposing forces but complementary design imperatives (Table 9.1). Fast phases accelerate exploration, option generation, and creative divergence, while slow phases provide evaluation, evidence-linking, and reflection that transform novelty into trustworthy action. The book's throughline—that modular architectures, role clarity, and governance rituals make this choreography durable—finds its fullest expression here. Through separating planning, retrieval, synthesis, critique, and verification into distinct components, institutions can measure, monitor, and improve their processes, rather than relying on enthusiasm or intuition.

The examples across education, healthcare, industry, government, and creative work reveal a consistent pattern: success depends on explicitly staging when to move quickly and when to slow down. In classrooms, students draft rapidly but must defend reasoning under rubrics. In hospitals, decision-support systems propose multiple care pathways, but human physicians retain final authority. In creative studios, artists branch widely but preserve rollback and recovery to safeguard originality. Each case illustrates that speed alone does not guarantee progress; without the counterweight of reflection, speed creates brittleness, inequity, and mistrust. Moreover, the significance of this synthesis lies in its

Table 9.1 Fast/Slow Synthesis in Modular, Agentic Systems

Element / Pattern	Purpose (what it solves)	Fast Phase (diverge)	Slow Phase (converge)	Roles and Modules (who/what)	Guardrails and Checkpoints (when to pause)	Key Metrics (how to know)	Core Artifacts (what to keep)	Cross-Domain Example
Choreography: Divergence → Convergence	Turn rapid option-making into trustworthy decisions	Generate multiple small alternatives; time-box ideation	Evaluate against evidence, constraints, and risk; select/rollback	Planner (ideas), Retriever (sources), Critic/Verifier (checks)	Named human-in-the-loop gates; escalation and rollback criteria	Time-to-first-draft; edit distance; error-catch rate; escalation frequency	Decision log with rationale; rubric scores; acceptance/rollback records	Students draft 3 thesis options (fast); instructor selects via rubric and sources (slow) (Kahneman; NIST)
Planning	Externalize tacit judgment into visible plans	Propose candidate plans with assumptions	Test assumptions; prune plans not meeting constraints	Planner module; Orchestrator	Gate before irreversible actions; pairwise plan comparison	Plan count; assumption coverage; proportion pruned	"Plan card" (assumptions, success criteria, risks)	Product team drafts 5 launch plans; leadership prunes to one plan with documented trade-offs
Retrieval-Augmented Generation (RAG)	Ground outputs in vetted sources; reduce hallucination	Fetch passages from curated corpora; frame candidate answers	Verify source coverage, relevance, and freshness	Retriever + Synthesizer	Abstain when coverage/confidence is low; require citations	RAG triad: context relevance, groundedness, answer relevance	Source map; citation list; coverage report	Clinic note drafting with citations to local guidelines; abstain on low coverage

Synthesis / Drafting	Turn options into reviewable artifacts	Produce several short drafts with tags (audience, tone)	Compare drafts with rubric; choose/merge with rationale	Solver/ Drafter + Critic	Gate before public release; tone/policy checklists	Pairwise win-rate; revision depth; policy violations	Draft set; rubric; change log	Marketing slogans: 10 options (fast), rubric pick + edits (slow)
Testing / Verification	Make quality falsifiable, not subjective	Generate candidate outputs; suggest tests	Run gold tests and synthetic evals; require pass to proceed	Verifier; Evaluator; Tool callers	Must-not-fail suite; shadow mode vs. baseline; conformal thresholds	Pass rate; abstention rate; override patterns	Gold set; synthetic battery; threshold table	Loan triage runs in shadow vs. human baseline before go-live
Critique / Reflection	Reduce error via legible reasoning	Produce multiple reasoning paths (Self-Consistency, ToT)	Critique traces; revise; keep veto authority human	Critic; Reflector; Verifier	Require trace for high-stakes outputs; one-click defer/ escalate	Latency; edit distance; post-critique accuracy	Reasoning traces; counter-argument set; negative tests	Moot-court: three argument chains + critiques before final brief
Selective Prediction and Abstention	Encode "slow down" when uncertainty is high	Flag borderline cases; propose options	Defer or escalate per policy; document reasons	Predictor; Orchestrator; Human owner	Confidence/ coverage gates; selective disclosure	Defer rate; adverse-event rate; subgroup deltas	Defer log; uncertainty note; clinician sign-off	Sepsis alert defers low-confidence cases; nurse escalates
Identity and Evidence-Linked Records	Tie fast outputs to slow accountability	Draft capability cards; link artifacts to skills	Verify, sign, and publish with selective disclosure	Agentic curator + Human reviewer	Publication gate; privacy scope; revocation and status checks	Verification rate; dispute/ appeal rate	Verifiable credential; e-portfolio entry; status proof	Candidate shares active certification proof, not full history

Table 9.1 (*Contd.*)

Table 9.1 (*Contd.*) Fast/Slow Synthesis in Modular, Agentic Systems

Element / Pattern	**Purpose (what it solves)**	**Fast Phase (diverge)**	**Slow Phase (converge)**	**Roles and Modules (who/what)**	**Guardrails and Checkpoints (when to pause)**	**Key Metrics (how to know)**	**Core Artifacts (what to keep)**	**Cross-Domain Example**
Culture and Roles	Turn practice into habit across teams	Ritualize divergence sprints; pattern reuse	Drift huddles; incident reviews; portfolio audits	Product Owner, Orchestrator, Evaluator, Data Steward	Predeclared rollback; supplier re-test gates	Artifact completeness; incident closure; drift counts	Model cards; datasheets; evidence briefs; playbooks	Agency benefits portal: weekly drift checks; public intended-use brief
Orchestration and Tool Use	Keep systems explainable and debuggable	Model routes tasks; tools compute deterministically	Verify pre/post-conditions; enforce budgets/ timeouts	Orchestrator; Deterministic tools	Cost ceilings; timeouts; allow-listed tools	Tool failure rate; cost/ latency vs. SLA	Signed prompt/config; tool contracts	ReAct pattern: think-act-check with tool calls and logs
Metrics and Dashboards	Balance speed with safety and equity	Track speed: time-to-draft, cycle time	Track safety/ quality/ equity: errors, overrides, subgroup deltas	Evaluator; Data steward	Conformal gates; limits displayed to users; public recourse	Value + Quality + Safety + Equity (V/Q/S/E)	Portfolio dashboard; negative test registry	Airline scheduling: faster routes **and** fair wait-time parity
Research and Policy Hooks	Sustain learning beyond pilots	Publish open rubrics/datasets; compare stacks	Standardize provenance; benchmark governance maturity	Standards bodies; Consortia	Impact assessments; audit summaries; complaint channels	Incident rate vs. rituals; ROI vs. maturity	Audit summary; model-card snapshot; mitigation log	Cross-sector hub studies credential portability & orchestration safety

reframing of human–machine interaction. Fast/slow is no longer a metaphor borrowed from psychology but an operational principle that can be encoded in workflows, agent architectures, and institutional culture. When implemented deliberately, this approach improves not only efficiency but also transparency, accountability, and equity. It equips learners to explain choices, managers to defend decisions, and organizations to adapt under pressure.

Future research must continue to test how different sectors implement this choreography at scale. What rituals and metrics most reliably balance speed with fairness? How should evaluation batteries evolve to capture both cognitive and operational performance? Which cultural scaffolds ensure that fast/slow remains a habit rather than a slogan? Addressing these questions will help institutions move from pilots to portfolios, ensuring that innovation compounds rather than stalls. Thus, synthesizing fast and slow within modular and agentic contexts points toward a new kind of system design—one where curiosity is celebrated, but judgment is institutionalized. It is in this balance that educational institutions, businesses, and governments can move beyond fragile novelty toward sustainable trust, creating systems that are not merely faster but wiser.

9.2 STRATEGIC VISION FOR FUTURE EDUCATION AND WORK ECOSYSTEMS

The strategic vision that emerges from this book is an ecosystemic one: modular, agent-orchestrated, and choreographed by fast/slow learning so that exploration scales while judgment remains accountable. The next phase requires aligning program design, data architecture, credentialing, and governance so that evidence travels with artifacts and decisions, not separately from them (Mitchell et al., 2019; Gebru et al., 2021). Institutions should implement management-system scaffolds that make fast/slow visible in roles, rituals, and metrics, while preserving academic and civic values. Education policy should connect classroom pilots to workforce mobility through verifiable, privacy-preserving credentials. Meanwhile, employers should restructure work around competencies and human-in-the-loop governance to ensure that productivity gains do not erode quality or equity. Finally, a shared research and transparency agenda must anchor this vision so that provenance, safety, and validity remain inspectable across vendors and time (C2PA, 2025; NIST, 2024). In short, the future ecosystem is not a single platform but a set of interoperable practices that bind human judgment to machine capability.

The first pillar is learner-centered design that treats fast/slow as a pedagogy: rapid drafting and formative feedback (fast) paired with rubric-guided revision and summative judgment (slow). Building on the earlier chapters, programs should require evidence-linked assessment where claims are grounded in sources, calculations, or prototypes that reviewers can audit (Panadero and Jonsson, 2013). Guidance from national and international bodies already frames how institutions can proceed responsibly while preserving teacher agency and student privacy (U.S. Department of Education, 2023; UNESCO, 2023). Pragmatically, this means course shells with RAG-grounded tutors, transparent intended-use statements, and escalation gates for higher-stakes assessments (Lewis et al., 2020; NIST, 2024). Faculty development should emphasize critique literacy—how to read model outputs, trace provenance, and use rubrics to separate surface fluency from warranted understanding (Kasneci et al., 2023). Program reviews should integrate outcome analytics, disaggregated for equity, so pedagogy is tuned by evidence rather than hype (NIST, 2024). Finally, institutions should publish portfolio exemplars that pair artifacts with the reasoning that produced them, making the slow half teachable. These moves converge to a culture where speed accelerates learning without outrunning validity.

A second pillar is credential and records architecture that makes learning portable and verifiable across contexts. VCs allow programs to issue cryptographically signed attestations of competencies while enabling selective disclosure of only what is needed in a given transaction (W3C, 2025). Open Badges and Comprehensive Learner Records from 1EdTech provide domain models that map achievements to frameworks, making micro-credentials interpretable by employers at scale (1EdTech, 2018; 1EdTech, 2025). Institutions should align badge metadata with program outcomes, evidence links, and assessment criteria so that credentials carry the "how we know" alongside the "what you did" (Panadero and Jonsson, 2013). Privacy-preserving flows—where only status or specific competencies are shared—reduce information hazards while keeping verification strong (W3C, 2025). Governance should include revocation/expiry, issuer audits, and sampling of evidence packets to prevent résumé inflation. Cross-registration via trust frameworks can allow consortia to honor each other's attestations, speeding transfer and recognition. Over time, VC-native records will shrink friction between education and employment while raising the signal-to-noise ratio of credentials.

A third pillar is management-system governance that embeds accountability into everyday operations. ISO/IEC 42001 establishes role clarity, documentation, and continual improvement cycles for AI systems, translating principles into auditable practice (ISO/IEC, 2023). NIST's AI RMF and Generative AI Profile supply risk controls, evaluation prompts, and measurement ideas that can be tailored to course, department, or enterprise (NIST, 2023, 2024). Public-sector actors already have direction to institutionalize these expectations through OMB M-24-10 and associated inventory guidance, which universities and vendors can mirror in procurement and stewardship (Office of Management and Budget [OMB], 2024). At the artifact level, model cards and datasheets make assumptions and limits legible to reviewers who must defend decisions later (Mitchell et al., 2019; Gebru et al., 2021). Together, these instruments operationalize the culture-first adoption stance advanced in earlier chapters. They also reduce the cost of caution by making "not yet" and rollback triggers normal outcomes of risk-aware practice. A management-system approach, in short, keeps speed from outpacing safety.

A fourth pillar is workforce alignment that links curricula to evolving labor-market signals without collapsing education into training. Macro-analyses indicate both disruption and opportunity, with productivity gains concentrated where copilots augment cognitively demanding tasks (MGI, 2023; WEF, 2023). Employer data show rapid skill turnover and a rising premium on durable skills—communication, problem-solving, and leadership—that complement automated systems (Lightcast, 2025a; Lightcast, 2025b). Programs should therefore balance domain depth, data and model fluency, and transferable competencies, with capstones that simulate real accountability contexts. Credential taxonomies tied to occupational families can help learners navigate mobility rather than chasing tool-du-jour volatility (W3C, 2025; 1EdTech, 2025). Employers, for their part, should rewrite job descriptions around competencies, embed human-in-the-loop checkpoints, and recognize VC-backed micro-credentials for advancement. Regional partnerships can then map inclusive pathways that reduce skills mismatch while protecting equity. This bidirectional alignment retains education's formative mission while enhancing employability.

A fifth pillar is platform and data architecture that grounds fast generation in trusted knowledge and verifiable provenance. Retrieval-augmented generation separates "fetch" from "frame," shrinking hallucination risk and making citations inspectable by teachers, auditors, and customers (Lewis et al., 2020). Content provenance standards such as C2PA attach cryptographically signed histories to media, allowing reviewers to see where an asset came from and how it changed (C2PA, 2025). Security baselines like the OWASP Top 10 for LLM Applications translate emerging risks—prompt injection, insecure output handling—into actionable controls for developers and IT (OWASP, 2025). For education, these choices make formative feedback safer and plagiarism adjudication more evidence-based. For enterprises, they stabilize copilot deployments and reduce downstream remediation costs. Architectures should also log tool calls and retrieval coverage, enabling negative testing and incident investigation. The outcome is an app stack where speed is enabled by structure, not undermined by it.

A sixth pillar is measurement that balances value, quality, safety, and equity—because what you measure will shape behavior. Program and product teams should track time-to-first-draft, edit distance, and cycle time (value) alongside groundedness, error-catch rate, and reviewer overrides (quality/safety) (NIST, 2024). Equity requires disaggregated outcome and wait-time metrics by subgroup, with monitoring for drift and disparate error patterns (Suresh and Guttag, 2021). Public bodies have modeled transparency through AI use-case inventories; analogous institutional dashboards can build trust with students, faculty, employees, and the public (OMB, 2024). Where possible, publish intended-use briefs, limitations, and complaint channels with turnaround targets (Mitchell et al., 2019). Combine these with negative tests and red-teaming focused on likely harms, not only average accuracy (NIST, 2024). In education, embed these metrics in program assessment cycles; in industry, tie them to risk registers and KPIs. Measurement literacy is thus part of cadence literacy.

A seventh pillar is a shared research agenda that treats fast/slow as a testable systems property, not a metaphor. Education needs longitudinal, quasi-experimental and RCT designs that compare evidence-linked tutoring and critique workflows to business-as-usual across different student groups (U.S. Department of Education, 2023; UNESCO, 2023). Human-AI governance studies should evaluate which rituals—shadow evaluations, drift huddles, incident postmortems—predict lower incident rates and better ROI over multiple years (NIST, 2024; ISO/IEC, 2023). Technical work should deepen retrieval evaluation and provenance resilience under adversarial pressure (Lewis et al., 2020; C2PA, 2025). Workforce research should quantify mobility and wage effects of VC-backed micro-credentials versus traditional degrees by sector and demographic (W3C, 2025; 1EdTech, 2025). And benchmarks must evolve beyond single-turn accuracy to agentic coordination, autonomy limits, and abstention behavior. In all cases, preregistration, open materials, and cross-sector consortia will accelerate credible learning. The payoff is a knowledge base that guides policy and practice rather than chasing headlines.

An eighth pillar is policy and interoperability that make good behavior the default path. The OECD AI Principles, UNESCO guidance, and national frameworks converge on human-centric, risk-based oversight; institutions should map local policies to these lodestars for coherence (OECD, 2024; UNESCO, 2023). Procurement should require ISO/IEC 42001 alignment, AI RMF profiles, model/dataset documentation, and C2PA/VC-compatible outputs where applicable (ISO/IEC, 2023; NIST, 2024; Mitchell et al., 2019). Education systems should prioritize open standards (1EdTech, W3C) to avoid lock-in and enable portability of learning records (W3C, 2025; 1EdTech, 2025). Public agencies can further institutionalize transparency via OMB inventories and minimum risk-management practices (OMB, 2024). Interoperability profiles should include privacy and selective disclosure by design, not as an afterthought (W3C, 2025). Finally, cross-border recognition schemes can reduce frictions in global mobility for learners and workers. Policy, in this sense, is the connective tissue that sustains ecosystems beyond single administrations or product cycles.

A ninth pillar is capability building for people and institutions so the paradigm survives leadership and vendor turnover. Faculty and manager development should emphasize orchestration skills: defining roles for planner, retriever, solver, critic, and verifier; writing intended-use briefs; and running incident reviews (Amershi et al., 2019; NIST, 2023). Communities of practice can maintain living pattern libraries—what worked, what failed, with metrics—so learning compounds institutionally rather than resetting each semester or quarter (NIST, 2024). Employers should redesign performance management to reward evidence-linked decision-making and safe escalation rather than performative speed. Sector alliances can co-fund shared retrieval indexes and evaluation harnesses that lower the cost of rigor for smaller organizations (Lewis et al., 2020). Finally, leadership should make reversibility a norm—time-boxed pilots, predeclared rollback triggers—so caution is a strength, not a stigma (ISO/IEC, 2023). This training agenda turns culture-first adoption into muscle memory. Over time, cadence literacy becomes a signature graduate and manager outcome.

The tenth pillar is a pragmatic roadmap that sequences the work for the next 12–24 months while leaving room for discovery. For education: adopt UNESCO/US-ED-aligned guardrails; pilot RAG-first tutors in two gateway courses; issue VC-backed micro-credentials with linked evidence; and publish program-level dashboards (U.S. Department of Education, 2023; UNESCO, 2023; W3C, 2025). For employers: stand up an ISO/IEC 42001-conformant AI management system; profile critical use cases with the NIST GenAI Profile; implement OWASP LLM controls in app pipelines; and publish intended-use briefs for customer-facing AI (ISO/IEC, 2023; NIST, 2024; OWASP, 2025). For both: require model cards/

datasheets from suppliers; integrate C2PA where content authenticity matters; and align HR to recognize VC-native learning (Mitchell et al., 2019; Gebru et al., 2021; C2PA, 2025; 1EdTech, 2025). Measure value, quality, safety, and equity every quarter, and use negative tests to catch regressions early (NIST, 2024). Convene cross-sector partners twice yearly to exchange metrics and anti-patterns, and retire pilots that do not outperform baselines. This is how modular, agentic, fast/slow systems become institutional infrastructure rather than isolated experiments. The vision is ambitious but buildable—optimistic with discipline.

The strategic vision that emerges here is ecosystemic rather than tool-centric: modular architectures, agent-orchestrated workflows, and fast/slow learning as the default cadence so exploration scales while judgment remains accountable (Table 9.2). The immediate implication is alignment: program design, data architecture, credentialing, and governance must be joined at the hip so evidence travels with artifacts and decisions, not separately from them (Mitchell et al., 2019; Gebru et al., 2021). Management-system scaffolds (e.g., ISO/IEC 42001; NIST AI RMF) should make the cadence visible in roles, rituals, and metrics, preserving academic and civic values while accelerating responsible practice. Education policy can close the loop by linking classroom pilots to workforce mobility via verifiable, privacy-preserving credentials; employers should reciprocate by writing jobs to competencies, not brands, and by keeping human-in-the-loop checkpoints where consequences are high. A shared research-and-transparency agenda—provenance standards, oversight batteries, and public evidence briefs—anchors the ecosystem so safety and validity are inspectable across vendors and time (C2PA, 2025; NIST, 2024). In short, the "platform" is a set of interoperable practices—retrieval, guardrails, measurement, and selective disclosure—that bind human judgment to machine capability.

Ten pillars translate that vision into practice. First, treat fast/slow as pedagogy: rapid drafting and formative feedback (fast) paired with rubric-guided revision and summative judgment (slow), all grounded in sources, calculations, or prototypes reviewers can audit (Panadero and Jonsson, 2013; UNESCO, 2023). Second, modernize credentials and records: Verifiable Credentials and Comprehensive Learner Records that carry the **how-we-know** alongside the **what-you-did**, with selective disclosure and revocation to protect privacy and trust (W3C, 2025; 1EdTech, 2025). Third, embed governance as a management system: role clarity, documented gates (shadow evals, drift huddles, incident reviews), and artifacts (model cards, datasheets) that make "not yet" and rollbacks normal outcomes of risk-aware practice (ISO/IEC, 2023; NIST, 2024). Fourth, align curricula and labor markets without collapsing education into training: blend domain depth, data/model fluency, and portable "power skills," with capstones that simulate real accountability contexts (MGI, 2023; WEF, 2023). Fifth, build platform/data stacks that make speed safe: RAG for grounding, C2PA for content lineage, and OWASP LLM controls for interface-level risks (Lewis et al., 2020; C2PA, 2025; OWASP, 2025). Sixth, measure what matters—value, quality, safety, and equity—so behavior optimizes to balanced outcomes, not just throughput (NIST, 2024; Suresh and Guttag, 2021). Seventh, commit to a shared research agenda that treats fast/slow as a testable systems property, not a metaphor; eighth, codify

Table 9.2 Strategic Vision for Future Education & Work Ecosystems: Pillars, Actions, Metrics, and Research

Pillar/Theme	*Plain-Language Meaning*	*Near-Term Actions (12–24 months)*	*Metrics (V/Q/S/E)**	*Core Artifacts & Standards*	*Primary Stakeholders*	*Future Research Focus*
Ecosystemic vision	Treat the "platform" as interoperable practices (retrieval, guardrails, measurement, selective disclosure) that bind human judgment to machine capability	Publish a program/ enterprise cadence: where to move fast vs. slow; map use cases to autonomy levels; set escalation/rollback rules	V: time-to-draft, cycle time • Q: groundedness, error-catch • S: abstention/ override, drift • E: subgroup deltas	Intended-use briefs, evidence briefs, negative test registry; NIST AI RMF, ISO/IEC 42001	Presidents/ Boards, CIO/ CTO, Deans/ Chairs, Risk/ Compliance	Which combinations of practices most strongly predict safety + ROI over 2–3 years?
1) Learner-centered fast/ slow pedagogy	Rapid drafting + formative feedback (fast) paired with rubric-guided revision + summative judgment (slow)	Pilot RAG-grounded tutors in gateway courses; require source-linked hints; add oral defenses for high-stakes work	V: time-to-feedback • Q: transfer, rubric alignment • S: integrity incidents • E: disaggregated outcomes	Course shells, rubrics, audit logs of feedback; UNESCO/US ED guidance	Faculty, Students, Teaching & Learning Centers	RCTs on transfer/ equity of evidence-linked tutoring vs. BAU
2) Credentials & records	Make learning portable/ inspectable with verifiable, privacy-preserving credentials	Issue VC-backed micro-credentials with evidence links; enable selective disclosure; define revocation/status	V: time-to-hire • Q: employer verification rate • S: revocations handled • E: subgroup recognition parity	Verifiable Credentials (W3C), Open Badges/CLR (1EdTech)	Registrars, Employers, Licensing bodies	Credential portability, hiring outcomes, privacy impacts
3) Management-system governance	Turn policy into repeatable practice (roles, rituals, audits)	Stand up ISO/ IEC 42001-aligned processes; run shadow evals, drift huddles, incident reviews; publish audit summaries	V: release velocity with gates • Q: doc completeness • S: incident closure time • E: appeal/ recourse usage	Model cards, datasheets, release gates; NIST AI RMF/ Profile	Program/ Enterprise governance, Legal, Audit	Which rituals/ artifacts correlate with fewer incidents & better ROI?

4) Workforce alignment	Connect curricula to labor signals without collapsing education into narrow training	Capstones simulating accountability; competency-based job descriptions; recognize VC-native learning	V: time-to-productivity • Q: supervisor ratings • S: supervised overrides • E: mobility across groups	Competency maps, role playbooks, VC frameworks	HR, Managers, Career Services	Wage/mobility effects of VC-backed evidence vs. degree proxies
5) Platform & data architecture	Ground generation in trusted knowledge with traceable provenance and secure interfaces	Adopt RAG; enforce C2PA for media lineage; apply OWASP LLM controls at orchestration seams	V: doc/analysis lead time • Q: citation accuracy • S: injection/leakage rates • E: parity of service	RAG pipelines, C2PA manifests, tool allow-lists	IT/Engineering, Security, Data Stewards	Provenance resilience and retrieval quality under adversarial pressure
6) Measurement (V/Q/S/E)*	Balance speed with quality, safety, and equity to avoid "throughput theater"	Stand up dashboards; set acceptance thresholds; tie metrics to rollbacks; publish intended-use & complaint channels	V: time-to-draft, cycle • Q: groundedness, error-catch • S: abstention/override, drift • E: subgroup deltas	Balanced scorecards, negative tests, public FAQs	Execs, Program Leads, Risk/Compliance	UX features (explanations, recovery) on trust & error containment
7) Shared research agenda	Treat fast/slow as a testable systems property across sectors	Form consortia; preregister studies; open rubrics/datasets; benchmark agent teams, abstention, coordination	V/Q/S/E as above + reproducibility metrics	Shared eval batteries (AISI), open corpora, preregistration	Universities, Labs, Agencies, Vendors	Longitudinal safety/value of modular stacks; governance benchmarks

Table 9.2 (*Contd.*)

Table 9.2(*Contd.*) Strategic Vision for Future Education & Work Ecosystems: Pillars, Actions, Metrics, and Research

Pillar/Theme	***Plain-Language Meaning***	***Near-Term Actions (12–24 months)***	***Metrics (V/Q/S/E)****	***Core Artifacts & Standards***	***Primary Stakeholders***	***Future Research Focus***
8) Policy & interoperability	Make good behavior the default path across orgs and borders	Require RMF/42001 alignment in procurement; mandate audit cooperation; prefer W3C/1EdTech standards	V: time-to-contract • Q: audit pass rate • S: supplier retest compliance • E: cross-jurisdiction reciprocity	Contracts with control clauses; inventories; impact assessments	Procurement, Legal, Regulators	Cross-border recognition, selective disclosure norms
9) Capability building	Elevate evaluators/stewards; encode practice in communities of learning	Fund evaluator/data-steward roles; credit rollbacks; publish pattern/anti-pattern libraries	V: time-to-decision • Q: pattern reuse • S: rollback agility • E: access to training	Pattern libraries, incident summaries, playbooks	L&D, Academics, Ops leaders	Which training mixes best improve orchestration & evaluation at scale?
10) 12–24 months roadmap	Sequence pilots → measures → publish → retire/refactor/scale	Education: UNESCO/US ED guardrails, RAG tutors, VC micro-creds, dashboards • Enterprise: 42001 system, NIST profile, OWASP controls, briefings	Quarterly V/Q/S/E reviews; "retire/refactor/scale" decisions	Evidence briefs, Kanban for portfolio triage	Deans, CIO/CTO, PMOs, Boards	What sequencing yields fastest safe scale across varied risk appetites?

****V/Q/S/E* = *Value/Quality/Safety/Equity***: *the balanced measurement set recommended for responsible scaling.*

policy and interoperability so good behavior is the default path; ninth, invest in capability building for evaluators and stewards so rigor survives vendor and leadership turnover; and tenth, sequence a pragmatic 12–24-month roadmap that pilots, measures, publishes, and either retires or scales.

Three cross-cutting takeaways deserve emphasis. First, provenance and privacy are architectural, not rhetorical—necessity/proportionality, selective disclosure, and logged access must be designed into data products so evidence can move without overexposure (W3C, 2025). Second, reversibility is maturity—predeclared rollback triggers, shadow modes, and supplier retests lower the political cost of caution and keep speed from outrunning safety (NIST, 2024). Third, evidence beats enthusiasm—balanced dashboards (value/quality/safety/equity), negative tests, and subgroup deltas ensure wins are real, portable, and legitimate across communities that must live with the results.

A focused future research agenda follows. Provenance: stress-test C2PA/VC pipelines under real editorial and hiring loads to see how lineage and selective disclosure perform at scale (C2PA, 2025; W3C, 2025). Oversight: develop shared evaluation batteries for agent teams—autonomy limits, abstention behavior, multi-agent coordination—beyond single-turn accuracy (Liu et al., 2023). Education: run longitudinal, equity-aware trials of evidence-linked tutoring and rubric-guided critique, measuring transfer and integrity rather than only term-end satisfaction (Kestin et al., 2025; UNESCO, 2023). Credential portability: quantify hiring and licensure outcomes for VC-backed micro-credentials versus traditional degrees, including employer verification costs and candidate privacy impacts. Security: advance threat models and mitigations at orchestration seams (prompt injection, tool misuse) for multi-agent workflows (OWASP, 2025). Governance maturity: benchmark which rituals (drift huddles, incident postmortems, quarterly audits) predict fewer incidents and better ROI over multi-year horizons. Measurement: evaluate UX features—explanations, recovery, escalation—on trust calibration and error containment in high-stakes settings.

The strategic significance is that wiser systems are possible now: ecosystems where modular design, evidence-linked identity, culture-first adoption, and balanced metrics let institutions move quickly where risks are low and evidence is strong, and deliberately where stakes are high. The task ahead is disciplined optimism—piloting with transparency, measuring with integrity, and sharing playbooks so judgment becomes reusable infrastructure. If the next decade achieves that, education and work will be defined not by smarter tools alone, but by systems that reliably align human judgment with machine capability—and earn the public trust to endure.

9.3 ACTIONABLE RECOMMENDATIONS FOR EDUCATORS, INDUSTRY LEADERS, TECHNOLOGISTS, AND POLICYMAKERS

This section translates the book's core moves—modularity, fast/slow choreography, evidence-linked identity, and culture-first adoption—into concrete, near-term actions for the four stakeholder groups that shape learning and work. The throughline is the same across contexts: use fast components to explore and draft, slow components to verify and govern, and modularize both so they can be audited, tuned, and taught. Because institutional change succeeds when it rides on existing scaffolds, each set of recommendations anchors to published frameworks that already carry organizational legitimacy and clarify roles, rituals, and artifacts. The overarching aim is not to "bolt AI on," but to re-platform practice so evidence, provenance, and credentials travel with the work product across classrooms and boardrooms (W3C, 2025). Readers will recognize the cadence from earlier chapters; the shift now is from argument to action, with explicit sequencing for the next 12–24 months. What follows begins with classroom-level moves, then scales to program governance, enterprise operating models, secure engineering, and policy instruments. Taken together, these steps turn optimistic possibility into disciplined progress.

For educators, the immediate classroom move is to institutionalize a fast/slow pedagogy: draft quickly, critique deliberately, and require visible evidence at each gate. In practice, this means pairing retrieval-augmented tutors for low-stakes exploration (fast) with rubric-guided review of sources, calculations, and reasoning (slow) (Lewis et al., 2020; Panadero and Jonsson, 2013). Course shells should include intended-use statements, escalation paths for higher-stakes assessments, and disclosure norms for tool use to preserve academic integrity and student agency (U.S. Department of Education, 2023; UNESCO, 2023). Faculty development should center critique literacy—how to read citations, trace provenance, and distinguish surface fluency from warranted understanding—so instructors can tune prompts, rubrics, and workflows rather than policing tools (Kasneci et al., 2023). Programs should monitor disaggregated outcomes to ensure speed does not erode equity, publishing summaries alongside remedies when subgroup deltas emerge (NIST, 2024). To move beyond pilots, departments can schedule "cadence studios" that rehearse draft-critique-revise loops on authentic assignments across a term. Finally, assessment design should reward process as well as product by grading evidence-linked revision, not just final answers. This combination keeps exploration brisk while making judgment teachable and auditable.

For program chairs and registrars, the near-term credential architecture is to issue portable, privacy-preserving proofs that travel with artifacts and rubrics. VCs provide signed attestations of outcomes with selective disclosure, allowing learners to show a skill or status without oversharing their dossier (W3C, 2025). Pair VCs with 1EdTech Open Badges and Comprehensive Learner Records (CLR) so micro-credentials map to competencies, link the underlying evidence, and remain interpretable by employers (1EdTech, 2018; 1EdTech, 2025). Governance should include revocation/expiry policies, issuer audits, and periodic sampling of evidence packets to deter résumé inflation and maintain trust. Procurement language can reference Open Badges and CLR conformance, plus VC-compatible wallets, to avoid lock-in and ensure portability across systems (1EdTech, 2025). Programs should publish exemplars—credential + artifact + rubric—so the verification burden shifts from ad-hoc narratives to standardized bundles. Over time, this architecture shrinks friction in internships, transfer credit, and hiring while improving the signal-to-noise ratio of claims. In effect, identity becomes the slow governance of trust for fast capability.

For industry leaders, the fastest way to scale value safely is to put an AI-management system under the work, not just tools on top of it. ISO/IEC 42001 aligns roles, documents, and improvement cycles so that "assist, don't decide" patterns, escalation rules, and rollback triggers become calendar-anchored habits rather than slogans. NIST's AI Risk Management Framework and Generative AI Profile supply concrete actions, risk statements, and evaluation prompts that can be profiled to a portfolio of use cases. Executives should require model cards and datasheets from suppliers, publish intended-use briefs for customer-facing features, and stage shadow evaluations before flipping high-impact defaults (Mitchell et al., 2019; Gebru et al., 2021). Public-sector guidance in OMB M-24-10 offers a template for inventories, Chief AI Officer responsibilities, and minimum practices that private firms can mirror to demonstrate due care. As covered earlier, culture carries these controls—so leaders should reward safe escalation and learning from incidents, not performative speed. Quarterly governance reviews should triage drift, incidents, and supplier changes, with authority to pause or roll back. The result is speed where optionality matters and rigor where accountability lives.

For workforce strategy, align curriculum and roles to labor-market signals without reducing education to narrow training. Macro-analyses show both disruption and opportunity, with copilots augmenting cognitively demanding tasks and shifting demand toward analytical thinking, communication, and collaboration—durable skills that pair with tool fluency. Lightcast data indicates that roughly one-third of job skills changed from 2021 to 2024, underscoring the need for modular learning and credential refresh (Lightcast, 2025). Employers should rewrite job architectures around competencies, recognize VC-backed micro-credentials, and budget for ongoing upskilling aligned to product roadmaps. Educators should map program outcomes to occupational families and publish mobility pathways that show how portfolios translate to roles. Regional partnerships can co-fund shared retrieval indexes and evaluation harnesses that lower the cost of rigor for small firms and districts. Capstones should simulate real accountability contexts—documentation, audits, and post-incident reviews—so graduates practice judgment, not just tool use. This approach preserves education's formative mission while increasing employability.

For technologists, the engineering baseline is "secure-by-design" with provenance by default and measurable risk controls. Adopt NIST CSF 2.0 to manage cyber risk across the stack, align software pipelines to SSDF (SP 800–218), and apply the new SSDF Profile for GenAI where models are produced or integrated. Implement OWASP Top 10 for LLM Applications to mitigate prompt injection, insecure output handling, supply-chain issues, and excessive agency at the app layer. For content and data integrity, attach C2PA Content Credentials to high-stakes media and publish verification flows in user-facing documentation. Instrument RAG pipelines to log retrieval coverage, tool calls, and negative tests, then review these traces in incident and drift huddles. Treat abstention policies and selective prediction as first-class outcomes when uncertainty is high, with routes to human escalation. Finally, build policy enforcement into orchestration—schema-constrained outputs, typed tools, and deterministic gateways—so many failure classes disappear by construction. This stack enables speed via structure rather than despite it.

For evaluators and safety teams, adopt the NIST Generative AI Profile as your master checklist and extend it with domain-specific tests. The profile enumerates risks that are novel to or exacerbated by generative systems and maps more than 200 actions across govern, map, measure, and manage, which teams can turn into living runbooks. Tie these to continuous red-teaming and shadow evaluations, publishing limits and intended-use briefs for any feature that touches customers or rights (Mitchell et al., 2019; OMB, 2024). Where decisions are consequential, pair conformal prediction or abstention thresholds with human review to make "slow down" a designed outcome rather than an ad-hoc exception. Evaluate equity by monitoring subgroup error rates and wait-time parity, reporting remediation steps alongside metrics. For public-sector deployments, mirror federal inventories and CAIO responsibilities even if not mandated, to normalize transparency and oversight. Across sectors, log overrides, escalations, and incident learnings to guide model/version retirements and supplier governance. Evaluation, in short, is the slow half made operational.

For policymakers, prioritize interoperability and risk-based oversight that makes good behavior the default. Use the OECD AI Principles as lodestar values and align national guidance to risk-proportionate controls already converging in standards and federal policy. Encourage or require ISO/IEC 42001 alignment for public procurement, plus AI RMF profiles and SSDF practices in vendor attestations, to lift baselines without prescribing a single stack. Where content authenticity matters, add C2PA compatibility to RFPs and support pilots that demonstrate end-to-end provenance flows for media and public records. In transatlantic contexts, ensure regulatory mapping to the EU AI Act's risk tiers to reduce friction for cross-border research and trade. Fund open evaluation harnesses, retrieval indexes for public data, and credential wallets that implement W3C VC 2.0 to catalyze ecosystems rather than lock-in. Finally, publish agency AI inventories, intended-use briefs, and complaint channels with service-level targets to strengthen procedural trust. Policy, in this framing, is connective tissue for culture-first adoption.

For procurement and supplier governance, encode fast/slow into contracts so speed never outruns accountability. Require supplier model cards, datasheets, and evaluation summaries; mandate notification windows for model updates; and specify rollback rights when drift or incidents cross thresholds (Mitchell et al., 2019; Gebru et al., 2021). Include references to ISO/IEC 42001 conformance, NIST AI RMF/GenAI Profile alignment, CSF 2.0, and SSDF adherence, with evidence artifacts at each delivery. Where content flows are high-stakes, require C2PA content credentials, repository support, and public verification paths for affected end users. Adopt OWASP LLM Top 10 controls as acceptance criteria for app-layer risks and require third-party penetration testing that exercises LLM-specific attack surfaces. In higher education, extend these controls to edtech contracts and require VC/CLR interoperability to keep learner records portable (1EdTech, 2025; W3C, 2025). Tie payments to evidence—tests passed, incidents resolved, metrics improved—so incentives match risk posture. In short, buy the cadence you want to operate.

For cross-sector coalitions, build communities of practice that turn isolated wins into shared infrastructure. Convene twice yearly to exchange pattern libraries, anti-patterns, and metrics on value, quality, safety, and equity, mirroring public-sector transparency models (OMB, 2024; NIST, 2024). Co-fund open retrieval indexes for public corpora, shared evaluation harnesses, and VC-compatible wallets to reduce the fixed costs of rigor for smaller institutions. Publish exemplar portfolios that pair artifacts, rubrics, and credentials so others can adopt by imitation, not reinvention (W3C, 2025; 1EdTech, 2025). Align workforce roadmaps to WEF/MGI signals while protecting the formative mission of education and civic institutions. Encourage secure-by-design norms across the consortium, including CSF 2.0 and SSDF, with OWASP LLM controls at the app layer and C2PA where media integrity matters. Track subgroup outcomes and publish remediation work, not just wins, to keep equity central. Over time, these coalitions will make cadence literacy a regional capability, not a single-firm advantage.

Lastly, sequence the next 12–24 months so learning compounds while risk stays bounded. Quarter 1–2: stand up an ISO/IEC 42001-conformant management system; profile priority use cases with the NIST GenAI Profile; pilot RAG-first tutors in two gateway courses; and issue VC-backed micro-credentials with linked evidence. Quarter 3–4: require model cards/datasheets from suppliers; implement OWASP LLM Top 10 controls; attach C2PA to high-stakes media; and publish intended-use briefs plus complaint channels. Year 2: expand CLR/VC interoperability across programs and HR; adopt CSF 2.0/SSDF for pipelines; and run biannual red-teaming with public summaries. Across all quarters: measure value, quality, safety, and equity; run negative tests; and normalize rollback triggers where uncertainty is high (OMB, 2024; NIST, 2024). Capstone this cycle with a cross-sector exchange of metrics and anti-patterns, pruning pilots that do not outperform baselines. The goal is a flywheel: faster exploration, stronger verification, and portable recognition that compounds across institutions. This is how wiser systems emerge—by design, not by accident.

As seen above, this section translates the main themes covered in the monograph—modularity, fast/slow choreography, evidence-linked identity, and culture-first adoption—into practical steps different groups can take right now. The consistent message is that speed should be used for brainstorming, drafting, and surfacing options, while slower processes—review, critique, testing, and verification—should keep outcomes accountable. By modularizing both the "fast" and "slow" parts, institutions can track what is working, fix what is failing, and teach the process to others. What matters most is not "adding AI" as a bolt-on, but rebuilding practice so evidence, provenance, and credentials travel with the work itself, whether that's a student's essay, a hospital discharge summary, or a corporate compliance report (Table 9.3).

For educators, the recommendation is to adopt a *fast/slow pedagogy*. That means letting students use tools to generate first drafts quickly (fast), but requiring them to revise, justify, and link evidence to sources before submission (slow). Courses should provide clear statements of what the tools are for, escalation

Table 9.3 Actionable Recommendations for Educators, Industry Leaders, Technologists, and Policymakers

Stakeholder Group	*Key Actions (Next 12–24 Months)*	*Supporting Frameworks/ Standards*	*Example Outcome*
Educators (faculty & instructors)	• Adopt fast/slow pedagogy: quick drafting + evidence-linked critique. • Use retrieval-augmented tutors for exploration; require rubric-based review. • Provide intended-use statements and disclosure norms in courses. • Train faculty in "critique literacy" (reading citations, tracing provenance). • Grade revision and reasoning, not just final answers.	UNESCO Guidelines; US Dept. of Education AI Guidance; Panadero & Jonsson (2013); Lewis et al. (2020).	A history course where students generate three draft theses with sources (fast), then revise with rubrics and instructor critique (slow).
Academic leadership & registrars	• Issue **Verifiable Credentials (VCs)** and Comprehensive Learner Records (CLR). • Align badges to competencies, evidence, and rubrics. • Enforce revocation/expiry and audit evidence packets. • Use procurement language to require VC/CLR interoperability. • Publish exemplar bundles (credential + artifact + rubric).	W3C Verifiable Credentials 2.0; 1EdTech Open Badges & CLR.	A nursing program issues a "Clinical Handoff" badge linked to a simulation video and rubric, portable to employer HR systems.
Industry leaders/ executives	• Establish ISO/IEC 42001–aligned AI management systems. • Profile use cases with NIST AI RMF & GenAI Profile. • Require supplier model cards and datasheets. • Publish intended-use briefs for customer-facing tools. • Reward escalation and safe rollback in governance reviews.	ISO/IEC 42001; NIST AI RMF & Generative AI Profile; OMB M-24-10.	A bank runs sepsis-style "shadow mode" pilots for customer risk alerts, pausing rollout until tests pass.
Workforce development/ employers	• Redesign job architectures around **competencies**, not tool brands. • Recognize VC-backed micro-credentials in hiring & promotion. • Budget for ongoing upskilling aligned to product roadmaps. • Partner regionally to share retrieval indexes & evaluation harnesses. • Capstones simulate accountability: audits, incident reviews, documentation.	Lightcast labor data (2025); WEF & MGI skills reports.	A logistics firm accepts a "Data Wrangling → Experiment Design → Risk Analysis" credential stack as proof of analyst readiness.
Technologists & engineers	• Build **secure-by-design** stacks with provenance by default. • Implement NIST CSF 2.0 and SSDF for pipelines. • Apply OWASP Top 10 for LLM Applications to mitigate risks. • Attach C2PA credentials to media. • Instrument RAG pipelines to log retrieval, tool calls, and coverage.	NIST CSF 2.0; SSDF (SP 800-218); OWASP LLM Top 10; C2PA provenance standard.	A newsroom adds C2PA credentials to images and logs retrieval coverage for audit trails.
Evaluators & safety teams	• Adopt the NIST Generative AI Profile as a living checklist. • Pair conformal prediction/abstention with human review. • Monitor subgroup error rates & report remedies. • Publish intended-use briefs & limits for customer-facing systems. • Log overrides, incidents, & retire weak model versions.	NIST Generative AI Profile; ISO/IEC 23894 Risk Mgmt; Mitchell et al. (2019).	A university safety team monitors model drift quarterly and publishes public summaries with subgroup equity data.

Policymakers/ regulators	• Align with OECD AI Principles & UNESCO guidance. • Require ISO/IEC 42001, AI RMF, SSDF, and C2PA compliance in procurement. • Fund open evaluation harnesses and VC wallets. • Map national policy to EU AI Act risk tiers for global coherence. • Publish inventories, intended-use briefs, and complaint channels.	OECD AI Principles; UNESCO 2023; OMB M-24-10; EU AI Act.	A national education ministry mandates VC-compatible learner records and funds an open-source credential wallet.
Procurement & supplier governance	• Encode fast/slow cadence in contracts: model cards, datasheets, incident notification, rollback rights. • Require supplier compliance with ISO/IEC 42001, NIST RMF, SSDF, and OWASP Top 10. • Demand C2PA credentials for media and VC/CLR interoperability for learning records. • Tie payments to evidence: tests passed, incidents resolved.	ISO/IEC 42001; NIST RMF; SSDF; OWASP LLM Top 10; C2PA; 1EdTech CLR/VC.	A university edtech contract requires suppliers to provide model cards, VC/CLR outputs, and support rollback on update failures.
Cross-sector coalitions	• Convene twice yearly to exchange metrics, patterns, and anti-patterns. • Co-fund open retrieval indexes & evaluation harnesses. • Publish exemplar credential bundles with artifacts & rubrics. • Align workforce pathways to WEF/MGI signals. • Normalize secure-by-design standards across participants.	NIST AI RMF; W3C & 1EdTech standards; WEF/MGI workforce reports.	A regional coalition funds a public RAG index for civic data and adopts shared fairness monitoring for all pilots.

paths for higher-stakes work, and rubrics that reward reasoning, not just polished answers. Faculty themselves should be trained in "critique literacy"—knowing how to read citations, spot weak logic, and separate style from substance—so they can coach rather than simply police. Departments should publish how different student groups are faring and fix inequities when they appear. The result is classrooms where students gain the confidence to move quickly but the discipline to slow down when it matters.

For universities and credentialing bodies, the priority is to issue portable, privacy-preserving credentials. Using standards like *Verifiable Credentials* (W3C) and *Comprehensive Learner Records* (1EdTech), schools can certify not only that a student has a skill but also attach proof of how that skill was demonstrated. Selective disclosure allows a graduate to show only what's relevant—for instance, that their certification is active—without oversharing personal details. Governance mechanisms such as expiration, audits, and evidence sampling keep credentials trustworthy. When done well, this system speeds hiring, simplifies transfer credit, and raises the credibility of micro-credentials while reducing résumé inflation.

For industry leaders, the lesson is that success comes from putting a management system under the tools. ISO/IEC 42001 and NIST's AI Risk Management Framework provide the scaffolds: clear roles, documented rules for when systems can act or must defer, and recurring reviews that turn slogans like "assist, don't decide" into practice. Executives should demand model documentation from vendors, stage shadow runs before rolling out new features, and make rollback triggers a norm, not a stigma. Rewarding employees for surfacing risks instead of punishing them for slowing things down strengthens organizational trust. In short, business leaders must build cultures where speed accelerates opportunity but rigor governs responsibility.

For the workforce, curricula and jobs should be redesigned around competencies and transferable skills, not just tools of the moment. Studies show job skill requirements are turning over rapidly, with an emphasis on communication, teamwork, and analytical thinking that complement new systems. Schools and employers should map outcomes to occupational families so learners understand how their portfolio translates to actual roles. Regional partnerships can share resources—retrieval indexes, evaluation harnesses—so smaller schools and firms can keep up. Graduates should leave with experience not only using tools, but also documenting their decisions, handling audits, and responding to simulated incidents. That kind of preparation makes them adaptable in volatile job markets.

For technologists and engineers, the baseline is secure-by-design. Systems should process only the data they need, log who accessed it and why, and attach provenance to content so its origins are clear. Security practices like those in NIST's CSF 2.0, the Secure Software Development Framework (SSDF), and the OWASP Top 10 for large models provide actionable checklists. Tool outputs should be schema-constrained (e.g., always producing valid JSON) so errors can be caught automatically. RAG pipelines should log what sources were retrieved and whether they covered the query. By designing these controls from the start, failures become containable and explainable rather than mysterious or systemic.

For evaluators and safety teams, the focus is on continuous testing and transparency. Use frameworks like NIST's Generative AI Profile to guide test design and coverage. Publish intended-use statements and make uncertainty visible so users know when to trust and when to escalate. Red-team regularly to expose edge cases, then convert those failures into new "must-not-fail" tests. Monitor subgroup error rates and service equity, and publish both wins and fixes to maintain legitimacy. Evaluation must be treated not as a one-off audit but as the slow, recurring counterweight to fast innovation.

For policymakers, the emphasis is on interoperability and accountability by default. Build on international principles (OECD, UNESCO) and national frameworks (OMB in the U.S.) to create rules that are risk-proportionate and transparent. Require verifiable records, audit cooperation, and provenance standards in public procurement. Ensure that learners and workers can carry their credentials across borders by aligning to W3C and 1EdTech standards. Fund open evaluation tools and credential wallets to support broad adoption. Policy, in this vision, is less about micromanaging tools and more about setting guardrails and building shared infrastructure.

The next steps across these groups converge: pilot small but authentic projects; measure value, quality, safety, and equity side by side; normalize rollbacks and pauses; and share what works through communities of practice. Success will come not from chasing novelty but from turning governance into a reusable rhythm. The significance is clear: only by embedding evidence, provenance, and accountability into everyday practice will education and industry realize durable gains. The future of learning and work lies not in faster tools alone, but in systems that are structured, transparent, and human-centered enough to earn trust at scale.

9.4 FINAL REFLECTIONS: IDENTITY-DRIVEN AI SOLUTIONS IN A DYNAMIC FUTURE

Identity-driven solutions can be thought of as the glue that holds everything together—tying modular system design, the balance of fast and slow learning, and governance practices into one durable whole. At the simplest level, it means linking what people do to actual evidence—proofs of skill, credentials, and verifiable records—so that speed never outruns accountability. Instead of treating identity as a one-time label like a degree or a résumé line, it becomes a living record: a bundle of work, feedback, and revisions that can travel from a classroom to a workplace or even to a civic institution. Imagine a student carrying a digital portfolio where each project is attached to the rubric and the teacher's feedback, or a professional who can show a credential that proves a license is active without giving away their whole employment history. That kind of identity doesn't just make recognition portable; it builds trust because anyone can check the evidence behind the claim. In this way, identity acts like the backbone that keeps speed, safety, and equity in balance even as conditions change.

The big idea is that speed should be used for brainstorming and exploring options, while slower processes make commitments, document reasoning, and verify outcomes. Identity makes those slower commitments portable, inspectable, and—when necessary—revocable. Rather than vague assertions of ability, we're talking about cryptographic proofs: digital receipts that show where a skill came from, how it was earned, and under what conditions. These proofs reduce confusion because they clearly connect people, organizations, and artifacts. They also give decision-makers something to check when questions arise—content lineage, permissions for who can do what, and selective disclosures that protect privacy. This is what allows institutions to move fast without losing track of where the guardrails are. Put simply, identity is the foundation that turns fast/slow into more than a metaphor: it makes it operational.

In practice, this starts with things like VCs, which are digitally signed attestations of achievements or statuses, and Decentralized Identifiers (DIDs), which act like permanent anchors not tied to any one platform. Wallets then give users control over what to share and with whom. With selective disclosure and zero-knowledge proofs, a person can prove, for example, that they have an active teaching certification without revealing grades, demographics, or unrelated history. Over time, credential portability means learners and workers can carry evidence of competence into new contexts without endless transcripts or manual verification. But these systems only stay trustworthy if governance is built in: rules for how credentials are issued, how they expire, how they can be revoked, and how samples are audited. Universities and employers can help by publishing real examples—a credential tied to a project artifact and rubric—so it's clear what is being verified. When handled this way, identity shifts from a static résumé line to a dynamic record that can be validated on demand.

Another key piece is provenance—showing where content came from and how it changed. Here, standards like C2PA make it possible to attach a "content credential" that records capture context, edits, and publishing lineage for photos, videos, or documents. In knowledge work, retrieval-augmented generation (RAG) separates "fetching" sources from "framing" an answer, making it easier to see which parts come from trusted references. Model cards and datasheets act as instruction manuals, spelling out assumptions, training data, and limits, so reviewers can decide whether a system is fit for purpose. Logs that record prompts, tool calls, and retrieval events then allow teams to retrace decisions after the fact. With these in place, reviewing work becomes much less guesswork and much more about reading structured evidence. In civic and creative settings, visible provenance helps fight misinformation by letting users verify authenticity without relying on secret detectors. Provenance, then, is how identity extends from people to content, making both more trustworthy.

Of course, identity systems only build trust if they are fair and protect privacy. That means being able to measure outcomes for different groups and correcting inequities when they appear. It also means collecting and sharing only what is necessary—no more, no less—so proving a skill doesn't require exposing personal histories. Transparency practices like public inventories of use cases, complaint channels, and clear timelines for review help keep institutions accountable. Identity wallets should show who accessed what credential, when, and why, giving individuals visibility and control. Hiring and assessment should focus on evidence of demonstrated competence rather than indirect proxies like the prestige of a school, which often reinforce bias. When uncertainty is high, the system should be designed to pause, escalate, or abstain rather than guess and risk harm. Equity and privacy, far from slowing things down, actually strengthen trust because they ensure participation is fair and safe.

For all of this to work, identity has to be embedded in governance. ISO/IEC 42001, NIST's AI Risk Management Framework, and other standards provide the scaffolding: roles, rituals, and artifacts that turn ideals into repeatable practice. Model cards, datasheets, intended-use briefs, and supplier contracts become the everyday paperwork that makes systems explainable. Supplier governance mirrors these expectations—requiring update notifications, rollback rights, and cooperation in audits. Public dashboards and inventories then close the loop, making both the value and the risks visible. Governance, in this sense, is the operating system that ensures identity isn't just a label but a living safeguard.

In education, identity-driven systems can make learning visible and portable. Students' portfolios would include not just their final papers but the feedback and revisions that show how they got there, carried forward as credentials into internships or job applications. E-portfolios provide the narrative, while micro-credentials capture specific competencies like "statistical reasoning" or "inclusive teaching." VC wallets allow students to share only what's relevant with employers or licensing bodies. Instructors get relief from manual verification, and students gain a way to prove learning beyond one classroom. Tutors can provide quick feedback (fast), while rubrics and checkpoints ensure final evaluations remain deliberate and evidence-based (slow). Analytics can then monitor for inequities, ensuring that faster processes don't inadvertently leave some groups behind. Education, in this framing, isn't just about a degree at the end—it's about carrying proof of learning along the way.

For industry, identity-driven solutions build trust in hiring, promotion, and compliance. Employers can verify achievements directly through VC-backed credentials, reducing resume inflation and onboarding delays. In high-stakes roles, thresholds and human review remain in place so uncertainty doesn't slip through. Model cards and datasheets give auditors the artifacts they need to understand system behavior and hold suppliers accountable. Compliance checks can even be partially automated by embedding identity proofs directly into records. Dashboards track not just productivity but also fairness and safety, ensuring speed doesn't come at the cost of quality. Incident reviews, tied to provenance and credential logs, provide clarity about what went wrong and how to fix it. In this sense, identity acts as a multiplier—streamlining processes while strengthening accountability.

Security, too, is inseparable from identity. Adversaries target the seams where credentials, prompts, and tools meet, so defenses must live there as well. OWASP guidelines point to prompt injection and insecure tool use as real risks, while frameworks like SSDF and CSF 2.0 give step-by-step practices for building resilient pipelines. Policy enforcement through schema-constrained outputs and typed tools keeps errors from cascading. Provenance credentials, meanwhile, provide a chain of custody for content that supports both user trust and forensic analysis. Wallets must be hardened, since identity stores are prime targets. Linking identity events to telemetry—who used what, when, and why—helps catch issues early and speed response. Treating identity and security as one problem ensures defenses are proportionate to evolving threats.

Looking ahead, research has to move beyond individual components to study entire ecosystems. How do credentials work across vendors and borders? How resilient is provenance under attack? Do identity artifacts improve audit quality or speed dispute resolution? Do VC-backed micro-credentials actually increase mobility and wage growth, and do they do so fairly? How do governance rituals like drift huddles and incident reviews reduce long-term risk? These are the questions that need empirical answers. Only with this evidence can identity-centered approaches move from promising pilots to verified infrastructure.

The larger takeaway is simple: the future is not about smarter tools alone, but about wiser systems. Identity is what ties evidence, context, and governance to the pace of change. By defaulting to verifiable claims, portable credentials, and risk-aware governance, institutions can move quickly where it's safe and deliberately where it's not. Communities of practice and shared repositories will keep lessons flowing, while portable credentials ensure people carry their judgment across jobs and sectors. Equity improves because verification focuses on actual competence rather than proxies, and privacy improves because selective disclosure reduces unnecessary exposure. Security strengthens because provenance and identity controls are built in from the start. The future will be dynamic, messy, and fast—but with identity at the center, institutions can stay coherent, credible, and human-centered. Optimism with discipline is the way forward.

REFERENCES

1EdTech. 2018. Open Badges v2.0 IMS Final Release (1EdTech). https://www.imsglobal.org/sites/default/files/Badges/OBv2p0Final/index.html

1EdTech. 2025. Comprehensive Learner Record (CLR) and Open Badges: FAQ (1EdTech). https://www.1edtech.org/clr/faq

Amershi, S., Weld, D.S., Vorvoreanu, M., Fourney, A., Nushi, B., Collisson, P., et al. 2019. Guidelines for human-AI interaction. *In*: Proceedings of the 2019 CHI Conference on Human Factors in Computing Systems, 1–13. https://doi.org/10.1145/3290605.3300233

Boston Consulting Group (BCG). 2024. Responsible AI at scale: Governance, risk, and performance. https://www.bcg.com/publications/2024/responsible-ai-at-scale

Coalition for Content Provenance and Authenticity (C2PA). 2025. C2PA Technical Specification 2.2 (C2PA). https://spec.c2pa.org/specifications/specifications/2.2/specs/_attachments/C2PA_Specification.pdf

Córdova-Esparza, D., Díaz-Morales, J. and López-García, J. 2025. E-portfolios as evidence-linked assessments in higher education. International Journal of Educational Technology in Higher Education. 22(1): 17. https://doi.org/10.1186/s41239-025-00432-1

Edmondson, A. 2019. The Fearless Organization: Creating Psychological Safety in the Workplace for Learning, Innovation, and Growth. Wiley.

Es, G., Dekker, A. and Sips, H. 2024. RAGAS: Framework for evaluating retrieval-augmented generation systems. *In*: Proceedings of the 2024 EMNLP Workshop on Evaluation. https://aclanthology.org/2024.ragas

Evans, J.S.B.T. 2008. Dual-processing accounts of reasoning, judgment, and social cognition. Annual Review of Psychology. 59: 255–278. https://doi.org/10.1146/annurev.psych.59.103006.093629

Gebru, T., Morgenstern, J., Vecchione, B., Vaughan, J.W., Wallach, H., Daumé III, H., et al. 2021. Datasheets for datasets. Communications of the ACM. 64(12): 86–92. https://doi.org/10.1145/3458723

International Organization for Standardization/International Electrotechnical Commission (ISO/IEC). 2023. ISO/IEC 42001: Artificial intelligence—Management system standard (ISO/IEC). https://www.iso.org/standard/42001

Kahneman, D. 2011. Thinking, Fast and Slow. Farrar, Straus and Giroux. Penguin.

Kasneci, E., Sessler, K., Küchemann, S., Bannert, M., Dementieva, D., Fischer, F., et al. 2023. ChatGPT for good? On opportunities and challenges of large language models for education. Learning and Individual Differences. 103: 102274. https://doi.org/10.1016/j.lindif.2023.102274

Kestin, G., Laski, E., Browne, W., Kim, J., Farmer, R. and O'Shea, B. 2025. AI tutoring outperforms in-class active learning. Scientific Reports. 15(1): 17458. https://doi.org/10.1038/s41598-025-97652-6

Labkoff, S., Oladimeji, B., Kannry, J., Solomonides, A., Leftwich, R., Koski, E., et al. 2024. Toward a responsible future: recommendations for AI-enabled clinical decision support. Journal of the American Medical Informatics Association, 31(11): 2730–2739.

Lewis, P., Perez, E., Piktus, A., Petroni, F., Karpukhin, V., Goyal, N., et al. 2020. Retrieval-augmented generation for knowledge-intensive NLP tasks. Advances in Neural Information Processing Systems. 33: 9459–9474. https://proceedings.neurips.cc/paper/2020/file/6b493230205f780e1bc26945df7481e5-Paper.pdf

Li, Y., Chen, M. and Zhao, J. 2025. Evidence-based AI tutors and student performance: A meta-analysis. Computers & Education. 209: 104800. https://doi.org/10.1016/j.compedu.2025.104800

Lightcast. 2025a. The speed of skill change: 32% of job skills changed since 2021 (Lightcast). https://lightcast.io/resources/blog/skills-change-us-press-release

Lightcast & America Succeeds. 2025b. Durable by design: An update on the high demand for durable skills (Lightcast/America Succeeds). https://theqacommons.org/wp-content/uploads/2025/08/2025_08-Durable-by-Design-America-Succeeds-Lightcast.pdf

Liu, X., Yu, H., Zhang, H., Xu, Y., Lei, X., Lai, H., et al. 2023. AgentBench: Benchmarking large language models as agents. arXiv preprint arXiv:2308.03688. https://arxiv.org/abs/2308.03688

Long, A., Smith, J. and Becker, R. 2024. Creative workflows with AI: Balancing originality and accountability. Digital Creativity. 35(2): 101–119. https://doi.org/10.1080/14626268.2024.1001234

Luk, T. and Chan, R. 2024. Trust in AI-mediated hiring: Verifiable credentials and employer practices. Journal of Business Ethics. 189(1): 77–95. https://doi.org/10.1007/s10551-024-05567-1

McKinsey Global Institute (MGI). 2023. The economic potential of generative AI: The next productivity frontier (MGI). https://www.mckinsey.com/~/media/mckinsey/business%20functions/mckinsey%20digital/our%20insights/the%20economic%20 potential%20of%20generative%20ai%20the%20next%20productivity%20frontier/the-economic-potential-of-generative-ai-the-next-productivity-frontier.pdf

Mitchell, M., Wu, S., Zaldivar, A., Barnes, P., Vasserman, L., Hutchinson, B., et al. 2019. Model cards for model reporting. *In*: Proceedings of the Conference on Fairness, Accountability, and Transparency (FAccT): 220–229. https://doi.org/10.1145/3287560.3287596

National Institute of Standards and Technology (NIST). 2023. Artificial Intelligence Risk Management Framework (AI RMF 1.0) (NIST). https://doi.org/10.6028/NIST.AI.100-1

National Institute of Standards and Technology (NIST). 2024. Artificial Intelligence Risk Management Framework: Generative AI Profile (NIST AI 600-1) (NIST). https://www.nist.gov/publications/artificial-intelligence-risk-management-framework-generative-artificial-intelligence

National Institute of Standards and Technology (NIST). 2024. The NIST Cybersecurity Framework (CSF) 2.0 (NIST). https://doi.org/10.6028/NIST.CSWP.29

Office of Management and Budget (OMB). 2024. M-24-10: Advancing governance, innovation, and risk management for agency use of AI (OMB). https://www.whitehouse.gov/wp-content/uploads/2024/03/M-24-10-Advancing-Governance-Innovation-and-Risk-Management-for-Agency-Use-of-Artificial-Intelligence.pdf

Office of Management and Budget (OMB). 2024. OMB guidance on use of AI in federal agencies. Executive Office of the President. https://www.whitehouse.gov/omb/ai-guidance

Open Worldwide Application Security Project (OWASP). 2025. OWASP Top 10 for Large Language Model (LLM) Applications (OWASP). https://owasp.org/www-project-top-10-for-large-language-model-applications/

Organization for Economic Co-operation and Development (OECD). 2024. OECD AI Principles (updated 2024) (OECD). https://oecd.ai/en/ai-principles

Panadero, E. and Jonsson, A. 2013. The use of scoring rubrics for formative assessment purposes revisited: A review. Educational Research Review. 9: 129–144. https://doi.org/10.1016/j.edurev.2013.01.002

Park, H., Kim, S. and Lee, J. 2025. Structured outputs for safe and efficient large language model deployment. Journal of Artificial Intelligence Research. 78(1): 200–225. https://doi.org/10.1613/jair.1.14212

Ramić, A., Vidas-Bubanja, M. and Petrović, D. 2024. Selective disclosure in verifiable credentials: Privacy-preserving digital identity in education and work. Information Systems Frontiers. 26(3): 667–683. https://doi.org/10.1007/s10796-024-10432-7

Ru, W., Sun, Y. and Jiang, X. 2024. RAGChecker: Diagnosing errors in retrieval-augmented generation pipelines. *In*: Proceedings of the 2024 ACL Workshop on Evaluation and Diagnostics. https://aclanthology.org/2024.ragchecker

Shinn, N., Cassano, F. and Chen, D. 2023. Reflexion: Language agents with verbal reinforcement learning. arXiv preprint arXiv:2303.11366. https://arxiv.org/abs/2303.11366

Sreenivasan, K., Zhao, L. and Thomas, P. 2025. Conformal prediction for reliable deployment of language models. Transactions on Machine Learning Research. 5(1): 45–67. https://openreview.net/forum?id=CP2025

Suresh, H. and Guttag, J. 2021. A framework for understanding sources of harm throughout the machine learning life cycle. *In*: Proceedings of the ACM Conference on Fairness, Accountability, and Transparency (FAccT): 1–9. https://doi.org/10.1145/3442188.3445939

Swaminathan, G., Rao, R. and Singh, A. 2024. Selective prediction for large language models: Balancing accuracy and safety. *In*: Proceedings of the International Conference on Learning Representations (ICLR). https://openreview.net/forum?id=SP2024

Tuccio, G., Martins, F. and Bauer, M. 2025. Deterministic interfaces for modular AI adoption in enterprises. AI and Society. 40(2): 155–176. https://doi.org/10.1007/s00146-024-01987-5

U.S. Department of Education, Office of Educational Technology. 2023. Artificial intelligence and the future of teaching and learning: Insights and recommendations (U.S. ED). https://www.ed.gov/sites/ed/files/documents/ai-report/ai-report.pdf

UNESCO. 2023. Guidance for generative AI in education and research (UNESCO). https://www.unesco.org/en/articles/guidance-generative-ai-education-and-research

Varadarajan, V., Kumar, P. and Banerjee, S. 2023. Credential portability in the digital era: Toward secure and interoperable standards. Educational Technology Research and Development. 71(4): 1813–1835. https://doi.org/10.1007/s11423-023-10245-2

Wang, X., Wei, J., Schuurmans, D., Le, Q., Chi, E. and Zhou, D. 2023. Self-consistency improves chain-of-thought reasoning in language models. arXiv preprint arXiv: 2203.11171. https://arxiv.org/abs/2203.11171

Wang, Z. 2025. Safe deployment of structured outputs in enterprise AI. Proceedings of the AAAI Conference on Artificial Intelligence. 39(1): 555–563. https://aaai.org/aaai-publications/aaai-conference-proceedings/

Watts, C., Evans, M. and Kim, H. 2024. Pairwise comparison as a convergence mechanism in collaborative decision-making. Decision Support Systems. 172: 113789. https://doi.org/10.1016/j.dss.2023.113789

World Economic Forum (WEF). 2023. The future of jobs report 2023 (WEF). https://www3.weforum.org/docs/WEF_Future_of_Jobs_2023.pdf

World Wide Web Consortium (W3C). 2025. Verifiable Credentials Data Model v2.0 (W3C). https://www.w3.org/TR/vc-data-model-2.0/

Wu, T., Liu, Y. and Ma, X. 2023. AutoGen: Enabling next-gen large language model applications through multi-agent conversation. arXiv preprint arXiv:2308.08155. https://arxiv.org/abs/2308.08155

Yang, J. 2024. E-portfolios and lifelong learning: A systematic review. Journal of Learning Analytics. 11(1): 1–23. https://doi.org/10.18608/jla.2024.7873

Yao, S., Zhao, J., Yu, D., Narasimhan, K. and Griffiths, T. 2023. Tree of thoughts: Deliberate problem solving with large language models. arXiv preprint arXiv:2305.10601. https://arxiv.org/abs/2305.10601

Index

S

T

V

W